ADMISSIONS TO PETERHOUSE

ADMISSIONS TO

PETERHOUSE

IN THE UNIVERSITY OF CAMBRIDGE

OCTOBER 1911–DECEMBER 1930

A Register consisting of abstracts from
the College Historical Registers, supplemented
by information from other sources

COMPILED BY
E. ANSELL, M.A.,
of Peterhouse

WITH A FOREWORD
BY
FIELD-MARSHAL LORD BIRDWOOD,
G.C.B., G.C.S.I., G.C.M.G., G.C.V.O., C.I.E., D.S.O.,
M.A., LL.D., D.C.L., LITT.D.
Master of Peterhouse 1931–8

CAMBRIDGE
AT THE UNIVERSITY PRESS
1939

CAMBRIDGE
UNIVERSITY PRESS

University Printing House, Cambridge CB2 8BS, United Kingdom

Cambridge University Press is part of the University of Cambridge.

It furthers the University's mission by disseminating knowledge in the pursuit of education, learning and research at the highest international levels of excellence.

www.cambridge.org
Information on this title: www.cambridge.org/9781107553897

First published 1939
First paperback edition 2015

A catalogue record for this publication is available from the British Library

ISBN 978-1-107-55389-7 Paperback

CONTENTS

FOREWORD

It is a source of real regret to me that my distinguished predecessor as Master, Lord Chalmers, is no longer with us. Had he been so, I, and I am sure all Peterhouse men, would have wished him to write a foreword to the Supplement to the Admission Books which has just been completed, which he could have done so very much better than I am able to do. But, as he has left us, the duty devolves on me.

On surveying the work accomplished by Mr Ansell, the first point that strikes me with reference to the publication of this Supplement, covering the years 1911–30 of the Admissions to the College, is that it carries on a continuous series from the year 1284 to within nine years of the present day. The first period dealt with by Dr Walker covered the years 1284–1574 and was published in 1927. This was a necessarily broken and imperfect record. The second period from 1574 to 1616, published in 1930, was much fuller, and contains most valuable information about Peterhouse men in the reigns of Elizabeth and James I. The full Admission Book covering the years 1615–1911 was published earlier than either of the above in the year 1912; and in these three works edited by Dr Walker, together with the Supplement now edited by Mr Ansell, the story of the College is displayed to us with an amplitude of detail that is most remarkable. In fact, there seems to remain only one more volume to make the account of the College activities in the past complete. There is still room for a volume containing a selection of the documents, deeds and statutes, illustrating the various phases of the College history. Dr Walker's history of the College has, as we all know, been republished in a revised edition in the year 1935.

The decision to publish the Register of Admissions from 1911 to 1930 was taken during the last year of the Mastership of my predecessor, and the first circular sent out to old Peterhouse men for information bore the signature of Lord Chalmers. I have myself been responsible for issuing further requests for information, and the work of editing and compilation was both begun and finished during the years 1931–8, which coincide with the period of my Mastership.

One of the most interesting features of the Supplement, and, as we may hope, a non-recurrent feature on anything like a great scale in future Supplements, is the record of War services of Peterhouse men together with the data referring to the Naval and other Officers who took up their temporary abode at Peterhouse after the War. The enquiries in this connection have been of a most exhaustive character and it is hoped that the results will prove satisfactory. The view taken by the Governing Body, which certainly accorded with my own, was that no pains should be spared to ensure the Register being as complete and accurate as possible and that the chief merit of such a record would lie in the fact that very little of the work would have to be done again. I believe that this aim has been achieved and that without the untiring devotion, the editorial experience and meticulous accuracy of Mr Ansell no such result would have been possible.

It is sometimes thought that a record of this kind, which deals with only a fragment of recorded time, and is confined to the members of a specialized corporation, would be of interest to them alone. Speaking as one who has stood outside this Society, and then become part of it, I can say with all sincerity that I believe this view to be erroneous. In the period covered by the work the members of this Society, as never before, were very many of them brought into contact with the world in a sense such as no similar community had previously experienced. I understand that the total number of Peterhouse men who served in the War, including those who were admitted after it, runs to no less than 447. Of these as many as 263 will be found in the pages of this volume: this is a high proportion of the total, and is no doubt largely due to the fact that our numbers have nearly doubled since the War and have included serving Naval, Military and Air Force Officers who came up on special courses. In all, seventy men received decorations and fifty-three gave their lives. I have nothing to add to these figures, which tell their own story.

It has been a fascinating task to read in these pages how the course of the War and the period of reconstruction varied the career of individuals. Two instances, earlier than the date where Mr Ansell begins, might be given here. One man, for instance, from a schoolmaster became a soldier and the Adjutant of his Regiment and subsequently returned to school life and has since compiled the history both of his Regiment and his School. A second individual, who was an elementary schoolmaster when the War began, became a Field Officer in France and has since obtained a business position where he controls 10,000 men. In all probability, these results would not have been possible but for the War and the way in which it developed character and threw careers open to those who had energy and talent.

These are two illustrations, and many others will be found in these pages. To me it has also proved a fascinating task to see what happens to the average man after he leaves College, and to see how far he seems to be helped by his academic career. There is much to be learnt by studying a register of this kind in this enquiring spirit.

If what I have written here be true, it will be seen that a record of this kind has its uses, interest and significance for those who are not members of the College as well as for those who are.

It only remains for me to express the great gratitude of all Peterhouse men to Mr Ansell for the great trouble and devotion he has given to what has, I believe, been a labour of love to him, and to Professor Harold Temperley, my successor as Master, who throughout has given constant valuable aid to Mr Ansell from the vast store of his great experience and knowledge of our College history.

BIRDWOOD, *F.M.*
Late Master of Peterhouse

DEAL CASTLE
23 *June* 1939

INTRODUCTION

Explanatory notes on specific points arising in the Register will be found on pp. xiv–xxiv.

When the Governing Body of the College decided in June 1930 upon the compilation of this Register, they entrusted the task to Mr G. W. Greenaway. Shortly after initiating the work, however, Mr Greenaway received an appointment away from Cambridge, and the present compiler was asked in March 1931 to act in his stead. He began his labours in May 1931; and a task which he thought to complete in a couple of years or so has, in fact, occupied the greater part of his leisure for the space of over eight. That he should so long have deferred the hopes of all those who have awaited the appearance of the Register has been a matter of sincere regret to the compiler, and one for which he tenders his profound apologies. He can only say that, but for the time spent, he could not have achieved even such a result as he offers; and in so good a cause he hopes he may be pardoned.

The sources on which the Register is based are fourfold, namely: College records, University records, questionnaires and correspondence, and private research by the compiler. These may all be briefly described.

(1) *College records*. For the purposes of the Register the College records most utilized have been as follows:

(i) The 'Historical Registers', in which are entered each man's names, particulars of birth, parentage, school, and academic record. Lacunae are occasionally found, especially, as might be expected, during the period of the Great War. The 'Historical Registers' constitute the backbone of the present work.

(ii) The 'Order Books', or minutes of the meetings of the Governing Body. These have provided the data concerning elections to Fellowships and other College offices, and sometimes supplementary details relating to Scholarships and other College awards.

(iii) The 'Exit and Redit Book', which shows the precise dates of each man's residence throughout every term.

(iv) The dossiers which have been formed for everyone from about 1920. In these are filed the correspondence, and occasionally other data, relating to each individual: the compiler has often found them especially valuable for the clues they offer regarding men's subsequent careers.

(2) *University records*. The *Cambridge University Reporter* and the two decennial Supplements to the *Historical Register of the University of Cambridge*,

covering respectively the years 1911–20 and 1921–30, have been used to check or obtain a multitude of details such as dates of matriculation, degrees, University Scholarships, etc. On a number of additional points, not wholly covered by published records, the compiler has derived help from the University Registrary's staff, to whom acknowledgements are made below.

(3) *Questionnaires and correspondence.* Printed questionnaires were sent out by Lord Chalmers in January 1931 to all those whose names appear in the Register and whose addresses were known. Lord Birdwood subsequently sent out three hundred manuscript questionnaires, each separately drafted by the compiler, calling for more information, or directed to men whose addresses had only been traced after prolonged research. In addition, either in the course of tracing men or in pursuit of still further details, the compiler wrote well over eight hundred personal letters to certain of the men concerned, to those who recommended them to the College, to their friends or relatives, and to Universities, Schools, etc., all over the world. The total number of names in the Register is 919*; and it may be of interest to note that, in consequence of the intensive effort just described, information was received from or concerning no less than 723. It may be mentioned that several letters were occasionally sent out in connection with but one man, and sometimes in regard to but one detail; and further, that the information received by no means always covered all the points on which it was sought.

(4) *Private research.* Alike with a view to tracing men, to acquiring information about those who remained untraced, and to filling in gaps or checking doubtful points, the compiler has engaged in extensive private research, primarily in the University Library. He estimates that the number of separate details investigated runs into thousands, and he has laid under contribution every source of information which was known to him.

In spite of the utmost care, errors of some kind are almost certain to have crept into the Register. They may have arisen through mistakes in the sources of information available to the compiler; and they may have been due to slips on the part of the compiler himself. The compiler has striven to guard against positive error, and to read no more into any statement than that statement contained. The reader, in his turn, is asked to preserve an open mind; and, if he suspects error, not to conclude it without confirmation from authoritative sources. Of the extreme difficulty of keeping up to date with every detail in a register of this kind, it is hardly necessary to speak: faults in this direction there must be, and every apology is offered for them.

The compiler's acknowledgements for assistance received in the course of his task are manifold. To the Governing Body of the College he expresses his sincere appreciation of the trust reposed in him, of the freedom in which he

---

* This figure excludes the Naval Officers listed on pp. 33–4, as the Officers there enumerated were not in fact admitted members either of the College or of the University.

has been allowed to work, and of their unfailing patience. To Field-Marshal Lord Birdwood, Master of the College during the period in which the Register was compiled, he owes his thanks for constant encouragement and interest, as well as for material aid. To Lord Birdwood's successor in the Mastership, Professor Harold Temperley, under whose direction the work was carried out, the compiler's debt can be acknowledged but now never paid in person; for it is tragic to have to record his death on 11 July while these sheets are passing through the press. The compiler relied continually upon Professor Temperley's encyclopaedic knowledge of all that concerns Peterhouse, referred innumerable points to his critical judgment, and has owed him thanks, in fact, at every stage of the work. For assistance with certain problems grateful thanks are also due to Mr P. C. Vellacott, D.S.O., M.A., who has just now, on 29 July, been elected Master of the College in succession to Professor Temperley; to Dr J. C. Burkill, Fellow and Tutor of the College, and to Mr R. Lubbock, M.A., also Fellow and Tutor of the College.

It is with particular pleasure that the compiler records his indebtedness to all those members of the College who responded so readily to the questionnaires and letters which were sent to them. Almost all of those who were traced gave unstinted help; and but for their remarkable co-operation the Register would have been far less complete than it is. He also acknowledges the help he has received from many private individuals and many authorities of Schools, Universities, Governmental and other public bodies in every part of the world: all have been thanked personally, and to name them all here would scarcely be practicable.

Grateful acknowledgements are further made as follows. To the University Registrary's staff, and in particular to Mr W. J. Baker, Registrary's Clerk, and to Mr S. P. Gilby, Assistant Clerk, for help in connection with certain matriculations, forms of names, and degrees. To the staff of the University Press for their unfailing courtesy and care throughout the printing. To his colleague in the University Library, Mr A. Tillotson, M.A., of Peterhouse, for assistance with the proof-reading. To the staff of the College Office, Mr E. B. Darby, Mr D. C. Baker and Miss P. A. Norman, for their ungrudging help on innumerable occasions, especial thanks being due to Mr Darby for typing the abstracts which were made from the 'Historical Registers'. Also, and not least, to his wife, whose opinion he has constantly sought, and who has helped in other and more than material ways.

Finally, to check a detail here or to glean a fact there, the compiler has availed himself of numerous printed reference works, such as: *The Air Force List, The Army List, Burke's Peerage, The British Imperial Calendar and Civil Service List, Crockford's Clerical Directory* (for fuller acknowledgement, see p. xvi), *Debrett's Peerage, The Dominions Office and Colonial Office List, The Foreign Office List, The India Office and Burma Office List, Kelly's Directories* (both county and trade), *The Law List*, *The Medical Directory*, *The Medical Register*, *The Navy List*, *The War List of the University of Cambridge*, 1914–18 (for fuller acknowledgement, see p. xxii), and *Who's Who*; besides the daily press, many School and College Registers, and the year-books, calendars and journals of many societies, institutions, Universities and professional bodies.

Incomplete as must needs be the record of any living society, the compiler trusts that this Register may adequately serve its purposes of interest and utility, alike to Peterhouse men and to others, to future generations as well as to our own. If it goes forth to all of these as a worthy record of but two decades in the long and honourable history of the College, he will have been well rewarded.

The following notes, intended for reference rather than consecutive reading, are inserted for the benefit of those who seek information on specific points arising in the Register.

Allowances for War Service, etc. Terms and examinations were, under certain conditions, allowed to men who served in one way or another in the Great War.* Such allowances of terms have been recorded only in the case of men who subsequently graduated; and, as the allowances were often claimed early in a man's residence, mention has only been made of the number of terms which in fact proved necessary to complete the requirements of residence. Any examinations similarly allowed have been omitted, because they were always either the Previous Examination (the 'Little-Go') or the Special Examination in Military Subjects.

Terms are also allowed to Commissioned Officers sent up to the University under orders from the War Office or the Air Ministry. Here again, in the case of Officers who have graduated, the number of terms allowed has been recorded.

Arrangement. The arrangement of names in the Register follows that of the College 'Historical Registers', where they are entered approximately in the chronological order of admission. Convenience rather than consistency has governed the detail, and slight divergencies of practice have occurred at different times. Thus, in the earlier years of the period covered in this Register, men's names were sometimes entered at the time of their admission and therefore sometimes before the commencement of residence; now, however, names are never entered until after residence has begun.

* The conditions were set out in the Report of the Council of the Senate, dated 31 May 1915 and approved by Grace of 11 June 1915, and in certain further official pronouncements. Details may be found in any contemporary volume of the *Student's Handbook to the University and Colleges of Cambridge*, but more especially in the volumes issued immediately after the conclusion of the War.

Degrees, diplomas, examinations. Degrees and Diplomas of the University are recorded with their dates; and, prior to the institution of the Diploma in Education in 1922, the Certificates issued by the Teachers' Training Syndicate have also been mentioned.

This is not the place to describe the examinations of the University, nor to explain what changes have occurred in the regulations governing them during the period 1911–30. Such details may usually best be found in the relevant volumes of the *Student's Handbook*, mentioned in the footnote to p. xiv. Altogether, and in no small part owing to the War, there has been a bewildering complexity of conditions under which it has been possible for men to graduate. For this reason, various methods of stating what examinations a man has passed have appeared desirable, and perhaps indeed inevitable.

Tripos examinations are always shown, except in the case of men who have graduated without passing an honours examination of some kind after the end of their first year; and the passing of an Intercollegiate examination in honours is also shown, when that and allowances made for War service, or for illness, or to Commissioned Officers, have together led to a degree. Where a Tripos examination passed after the end of a candidate's first year has been followed by either a Special or a Principal Subject examination, the Special or Principal Subject examination has also been mentioned, but any Subsidiary Subject examination has been omitted. Oral examinations in the Modern and Medieval Languages Tripos and Certificates in Foreign Languages have likewise been omitted.

The letters or other symbols (as (a), f, †) which sometimes appear in the statements of Tripos particulars denote the section, language, etc., in which the candidate was examined. These sigla have not all been in use throughout the period covered by this Register, and even in the same Triposes the same sigla have not necessarily always stood for the same thing: it has, therefore, hardly been practicable to indicate their meanings. Anyone desiring such information should consult the 'Tripos lists' in the relevant issues of the *Cambridge University Calendar* or in the decennial Supplements to the *Historical Register of the University of Cambridge*.

Degrees obtained through examinations for the Ordinary degree, or for which no honours examination was passed after the end of the candidate's first year, are recorded simply as Ordinary degrees. It should be observed, however, that any B.A. degree is technically regarded as an Ordinary one unless it was obtained wholly by passing honours examinations.

Special cases have occasionally called for special methods of statement. Such, for example, are those in which allowances have been made in Tripos examinations to candidates who failed to reach honours standard; such, again, are Aegrotat degrees; and there are other and more unusual instances.

Prior to the Statutes of 1926, the dates given for Masters' degrees are those of the years in which the complete degrees were acquired by creation—creation, in certain circumstances, taking place in the year following that of inception. (For explanation, see the *Student's Handbook* of the period.)

For the allowances of examinations made to men with service in the Great War, see the section entitled **Allowances for War Service, etc.**

Fellowships, etc. The list of Masters and Fellows (on pp. 1–3) includes the full dates of their election to these offices. In the body of the Register, however, the year of election is shown in the case of those who were already members of the College; while, in the case of those elected from other Colleges, the dates of admission have been recorded.

In all cases where a Mastership or Fellowship has expired, the terminating year appears.

In the body of the Register, the category of a Fellowship under the 1926 Statutes (as 'Internal', 'External', 'Professorial' or 'Research') has always been indicated. Also, in the statements of College and University offices held by Fellows, the College offices precede the University ones; and, in the case of Fellows elected from other Colleges, the details of birth, parentage, etc., follow, instead of preceding, the statement of offices held.

Occupations, professions. The details about men's careers after 'going down' may not improbably be regarded as amongst the most interesting in the Register. In hardly any other matter, however, have men differed more widely in the nature and extent of the information which they have supplied. So far as possible, the compiler has standardized the details in question along broad lines suitable to different classes of occupation or profession: sometimes he has abbreviated the information he has received, but quite as often he has amplified it by private research. In reaching his decisions he has striven to respect the expressed or implied desires of his correspondents, and for any faults of omission or commission he asks that his full apologies may be accepted.

Where, under any name, there is note of only one occupation, it may be assumed that this is the present one: in these cases, a commencing date has occasionally been inserted, but its absence means no more than that the stated occupation has, so far as known, been followed at least for some while. Where no occupation at all is recorded, this may be either because the man has remained untraced, or because, for various reasons, he has no occupation.

In so far as concerns the ecclesiastical details relating to men in Anglican Orders, the compiler would here emphasize his indebtedness (already briefly mentioned on p. xiii) to the proprietors and the editor of *Crockford's Clerical Directory*: they have generously allowed him not only to follow the general method of statement adopted in the *Directory*, but also to derive certain data therefrom. For his deviations from their method, as also for any errors in the data, the compiler of this Register must alone be held responsible.

Personal names. The aim of the Register has been to state each man's full names, together with any titles, in the form which was correct at the date of his admission to the College, even although that form may not be found in the College and University records. As might be expected, very few discrepancies have in fact come to light; and these have concerned only forenames and compound surnames. Where the discrepancy lies in the number, order or spelling of the forenames, or in the number of names which constitute the surname, an indication of the fact is given; but where it concerns merely the insertion or omission of hyphens in compound surnames, no such indication has seemed necessary.

All surnames, whether simple or compound, are entered in larger type than the forenames. In the case of certain Oriental names, however, the name printed in larger type may be only what has been reckoned as the surname in this country.

Accents on Oriental names have been omitted, if only because they are seldom consistently applied.

Changes of name legalized after the date of admission are duly recorded, so far as they are known.

Fathers' forenames, and also their titles, orders, decorations and certain other distinctions, are stated as fully as known, and in the forms borne at the date when their sons were admitted. A few titles known to have been conferred at a later date have been included, but always with due indication of the fact; and it may be observed that the title 'Dr' has been omitted from the names of medical men, if the compiler has known that no actual doctorate was held. When a man's father was at Peterhouse, the fact is shown after the father's name, normally with the latter's highest degree alone and its date, or, if he never graduated, with the date of his admission; otherwise, except in special circumstances, the letters of parents' degrees have been omitted. A note of decease against a parent's name means that death was prior to the son's admission.

Orders and decorations conferred during the Great War are normally entered with the particulars of a man's War service, and not after his name as part of the heading.

Place-names, addresses. In general, place-names are spelt, and addresses given, as found in the College 'Historical Registers'. Birthplaces are usually named as they were known at the date of birth (e.g. 'St Petersburg, Russia' for an instance of birth in 1896); and the addresses are always those which obtained at the date of admission.

It may be observed that the 'Historical Registers' normally derive these data from men's application forms for admission to the College; but the application forms naturally vary greatly in legibility, in accuracy, and in the degree of detail provided; and it is to be remembered, too, that the same place has sometimes more than one recognized form or spelling. The compiler has occasionally emended a definitely incorrect spelling, but he has admitted all reasonable transliterations of Greek, Slavonic and Oriental names, whether or not these accord with current fashions; he has sought to spell the same place in the same way when it occurs more than once in the Register; and when different places exist with the same name, and there might be a doubt as to which is intended, he has inserted sufficient further description to identify the place concerned. The London metropolitan boroughs (e.g. Chelsea, Hampstead, Islington) have, however, been deemed sufficiently well known without the addition after them of the word 'London'.

Publications. While this Register lays no claim to being a bibliography, it attempts to include under men's names as full a list as possible of books which they have written or edited: in a few instances contributions to collective undertakings of an encyclopaedic nature are also named: and sometimes the editorship of a journal, or some other like fact, has been recorded. Contributions to periodicals have been omitted, if only because of the difficulty of obtaining anything approaching a complete list of them, and on account of the additional printing costs which would have been involved.

Within the sphere indicated, the compiler's aim has been that of exhaustiveness, except in so far as a few of the more voluminous authors comprehended their minor writings under the phrase 'And other works', while one or two others desired the exclusion of their works altogether. Merit could have been no criterion, except for a hypothetical omniscient observer; nor, on the long view, can any work be insignificant, since it represents at least a facet of its author's interests.

Some of the data relating to publications have been derived from notes sent in by the men themselves; but the greater part of them has been gathered by the compiler, who has looked up each man's name in the Catalogues of the University Library, examining everything which was relevant to his purpose. No doubt a few items, particularly foreign ones, may not have come within his view; and a few others which might have found a place have been excluded, because the identity of the author was neither certain nor susceptible of confirmation.

The titles and imprints of the works listed are drafted in accordance with the cataloguing rules which obtain in the University Library at Cambridge; and the works themselves are arranged in the chronological order of their publication, and not in the alphabetical order of their titles.

Recommendations. Sometimes, and especially in the earlier years of the period covered by this book, the College 'Historical Registers' name the person recommending a man for admission to the College. In the ordinary way, these recommendations are usually made by the head or a house master of the man's school. The compiler has therefore omitted particulars of recommendations except (1) When the recommender was a Peterhouse man; (2) When the entrant was a serving Officer recommended to the College respectively by the Admiralty, the War Office or the Air Ministry; (3) When the compiler has derived valuable information from the recommender; (4) When the compiler has known that some special interest attached to the recommendation; or (5) When the compiler has believed that the person recommending an entrant was, in fact, the man's private tutor.

In all but the first two of the above cases, the reader may be unaware which is the reason that has prompted the insertion of the recommender's name; but the appearance of such a name may serve useful purposes, even providing some future biographer with suggestive lines of enquiry.

Residence. The full date of beginning residence is always shown.

In the case of graduates, residence may normally be assumed until the date of the first degree; but if that was postponed for more than about a year after the requirements of residence had been fulfilled, the actual terms kept have been inserted. Residence after graduation has not been specifically indicated, except in the case of Bachelors of Arts who returned after War service; but post-graduate residence is not uncommon, and may sometimes be deduced (as from the subsequent award of Scholarships, etc.).

When residence was interrupted by War service and resumed after it, the term of resumption has been stated; save that if the man was a Bachelor of Arts, his actual terms of subsequent residence have been named.

'Resided [such and such terms]' is the phrase used to indicate the residence (1) of men who graduated more than about a year after fulfilling the requirements of residence, (2) of certain migrants from Peterhouse, and (3) of men who came up for a special course only, e.g. certain Probationers, and the Naval Officers sent up to the College after the War. The phrase does not necessarily imply that all the terms were technically 'kept'; nor does it imply that partial residence never occurred in any other terms. The compiler's intention has merely been to indicate within concise limits the significant period of residence, if this would otherwise not be clear.

'Went down after *or* during [such and such a term]' means always that the man in question, not being resident under special conditions, went down without graduating. This phrase, again, does not necessarily imply either that all the terms were technically 'kept', or that partial residence never occurred in any other terms; and the aim, here too, has merely been to indicate the significant period of residence. Where the phrase occurs during the War years, it may connote service, which is mentioned; and in these cases it affords no evidence that the man in question never intended to reside again.

Expulsions from the College have happily been few, and for obvious reasons they have not been recorded here.

For the allowances of terms made to men with service in the Great War and to Commissioned Officers sent up to the College under Orders, see the section entitled **Allowances for War Service, etc.**

Scholarships, Exhibitions, Studentships, Prizes. During the period covered by this Register, the College has been governed by two successive bodies of Statutes, namely, those of 1882 and those of 1926.* Under the Statutes of 1882 all Scholarships and Exhibitions were of definite stated values; but under those of 1926 the values of these awards have been only nominal, the amount actually paid to a Scholar or Exhibitioner being dependent upon his financial circumstances. For this reason the compiler has stated the values of Scholarships and Exhibitions awarded under the Statutes of 1882, but has omitted them in the case of such awards under the Statutes of 1926.

Dates attached in this Register to Scholarships, Exhibitions, Studentships, University Prizes and the like, are the dates of election.

Entrance Scholarships and Entrance Exhibitions stand in no need of definition; but, so far as concerns the Statutes of 1926, it may be observed that the titular annual value of a Major Entrance Scholarship is £100, while that of a Minor Entrance Scholarship is £60, and that of an Exhibition is £40. Under the Statutes of both 1882 and 1926 the normal tenure of an Entrance award is for two years. Honesty prompts the observation that in a few cases the emoluments have been reduced, or even forfeited, for disciplinary or other reasons; but such facts have here been overlooked.

Foundation and Senior Scholarships call for a word of explanation. Under the 1882 Statutes, Scholarships awarded to men already in residence were termed Foundation Scholarships, and these are denoted in this Register by an asterisk (*). Under the 1926 Statutes, however, Scholarships awarded to men already in residence have been called Senior Scholarships, and the names of particular benefactors are usually associated with them: such Senior Scholarships, however, as are unnamed the compiler has denoted by an obelus (†). It should be mentioned that Entrance Scholars promoted to Scholarships of higher value after only one year's residence do not by that promotion become Foundation or Senior Scholars, as the case may be.

Re-elections effected under the 1882 Statutes to Scholarships, etc., of the same value as those held hitherto, are shown simply by the words 'Re-elected', without fresh statement of the amount; in the case of Scholars, an asterisk betokens that the new tenure is as Foundation Scholar. But under the 1926 Statutes, since the values of Scholarships and Exhibitions are not shown, the term 'Re-elected' has been practically confined to the continuance of Senior Scholars in their Scholarships or of Students in their Studentships; and, in these cases, the word 'Re-elected' does not necessarily imply that there was no alteration in the value of the emoluments.

Scholarships awarded to certain men, normally at the commencement of

* The Statutes of 1926 came into force on 1 October 1926.

their University career, by the Trustees of the Lord Kitchener National Memorial Fund have been recorded: so also have the awards generously instituted by the Worshipful Company of Goldsmiths, the Worshipful Company of Ironmongers, and certain other Companies.

Studentships have hardly, for practical purposes, been affected by the new Statutes of 1926; and their values have accordingly been inserted throughout the Register.

University Prizes, Scholarships and Studentships appear in italics: so also do a few major awards not made by the University, but more or less officially recognized by it (as through advertisement in the *Cambridge University Reporter*), such as the 'Studentship of the British School at Athens' and the 'Senior Studentship of the Royal Commissioners for the Exhibition of 1851'.

As far as reasonably practicable, awards granted subsequently to a man's admission have been arranged in chronological order after the statement of his highest degree.

College Prizes and Choral Exhibitions have not been inserted.

Schools, Colleges, Universities. The names of several Schools and Colleges and of a few Universities occur repeatedly throughout the Register; and some of these institutions are occasionally, if only popularly, known by variant forms of name (e.g. 'Lancaster Grammar School' or the 'Royal Grammar School, Lancaster'). Wherever this is the case, the compiler has adhered to one form of name throughout, his chief deciding authorities being the *Public Schools Year Book...* and the *Schoolmasters' Yearbook and Educational Directory....* Where, however, a school or other place of education has definitely changed its name, the compiler has normally adopted the name in use when the man concerned left: the exception here implied by the word 'normally' is, that if Peterhouse men have come from the school both before and after the change of name, and if the change is not material, then the compiler has chosen the later name for every instance.

Preparatory schools are very occasionally recorded in the College 'Historical Registers'. If known to be such, they have been omitted; but doubtful cases—usually of private or foreign schools, sometimes no longer in existence—have been allowed to stand.

Naval Officers having their own special training, their 'schools' have called for somewhat exceptional treatment. The Royal Naval Colleges of Osborne, Dartmouth and Keyham occur most often; but public schools and a training ship are also found. The relevant facts have been recorded as was necessary in each individual instance.

Migrations to and from Peterhouse have been few in number. Where they occur, the other Colleges named are of this University unless otherwise stated. In the case of migrations from Peterhouse, the compiler has omitted details subsequent to the migration.

Sports, athletics. The compiler has recorded participation in Inter-University contests, and also in the Olympic Games: to the best of his knowledge the record of these is complete. In addition, though in this respect without any claim to completeness, notes have been made of a few other sporting events of especial interest, e.g. the University Lowe Double Sculls, the Diamond Sculls, regular membership of a county team. Participation in College contests, and the holding of office in College clubs, have not been recorded.

So far as concerns Inter-University contests, it may be noted that Blues and Half-Blues are only awarded for what are considered the more important events. The most important are those in which full Blues are awarded to all or some of the players participating, namely: Association Football, Athletics, Cricket, Cross Country, Hockey, Lawn Tennis, Rackets, Rowing, Rugby Football and Tennis. Half-Blues are awarded to 'second strings' or subordinate players in some of the foregoing events, and to all of the participants in certain others, e.g. Boxing, Fencing, Golf, Lacrosse, Water Polo, etc. Less generally known is the fact that participation in some Inter-University contests carries with it no award either of a Blue or of a Half-Blue: amongst such contests are Ice Hockey, Jiu-Jitsu, Shooting, etc.

In all Inter-University contests the dates shown are those of the years in which the participants competed against Oxford, whether or not a Blue or a Half-Blue was in fact awarded earlier than the contest.

Difficulties have occasionally arisen, chiefly in respect of dates and of ascertaining whether Blues or Half-Blues were awarded. In uncertain cases the compiler has checked his data with those in the admirable record compiled and arranged by Mr H. M. Abrahams and Mr J. Bruce-Kerr under the title *Oxford versus Cambridge: a Record of Inter-University Contests from* 1827–1930 (afterwards supplemented for 1931); and more than once he has been indebted to the officers of certain Clubs for their helpful answers to specific enquiries. But here and there a doubt has been unresolved, and for any faults the compiler accepts the responsibility.

War Service. Service in the European or Great War of 1914–19 has been recorded in the manner explained further on in this section; and, owing alike to the fullness of the details supplied by the returned questionnaires and to the extensive published sources of information, it is believed that the facts set forth may be accepted as tolerably complete. For his general method of statement, and for certain details as well, the compiler is indebted to *The War List of the University of Cambridge,* 1914–18; and for permission to make use of this he expresses his sincere gratitude alike to the editor, Mr G. V. Carey, M.A., sometime Fellow of Clare College and lately Headmaster of Eastbourne College, and to the publishers, the Syndics of the Cambridge University Press. To the *War List*'s excellence of method, its essential balance, and to the prodigious industry which went to its making, the present writer here pays the highest tribute in his power. In his own task of minor magnitude he may sometimes have secured more information, and he has not always followed his model; moreover, the ground covered is not always quite the same. Anyone, therefore, who should compare the details in this Register with those in the *War List* is cautioned to examine the principles of each.

Peterhouse numbered many men who served their country. Some of these had already gone out of residence before the War began; some had been admitted but had not as yet resided; some had their studies interrupted in mid career; and of all of these some laid down their lives. Then, while the War was still in progress, a few men, already members of the College, were drafted for duty to Cambridge, where they were able to count as residence their period of service, or some part of it; but it should be noted that the fact of a service man's taking an examination during the War is no proof of his residence then—he may have come up for the examination only. When the War was at last over, many Peterhouse survivors were seen again in the College; but there were not a few who gave up further residence altogether. Finally, amongst those admitted only at the conclusion of the War, a substantial number had also taken part in it. These divergent circumstances have lent themselves to no harshly uniform mode of statement; but the general principles on which the compiler has sought to draft the details are as follows.

Nature of service. Crossed swords (⚔) have been used to denote service with the military, naval or air forces of this or of other countries; save that service with the Junior Division of the Officers Training Corps has not been reckoned. Services rendered in a civilian capacity, as with the Y.M.C.A. or on munition work, have been indicated when known, but without the crossed swords.

Period of service. Dates of service, reckoned in years, have been stated so far as possible. When the commencing year is followed by a query within square brackets, it may be understood that the man in question was serving then, although the possibility of his having served earlier is not excluded. The concluding year of service has been more difficult to assess: death, and sometimes other causes, set a final date past all dispute: but, of the survivors, a few gave up return to Peterhouse and remained with the Forces permanently, while many others continued serving long after both the Armistice (11 November 1918) and the Peace Treaty of Versailles (28 June 1919): and Officers, moreover, were frequently not gazetted out of the Forces till long after they had been demobilized. In the case of men who remained with the Forces permanently, the year 1919 has been reckoned as the concluding year of service; so too in the case of the Regular Naval, Military and Air Force Officers who were sent up to the College under Orders after the War. In all other instances the year of demobilization has been recorded, whenever known; and when this is not known, the year in which an Officer was gazetted out has been stated. A query within square brackets after the concluding date implies some uncertainty; if the date is after 1919, the query means that the year shown is that in which an Officer was gazetted out.

Rank and regiment. Rank and regiment follow the period of service. The rank shown is the highest held within the regiment or Force concerned; and as substantive, temporary, and acting rank were equivalent for practical purposes, no differentiation has been made between them. Honorary rank, however, has been designated as such. Regiments of the British Army are, in general, named as they were commonly known during the War. A semi-colon separates successive stages of service, such as transfer to another arm or sometimes to another regiment, employment in some special capacity, Staff appointments, and the like. Battalion numbers and theatres of war have been omitted; and service in the ranks has normally been omitted, if this was followed by commissioned service. There were probably few men who saw much service without some change at least of rank, battalion or regiment. The compiler would be the last to maintain that he has been entirely consistent in his treatment of the details mentioned in this paragraph: he may not always have had full knowledge of the facts, and vicissitudes of short duration may not always have seemed to warrant mention.

Casualties. Casualties have been recorded. In the case of death, the date and sometimes the place have been stated, always in italics: in the case of wounds, a numeral indicates the number of occasions on which a man was wounded, if this was more than once. Casualties from gassing have been reckoned as wounds. Prisoners of War have been so denoted.

Orders and decorations. Orders, decorations and mentions in despatches conclude the particulars of War service: they are shown in italics, and are arranged as far as possible in the order of dignity, and not in the chronological order of their award. Medals have not been indicated, because their award was general to all those whose services fulfilled recognized conditions.

Service in campaigns other than the Great War has been indicated, so far as known: the particulars follow those of service in the Great War.

For the allowances of terms and examinations made to men with service in the Great War, see the section entitled **Allowances for War Service, etc.**

E. ANSELL

CAMBRIDGE

10 *August* 1939

ABBREVIATIONS

To obviate the necessity of consulting other reference works, this list has been made virtually exhaustive. In the body of the Register titles and distinctions appearing in the name headings are shown in italics; and distinctions awarded for service in the Great War are italicized in the statements relating thereto.

A.A.Dipl.	Architectural Association Diploma.
A.A.G.	Assistant Adjutant-General.
A.A.I.	Associate of the Auctioneers' Institute.
A.B.	Bachelor of Arts.
A.C.A.	Associate of the Institute of Chartered Accountants.
A.D.C.	Aide-de-Camp.
Adjt.	Adjutant.
Adm., adm.	Admitted.
Adv.	Advanced.
Aegr., aegr.	Aegrotat.
A.F.C.	Air Force Cross.
Aff.	Affiliated.
A.F.R.Ae.S.	Associate Fellow of the Royal Aeronautical Society.
Agric.	Agricultural; *or* Agriculture.
A.H.Q.	Army Headquarters.
A.I.C.	Associate of the Institute of Chemistry.
A.Inst.P.	Associate of the Institute of Physics.
all.	allowed.
A.M.	Alpes Maritimes.
A.M.I.E.E.	Associate Member of the Institution of Electrical Engineers.
A.M.I.Mech.E.	Associate Member of the Institution of Mechanical Engineers.
A.M.Inst.T.	Associate Member of the Institute of Transport.
A.M.R.S.T.	Associate Member of the Royal Society of Teachers.
Anthropol.	Anthropological.
A.P.M.	Assistant Provost-Marshal.
appt.	appointment.
Apptd, apptd	Appointed.
Archaeol.	Archaeological.
Architect.	Architectural.
A.R.C.M.	Associate of the Royal College of Music.
A.R.C.O.	Associate of the Royal College of Organists.
A.R.I.B.A.	Associate of the Royal Institute of British Architects.
Assoc.	Association.

Assoc.M.Inst.C.E.	Associate Member of the Institution of Civil Engineers.
Asst	Assistant.
attd	attached.
B.A.	Bachelor of Arts.
Bapt.	the Baptist.
Bart	Baronet.
B.B.C.	British Broadcasting Corporation.
B.C.	Boat Club.
B.Chir.	Bachelor of Surgery.
Bde	Brigade.
Biol.	Biology.
Bn	Battalion.
Bp	Bishop.
Brig.-Gen.	Brigadier-General.
Bro.	Brother.
B.Sc.	Bachelor of Science.
Bt	Brevet.
B.W.I.	British West Indies.
C.	Curate.
Capt.	Captain.
C.B.	Companion of the Order of the Bath.
C.B.E.	Companion of the Order of the British Empire.
Cdr	Commander.
Cert., cert.	Certificate.
Ch.B.	Bachelor of Surgery.
C.I.	Channel Islands.
C.I.E.	Companion of the Order of the Indian Empire.
C.-in-C.	Commander-in-Chief.
Cl.	Class.
Class.	Classical.
cmdg.	commanding.
C.M.G.	Companion of the Order of St Michael and St George.
C.M.S.	Church Missionary Society.
C.O.	Commanding Officer.
Co.	Company.
Co., co.	County.
Coll.	College.
Commiss.	Commissioned.
Conn.	Connecticut.

Corpl	Corporal.	F.R.A.I.	Fellow of the Royal Anthropological Institute.
C.Q.M.S.	Company Quartermaster-Sergeant.	F.R.A.M.	Fellow of the Royal Academy of Music.
Cr., cr.	Created.		
C.S.I.	Companion of the Order of the Star of India.	F.R.C.O.	Fellow of the Royal College of Organists.
C.U.B.C.	Cambridge University Boat Club.	F.R.C.S.	Fellow of the Royal College of Surgeons.
		F.R.Econ.S.	Fellow of the Royal Economic Society.
d.	deacon.		
D.A.A.G.	Deputy Assistant Adjutant-General.	F.R.E.S.	Fellow of the Royal Empire Society.
D.A.Q.M.G.	Deputy Assistant Quartermaster-General.	F.R.G.S.	Fellow of the Royal Geographical Society.
D.C.	District of Columbia.	F.R.Hist.Soc.	Fellow of the Royal Historical Society.
D.C.L.	Doctor of Civil Law.		
D.C.M.	Distinguished Conduct Medal.	F.R.Met.Soc.	Fellow of the Royal Meteorological Society.
D.D.	Doctor of Divinity.		
dec^d	deceased.	F.R.S.	Fellow of the Royal Society.
Dept	Department.	F.S.A.	Fellow of the Society of Antiquaries.
D.F.C.	Distinguished Flying Cross.		
Dilig.	Diligent.	F.S.I.	Fellow of the Chartered Surveyors' Institution.
Dio.	Diocese.		
Dipl.	Diploma.	Fus.	Fusiliers.
Dist.	District.		
Dist. Serv. Medal.	Distinguished Service Medal.	G.C.B.	Knight Grand Cross of the Order of the Bath.
Div.	Division.	G.C.M.G.	Knight Grand Cross of the Order of St Michael and St George.
D.L.	Deputy Lieutenant.		
D.Litt.	Doctor of Letters.		
D.Mus.	Doctor of Music.	G.C.S.I.	Knight Grand Commander of the Order of the Star of India.
D.O.	Doctor of Osteopathy.		
D.S.C.	Distinguished Service Cross.		
D.S.O.	Distinguished Service Order.	G.C.V.O.	Knight Grand Cross of the Royal Victorian Order.
		Gds	Guards.
E.	East; or Easter Term.	Gen.	General.
Econ.	Economics.	Geog.	Geographical; or Geography.
ed.	edition.	Geol.	Geology.
Educ.	Educated.	G.H.Q.	General Headquarters.
empld	employed.	G.I.E.E.	Graduate of the Institution of Electrical Engineers.
Eng.	England.		
Eng. Capt.	Engineer Captain.	G.I.Mech.E.	Graduate of the Institution of Mechanical Engineers.
Eng. Cdr	Engineer Commander.		
Engl.	English.	G.Inst.T.	Graduate of the Institute of Transport.
Evang.	the Evangelist.		
Exam(s).	Examination(s).	G.M.I.Auto.E.	Graduate Member of the Institution of Automobile Engineers.
Exhib.	Exhibition(er).		
		Gnr	Gunner.
F.A.I.	Fellow of the Auctioneers' Institute.	G.O.C.	General Officer Commanding.
		G.S.O.3	General Staff Officer, 3rd grade.
F.B.A.	Fellow of the British Academy.		
F.I.A.	Fellow of the Institute of Actuaries.		
F.I.C.	Fellow of the Institute of Chemistry.	H.A.C.	Honourable Artillery Company.
F.L.A.	Fellow of the Library Association.	H.E.H.	His Exalted Highness.
		H.H.	His Highness.
Flg. Off.	Flying Officer.	Hist.	Historical.
F.L.S.	Fellow of the Linnean Society.	H.M.	His Majesty('s).
Flt	Flight.	Hon.	Honourable; or Honourably; or Honorary.
F.M.S.	Federated Malay States.		

H.R.H.	His Royal Highness.	Maths	Mathematics.
		Matric., matric.	Matriculated.
I.A.	Indian Army.	M.B.	Bachelor of Medicine.
I.A.R.O.	Indian Army Reserve of Officers.	M.B.E.	Member of the Order of the British Empire.
I.C.S.	Indian Civil Service.	M.C.	Military Cross.
I.M.S.	Indian Medical Service.	M.D.	Doctor of Medicine.
incorp.	incorporated.	Mech.	Mechanical.
Intercoll.	Intercollegiate.	Med.	Medieval.
I.O.W.	Isle of Wight.	M.G.C.	Machine Gun Corps.
		Mid.	Midshipman.
Jun. Opt.	Junior Optime.	Mineral.	Mineralogy.
		Mod.	Modern.
K. (in names of regiments) King.		M.P.	Member of Parliament.
K.B.E.	Knight Commander of the Order of the British Empire.	M.R.C.P.	Member of the Royal College of Physicians.
K.C.	King's Counsel.	M.R.C.S.	Member of the Royal College of Surgeons.
K.C.B.	Knight Commander of the Order of the Bath.	M.R.San.I.	Member of the Royal Sanitary Institute.
K.C.M.G.	Knight Commander of the Order of St Michael and St George.	M.Sc.	Master of Science.
		M.Sc.Tech.	Master of Technical Science.
K.C.S.I.	Knight Commander of the Order of the Star of India.	(M.T.)	Mechanical Transport.
		Mt	Mount.
K.G.O.	King George's Own.	Mtd	Mounted.
K.S.	King's Scholar (at Eton College).	Mus.B.	Bachelor of Music.
		M.V.O.	Member of the Royal Victorian Order.
Kt	Knight.		
L.	Lent Term.	N.	North(ern).
Lang.	Languages.	Nat.	Natural.
Lce-Corpl	Lance-Corporal.	Non-Coll.	Non-Collegiate.
Ldr	Leader.	nr	near.
L.D.S.	Licentiate in Dental Surgery.	N.R.	North Riding.
L.I.	Light Infantry.	(N.R.)	New Regulations.
Lic.	Licence.	N.W.F.P.	North West Frontier Province, India.
Lieut.	Lieutenant.		
Lieut.-Cdr	Lieutenant-Commander.	N.Y.	New York State.
Lieut.-Col.	Lieutenant-Colonel.	N.Z.	New Zealand.
Lieut.-Gen.	Lieutenant-General.		
Litt.D.	Doctor of Letters.	O.B.E.	Officer of the Order of the British Empire.
LL.B.	Bachelor of Laws.		
LL.D.	Doctor of Laws.	O.C.B.	Officer Cadet Battalion.
LL.M.	Master of Laws.	Off.	Officer.
L.M.S.S.A.	Licentiate in Medicine, Surgery and Midwifery of the Society of Apothecaries of London.	Offic.	Officiate.
		(O.R.)	Old Regulations.
		Ord.	Ordinary.
		O.S.B.	Order of St Benedict.
L.R.A.M.	Licentiate of the Royal Academy of Music.	O.T.C.	Officers Training Corps.
L.R.C.P.	Licentiate of the Royal College of Physicians.	p.	priest.
		(P.)	Prisoner of War.
		Pa.	Pennsylvania.
M.	Michaelmas Term.	P.A.S.I.	Professional Associate of the Chartered Surveyors' Institution.
M., M2, etc. (in details of War service) Mentioned in despatches once, twice, etc.			
		Pathol.	Pathology.
M.A.	Master of Arts.	P.B.A.	President of the British Academy.
Major-Gen.	Major-General.		
Mart.	the Martyr.	P.C.	Privy Councillor; or (with ecclesiastical details) Perpetual Curate.
Mass.	Massachusetts.		
Math.	Mathematical.		

Perm.	Permission.	S.	Son; *or* South.
Ph.B.	Bachelor of Philosophy.	(S.)	Seaplane Officer.
Ph.D.	Doctor of Philosophy.	S.A.	Sociedad anónima (Ltd).
P.O.	Post Office.	S. and T. Corps	Supply and Transport Corps.
Pol. Econ.	Political Economy.	Sc.D.	Doctor of Science.
Polit.	Political.	Schol.	Scholar(ship).
Preb.	Prebendary.	Schol.*	Foundation Scholarship.
Prof.	Professor.	Schol.†	Senior Scholarship without
P.S.	Principal Subject.		Benefactor's name attached.
(P.S.Bn)	Public Schools Battalion.	Sci.	Sciences.
Pt	Part.	Sec.	Secretary; *or* Section.
Pte	Private.	Sen. Opt.	Senior Optime.
(Pty)	Proprietory.	Ser.	Series.
publ.	published.	Sergt	Sergeant.
		serv.	service.
Q.M.G.	Quartermaster-General.	S.J.	Society of Jesus.
(Q.V.R.)	Queen Victoria's Rifles.	S.M.E.	School of Military Engineering.
R.	Rector; *or* (in names of regiments) Royal.	Soc.	Society.
		Spec.	Special.
R.A.	Royal Artillery.	S.P.G.	Society for the Propagation of the Gospel.
R.A.C.D.	Royal Army Chaplains' Department.	Sqdn	Squadron.
R.A.F.	Royal Air Force.	St	Saint.
R.A.M.C.	Royal Army Medical Corps.	Stud.	Student(ship).
R.A.S.C.	Royal Army Service Corps.	Sub-Lieut.	Sub-Lieutenant.
R.C.	Roman Catholic.		
R.C. of S.	Royal Corps of Signals.	T.	Transport.
R.C.S.Eng.	Royal College of Surgeons of England.	T.A.	Territorial Army.
		Theol.	Theological.
R.E.	Royal Engineers.	Toc H.	Talbot House.
Rec.	Recommended.	Tr.	Training.
Regt	Regiment.	Tri.	Tripos.
res.	residence.		
Res.	Reserve.	Univ.	University.
ret.	retired.	U.S.A.	United States of America.
Rev.	Reverend.		
R.F.A.	Royal Field Artillery.	V.	Vicar.
R.F.C.	Royal Flying Corps.	Vac.	Vacation.
Rfn	Rifleman.	Ven.	Venerable.
R.G.A.	Royal Garrison Artillery.	Virg.	the Virgin.
R.M.A.	Royal Military Academy.	Vol.	Volume.
R.M.C.	Royal Military College.		
R.N.	Royal Navy.	*w.*	with.
R.N.A.S.	Royal Naval Air Service.	W.	West(ern).
R.N.C.	Royal Naval College(s).	(W.),(W2.),etc.	Wounded once, twice, etc.
R.N.R.	Royal Naval Reserve.	Wrang.	Wrangler.
R.N.V.R.	Royal Naval Volunteer Reserve.		
		Yeo.	Yeomanry.
Rt	Right.	Y.M.C.A.	Young Men's Christian Association.
(R.T.O.)	Railway Traffic Officer; *or* Railway Transport Officer.		

NOTE. References to *Walker* are to Dr T. A. Walker's *Admissions to Peterhouse*...1615 *to* 1911. Cambridge, 1912.

MASTERS AND FELLOWS

ELECTED DURING THE PERIOD
OCTOBER 1911 TO DECEMBER 1938

* Names marked with an asterisk do not appear in the body of the Register owing to admission having been before October 1911 or after December 1930.

ELECTED	MASTERS	VACATED
5 July 1924	*Rt Hon. Baron* CHALMERS (*Sir* Robert Chalmers), *P.C.*, *G.C.B.*, M.A., Hon. LL.D. (Cambridge, Glasgow and St Andrews), Hon. D.Litt. (Oxford), F.B.A.	31 March 1931
9 March as from} 1 April 1931	*Field-Marshal Baron* BIRDWOOD (*Sir* William Riddell Birdwood), *Bart*, *G.C.B.*, *G.C.S.I.*, *G.C.M.G.*, *G.C.V.O.*, *C.I.E.*, *D.S.O.*, M.A., Hon. LL.D. (Cambridge, Melbourne, Sydney and Bristol), Hon. D.C.L. (Durham), Hon. Litt.D. (Reading).	30 June 1938
1 July 1938	*HAROLD WILLIAM VAZEILLE TEMPERLEY, *O.B.E.*, M.A., Litt.D., Hon. D.Litt. (Durham), Hon. LL.D. (St Andrews), F.B.A., Hon. Fellow of Czecho-Slovak, Danish, Norwegian, Polish and Rumanian National Academies; Professor of Modern History in the University since 1930.	

HONORARY FELLOWS

29 Oct. 1915	**Rt Hon. Sir* WILLIAM HENRY SOLOMON, *P.C.*, *K.C.S.I.*, *K.C.M.G.*, M.A.	Died 13 June 1930
,,	*GEORGE HARTLEY BRYAN, M.A., Sc.D., F.R.S. Formerly **Fellow** 1889–95.	Died 13 Oct. 1928
29 Oct. 1919	**Rt Rev.* ERNEST HAROLD PEARCE, *C.B.E.*, M.A., Litt.D., D.D., Lord Bishop of Worcester.	Died 28 Oct. 1930
,,	**Most Rev.* FOSS WESTCOTT, M.A., Hon. D.D., Lord Bishop of Calcutta, and Metropolitan of India, Burma and Ceylon.	
31 Jan. 1927 and 1 July 1938	*Field-Marshal Baron* BIRDWOOD. Resigned on election as **Master**: Re-elected Honorary Fellow, after resignation as Master.	1931
4 Feb. 1935	*Rt Hon. Baron* CHALMERS. Formerly **Master** as above.	Died 17 Nov. 1938

Elected	FELLOWS	Vacated
30 Oct. 1911	*GEORGE FREDERICK CHARLES SEARLE, M.A., Sc.D., F.R.S.	1917
29 Oct. 1914	*CHARLES SPROXTON, *M.C.*, B.A.	Killed in action 1917
29 Oct. 1919	*PAUL CAIRN VELLACOTT, *D.S.O.*, M.A.	1934
„	ROY LUBBOCK, M.A.	
30 Oct. 1922	EDWARD CAREY FRANCIS, M.A.	1930
„	*Rev.* CHARLES SCOTT GILLETT, M.A.	1932
29 Oct. 1923	HERBERT BUTTERFIELD, M.A.	
„	BERTRAND LESLIE HALLWARD, M.A. Resigned on appointment as Head Master of Clifton College:	1939
6 Oct. 1927	ERNEST BARKER, Litt.D.; M.A., D.Litt. (Oxford); Hon. LL.D. (Edinburgh, Harvard, Calcutta, and Dalhousie, Nova Scotia); Professor of Political Science in the University, 1927–39.	1939
11 July 1928	HUBERT STANLEY MIDDLETON, M.A., Mus.B.; D.Mus. (Oxford).	1933
12 March as from } 1 Oct. 1928	*Sir* THOMAS ANTON BERTRAM, M.A., K.C.	1929
18 Feb. as from } 1 Oct. 1929	JOHN CHARLES BURKILL, M.A., Sc.D.	
23 Nov. 1931	*Sir* HUBERT ARTHUR SAMS, *C.I.E.*, M.A.	
22 Feb. as from } 1 Oct. 1932	WILLIAM KEITH CHAMBERS GUTHRIE, M.A.	
27 Sept. 1935	*Rev.* RICHARD GRENVILLE HEARD, M.A.	
21 Oct. 1935	*MICHAEL MOÏSSEY POSTAN, M.A., Professor of Economic History in the University since 1938.	
20 Jan. 1936	*PHILIP ULLYOTT, M.A.	1937
9 May 1938	BRIAN HARVEY GOODWIN WORMALD, M.A.	

EMERITUS FELLOWS

15 Oct. 1934	*Rev.* WILLIAM EMERY BARNES, M.A., D.D. Formerly **Fellow** 1889–1934. Emeritus Professor of Divinity in the University since 1934.	
14 Jan. 1935	*PAUL CAIRN VELLACOTT, *D.S.O.*, M.A. Formerly **Fellow** as above. Head Master of Harrow School since 1934.	

ELECTED	BYE-FELLOWS	VACATED
5 May as from 1 Oct. 1930	WILLIAM KEITH CHAMBERS GUTHRIE, M.A. Afterwards **Fellow** as above.	1932
30 May as from 1 Oct. 1932	JOHN GRAHAME DOUGLAS CLARK, M.A., Ph.D., F.S.A.	1935
18 May as from 1 Oct. 1936	*HARRY RAYMOND PITT, B.A., Ph.D.	
19 April as from 1 Oct. 1938	*JOSEPH NEWBOULD SANDERS, M.A.	

ADMITTED	FELLOW COMMONERS	
4 Oct. 1919	*Field-Marshal Baron* BIRDWOOD. Resigned on election as **Honorary Fellow**:	1927
22 Oct. 1928	JOSEPH DANIEL UNWIN, Ph.D. 1931.	1931

ADMISSIONS
OCTOBER 1911 TO DECEMBER 1930

MASTERSHIP OF

SIR ADOLPHUS WILLIAM WARD, KT,

M.A., Litt.D., Hon. Litt.D. (Manchester), Hon. LL.D.

(Glasgow and St Andrews), Hon. Ph.D. (Leipzig),

F.B.A. (P.B.A. 1911).

Master, 1900–24

All personal names, titles and addresses are entered as they applied at the date of admission. Changes of name legalized after admission are recorded so far as known. A note of decease against a parent's name means that death was prior to the son's admission.

An asterisk (*) against a Scholarship denotes that this was on the Foundation under the Statutes of 1882; an obelus (†) that it was a Senior Scholarship, without a Benefactor's name attached, under the Statutes of 1926. University Scholarships, etc., are italicized.

For fuller explanations, see the Introduction.

WILLIAM ROBERT BROWN MᶜBAIN. Born 31 Oct. 1891, at Shanghai. S. of George Mᶜbain (decᵈ). Stepfather: R. J. F. MᶜBain, Wyfold Court, nr Reading. Educ. privately. Adm. 14 Oct. 1911, by *bene discessit* from Jesus College: began res. 2 Oct. 1911. Matric. 22 Oct. 1910 (from Jesus College, where he resided M. 1910, L. and E. 1911).

Went down after E. 1913.
⚔ 1915 [?]–21 [?]. Lieut., R.F.A.; Major, R.A.F. *M.C. A.F.C. M* 3. *French Croix de Guerre, avec Palme.*

WILLIAM POLSON. Born 11 May 1889, at Burgh of Kintore, Aberdeenshire. S. of David Polson. Guardian: William Spence, Ashgrove, Kintore. Educ. at Central Higher Grade School, Aberdeen; and Aberdeen Univ. (M.A. degree). Adm. 26 Oct. 1911: began res. 13 Jan. 1912. Matric. 29 Jan. 1912.

2ⁿᵈ Cl. Math. Tri. Pt I, 1912. Went down after E. 1912.

SYED AHMAD HOSAIN. Born Feb. 1888, at Patna City. S. of Syed Hamid
Hosain. Guardian: S. L. Huda, The Shelter, Bakhtayarpore, Dist. Patna, Bengal.
Educ. at Government City School, Patna; and Behar National Collegiate School.
Adm. 28 Oct. 1911: began res. 16 Jan. 1912. Matric. 29 Jan. 1912.
Went down after E. 1913.

EDWARD MELVILLE WALKER. Born 8 Oct. 1891, at Kirkee, India. S. of
Lieut.-Col. Melville Walker, R.A., Small Arms and Ammunition Factory, Kirkee.
Educ. at King Edward VI. Grammar School, Louth, Lincs; and Bedford School.
Adm. 24 Nov. 1911: began res. 15 Jan. 1912. Matric. 29 Jan. 1912.
Went down after E. 1913.
✂ 1914–22 [?]. Capt., I.A.R.O., attd S. and T. Corps.

JOHN LANCELOT ANDREWS. Born 18 Dec. 1893, at Chelsea. S. of Dr
Lancelot William Andrews (dec^d) and Mrs Andrews, 31 Cotterill Road, Tolworth,
Surbiton. Educ. at Rugby School. Adm. (for Previous Exam.) 16 Feb. 1911:
began res. 4 Oct. 1912. Matric. 21 Oct. 1912. Resided again (after War serv.)
during Long Vac. and M. 1919.
B.A. (2nd Cl., 1st Div., Hist. Tri. Pt I, 1914; all. 3 terms for War serv.) 1915. M.A. 1925. Exhib.
of £25, 1914.
✂ 1914–19. Capt., Hampshire Regt; attd 72nd Punjabis, I.A. (W.)
Asst Principal, Board of Education, 1920–1. Asst Master, Rugby School, 1922; and at Marlborough
College, 1923–7. Headmaster, Exeter School, 1927–.
First cousin once removed of Rev. G. H. Clayton, Fellow (*Walker*, p. 671).

ROBERT JACOB REICHERT. Born 9 Dec. 1893, at New York. S. of William
Reichert, 34 Douglas Road, Canonbury, N. Educ. at Central Foundation School,
London. Rec. by W. H. Wagstaff, M.A. (Peterhouse), Head Master. Adm. Dec.
1911: began res. 8 Oct. 1912. Matric. 21 Oct. 1912. Entrance Schol., Maths, £60.
1st Cl. Math. Tri. Pt I, 1913. Re-elected to Schol.*, 1914. Went down after M. 1914.

CHRISTOPHER LUKE WISEMAN. Born 20 April 1893, at Birmingham.
S. of Rev. Frederick Luke Wiseman (Wesleyan Methodist Minister), 12 Greenfield
Crescent, Edgbaston, Birmingham. Educ. at King Edward's School, Birmingham.
Adm. Dec. 1911: began res. 9 Oct. 1912. Matric. 21 Oct. 1912. Entrance Schol.,
Maths, £50.
B.A. (1st Cl. Math. Tri. Pt I, 1913; Sen. Opt. Pt II, 1915) 1915. M.A. 1919. 2nd Cl. Nat. Sci. Tri.
Pt II (Physics), 1921. Re-elected to Schol.*, 1914.
✂ 1915–19. Instructor Lieut., R.N. (Instructor Lieut.-Cdr for the Naval Officers' course at
Cambridge, 1919.)
Senior Math. Master, Kingswood School, Bath, 1921–6. Headmaster, Queen's College, Taunton,
1926–.
Bro. of F. D. Wiseman (p. 39).

HAROLD THOMAS. Born 31 March 1893, at Menston, Yorks. S. of John
Thomas, 114 Bowling Hall Road, Bradford, Yorks. Educ. at Bradford Grammar
School. Adm. Dec. 1911: began res. 9 Oct. 1912. Matric. 21 Oct. 1912. Entrance
Schol., Nat. Sciences, £50.
B.A. (1st Cl. Nat. Sci. Tri. Pt I, 1914; 1st Cl. Pt II (Geol.), 1915) 1915. M.A. 1919. Schol.*
of £60, 1914. *Wiltshire Prize*, 1914. *Harkness Schol.*, 1916.
Congregational Minister: at Dogley Lane, Huddersfield, 1919–24; Hillsborough, Sheffield, 1924–34;
Springfield, Dewsbury, 1934–5; and Dist. Sec., N.W. Area, London Missionary Soc., 1935–.
Author:
   History of Dogley Lane Congregational Church, 1816–1918. Huddersfield, 1918.
   The jubilee history of the Sheffield Congregational Association, 1878–1928. Sheffield, 1928.

THOMAS GARRETT ELKINGTON. Born 22 June 1893, at King's Norton, nr Birmingham. S. of Hyla Garrett Elkington, Birch Tree Cottage, Rednal, nr Birmingham. Educ. at Bromsgrove School. Adm. Dec. 1911: began res. 9 Oct. 1912. Matric. 21 Oct. 1912. Entrance Schol., Classics, £40.

> Re-elected to Schol.*, 1914. Went down after E. 1914.
> ✕ 1914–16. Pte, R. Fusiliers (P.S.Bn); 2nd Lieut., Suffolk Regt. *Died 4 March 1916 of wounds received in action 3 March 1916.*

GERALD VERNON WILLIAMS. Born 13 Nov. 1893, at Lancaster. S. of Rowland Williams, Hale Cote, Haverbreaks, Lancaster. Educ. at Royal Grammar School, Lancaster. Rec. by Rev. H. A. Watson, D.D. (Peterhouse), Head Master. Adm. Dec. 1911: began res. 4 Oct. 1912. Matric. 21 Oct. 1912. Entrance Exhib., Classics, £30.

> B.A. (Intercoll. Exam. in Classics, 1914; all. 3 terms for War serv.) 1919. Re-elected to Exhib., 1914.
> ✕ 1914–18. Capt., Loyal N. Lancs Regt.
> H.M. Inspector of Taxes.

RONALD FLOWER MARTYN. Born 20 April 1893, at Blo' Norton Hall, Norfolk. S. of Charles Harrison Martyn, The Lawn, Aspley Guise, Beds. Educ. at Bedford School. Adm. 10 Jan. 1912: began res. 9 Oct. 1912. Matric. 21 Oct. 1912. Entrance Exhib., History, £30.

> B.A. (2nd Cl., 2nd Div., Hist. Tri. Pt I, 1914; all. 3 terms for War serv.) 1916. Re-elected to Exhib., 1914.
> ✕ 1914–20. Trooper, K. Edward's Horse; Lieut., R.A.S.C.; Capt., R.F.A. (Spec. Res.); empld as Education Officer. *M. Italian Medal for Military Valour.*
> Egyptian Civil Service, 1920–30. With the Sun Life Assurance Co. of Canada, 1930–5. Education Officer, R.A.F., 1935–.
> Author:
> (With W. F. Synge) '*Let my people go!*' [*A portrayal of Pharaonic life.*] London (1937).

AHMAD KHAN SHAHZAD. Born 1891, at Gwalior. S. of Sahibzada Aftab Ahmad Khan. Educ. at Mohammedan Anglo-Oriental School and College, Aligarh. Rec. by H. J. Edwards, M.A., Fellow and Tutor of Peterhouse. Adm. 1 March 1912: began res. 11 Oct. 1912. Matric. 21 Oct. 1912.

> B.A. (Ord. degree) 1915.
> ✕ 1915 [?]–17 [?]. Indian Voluntary Aid Detachment.
> Bro. of Ahmad Khan Shamshad (*Walker*, p. 673).

FREDERICK RICHARD CROCOMBE. Born 16 March 1893, at Stratford-on-Avon. S. of George Whitefield Crocombe, Hednacott, Stratford-on-Avon. Educ. at King Edward VI. School, Stratford-on-Avon. Adm. 3 March 1912, by *bene discessit* from Selwyn College: began res. 8 Oct. 1912. Matric. 24 Oct. 1911 (from Selwyn College, where he resided M. 1911, L. and E. 1912).

> B.A. (Ord. degree; all. 3 terms for War serv.) 1917. M.A. 1920.
> ✕ 1914–19. Lieut., 45th Victoria Regt of Infantry (Ontario Rifles), Canadian Force; Lieut., Oxford and Bucks L.I.; Lieut., 76th Punjabis, I.A.

KHOO SOON CHEE. Born 21 Jan. 1895, at Rangoon. S. of Khoo Jin Sun, 61, 23rd Street, Rangoon. Educ. at St Xavier's Institution, Penang; and privately, with B. N. Langdon-Davies, M.A., Copthill, Burgh Heath, Epsom, Surrey. Adm. 5 March 1912: began res. 10 Oct. 1912. Matric. 21 Oct. 1912.

> B.A. (Ord. degree) 1915. M.A. 1919.
> Called to the Bar, Gray's Inn, 28 Jan. 1918. Advocate and Solicitor of the Supreme Court, Straits Settlements.

PERCY DAWSON. Born 19 Nov. 1892, at Louth, Lincs. S. of Benjamin Hewson Dawson, 67 Upgate, Louth. Educ. at King Edward VI. Grammar School, Louth. Adm. 5 May 1912: began res. 1 Oct. 1912. Matric. 21 Oct. 1912.

B.A. (2nd Cl., 2nd Div., Hist. Tri. Pt I, 1914; 3rd Cl. Pt II, 1915) 1915.
Solicitor (adm. Feb. 1923); practising at Louth.

GEORGE EDMUND JAMES HODGES. Born 1 Jan. 1894, at Bury St Edmunds. S. of Ven. George Hodges (Archdeacon of Sudbury), The College, Ely. Educ. at King Edward VI. Grammar School, Bury St Edmunds. Adm. 12 May 1912: began res. 2 Oct. 1912. Matric. 21 Oct. 1912.

B.A. (Ord. degree) 1915.
Asst Master, King's School, Ely, 1915–16; and at Hildersham House, Broadstairs, 1916–19. Joined the Egyptian Educational Service as English Master, 1919; apptd English Lecturer, Higher Training College, Cairo, 1928; and Inspector of Secondary Schools, Egyptian Government Service, 1934.

JOHN CEDRIC GURNEY. Born 25 March 1893, at Swanage. S. of Rev. Thomas Alfred Gurney, St Giles' Vicarage, Northampton. Educ. at Sherborne School. Adm. 29 May 1912: began res. 1 Oct. 1912. Matric. 21 Oct. 1912. Resided again (after War serv.) M. 1919, L. and E. 1920.

B.A. (Ord. degree; all. 2 terms for War serv.) 1916. M.A. 1920.
✕ 1914–19. Capt., Northamptonshire Regt; G.S.O. 3. O.B.E. M 3. *Belgian Croix de Guerre.*
Asst Master, Cheltenham College, 1920– (and House Master, 1927–). Lately Major, T.A. Res. of Officers.
Cousin of W. A. Forbes (p. 91) and D. B. Forbes (p. 136).

THOMAS MARTIN WILSON. Born 23 Oct. 1892, at Blackburn. S. of William Wilson, 127 Harwood Street, Blackburn. Educ. at Queen Elizabeth's Grammar School, Blackburn. Adm. 18 June 1912: began res. 1 Oct. 1912. Matric. 21 Oct. 1912.

B.A. (2nd Cl. Math. Tri. Pt I, 1913; 1st Cl. Mech. Sci. Tri., 1915) 1915. Exhib. for Mech. Sciences, £30, 1914.
✕ 1915–18. Capt., R.A.F.
Executive Director and Chief Engineer, Synthetic Ammonia & Nitrates Ltd (a subsidiary Co. of Imperial Chemical Industries Ltd), Billingham, Stockton-on-Tees.
Bro. of R. F. Wilson (p. 48).

CALEB HOWARD CASH. Born 11 July 1878, at Netherton, Dudley, Worcs. S. of Caleb Cash. Educ. at Technical Schools, Birmingham; and Carmarthen College. Adm. 19 June 1912: began res. 1 Oct. 1912. Matric. 21 Oct. 1912.

B.A., LL.B. (2nd Cl. Med. & Mod. Lang. Tri. (a), 1914; 2nd Cl. Law Tri. Pt II, 1915) 1915.

CHARLES NEVILLE JOLLY. Born 3 Oct. 1893, at Thornton, Bradford, Yorks. S. of Rev. John Jolly (decd) and Mrs Jolly, 3 Brompton Avenue, Sefton Park, Liverpool. Educ. at Bradford Grammar School, and King Edward's School, Birmingham. Adm. 7 July 1912: began res. 1 Oct. 1912. Matric. 21 Oct. 1912. Resided again (after War serv.) E. 1919.

B.A. (2nd Cl., 2nd Div., Hist. Tri. Pt I, 1914; 1st Cl. Theol. Tri. Pt II (b) (4), 1916) 1916. *Carus Greek Testament Prize*, 1915. Hugo de Balsham Stud. (for research in Theology), £80, 1919.
Served with the Y.M.C.A. in the War 1916–18, after repeated rejections for the Army. *Died 10 Feb. 1920 in Liverpool, his health having been undermined by service on the Western and Italian fronts.*

MONTAGU CLARE CALLIS. Born 25 Nov. 1893, at Wymondham, Norfolk. S. of Rev. Arthur Wright Callis, Sproughton Rectory, Ipswich. Educ. at King Edward VI. Grammar School, Bury St Edmunds. Adm. 20 July 1912: began res. 10 Oct. 1912. Matric. 21 Oct. 1912.

> B.A. (3ʳᵈ Cl. Intercoll. Exam. in Classics, 1914; all. 3 terms for War serv.) 1915.
> ✂ 1914–19. Capt., R.E. (W.)
> Asst Principal, Board of Customs and Excise, 1919–22. Dipl. in Industrial Welfare, Manchester College of Technology, 1923. With Toc H. (finally as Area Pilot and Sec., Yorks Area), 1923–34. Lincoln Theol. Coll., 1934. Ordained d. 1935 Whitby for York, p. 1936 York. C. of St John Evang., Middlesbrough, Dio. York, 1935–.

Mom Chao TONGTOR. Born 26 Sept. 1892, at Bangkok, Siam. S. of H.R.H. Prince Sanparsartr. Educ. at Shrewsbury School. Adm. 21 July 1912: began res. 1 Oct. 1912. Matric. 21 Oct. 1912.

> B.A. (Ord. degree) 1916.
> Served as a Student Interpreter in the War 1916[?]–[?], being attached to the Siamese Legation in Paris.
> Third Secretary, Siamese Legation in London, 1926–32. Returned to Siam, 1932.

SYED ALI AKBAR. Born 16 Oct. 1890, at Hyderabad, Deccan, India. S. of Capt. Syed Mohamed (decᵈ). Educ. at Madrasa-i-Aliya, Hyderabad; and Wilson College, Bombay. Adm. 31 July 1912: began res. 1 Oct. 1912. Matric. 21 Oct. 1912.

> B.A. (3ʳᵈ Cl. Econ. Tri. Pt I, 1914; 2ⁿᵈ Cl., 2ⁿᵈ Div., Pt II, 1915) 1915. M.A. 1927.
> Divisional Inspector of Schools, Hyderabad, 1920–. President, Hyderabad Teachers' Assoc.
> Bro. of S. M. Hadi (p. 67).
> Author:
>   *The German school system...* Calcutta, 1932.
> Editor:
>   *The Hyderabad teacher; a quarterly organ of the Hyderabad Teachers' Association.*

FREDERICK CROSSFIELD HAPPOLD. Born 15 Feb. 1893, at Lancaster. S. of Albert Conrad Happold, 22 Penny Street, Lancaster. Educ. at Rydal Mount School, Colwyn Bay; and Royal Grammar School, Lancaster. Rec. by Rev. H. A. Watson, D.D. (Peterhouse), Head Master, Royal Grammar School, Lancaster. Adm. 8 Aug. 1912: began res. 1 Oct. 1912. Matric. 21 Oct. 1912.

> B.A. (2ⁿᵈ Cl., 1ˢᵗ Div., Hist. Tri. Pt I, 1914; all. 3 terms for War serv.) 1918. M.A. 1922.
> ✂ 1914–19. 2nd Lieut., Loyal N. Lancs Regt; Capt., Gen. Staff (Intelligence); G.S.O. 3 (Intelligence). (W.) *D.S.O. M.*
> Asst Master, Perse School, Cambridge, 1920–8. Headmaster, Bishop Wordsworth's School, Salisbury, 1928–. Hon. LL.D., Melbourne, 1937.
> Bro. of E. C. Happold (p. 29).
> Author:
>   *The adventure of man: a brief history of the world.* London (1926).
>   *The approach to history...* London (1928).
>   *Citizens in the making.* London (1935).
>   *And other works.*

MICHAEL DODD. Born 26 Aug. 1893, at Lemington, Northumberland. S. of Thomas Robert Dodd (decᵈ) and Mrs Dodd, 185 Osborne Road, Newcastle-on-Tyne. Educ. at Royal Grammar School, Newcastle; and College for the Blind, Worcester. Adm. 12 Aug. 1912: began res. 10 Oct. 1912. Matric. 21 Oct. 1912.

> B.A., LL.B. (3ʳᵈ Cl. Law Tri. Pt I, 1915; 3ʳᵈ Cl. Pt II, 1916) 1916.
> Was on the staff of the National Institute for the Blind, London, 1916–31; retired on account of ill health. Died 12 Nov. 1933 at Ilford, Essex.

BASIL ARTHUR RIDGE. Born 13 Nov. 1893, at Wimbledon. S. of Capt. Samuel Snashell Ridge, 112 Christchurch Road, Tulse Hill, S.W. Educ. at College for the Blind, Worcester. Adm. 14 Aug. 1912: began res. 1 Oct. 1912. Matric. 21 Oct. 1912.

B.A. (Ord. degree) 1915.

CONSTANTIN PETER DE HAHN. Born 21 June 1893, at Karkow, Ukraine. S. of Peter de Hahn, Aloupka, Crimea. In England educ. privately with Rev. S. Stewart Stitt, M.A., Stretham Rectory, Ely; then with C. S. Hayward, M.A., Bengeo, Hertford. Rec. by Rev. S. Stewart Stitt, M.A. Adm. 29 Aug. 1912: began res. 3 Oct. 1912. Matric. 21 Oct. 1912.

Went down after E. 1914.
✗ 1915–17. Lieut., Imperial Russian Mtd Grenadier Gds. (W.) *Order of St Anne, with swords (Russia). Cross of St Stanislas (Russia).*
Escaped penniless from Russia during or after the Revolution of Nov. 1917; then acted for a time as interpreter with the British Navy in the Black Sea. Last heard of as a journalist in the U.S.A. His relatives appear to have been murdered by the Bolsheviks, his father being owner of large estates in the Crimea.

WILFRID HERBERT SEALY. Born 23 Sept. 1890, at Boston, Lincs. S. of Rev. William Bellett Sealy (Peterhouse, M.A. 1883), Christ Church Vicarage, Newark-on-Trent. Educ. at St Lawrence College, Ramsgate. Adm. Sept. 1912: began res. 9 Oct. 1912. Matric. 21 Oct. 1912.

2ⁿᵈ Cl., 2ⁿᵈ Div., Hist. Tri. Pt I, 1914. Went down after E. 1914.
✗ 1914–19. Capt., R.A.S.C. *M.*
Remained in the Army. Transferred to Indian Army, 10 May 1927: Major (1932–), Indian Army Service Corps.
For his father, grandfather (S. B. Sealy) and bro. (P. T. Sealy), see *Walker.*

WALTER EDMUND RHODES. Born 6 Sept. 1895, at Cambridge. S. of William Atkinson Rhodes, Brocodale, Selwyn Gardens, Cambridge. Educ. at Weymouth College. Adm. 3 Oct. 1912: began res. 11 Oct. 1912. Matric. 21 Oct. 1912.

B.A. (Ord. degree; all 3 terms for War serv.) 1915. M.A. 1921.
✗ 1914–19. Lieut., R.E. (W.)
Dental Surgeon (L.D.S., R.C.S.Eng. 1921); practising in London.

Rev. CARL OTTO HEINRICH JOPPEN, *S. J.* Born 20 May 1878, at Strassburg. S. of Dr Thomas Joppen (dec^d), Strassburg, Oberkatasterinspektor for the Province of Alsace-Lorraine. Educ. at Strassburg Gymnasium. Rec. by Dr (*and later* Sir) A. W. Ward, Master of the College. Adm. Oct. 1912: began res. 2 Oct. 1912. Matric. (as Adv. Stud.) 14 Nov. 1912.

B.A. (as Research Stud.) 1914.
Between leaving Strassburg Gymnasium in 1897 and entering Peterhouse, he studied 1897–1903 successively at Feldkirch (Austria), Exaten and Valkenburg (Holland), and Stonyhurst; taught at St Xavier's High School, Bombay, 1903–7; studied again at St Beuno's (N. Wales) and Exaten till 1912. During the War was interned for a short time in 1914 near Huddersfield, then left for Germany. From 1915 until now (1932) has been teaching at the Höhere Katholische Knabenschule, Hamburg.
In the College and Univ. records he appears as Charles JOPPEN.
Author:
  Historical atlas of India for the use of High Schools, Colleges, and private students. London, 1907. (2nd ed.) Ib., 1910. 3rd...ed. Ib., 1914.

GEORGE WILFRED DYMOND. Born 20 Nov. 1893, at Upton, Birkenhead.
S. of George Cecil Dymond, Carrwood, Boundary Road, Bidston, Birkenhead.
Educ. at Haileybury College. Adm. 9 Dec. 1911: began res. 7 Oct. 1913. Matric.
21 Oct. 1913. Resumed res. (after War serv.) E. 1919. Entrance Exhib. (1913),
History, £30.

> B.A. (Ord. degree; all. 2 terms for War serv.) 1920. M.A. 1923.
> ✕ 1914–19. Capt. and Adjt., Cheshire Regt. *M.C.*
> Cuddesdon Theol. Coll., 1920. Ordained d. 1921, p. 1922 Ripon. C. of All Souls, Leeds, 1921–5;
> Chesterfield, 1925–7; P.C. of St Leonard, Grimsbury, 1928–34; R. of St Mary, Jeppestown, Dio.
> Johannesburg, 1934–.

GUY MALLABEY PLASKITT. Born 8 March 1895, at West Hampstead.
S. of William Levers Plaskitt (Peterhouse, M.A. 1887), 5 Fenchurch Street, E.C.
Educ. at Westminster School. Adm. 1 Feb. 1912: began res. 9 Oct. 1913. Matric.
21 Oct. 1913.

> Went down after E. 1914.
> ✕ 1914–19. 2nd Lieut., Essex Regt; R.M.C., Sandhurst; Lieut., Middlesex Regt.
> Solicitor (adm. Jan. 1922); being partner in Foss, Bilbrough, Plaskitt & Co., Moorgate Station
> Chambers, London, E.C. 2.

FREDERIC JAMES BENNETT. Born 29 June 1895, at Bollington, Cheshire.
S. of George Bennett, Laurel Bank, Longshut Lane West, Stockport. Educ. at
Stockport Grammar School. Adm. 7 March 1912: began res. 9 Oct. 1913. Matric.
21 Oct. 1913.

> B.A. (Ord. degree) 1916. M.A., M.B., B.Chir. 1920.
> Half-Blue: Lacrosse, 1914.
> M.R.C.S., L.R.C.P. 1918. In general practice at Colwyn Bay, N. Wales.

HERBERT FREDERICK BIRDWOOD. Born 11 Feb. 1894, at Harlesden,
Middlesex. S. of Roger Alan Birdwood (Peterhouse, M.D. 1889), Park Hospital,
Hither Green, S.E. Educ. at Mount St Mary's College, Chesterfield; and City of
London School. Adm. 30 Dec. 1912: began res. 8 Oct. 1913. Matric. 21 Oct. 1913.

> Went down after E. 1914.
> ✕ 1914–16. Lieut., London Regt (Blackheath and Woolwich Bn); attd R.F.C. *Killed in action
> over Valenciennes 2 March* 1916.
> The fifth of his family at Peterhouse: for the connections, see *Walker* and pp. 45 and 90 of this
> Register.

ROBERT ARTHUR LLOYD. Born 2 April 1895, at Waterloo, Seaforth, Lancs.
S. of Walter Edmund Lloyd, Glenallon, Greenbank Drive, Liverpool. Educ. at
Mill Hill School. Adm. Jan. 1913: began res. 7 Oct. 1913. Matric. 21 Oct. 1913.
Entrance Schol., Classics, £60.

> Went down after E. 1914.
> ✕ 1914–15. 2nd Lieut., The King's (Liverpool Regt). *Killed in action near Ypres 27 April* 1915.

SIMON SHERMAN. Born 18 March 1895, in London. S. of Morris Sherman,
32 Wellesley Street, Stepney, E. Educ. at Central Foundation School, London.
Rec. by W. H. Wagstaff, M.A. (Peterhouse), Head Master. Adm. Jan 1913: began
res. 9 Oct. 1913. Matric. 21 Oct. 1913. Entrance Schol., Maths, £50.

> B.A. (1ˢᵗ Cl. Math. Tri. Pt I, 1914; Wrang. Pt II (*b*), 1916) 1916. Schol.* of £60, 1915; re-elected,
> 1916.
> B.Sc., London, 1916. Apptd H.M. Inspector of Naval Ordnance, Admiralty, 1916. Principal,
> G.H.Q. School for British Army on the Rhine, and also Reuter's Special Correspondent with the

Allied Armies on the Rhine, 1919–20. Sec. of Education Committee, League of Nations Union, 1920–8. Drowned in a boating accident on the Cherwell, near Oxford, 1 Aug. 1928.

After leaving Cambridge he used the names Stanley Simon SHERMAN.

Author:

(With R. Jones) *The League of Nations, from idea to reality; its place in history and in the world of to-day*... London, 1927. 2nd ed. Ib., 1929.

(With R. Jones) *The League of Nations school book.* London, 1928. New and enlarged ed. Ib., 1934.

(With H. Spaull) *The united world*... London (1929).

MAURICE RAYMOND NEVILLE. Born 9 Jan. 1894, at Bow, London. S. of Mynott Neville, Silverleigh, 42 Constantine Road, Hampstead, N.W. Educ. at William Ellis School, Gospel Oak, London. Adm. Jan. 1913: began res. 9 Oct. 1913. Matric. 21 Oct. 1913. Entrance Schol., Maths, £40.

B.A. (1st Cl. Math. Tri. Pt I, 1914; 3rd Cl. Intercoll. Exam. in Maths, 1915; all. 3 terms for War serv.) 1916. M.A. 1920. Re-elected to Schol.*, 1915.

✂ 1916–19. Lieut., R.G.A. *M.C.*

With the General Electric Co., Ltd, Magnet House, Kingsway, London, W.C. 2.

KENNETH LLOYD. Born 16 April 1894, at Hampstead. S. of Herbert John Lloyd, 26 Marriott Road, High Barnet, Herts. Educ. at Gresham's School, Holt. Adm. Jan. 1913: began res. 8 Oct. 1913. Matric. 21 Oct. 1913. Resided again (after War serv., with 2 terms kept whilst on military duty in Cambridge) L. and E. 1919. Entrance Schol., Nat. Sciences, £40.

B.A. (Ord. degree; all. 4 terms for War serv.) 1917.

✂ 1914–18. Capt., London Regt (Q.V.R.); empld O.C.B. (W.)

Managing Director in Williams, Standring, Sandeman & Heatley, Ltd (wine merchants), 59 Duke Street, Grosvenor Square, London, W. 1.

Bro. of G. Lloyd (p. 41).

HARRY EDWARD KING REYNOLDS. Born 18 Feb. 1894, at York. S. of Harry Williams Reynolds, 18 St Saviourgate, York. Educ. at St Peter's School, York. Adm. Jan. 1913: began res. 11 Oct. 1913. Matric. 21 Oct. 1913. Resided again (after War serv.) E. 1917. Entrance Schol., History, £40.

B.A. (Ord. degree; all. 4 terms for War serv.) 1917. 2nd Cl., 2nd Div., Hist. Tri. Pt II, 1918. M.B. 1924.

✂ 1914–16. 2nd Lieut., York and Lancaster Regt. Invalided out.

M.R.C.S., L.R.C.P. 1922. Apptd Police Surgeon for York, 1931.

REGINALD FRANK MASON. Born 14 March 1894, at Penarth. S. of Frank Mason, 7 Stanley Crescent, Kensington, W. Educ. at King's School, Canterbury. Adm. Jan. 1913: began res. 1 Oct. 1913. Matric. 21 Oct. 1913. Resumed res. (after War serv.) L. 1919. Entrance Exhib., Maths, £30.

B.A. (Ord. degree; all. 5 terms for War serv.) 1919. M.A. 1935.

✂ 1914–19. R.M.A., Woolwich; Capt., R.F.A.; Staff Capt. (W.) *M.C. M.*

Was Chairman and Managing Director of Frank Mason & Co., Ltd (advertising contractors), 33 Norfolk Street, Strand, London, W.C. 2. Killed 31 Dec. 1935 in an accident to the air liner 'City of Khartoum' at sea off Alexandria.

JOHN THEODORE ST CLAIR TISDALL. Born 9 Oct. 1893, at Ispahan, Persia. S. of Rev. Dr William St Clair Tisdall, St George's Vicarage, Deal. Educ. at Bedford School. Adm. Jan. 1913: began res. 9 Oct. 1913. Matric. 21 Oct. 1913. Entrance Exhib., Classics, £30.

Bell Schol., 1914. Went down after E. 1914.

✂ 1914–16. Corpl [?], K. Edward's Horse; R.M.C., Sandhurst; Lieut., The King's (Liverpool Regt). (W.) *Killed in action 8 Aug. 1916.*

LOUIS ARNOLD ABRAHAM. Born 26 Nov. 1893, in London. S. of William Abraham, 26 Ashmount Road, Hornsey Lane, N. Educ. at Owen's School, Islington. Adm. Jan. 1913: began res. 9 Oct. 1913. Matric. 21 Oct. 1913. Resided again (after War serv.) E. 1919 to E. 1920, and partially M. 1920. Entrance Exhib., History, £30.

B.A. (2nd Cl., 1st Div., Hist. Tri. Pt I, 1915; all. 3 terms for War serv.) 1916. 1st Cl., 2nd Div., Hist. Tri. Pt II, 1920. Re-elected to Exhib., 1915. Hugo de Balsham Grant (for research in History), £60, 1920.
President of Union Soc., M. 1920.
✕ 1915–19. Lieut., Gen. List; empld Ministry of National Service.
Asst Clerk, House of Commons, 1920–32; and Senior Clerk, 1932–. Called to the Bar, Inner Temple, 26 Jan. 1928. President of Hardwicke Soc., 1928–9. Joint Sec. (1929), Departmental Committee on House of Commons Personnel and Politics, 1264–1832.

RICHARD KENAH STUART EXHAM. Born 29 May 1894, at Market Drayton, Salop. S. of Dr Arthur Richard Frederic Exham, Brooklyn House, Market Drayton. Educ. at Repton School. Adm. Jan. 1913: began res. 1 Oct. 1913. Matric. 21 Oct. 1913. Resumed res. (after War serv.) L. 1923. Entrance Exhib., Classics, £30.

B.A. (Ord degree; all. 4 terms for War serv.) 1923. M.A. 1926.
✕ 1914–22. Lieut., The King's (Shropshire L.I.); Lieut., Army Educational Corps, attd Middlesex Regt. (W.)
Schoolmaster.

JOHN HODSON ALCOCK. Born 9 June 1894, at Mansfield, Notts. S. of John Edward Alcock, Sunnycroft, The Park, Mansfield. Educ. at Leys School. Adm. 20 Jan. 1913: began res. 7 Oct. 1913. Matric. 21 Oct. 1913. Resided again (after War serv.) L. 1920.

B.A., LL.B. (2nd Cl. Law Tri. Pt II, 1920; all. 4 terms for War serv.) 1920.
✕ 1915–19. Lieut., Lincolnshire Regt. (P.)
Solicitor (adm. Dec. 1920); practising at Mansfield (J. E. Alcock & Son).

RAYMOND JOHN GARMONDSWAY TEMPLE. Born 15 Sept. 1894, at Bridport, Dorset. S. of Major Arthur Waldie Temple, Warburton House, Bridport. Educ. at Weymouth College. Adm. Jan. 1913: began res. 8 Oct. 1913. Matric. 21 Oct. 1913.

Went down after E. 1914.
✕ 1914–19. Trooper, Dorset Yeo.; 2nd Lieut., R.G.A.; Capt., R.A.F.; Instructor, School of Military Aeronautics, Toronto.
Remained in the Army: Major (1936–), R.A.

VIVIAN ST CLARE HILL. Born 13 March 1894, at Southwark. S. of Rev. James William St Clare Hill (Peterhouse, M.A. 1890), St Margaret's, Leatherhead, Surrey. Educ. at St Paul's School. Adm. 25 Feb. 1913: began res. 7 Oct. 1913. Matric. 21 Oct. 1913. Resumed res. (after War serv.) E. 1919.

B.A. (Ord. degree; all. 4 terms for War serv.) 1919.
✕ 1914–19. 2nd Lieut., S. Lancs Regt; Capt., M.G.C. *M.C. M.*
Westcott House, Cambridge, 1921. Ordained d. 1922, p. 1923 Winchester. Asst Principal, Royal School for the Blind, Leatherhead, 1922–4. Became Roman Catholic, 1924. Catholic Seminary, Wonersh, Guildford, 1924–6. Ordained R.C. p. 1929 St George's, Southwark. C. of St Joseph, Bromley, Kent, 1929–32; English Martyrs, Streatham, 1932–5; Convent Chapel, Our Lady Star of the Sea, Rottingdean, 1935–.

ROBERT LINNINGTON GRAHAM LINDSAY. Born 15 Feb. 1895, at Kensington. S. of William Arthur Lindsay (Peterhouse, adm. 1885), Tyrone House,

Belfast. Educ. at Charterhouse and Leys School. Adm. 1 March 1913: began res. 9 Oct. 1913. Matric. 21 Oct. 1913.

Went down after E. 1914.

✕ 1914–19. Lieut., R.E. (Signals); invalided out, 1916; A.P.M.'s Staff (as civilian), 1917–18; rejoined as Lieut., R.E. (Signals), 1918.

Remained in the Army as Lieut., R.E. (Signals), 1919–22. Lieut., Regular Army Res. of Officers, 1922–33; was Capt. 1926–33 (and local Major 1931–3), Cambridge Univ. O.T.C., cmdg. the Signal Co. from 1929. Died 17 June 1933 at Cambridge.

He matric. as Robert Graham Linnington LINDSAY.

Cousin of J. H. Lindsay (p. 54).

JOHN YORK SMITH. Born 23 June 1894, at Bury, Lancs. S. of John Edmund Smith, 138 Manchester Road, Bury. Educ. at Bury Grammar School. Adm. 1 March 1913: began res. 1 Oct. 1913. Matric. 21 Oct. 1913. Resided again (after War serv.) E. 1919 to E. 1920 inclusive.

B.A. (3rd Cl. Hist. Tri. Pt I, 1915; all. 2 terms for War serv.) 1916. 2nd Cl., 1st Div., Hist. Tri. Pt II, 1920. M.A. 1920.

✕ 1916–19. Pte, R.A.S.C. (M.T.); empld G.H.Q. (Records).

Asst Master, Silcoates School, nr Wakefield.

HUBERT STANLEY MIDDLETON, subsequently **Fellow**. Born 11 May 1890, at Windsor. S. of Joseph Middleton, 34 Temple Road, Windsor. Educ. at United Services College, Windsor. Adm. 11 March 1913: began res. 1 Oct. 1913. Matric. 21 Oct. 1913. Resided again (after War serv.) E. 1919 to E. 1920 inclusive. Organ Scholar.

B.A. (3rd Cl. Hist. Tri. Pt I, 1915; all. 3 terms for War serv.) 1916. M.A., Mus.B. 1920. Re-elected Organ Scholar, 1915.

✕ 1915–19. Capt., Suffolk Regt; empld as Education Officer.

Organist and Master of the Choir, Truro Cathedral, 1920–6. Organist and Magister Choristarum, Ely Cathedral, 1926–31. Organist of Trinity College, Cambridge, 1931–. F.R.C.O. 1911. F.R.A.M. 1928. Matric. and incorp. M.A., Merton College, Oxford, 17 Oct. 1934. D.Mus., Oxford, 1937.

Fellow (External), 1928–33. Director of Studies in Music, 1928–33; and Director of Music, 1933–.

University Lecturer in Music, 1938–.

Composer:

Carmen Petrinum. Cambridge, 1920.

Let my prayer be set forth; motet for double choir. (Year Book Press Ser. of Anthems and Church Music.) London, 1928.

Praise to the Holiest in the Height; anthem for double choir and organ. (Year Book Press Ser. of Anthems and Church Music.) London, 1930.

(With T. Grigg-Smith and C. Wood) Hosanna: a book of praise for young children. London [1931]. And other compositions for voice.

RICHARD NORMAN SCOTT TEBB. Born 14 July 1894, at Boscombe, Bournemouth. S. of William Scott Tebb (Peterhouse, M.D. 1890), Hopedale, Worple Road, Epsom. Educ. at King's College School. Adm. 3 April 1913: began res. 1 Oct. 1913. Matric. 21 Oct. 1913. Resided again (after War serv., with some terms kept whilst on military duty in Cambridge) M. 1919 to M. 1920 inclusive.

B.A. (Ord degree) 1916. M.A. 1921. Dipl. in Agric. 1921.

✕ 1915–19. Capt., Spec. List (O.C.B.) and Hampshire Regt.

Farming 1922– (now in Shropshire) with his brother, B. M. Tebb (p. 25).

VINCENT LEWIS. Born 13 Dec. 1893, at Caythorpe, Lincs. S. of Rev. Edward Thomas Lewis (decd), Rector of Caythorpe. Educ. at Brighton College, and R.M.A., Woolwich. Adm. 10 April 1913: began res. 2 Oct. 1913. Matric. 21 Oct. 1913.

Went down after E. 1914.

✕ 1914–22 [?]. Lieut., R.F.A.

WALTER HAMILTON LILLIE. Born 4 May 1895, at Richmond, Surrey. S. of John Lillie, Ivy Hall, Richmond. Educ. at Rugby School. Adm. 5 May 1913: began res. 6 Oct. 1913. Matric. 21 Oct. 1913.

Went down after M. 1914.
✕ 1915 [?]–[?]. Driver, American Field Ambulance, attd French Army; 2nd Lieut., United States Air Service.

JAMES EDWARD BAKER BERE MACLEAN. Born 26 Oct. 1894. S. of James Maclean (dec^d). Guardians: Charles Mackintosh, 31 Lombard Street, E.C., and William Macdonald Ballingall, 3 Highbury Place, N. Educ. at Dulwich College. Adm. 8 May 1913: began res. 3 Oct. 1913. Matric. 21 Oct. 1913.

Went down during M. 1914.
✕ 1914–19. Sqdn Cdr, R.N.A.S.; Major (S.), R.A.F. (W.) *D.S.C. M* 2.
Remained in the R.A.F. till 1924, when he retired with the rank of Flt Lieut.

TETE MENSA-ANNAN. Born 1 Jan. 1894, at Accra, Gold Coast. S. of Robert Mensa-Annan. Educ. at the Collegiate School, Accra; High School, Freetown; and King Edward VII. Grammar School, King's Lynn. Adm. 21 May 1913: began res. 1 Oct. 1913. Matric. 21 Oct. 1913.

B.A. (Ord. degree) 1916.

GEORGE ARTHUR HYDE. Born 31 July 1893, at Thornton Dale, Yorks, N.R. S. of Rev. Robert Hyde, Riccall Vicarage, nr York. Educ. at St Peter's School, York. Adm. 1 July 1913: began res. 8 Oct. 1913. Matric. 21 Oct. 1913. Resumed res. (after War serv.) M. 1919.

B.A. (Ord. degree; all 3 terms for War serv.) 1920. M.A. 1928.
✕ 1914–19. 2nd Lieut., King's Royal Rifle Corps; Capt., R.A.F. *M.C.*
Salisbury Theol. Coll., 1920. Ordained d. 1921, p. 1922 York. C. of St Mary, Bishophill Senior, *w.* St Clement, York, 1921–5; Great Ayton *w.* Newton, 1925–7; R. of South Milford, 1927–36; V. of St Chad, City and Dio. York, 1936–.

HENRY NURALAZEEM KHUNDKAR. Born 17 March 1890, at Calcutta. S. of Eusuf Ali Khundkar (dec^d). Educ. at St Xavier's College, Calcutta; Scottish Churches College, Calcutta; and Calcutta Univ. (B.A. degree). Adm. 19 July 1913: began res. 9 Oct. 1913. Matric. 21 Oct. 1913. Aff. Stud.

B.A., LL.B. (2nd Cl., 1st Div., Econ. Tri. Pt I, 1915; 2nd Cl. Law Tri. Pt II, 1917) 1917.
Called to the Bar, Lincoln's Inn, 28 Jan. 1918. Judicial Dept, Bengal, 1921–; with appt. as Judge, High Court, Calcutta, 1937–.
Since going down he has used only the names Nural Azeem KHUNDKAR.

GUY DU SAUTOY ATTHILL. Born 5 Sept. 1885, at Brandiston, Norfolk. S. of William Atthill, St Peter's School, Lee Park, Blackheath, S.E. Educ. at Christ's Hospital. Adm. 18 Aug. 1913: began res. 9 Oct. 1919. Matric. 21 Oct. 1919.

Went down after E. 1920.
✕ 1914–18. Major, Hampshire Regt. (W.)

RENÉ ANTON VAN RIJCKEVORSEL. Born 5 Feb. 1896, at 's Hertogenbosch, Holland. S. of Jonkheer Mr F. J. J. M. van Rijckevorsel (Member of the Provincial State), Hinthamerstraat, den Bosch, Holland. Educ. at St Willibrord's College, Katwijk a/d Rijn. Adm. 15 Oct. 1913: began res. 15 Oct. 1913. Matric. 21 Oct. 1913.

Went down after E. 1914.

HENRY SUTCLIFFE HAY. Born 5 March 1893, at Clayton, Bradford, Yorks. S. of Henry Hay, Clayton House, Clayton, Bradford. Educ. at Dollar Academy; and Bradford Grammar School. Adm. 9 Jan. 1914: began res. 15 Jan. 1914. Matric. 28 Jan. 1914.

B.A. (Ord. degree) 1916. M.A. 1920.
Ridley Hall, Cambridge, 1917. Ordained d. 1917, p. 1918 St Albans. C. of Luton, 1917–20; Ilkley, 1920–6; V. of St John Evang., Yeadon, 1926–32; R. of Dollar, Dio. St Andrews, 1932–.

FRANCIS LEOPOLD MOND. Born 20 July 1895, in London. S. of Emile Schweich Mond, 22 Hyde Park Square, W. Educ. at Rugby School. Adm. 18 Jan. 1914, by *bene discessit* from King's College: began res. 20 Jan. 1914. Matric. 21 Oct. 1912 (from King's College, where he resided M. 1912, L. and E. 1913).

Went down after E. 1914.
✕1914–18. Lieut., R.F.A.; Staff Lieut.; Lieut., R.A.F. *Killed in action over Bouzencourt-sur-Somme 15 May 1918.*
Bro. of A. W. Mond (p. 32), and first cousin once removed of Sir R. L. Mond (cr. Kt 1932; *Walker*, p. 583).
The Francis Mond Professorship of Aeronautical Engineering was founded and endowed in 1919 by Mr Emile Schweich Mond as a memorial of his son.

ARCHIBALD BUCHERER. Born 11 May 1894, at Ithaca, N.Y. S. of Alfred Henry Bucherer, Hon. Prof. of Physical Chemistry, Univ. of Bonn. Educ. at Gymnasium, Bonn. Rec. by G. F. C. Searle, M.A., Sc.D., Fellow of Peterhouse. Adm. 1914: began res. 22 April 1914. Matric. 5 May 1914.

Went down after E. 1914.
✕. Served in the German Army. Prisoner of War in Shropshire c. 1917.

GEORGE LESLIE BOYLE. Born 20 Nov. 1895, at Swansea. S. of William Boyle, 13 Windsor Terrace, Swansea. Educ. at Swansea Grammar School. Adm. 12 Jan. 1914: began res. 9 Oct. 1919. Matric. 21 Oct. 1919. Entrance Schol., Maths, £60.

B.A. (2nd Cl. Math. Tri. Pt I, 1920; 1st Cl. Geog. Tri. Pt I, 1922) 1922. M.A. 1926. Re-elected to Schol.* (and all. to change subject to Geography), 1921.
✕ 1914–19. Capt. and Adjt., Welsh Regt. (W 2.)
Asst Master, Silcoates School, nr Wakefield, 1922–6; and at Cambridge and County High School, 1926–. F.R.G.S. 1924. Capt. (1927–), Cambridge and County High School O.T.C. (T.A.).
College Director of Studies in Geography, 1929–30 and 1934–.

VAUGHAN PALMER DAVIES. Born 2 April 1895, at Luayuni Tea Estate, Sylhet, Assam, India. S. of Augustus Granville Harvey Davies, Luayuni Tea Estate. Educ. at Rossall School. Adm. 12 Jan. 1914: began res. 23 April 1919. Matric. 8 May 1919. Entrance Schol., Classics, £60.

Went down after E. 1919.
✕ 1914–19. Major, M.G.C. (W.)
Caterer, of 'Dean Incents', High Street, Berkhamsted, 1937–.

HUMPHREY PROCTER-GREGG. Born 31 July 1895, at Kirkby Lonsdale. S. of Oliver Procter-Gregg (formerly Procter, of Kirkby Lonsdale), Westham, Castletown, Isle of Man. Educ. at King William's College, Isle of Man. Adm. 12 Jan. 1914: began res. 1 Oct. 1914. Matric. 21 Oct. 1914. Entrance Schol., History, £50.

B.A. (2nd Cl., 2nd Div., Hist. Tri. Pt I, 1916; Spec. Exam. Music, 1916) 1917. Mus.B. 1920. Elected

Organ Scholar (during H. S. Middleton's absence on War serv.) *vice* History Scholar, Jan. 1916. Re-elected to Schol.* for History, June 1916. Re-apptd Organist, Oct. 1916; and again, June 1917.

Engaged 1919–30 mostly in opera companies, stage-managing and producing, e.g. British National Opera Co., Covent Garden Opera Co., Imperial League of Opera, 'Grand season' Covent Garden, Carl Rosa, manager of Royal College of Music Opera School, producer for Royal Manchester College of Music, etc.; also engaged in musical journalism, teaching and study. Lecturer in Music, Manchester Univ., 1935–. Hon. A.R.C.M. 1924.

Works:
English text (acting version) of Borodin's 'Prince Igor'. London [1933].
English translation of A. Boito's libretto of Verdi's 'Falstaff'. London [1936].
Sonata in A minor, for violin and piano. London, 1936.
And the music to several songs.

HENRY ALPHEGE UTTING. Born 29 Nov. 1895, at Liverpool. S. of (*later* Sir) John Utting, St Anne's Hill, Anfield Road, Liverpool. Educ. at Liverpool College. Adm. 12 Jan. 1914: began res 1 Oct. 1914. Matric. 21 Oct. 1914. Resumed res. (after War serv.) E. 1919. Entrance Schol., Maths, £40.

B.A. (Ord. degree; all. 4 terms for War serv.) 1920. M.A. 1923.
✗ 1915–19. Capt. and Adjt., R.F.A.
With Imperial Chemical Industries Ltd, Cunard Building, Liverpool. Capt., T.A. Res. of Officers.

EDWARD ARTHUR LUGARD GASKIN. Born 26 Nov. 1895, at Raipur, Central Provinces, India. S. of Lionel Edward Palmer Gaskin, I.C.S. Educ. at St Paul's School; and privately, with Rev. T. M. Bromley, M.A. Adm. 12 Jan. 1914: began res. 21 Oct. 1914. Entrance Schol., Classics, £40.

Did not matric. Went down during M. 1914.
✗ 1914–19. Corpl, R.E. (Motor Cyclist Section); Lieut., Spec. List (R.T.O.).

FRANCIS WILLIAM CHARLES LONG. Born 4 Feb. 1895, at Nottingham. S. of Francis John Long, St Mary's Square, Lichfield. Educ. at King Edward's School, Birmingham. Adm. 12 Jan. 1914: began res. 1 Oct. 1914. Matric. 21 Oct. 1914. Entrance Schol., Nat. Sciences, £40.

3rd Cl. Math. Tri. Pt I, 1915. Went down after E. 1915.
✗ 1917–19. Sapper, R.E. (Signals). (W.)
In business at Lichfield.

ARTHUR HAMMOND BUTLER SHIPLEY. Born 26 Aug. 1895, at Ledbury, Herefordshire. S. of Rev. Arthur Granville Shipley, All Saints' Vicarage, Pontefract, Yorks. Educ. at Haileybury College. Adm. 12 Jan. 1914. Entrance Schol., History, £40.

Did not matric.
✗ 1914–16. Pte, R. Fusiliers (P.S. Bn); 2nd Lieut., Yorkshire Regt. *Killed in action 27 Sept. 1916.*

ROY ETRICK BENEY WILLIS. Born 24 Aug. 1895, at Hove, Sussex. S. of George Richard Willis (dec^d) and Mrs Willis, St David's, London Road, Guildford. Educ. at Linton House School and St Paul's School, London. Rec. by A. D. Hardie, M.A. (Peterhouse), Head Master of Linton House School. Adm. 1913.

Did not matric.
✗1914–20. Capt., R. Warwickshire Regt.

Kumar Shri PRATAPSINHJI. Born 1 Sept. 1893, at Sarodad, Kathiawar, India. S. of Kumar Shri Joovansinhji, and nephew of H.H. The Maharaja Jam Sahib of Nawanagar (Ranjitsinhji). Educ. at Rajkumar College, Rajkot; then privately, with Rev. H. Foster, M.A., Malvern, then with R. S. Goodchild, M.A., Cambridge. Adm. 1913: began res. 12 Oct. 1914. Matric. 21 Oct. 1914.

Went down after M. 1918.
Served in the Indian Army 1919–30, retiring with the rank of Lieut. Now (1932) in command of the Nawanagar State Lancers at Jamnagar.

WILLIAM GEORGE BOLLARD. Born 26 July 1894, at Burton-on-Trent. S. of George Bollard. Educ. at Kettering Grammar School. Adm. 1914: began res. 7 Oct. 1914. Matric. 21 Oct. 1914.

B.A. (Ord. degree; all. 3 terms for War work) 1917.
Was serving with the Church Army in France during 1917.

JOB (WESTWOOD) WATTS. Born 3 July 1894, at Roseville, Coseley, Staffs. S. of John Watts, Providence Road, Coseley. Educ. mostly privately. Adm. March 1914: began res. 17 Jan. 1920. Matric. 28 Jan. 1920.

B.A. (2ⁿᵈ Cl. Math. Tri. Pt I, 1920; Jun. Opt. Pt II (b), 1922; allowed 1 term for War serv.) 1922. M.A. 1933.
✕ 1918–19. Lieut., R.A.F.
Asst Master, Tonbridge School, 1922–. F.R.Met.Soc.1919.
He matric. as Job WATTS; the name Westwood added since baptism.
Author:
    Epithalamium omnium; a poem. (Tonbridge, 1927.)
    The rose and the thistle; poems. (Tonbridge, 1927.)

ROBERT ROGERSON JORDAN. Born 5 Sept. 1890, at Carlisle. S. of William Hill Jordan (decᵈ) and Mrs Jordan, 8 Fisher Street, Carlisle. Educ. at Carlisle Grammar School, and Grosvenor College, Carlisle. Adm. Oct. 1914.

Matric. 22 Oct. 1920 from Queens' College.

CHARLES HUBERT WYNN KENRICK. Born 20 Feb. 1894, at Anerley, Surrey. S. of Cdr Hubert Wynn Kenrick, R.N.R. Educ. at Haileybury College. Adm. 1914: began res. 1 Oct. 1914. Matric. 21 Oct. 1914.

Went down after M. 1914.
✕ 1914–16. 2nd Lieut., The Buffs (E. Kent Regt). Invalided out.
Still an invalid. Lately Asst Master, Malvern School, Sydney, Australia; and Head Master, Berwick Grammar School, Victoria, Australia. Now (1932) engaged in various kinds of honorary work, especially relief work.

JACK LESLIE SOWDEN. Born 23 Dec. 1895, at Criffel Avenue, Streatham Hill, S.W. S. of William John Sowden, 66 Basinghall Street, E.C. Educ. at College for the Blind, Worcester. Adm. 1914: began res. 12 Oct. 1914. Matric. 21 Oct. 1914.

B.A. (Ord. degree) 1917. M.A. 1922.
Ordained d. 1919, p. 1920 London. C. of St Anne, Hoxton, 1919–20; St Peter, Hornsey, 1920–4; Christ Church, Crouch End, 1924–8; Bishop's Hatfield, 1928–30; R. and V. of Freckenham (a Peterhouse living), 1930–, w. Worlington since 1932, Dio. St Edmundsbury and Ipswich.
Freeman of City of London, and Member of Worshipful Co. of Makers of Playing Cards, 1917–. Governor of Christ's Hospital, 1921–.

Mom Luang OON ISRASENA. Born 31 Oct. 1893, at Bangkok, Siam. S. of Mom Rachawong Yen Israsena. Educ. at King's College, Bangkok; Château de Lancy, Paris; Geneva; and Haileybury College. Adm. 1914: began res. 2 Oct. 1914. Matric. 21 Oct. 1914.

B.A. (Ord. degree) 1917.
✕ 1918–19. Interpreter (rank of Naisib), Siamese Expeditionary Force. *Died in France* 8 *March* 1919 *as the result of an accident on service.*
The College 'Historical Register' gives the year of his birth as 1895; Haileybury College Register gives 1894; information from Bangkok 1893.

ERIC READ. Born 5 Sept. 1895, at Blackpool. S. of William John Read, 32 Birley Street, Blackpool. Educ. at Leys School. Adm. 1914: began res. 21 Jan. 1919. Matric. 29 Jan. 1919.

> B.A. (Ord degree; all. 4 terms for War serv.) 1920. M.A. 1927.
> Half-Blue: Water Polo, 1919, 1920.
> ✕ 1914–19. Capt., R.F.A. (W.) *Belgian Croix de Guerre.*
> Solicitor (adm. Oct. 1922); practising at Blackpool (W. J. Read & Son).

WALDEMAR FRANKLIN. Born 29 Dec. 1896, at St Petersburg, Russia. S. of Frank Franklin (dec^d) and Mrs Franklin, Abbotsbury, Nelson Road, Bournemouth. Educ. at Marlborough College. Adm. 1914.

> Did not matric.
> ✕ 1914–19. Lieut., Dorsetshire Regt; Lieut., R.A.F. (W 2.)
> Petroleum Geologist.

CHARLES HENRY ARTHUR FRENCH. Born 7 Sept. 1884, at Gloucester. S. of John Edwin French, Moseley, Birmingham. Educ. at King Edward's Camp Hill Grammar School, Birmingham. Adm. 1914.

> Did not matric.
> ✕ 1914–21 [?]. Capt., Lincolnshire Regt; Capt., Gen. List (R.E., Signals); Major, D.A.Q.M.G.; Capt., R. Warwickshire Regt. (W.) *M.C. M* 2.

ARTHUR JOHN WAKERLEY. Born 31 Oct. 1893, at Leicester. S. of Arthur Wakerley, 14 Market Place, Leicester. Educ. at Leys School. Adm. 1914: began res. 2 Oct. 1914. Matric. 21 Oct. 1914.

> Went down after L. 1915.
> ✕ 1915–17. Capt., Leicestershire Regt. *Killed in action* 8 *June* 1917.

ALFRED SIDELL MASON. Born 8 June 1886, at Wivenhoe, Essex. S. of Robert James Mason, 14 High Street, Wivenhoe. Educ. at Royal Grammar School, Colchester. Adm. 1914.

> Matric. 21 Oct. 1920 from Gonville and Caius College.
> ✕ 1914–19. Major, Devonshire Regt; D.A.Q.M.G. (W.) *O.B.E.*

WILLIAM OSCAR COSGROVE. Born 6 Feb. 1894, at New Southgate, Middlesex. S. of William Owen Cosgrove, Hillside, Colney Hatch Lane, Muswell Hill, N. Educ. at Owen's School, Islington. Adm. 1 June 1914: began res. 1 Oct. 1914. Matric. 21 Oct. 1914. Resumed res. (after War serv.) E. 1919.

> B.A (2nd Cl., 2nd Div., Hist. Tri. Pt II, 1920; all. 3 terms for War serv.) 1920. 2nd Cl. Theol. Tri. Pt II (*c*), 1921. M.A. 1923.
> ✕ 1914–19. Lieut., R.F.A.
> Westcott House, Cambridge, 1922. Ordained d. 1922, p. 1923 Canterbury. Asst Master, Sutton Valence School, 1921–4. Chaplain and Asst Master, Malvern College, 1925– (and House Master, 1933–).

WALTER WOODS McKEOWN. Born 2 Oct. 1894, at Toronto, Canada. S. of Dr Walter McKeown, 7 College Street, Toronto. Educ. at Upper Canada College, Toronto; Toronto Univ.; and l'Institut Saint-Louis, Brussels. Adm. 4 June 1914: began res. 5 Oct. 1914. Matric. 21 Oct. 1914. Resumed res. (after War serv.) E. 1919.

> B.A. (Ord. degree; all. 4 terms for War serv.) 1921.
> ✕ 1914–19. Lieut., R.F.A. *M.C.*

FRANCIS MUSTAPHA BELARIBI. Born April 1874, at Ain M'lila, Department Constantine, Algeria. Of Bartlands, Shrawley, Worcs. S. of Bouzid Belaribi, Sheekh of Ain M'lila. Educ. privately, with Rev. J. D. Lambi Leyland, M.A., and E. A. Reuneman, B.A. Rec. by Rev. J. B. Frith, M.A., Shrawley Rectory, and W. R. Crowdy, B.A. Adm. 1914: began res. 12 Oct. 1914. Matric. 21 Oct. 1914.

Went down after M. 1914.
✕ 1915–16. French Army. Apptd an Interpreter. *Died 12 Aug. 1916 in hospital at Hauteville, Ain, France.*
He was a French subject until granted a cert. of naturalization in this country on 12 Dec. 1912, and was a landed proprietor in Tashamana, Department Constantine, Algeria, and also in Worcs.
He matric. as Francis BELARIBI.

OSCAR ERIC HARVEY. Born 12 Jan. 1895, at Great Harwood, nr Blackburn. S. of Samuel Henry Harvey, 18 St Hubert's Road, Great Harwood. Educ. at Queen Elizabeth's Grammar School, Blackburn. Adm. 1914: began res. 12 Oct. 1914. Matric. 21 Oct. 1914. Resumed res. (after War work) M. 1919.

B.A. (3rd Cl. Mod. & Med. Lang. Tri., 1920; all. 3 terms for War work) 1920. M.A. 1923.
On munition work during the War, at Barrow-in-Furness, 1915–18.
Schoolmaster; with appt. as Asst Master, Oswestry High School, 1929–.

FREDERICK ELFORD COPLESTON. Born 30 Oct. 1894, at Willand, Devon. S. of William Chester Copleston, Elford House, Exeter. Educ. at St John's School, Leatherhead. Adm. 1914.

Did not matric. Migrated to Oriel College, Oxford, after the War.

RAYMOND MEADOWS. Born 29 June 1895, at Stratford-on-Avon. S. of Thomas Henry Meadows, 44 Wood Street, Stratford-on-Avon. Educ. at King Edward VI. School, Stratford-on-Avon. Adm. 4 Sept. 1914: began res. 10 Oct. 1914. Matric. 21 Oct. 1914. Resumed res. (after War serv.) M. 1919.

B.A. (3rd Cl. Mod. & Med. Lang. Tri., *f*, 1920; all. 5 terms for War serv.) 1920.
✕ 1914–19. Capt., R. Warwickshire Regt; attd King's Own (Yorkshire L.I.). (W.)
Clerk with N. M. Rothschild & Sons (merchants and bankers), New Court, St Swithin's Lane, London, E.C. 4.

HUGH NEVILLE PACKARD. Born 5 July 1895, at Watford, Herts. S. of Henry Charles Packard, Fotherington, Osterley Park Road, Southall, Middlesex. Educ. at Highgate School. Adm. 1914: began res. 1 Oct. 1914. Matric. 21 Oct. 1914. Resumed res. (after War serv., with some terms kept whilst on military duty in Cambridge) L. 1919.

B.A. (Ord. degree) 1919. 2nd Cl., 2nd Div., Hist. Tri. Pt II, 1920.
✕ 1914–18. Capt., Special List (O.C.B.).
Private Sec. to 1st Lord Hollenden, senior partner of I. & R. Morley (warehousemen, of 18 Wood Street, London, E.C. 2), 1923–8; thereafter Advertising Manager of that firm.

ARTHUR EDWIN MARLEY. Born 14 Dec. 1872, at Sherburn Hill, Co. Durham. S. of John Marley. Educ. at Univ. of Durham College of Physical Science, Newcastle-on-Tyne. Adm. 1914: began res. 13 Oct. 1914. Matric. 21 Oct. 1898 (as Non-Coll. Student, and kept 9 terms as such).

Went down during M. 1914.
✕ 1915–19. Lieut., Special List (Interpreter).

SURESHCHANDRA SEN. Born 1 Jan. 1894, at Gauhati, Assam, India. S. of Aswinikumar Sen, 4 Amherst Row, Calcutta. Educ. at Kishori-lal Jubilee School, Dacca; and Dacca College (B.Sc. degree, Calcutta Univ.). Rec. by W. A. J. Archbold, M.A. (Peterhouse), Principal of Dacca College. Adm. Oct. 1914: began res. 10 Oct. 1914. Matric. 21 Oct. 1914. Aff. Stud.

> B.A. (3ʳᵈ Cl. Nat. Sci. Tri. Pt I, 1916; Cert. of Dilig. Study, 1917) 1917.
> Industrial Chemist: now (1932) Quinologist to the Government of Bengal.

CLIFFORD RICHMOND MAGGS. Born 4 Aug. 1896, at Pretoria, Transvaal. S. of Joseph Maggs. Educ. at St Marylebone Grammar School, London; and Athénée Royal d'Ixelles, Brussels. Adm. Oct. 1914: began res. 16 Jan. 1915. Matric. 28 Jan. 1915.

> Resided till L. 1916 inclusive; thereafter migrated to Non-Coll. Students.

NORMAN GROVE DUNNING. Born 17 Dec. 1894, at Barrow-in-Furness. S. of Elisha Dunning, 46 Hawcoat Lane, Barrow-in-Furness. Educ. at Victoria Grammar School, Ulverston. Adm. 16 Jan. 1915, by *bene discessit* from Non-Coll. Board: began res. 15 Jan. 1915. Matric. 22 Oct. 1914 (as Non-Coll. Student, residing as such M. 1914). Resumed res. (after War work) L. 1919.

> B.A. (3ʳᵈ Cl. Hist. Tri. Pt II, 1919; all. 4 terms for War work) 1919. LL.B. (3ʳᵈ Cl. Law Tri. Pt II, 1920) 1920. M.A. 1922.
> On War work, 1915–18.
> Methodist Minister: under direction of the Home Mission Committee, 1919–26; travelling in Africa, Australia and the East in the interests of the Methodist Missions, 1926–9; Biblical and Theological Tutor, Cliff College, Calver, 1929–34; Home Mission Committee again, 1934; London Mission, West, 1935–.
> Bro. of J. G. Dunning (p. 103).
> Author:
> *Samuel Chadwick*... London, 1933.

JOHN BRABYN NORTH. Born 23 Dec. 1896, at Kenfield Hall, Petham, Kent. S. of Colonel Bordrigge North North, C.B., M.V.O., Newton Hall, Kirkby Lonsdale. Educ. privately, with Rev. F. Meyrick Jones, M.A., Holt, Norfolk. Adm. 4 Dec. 1914: began res. 15 Jan. 1915. Matric. 28 Jan. 1915.

> Went down after E. 1915.
> ✗ 1915–19. 2nd Lieut., Grenadier Gds; R.M.C., Sandhurst; 2nd Lieut., 2nd Dragoons (R. Scots Greys). (W.)
> Remained in the Army. Placed on half pay on account of ill health, 25 Sept. 1919. *Died 17 May 1921 at Toulon, France, from the effects of having been gassed in the War.*

HARRY EDWARD WHITEHOUSE. Born 11 Sept. 1896, at St Nicholas, Glam. S. of Harry Whitehouse, The School House, Barry, Glam. Educ. at Barry County School; and privately. Adm. 12 Jan. 1915: began res. 1 Oct. 1915. Matric. 21 Oct. 1915. Resumed res. (after War serv.) E. 1919. Entrance Schol., Maths, £60.

> B.A. (1ˢᵗ Cl. Math. Tri. Pt I, 1916; 1ˢᵗ Cl. Mech. Sci. Tri., 1920; all. 2 terms for War serv.) 1920. M.A. 1926.
> ✗ 1916–19. Lieut., R.G.A. *M.C.*
> Civil Engineer. Assoc.M.Inst.C.E. 1926. A.M.I.Mech.E. 1926.

ALEXANDER JAMES BARTLET BEGG. Born 14 Sept. 1896, at Usworth, Co. Durham. S. of Rev. Alexander Begg, Usworth Rectory, Washington, Co. Durham. Educ. at Christ's Hospital. Adm. 12 Jan. 1915. Entrance Schol., Maths, £60.

> Did not matric.
> ✗ 1915–18. Lieut., Northumberland Fus. (W.) *M.C. Killed in action 21 March 1918.*

FREDERICK MALLINSON MARRS. Born 26 Aug. 1896, at Nottingham. S. of Rev. Francis Marrs, 191 Stamford Street, Brooke's Bar, Manchester. Educ. at King Edward VII. School, Sheffield. Adm. 12 Jan. 1915. Entrance Schol., Classics, £40.

Did not matric.
✕ 1915–17. R.M.C., Sandhurst; 2nd Lieut., Worcestershire Regt. *Killed in action at Bouchavesnes 4 March* 1917.

ROBERT CECIL THOMAS PETTY. Born 10 May 1896, in London. S. of William Robert Petty, Rockbourne, Park Avenue, Enfield, Middlesex. Educ. at Southgate County School, Middlesex. Adm. 12 Jan. 1915: began res. 28 April 1919. Matric. 8 May 1919. Entrance Schol., Nat. Sciences, £40.

B.A. (3rd Cl. Nat. Sci. Tri. Pt I, 1920; 3rd Cl. Pt II (Chemistry), 1921; all. 2 terms for War serv.) 1921. Re-elected to Schol.*, 1920.
✕ 1915–19. 2nd Lieut., King's Own (Yorkshire L.I.); Lieut., M.G.C. (W.)
Apptd Asst Bacteriologist, Indian Agricultural Service, 1921. Died 15 March 1922 at Pusa, Bihar, India, after an operation for appendicitis.

HERBERT DENNIS NORTHFIELD. Born 4 Sept. 1896, at Harrogate. S. of Herbert John Northfield, Applehurst, Flora Avenue, Darlington. Educ. at Darlington Grammar School. Adm. 12 Jan. 1915: began res. 9 Oct. 1915. Matric. 21 Oct. 1915. Resumed res. (after War serv.) E. 1919. Entrance Exhib., History, £30.

B.A. (1st Cl., 2nd Div., Hist. Tri. Pt II, 1920; all. 3 terms for War serv.) 1920. Cert. (with endorsement for History) of Teachers' Tr. Syndicate, 1921. M.A. 1923. Schol.* of £40, 1920.
✕ 1916–19. Pte, R. Scots.
Missionary, Baptist Missionary Soc., Dacca, Bengal, 1924–. Headmaster, Baptist Mission Boys' School, Barisal, 1925–6. Warden, Baptist Mission Hostel, Dacca, 1927–30. Nominated member of Dacca Univ. Court, 1930; and of Dacca Board of Intermediate and Secondary Education, 1933.
Author:
A front-line post: Mission work in Dacca, India. London (1938).

JOHN GAVIN DRUMMOND CURRIE. Born 25 April 1895, at Buxton. S. of John Currie, Holmedale, New Park Road, Clapham Park, S.W. Educ. at Eastbourne College; and privately, with A. W. Benson. Adm. June 1914: began res. 1 Oct. 1915. Matric. 21 Oct. 1915.

B.A. (Ord. degree) 1918.
M.R.C.S., L.R.C.P. 1922. In practice at Cheltenham.

RICHARD HURD. Born 15 March 1894, at Flowton Rectory, Ipswich. S. of Rev. Walter Robert Hurd, Tasburgh Rectory, Norwich. Educ. at St John's School, Leatherhead. Adm. 29 June 1914: began res. 11 Oct. 1915. Matric. 21 Oct. 1915.

B.A. (Ord. degree) 1918. M.A. 1923.
Ridley Hall, Cambridge, 1919. Ordained d. 1919, p. 1920 Norwich. C. of Cromer, 1919–26; V. of St Thomas, Heigham, Dio. Norwich, 1926–.

SAMUEL WILLIAM BOWER. Born 29 Dec. 1895, at Alwalton, Hunts. S. of Felix Bower, 17 Oundle Road, Peterborough. Educ. at Huntingdon Grammar School. Adm. 28 Jan. 1915. Miller Exhib.

Did not matric.
✕ 1915–19. Lieut., Northamptonshire Regt; Lieut., 7th Rajputs, I.A. (W.)
Remained in the Indian Army: Major (1934–), I.A.

Mom Luang CHAROON SNIDWONGS. Born 18 Nov. 1896, at Bangkok, Siam. S. of Chao Phya Wongsa. Educ. at King's College, Bangkwang; and privately with D. Daniell, Daresbury, Pinecliffe Avenue, Bournemouth. Adm. Dec. 1914: began res. 11 Oct. 1915. Matric. 21 Oct. 1915.

> B.A. (Ord. degree) 1919.
> With the Siamese State Railways, 1922–; apptd Superintending Engineer of Workshops, 1930.

REGINALD CHARLES WARREN JERVOIS. Born 25 Dec. 1896, at Dover. S. of Major Charles Edwin Jervois, c/o Lloyds Bank, Newquay, Cornwall. Educ. at Marlborough College. Adm. 24 May 1915: began res. 12 Oct. 1915. Matric. 21 Oct. 1915. Resumed res. (after War serv.) M. 1919.

> B.A. (2nd Cl. Engl. Tri. (a), 1921; all. 1 term for War serv.) 1921. LL.B. (2nd Cl. Law Tri. Pt II, 1922) 1922. M.A. 1924.
> ✗ 1916–19. 2nd Lieut., R.G.A.; Lieut., R.A.F.
> Chartered Accountant. A.C.A. 1926. Financial Sec. of the Society for the Propagation of the Gospel, 1929–.

ERNEST GEOFFREY ADAMS. Born 31 March 1897, at Bedford. S. of Rev. Ernest William Adams, St John's Vicarage, Bury St Edmunds. Educ. at King Edward VI. Grammar School, Bury St Edmunds. Adm. 1915: began res. 11 Oct. 1915. Matric. 21 Oct. 1915.

> Went down during L. 1916; but also kept M. 1917 whilst in O.C.B. at Cambridge.
> ✗ 1916–18. Pte, Cambridgeshire Regt; 2nd Lieut., Norfolk Regt. (W.) *Died 26 June 1918 of wounds received in action.*

WALTER AUBREY FOOKS. Born 21 May 1896, at Dawlish. S. of Charles Job Fooks, Larchdale, Park Road, Woking. Educ. at College for the Blind, Worcester. Adm. 25 April 1915: began res. 11 Oct. 1915. Matric. 21 Oct. 1915.

> B.A., LL.B. (2nd Cl., 2nd Div., Hist. Tri. Pt I, 1917; 2nd Cl. Law Tri. Pt II, 1918) 1918. M.A. 1922.
> Solicitor (adm. Jan. 1922); but does not practise.

AJIT NATH MALLIK. Born 3 May 1897, at Patna, Bihar and Orissa, India. S. of Prof. Devendra Nath Mallik (Peterhouse, B.A. 1892), 11 Williams Lane, Bow Bazar, Calcutta. Educ. at St Joseph's Convent, Patna; St Michael's High School, Digha Ghat, Patna; St Joseph's High School, Calcutta; and Presidency College, Calcutta. Adm. 1915: began res. 7 Oct. 1915. Matric. 21 Oct. 1915.

> Resided till L. 1919 inclusive. B.A. (Ord. degree) 1924.
> Asst Traffic Superintendent, East Indian Railway, Calcutta, 1921–5; and with Martin & Co's Light Railways, 1926–7. Apptd Traffic Manager, Gwalior State Railways, but deputed as Gen. Manager of Matheran Railway, 1927–8. Personal Asst to American Consul General, Calcutta, 1928–33. Lecturer in Railway Transport and Inland and Foreign Trade, Calcutta Univ., 1933–.

SANT RAM KHARBANDA. Born 1893. S. of Gobind Ram, Lahore. Educ. at Government School, Lahore. Adm. 9 Jan. 1916: began res. 14 Jan. 1916. Matric. 31 Jan. 1916.

> Went down after M. 1918.

VICTOR HENRY THOMPSON BOYTON. Born 13 April 1897, at Wandsworth. S. of Charles Taylor Boyton, Bank House, Horsefair, Birmingham. Educ. at King Edward's School, Birmingham. Adm. 10 Jan. 1916. Entrance Schol., Maths, £60.

> Did not matric.
> ✗ 1916–17. 2nd Lieut., R.G.A. *Killed in action 30 May 1917.*

ERNEST CHARLES REGAN. Born 21 Nov. 1897, in London. S. of William James Regan, 95 Woodside, Wimbledon. Educ. at Wimbledon College and St Paul's School. Adm. 10 Jan. 1916. Entrance Schol., Classics, £60.

Did not matric.
✖ 1916–18. 2nd Lieut., R. Sussex Regt. *Killed in action 21 March* 1918.
Bro. of L. O. Regan (p. 81).

RICHARD HARDCASTLE SETTLE. Born 12 July 1897, at Horwich, Lancs. S. of Robert Hardcastle Settle (dec^d) and Mrs Settle (now Mrs Ashworth), 174 Westminster Road, Morecambe. Educ. at Royal Grammar School, Lancaster. Adm. 10 Jan. 1916: began res. 9 Oct. 1916. Matric. 23 Oct. 1916. Resumed res. (after War serv.) E. 1919. Entrance Schol., Nat. Sciences, £50.

B.A. (2nd Cl. Nat. Sci. Tri. Pt I, 1920; 2nd Cl. Pt II (Chemistry), 1921) 1921. Re-elected to Schol., 1920.
✖ 1917–19. 2nd Lieut., R.G.A.
Chemist, Government Laboratory, 1922–. A.I.C. 1922.

WILLIAM LANGSTAFF. Born 7 Nov. 1897, at Ramsgate. S. of William Henry Langstaff, Eskdale, Grove Road, Ramsgate. Educ. at Sir Roger Manwood's Grammar School, Sandwich. Adm. 10 Jan. 1916: began res. 2 Oct. 1916. Matric. 23 Oct. 1916. Resumed res. (after War serv.) E. 1919. Entrance Schol., Nat. Sciences (Maths and Physics), £40.

B.A. (1st Cl. Math. Tri. Pt I, 1917; Sen. Opt. Pt II, 1920; all. 2 terms for War serv.) 1920. 3rd Cl. Nat. Sci. Tri. Pt II (Physics), 1921. Re-elected to Schol.*, 1920.
✖ 1917–19. 2nd Lieut., R.E. (Signals).
Asst Examiner, Patent Office, 1921–6; and Examiner, 1926–.

PAUL HERBERT STEELE. Born 5 May 1897, in London. S. of Herbert George Steele, Garden Court, Warwick's Bench, Guildford. Educ. at Dulwich College. Adm. 10 Jan. 1916: began res. 10 Oct. 1919. Matric. 21 Oct. 1919. Entrance Schol., Classics, £40.

B.A. (Ord. degree; all. 3 terms for War serv.) 1921. M.A. 1926.
✖ 1916–19. Gnr, R.G.A.; Lieut., Middlesex Regt. (W.)
Sec., British Home and Hospital for Incurables, Streatham, 1933–.

BASIL WILLEY. Born 25 July 1897, in London. S. of William Herbert Willey, Rozel, Grove Avenue, Church End, Finchley, N. Educ. at University College School. Adm. 10 Jan. 1916: began res. 20 Jan. 1919. Matric. 23 Oct. 1916. Entrance Schol., History, £40.

B.A. (1st Cl., 2nd Div., Hist. Tri. Pt II, 1920; all. 4 terms for War serv.) 1920. 1st Cl. Engl. Tri (A), 1921. M.A. 1923. Re-elected to Schol.*, 1920. Hugo de Balsham Stud. (for research in English Literature), £100, 1921. *Le Bas Prize*, 1922.
✖ 1916–18. 2nd Lieut., W. Yorks Regt. (W.) (P.)
College Director of Studies in English, 1922–6.
Lecturer for English Tripos, 1923–. Lecturer for Extra-Mural Board, 1926–32. Probationary Lecturer in Faculty of English, 1926–31; and Asst Lecturer, 1931–4. University Lecturer in English, 1934–.
Fellow of Pembroke College, 1935–.
Author:
　　Tendencies in Renaissance literary theory. (Le Bas Prize, 1922.) Cambridge, 1922.
　　The seventeenth century background; studies in the thought of the age in relation to poetry and religion.
　　London, 1934.

HENRY CHARLES TUER SEYMOUR. Born 13 April 1897, at Chelsea. S. of Harry Tuer Seymour, 11 Dartrey Road, Chelsea, S.W. Educ. at Westminster City School. Adm. 10 Jan. 1916: began res. 28 Jan. 1919. Matric. 29 Jan. 1919. Entrance Schol., Maths, £40.

B.A. (1st Cl. Math. Tri. Pt I, 1919; Sen. Opt. Pt II, 1920; all. 5 terms for War. serv.) 1920. M.A. 1926.
⚔ 1916–19. 2nd Lieut., R. Berkshire Regt; Lieut., M.G.C.
Sec. of a Life Assurance Office.

LEWIS GUY PEIRSON. Born 19 Nov. 1897, at Bodmin, Cornwall. S. of Rev. Ernest Goodwyn Peirson (Peterhouse, M.A. 1905), Bothwicks, Newquay, Cornwall. Educ. at Oundle School. Adm. 10 Jan. 1916: began res. 9 Oct. 1916. Matric. 23 Oct. 1916. Entrance Exhib., Nat. Sciences, £30.

B.A. (3rd Cl. Nat. Sci. Tri. Pt I, 1918; 3rd Cl. Pt II (Chemistry), 1919) 1919. Re-elected to Exhib., 1918.
Asst Master, Marlborough College, 1919–. A.I.C. 1919. F.L.S. 1927.

EVELYN ANSELL. Born 23 Aug. 1898, at Esher, Surrey. S. of John Evelyn Ansell, 4 Glenloch Road, Hampstead, N.W. Educ. at University College School. Adm. 15 Aug. 1916: began res. 7 Oct. 1916. Matric. 23 Oct. 1916. Resumed res. (after War serv.) L. 1919.

B.A. (2nd Cl., 1st Div., Moral Sci. Tri. Pt I, 1920; all. 2 terms for War serv.) 1920. 2nd Cl. Moral Sci. Tri. Pt II, 1921. M.A. 1923.
⚔ 1917–18. 2nd Lieut., The King's (Liverpool Regt); attd R. Irish Rifles. (W.)
With Library Bureau, Ltd, London, 1921–2. Handloom weaver, 1922–3. Studied at Univ. of Freiburg i. Br., 1923–4; and at University College, London (School of Librarianship), 1924–5. Library Asst, London School of Economics, 1925–6. Asst Under-Librarian, University Library, Cambridge, 1926–33; and Under-Librarian, 1933–. F.L.A. 1930.
Compiler of this Register.

MOHAMAD ABDUL AZIM. Born 25 Nov. 1895. S. of Mohamad Mahmood Khan Bahadur. Educ. at Mohammedan Anglo-Oriental School and College, Aligarh (B.A. degree, Allahabad Univ.). Adm. 1916: began res. 10 Oct. 1916. Matric. 23 Oct. 1916.

B.A. (3rd Cl. Econ. Tri. Pt I, 1918; 3rd Cl. Pt II, 1919) 1919. LL.B. (3rd Cl. Law Tri. Pt II, 1920) 1920.

ROBERT HILARY CLEMENT JOHNSTON. Born 6 Jan. 1898, at Cambridge. S. of James Clement Johnston, 54 Bateman Street, Cambridge. Educ. privately, with Rev. H. Bedford. Adm. Jan. 1917: began res. 16 Jan. 1917. Matric. 24 Feb. 1917.

B.A. (Ord. degree) 1919.
Was a Business manager. Died 25 April 1929 at Hornsey, Middlesex.

BRIAN MAXWELL TEBB. Born 3 Dec. 1898, at Anerley, Surrey. S. of William Scott Tebb (Peterhouse, M.D. 1890), The Old Lodge, Church Street, Epsom. Educ. at King's College School. Rec. by H. J. Edwards, M.A., Fellow and Tutor of Peterhouse. Adm. Feb. 1917: began res. 15 Feb. 1917. Matric. 5 May 1917. Resumed res. (after War serv.) L. 1919.

B.A. (Ord. degree; all. 5 terms for War serv.) 1920.
⚔ 1917–18. 2nd Lieut., Suffolk Regt.
Farming 1922– (now in Shropshire) with his brother, R. N. S. Tebb (p. 14).

WILLIAM JOSEPH HODGETTS. Born 6 May 1900, at St Helens, Lancs. S. of Charles Hodgetts, 98 Park Road, St Helens. Educ. at Cowley School, St Helens. Adm. 15 Jan. 1917: began res. 1 Oct. 1917. Matric. 22 Oct. 1917. Resumed res. (after War serv.) L. 1919. Entrance Schol., Maths, £70.

B.A. (1st Cl. Math. Tri. Pt I, 1918; Wrang. Pt II, 1920; all. 1 term for War serv.) 1920. M.A. 1931.
✕ 1918–19. Driver, H.A.C.
Asst Master, Cowley School, St Helens, 1920–4; at Bristol Grammar School, 1924–8; and at Merchant Taylors' School, 1929–.

ERIC HERBERT WARMINGTON. Born 15 March 1898, at Cambridge. S. of John Herbert Warmington (Peterhouse, M.A. 1894), 56 Glisson Road, Cambridge. Educ. at Perse School, Cambridge. Adm. 15 Jan. 1917: began res. 10 Oct. 1919. Matric. 21 Oct. 1919. Entrance Schol., Classics, £60.

B.A. (1st Cl. Class. Tri. Pt I, 1921; 1st Cl. Pt II (c), 1922) 1922. M.A. 1926. Schol.* of £70, 1921.
Hon. mentioned for Porson Prize and Browne Medal (Latin Epigram), 1920. Le Bas Prize, 1925.
✕ 1917–19. Lieût., King's Own (Yorkshire L.I.).
Asst Master, Charterhouse, 1922–3; and at Mill Hill School, 1923–5. Reader in Ancient History, London Univ. (King's College), 1925–35. Professor of Classics, London Univ. (Birkbeck College), 1935–. F.R.Hist.Soc. 1928.
    Author:
      Athens: a picture of a great Greek city. (Benn's Sixpenny Library.) London (1928).
      The commerce between the Roman Empire and India. Cambridge, 1928.
      (With M. Cary) The ancient explorers. London (1929).
      Greek geography. (Library of Greek Thought.) London (1934).
    Editor:
      Remains of old Latin; newly edited and translated by E. H. Warmington. Vols. 1 & 2. (Loeb
        Classical Library.) London, 1935 & 1936.

PERCIVAL JOSEPH GRIFFITHS. Born 15 Jan. 1899, in London. S. of Joseph Thomas Griffiths, 11 Denver Road, Stamford Hill, N. Educ. at Central Foundation School, London. Rec. by W. H. Wagstaff, M.A. (Peterhouse), Head Master. Adm. 15 Jan. 1917: began res. 15 Jan. 1919. Matric. 29 Jan. 1919. Entrance Schol., Maths, £50.

B.A. (1st Cl. Math. Tri. Pt I, 1919; Sen. Opt. Pt II (b), 1921; all. 1 term for War serv.) 1921.
Schol.* of £60, 1920.
✕ 1917–19. Rfn, London Regt (Queen's Westminster Rifles); 2nd Lieut., R.A.F.
B.Sc., London, 1921. I.C.S., 1922–; with appt. as Magistrate and Collector, Bengal, 1936–.
Bro. of R. W. Griffiths (p. 34).

CHARLES SINGLETON KNOTT. Born 28 July 1898, at Cambridge. S. of Hammett Charles Knott (Peterhouse, M.A. 1887), Fellow and Bursar of Selwyn College, 8 Cranmer Road, Cambridge. Educ. at Perse School, Cambridge. Adm. 15 Jan. 1917. Entrance Schol., Maths, £40.

Did not matric.
✕ 1917–18. 2nd Lieut., R. Fusiliers. (W.) Missing, presumed killed in action, 23 March 1918.
Bro. of A. J. Knott (p. 91).

CHARLES FRANCIS KNOX WATSON. Born 25 Oct. 1898. S. of Thomas Pickles Watson, Oakville, Exley Head, Keighley, Yorks. Educ. at Keighley Trade and Grammar School, and Bradford Grammar School. Adm. 15 Jan. 1917: began res. 26 April 1919. Matric. 8 May 1919. Entrance Schol., Classics, £40.

B.A. (1st Cl. Class. Tri. Pt I (N.R.), 1920; 1st Cl. Pt II (N.R.), 1921; all. 2 terms for War serv.)
1921. Schol.* of £60, 1920.
Blue: Rugby Football, 1919, 1920.
✕ 1917–19. 2nd Lieut., R.G.A.
Was Lecturer in Classics, Cape Town Univ., 1922–5.

RONALD EWART FRAMPTON. Born 16 April 1898, at Worthing. S. of Joseph Frampton, Kenilworth, Church Walk, Worthing. Educ. at King William's College, Isle of Man. Adm. 15 Jan. 1917. Entrance Schol., History, £40.

Did not matric.
✗ 1917–19. 2nd Lieut., R.G.A.; Lieut., R.A.F.
Engaged in horticulture.

WILLIAM ERIC JOSEPH. Born 5 Feb. 1898, at Oxford. S. of Rev. William Joseph, 22 Northumberland Road, Sheffield. Educ. at Taunton School. Adm. 15 Jan. 1917: began res. 8 Oct. 1919. Matric. 21 Oct. 1919. Entrance Schol., Nat. Sciences, £40.

B.A. (Ord. degree) 1922. M.A., M.B., B.Chir. 1937. Re-elected to Schol.*, 1921.
✗ 1917–19. 2nd Lieut., R.F.A.; Capt., R.A.F. (W.)
M.R.C.S., L.R.C.P. 1924. Senior Medical Officer, Whipps Cross Hospital, Leytonstone, E. 11.

CHARLES COLEGRAVE-SCOTT. Born 5 Nov. 1897, at Gosforth, Northumberland. S. of Cecil Thring Scott, 21 Wolveleigh Terrace, Gosforth. Educ. at Royal Grammar School, Newcastle-on-Tyne. Adm. 15 Jan. 1917: began res. 4 Oct. 1917. Matric. 22 Oct. 1917. Resumed res. (after War serv.) L. 1920.

B.A. (2nd Cl., 2nd Div., Hist. Tri. Pt I, 1921; 2nd Cl., 2nd Div., Pt II, 1922) 1922. Dipl. in Geog. 1923. M.A. 1925.
✗ 1917–19. Lieut., 9th Russian Labour Bn.
Asst Master, Great Yarmouth Grammar School, 1923–5; and at Carlisle Grammar School, 1925–. F.R.G.S. 1924.

NAI NABH KRAIRIKS. Born 5 Dec. 1899, at Bangkok, Siam. S. of Phya Burus Ratanaroyabanlobh. Educ. at Cheltenham College. Adm. 26 July 1917: began res. 8 Oct. 1917. Matric. 22 Oct. 1917.

B.A. (3rd Cl. Mech. Sci. Tri., 1920) 1920.

RAOUL ROTTNER-SMITH. Born 8 June 1900, at Neuilly, Paris. S. of Harold Rottner-Smith, 6 Place du Palais Bourbon, Paris. Educ. at Gymnase Scientifique, Lausanne. Adm. 19 Sept. 1917: began res. 8 Oct. 1917. Matric. 22 Oct. 1917.

B.A. (3rd Cl. Nat. Sci. Tri. Pt I, 1921) 1921.

MOHAMMED SAJJAD MIRZA. Born 30 Aug. 1897, at Hyderabad, Deccan, India. S. of Mohamed Aziz Mirza (decd). Educ. at Mohammedan Anglo-Oriental College, Aligarh; and Nizam's College, Hyderabad. Rec. by S. A. Akbar, B.A. (Peterhouse), and others. Adm. 4 Oct. 1917: began res. 9 Oct. 1917. Matric. 22 Oct. 1917.

B.A. (3rd Cl. Hist. Tri. Pt I, 1919; 3rd Cl. Pt II, 1920) 1920. M.A. 1924.
In the Educational Service of H.E.H. The Nizam's Government, Hyderabad.
Editor:
  Al-Muallim. [An Indian monthly.]

CATHIRAVELU SITTAMPALAM. Born 13 Sept. 1898, at Jaffna, Ceylon. S. of Arumugam Cathiravelu, Crown Proctor, Jaffna. Educ. at Royal College, Colombo, Ceylon. Adm. 6 Oct. 1917: began res. 12 Oct. 1917. Matric. 22 Oct. 1917.

B.A. (2nd Cl. Math. Tri. Pt I, 1919; aegr. Pt II, 1920) 1920.
Called to the Bar, Middle Temple, 26 Jan. 1923. Ceylon Civil Service, 1923–; with appt. as Asst Government Agent, 1932– (serving at Batticaloa, 1934–).

CHRISTOPHER CHARLES FYSON. Born 9 Aug. 1899, at Great Barton, Bury St Edmunds. S. of Robert Paul Fyson, Manor House, Great Barton. Educ. at St Edmund's School, Canterbury. Adm. 1 Aug. 1917: began res. 12 Oct. 1917. Matric. 22 Oct. 1917.

> Went down after L. 1918.
> ✕ 1918–20 [?]. 2nd Lieut., Suffolk Regt.

HAROLD JOHN BIRD. Born 6 Sept. 1899, at Carbrooke, Watton, Norfolk. S. of Charles Flindell Bird, Honington, Bury St Edmunds. Educ. at King Edward VI. Grammar School, Bury St Edmunds. Adm. 1 Aug. 1917: began res. 12 Oct. 1917. Matric. 22 Oct. 1917.

> Went down after E. 1918.
> ✕ 1918–19. 2nd Lieut., Suffolk Regt.
> Farming at Troston, Bury St Edmunds.

KENNETH JACK SMITH GOUGH. Born 7 Oct. 1899, at Bury St Edmunds. S. of Charles Smith Gough, 118 Northgate Street, Bury St Edmunds. Educ. at King Edward VI. Grammar School, Bury St Edmunds; and Bishop's Stortford College. Adm. 1 Aug. 1917: began res. 12 Oct. 1917. Matric. 22 Oct. 1917.

> Went down after M. 1917.
> ✕ 1917–19. Pte, Scottish Horse.
> Fruit and cattle farming at Kaimosi, Kenya Colony, 1919–.

REGINALD GEORGE GREEN. Born 12 Aug. 1899, at Theddingworth, nr Rugby. S. of William Green, Theddingworth. Educ. at Wellingborough School. Adm. 28 July 1917: began res. 12 Oct. 1917. Matric. 22 Oct. 1917.

> Went down after L. 1918.
> ✕ 1918–19. 2nd Lieut., M.G.C.
> Chartered Surveyor; being partner in Holloway, Price & Co., Market Harborough, Leics. F.S.I., F.A.I.

SIDNEY CHARLES HAROLD FRENCH. Born 17 Nov. 1899, at Colchester. S. of Alfred French, 40 St Botolph's Street, Colchester. Educ. at Royal Grammar School, Colchester. Adm. 14 Jan. 1918: began res. 9 Oct. 1919. Matric. 21 Oct. 1919. Entrance Schol., Maths, £70.

> 1st Cl. Math. Tri. Pt I, 1920. Went down after L. 1921.
> ✕ 1918–19. Pte, Queen's Own (R.W.Kent Regt). (W.) *Died 1 June 1924 at Montana-Vermala, Switzerland, from the effects of having been gassed in the War.*

GEORGE VALE. Born 2 Dec. 1899, at Liverpool. S. of Thomas William Vale, 87 Ullswater Street, Anfield, Liverpool. Educ. at Liverpool Collegiate School. Adm. 14 Jan. 1918: began res. 17 Jan. 1919. Matric. 29 Jan. 1919. Entrance Schol., Classics, £70.

> B.A. (2nd Cl. Class. Tri. Pt I (N.R.), 1920; 2nd Cl. Pt II (N.R.), 1921; all. 1 term for War serv.) 1921. M.A. 1926. Re-elected to Schol.*, 1920.
> ✕ 1918. Trooper, 1st (King's) Dragoon Gds.
> Asst Master, Taunton School, 1921–5; and at Reading School, 1925–.

DONALD RICHARDSON GRIGG. Born 2 Nov. 1899, at Whetstone, Middlesex. S. of Frederick Richardson Grigg, Inglewood, High Road, Whetstone, N. 20. Educ.

at Christ's Hospital. Adm. 14 Jan. 1918: began res. 16 Jan. 1919. Matric. 29 Jan. 1919. Entrance Schol., Maths, £60.

> B.A. (1st Cl. Math. Tri. Pt I, 1919; Jun. Opt. Pt II, 1921; all. 1 term for War serv.) 1921. 2nd Cl., 2nd Div., Hist. Tri. Pt II, 1922. M.A. 1927. Re-elected to Schol.*, 1920.
> ✕ 1918. Pte, R.G.A.
> Asst Master, St John's School, Leatherhead, 1923–.

GEORGE ALFRED REA FOSTER. Born 24 Nov. 1899, at Rochester. S. of David Foster, Tyneholme, Campbell Road, Gravesend. Educ. at Gravesend County School. Adm. 14 Jan. 1918: began res. 14 Jan. 1919. Matric. 29 Jan. 1919. Entrance Schol., Nat. Sciences, £60.

> B.A. (1st Cl. Nat. Sci. Tri. Pt I, 1920; aegr. Pt II (Physics), 1921; all. 1 term for War serv.) 1921. Re-elected to Schol.*, 1920.
> ✕ 1918–19. Pioneer, R.E. (Spec. Bde).
> Research Physicist, British Cotton Industry Research Assoc., Manchester. A.Inst.P. 1923.
> Bro. of W. R. Foster (p. 46).

NOEL ATHERTON. Born 8 May 1899, at Bradford, Yorks. S. of John William Atherton, Airedale, Croft Road, Sutton, Surrey. Educ. at Whitgift Grammar School, Croydon. Adm. 14 Jan. 1918: began res. 14 Jan. 1920. Matric. 28 Jan. 1920. Entrance Schol., Nat. Sciences, £40.

> B.A. (Ord. degree; all. 1 term for War serv.) 1922. Re-elected to Schol.*, 1921.
> ✕ 1918–19. 2nd Lieut., R.E. (Signals).
> In the Hydrographic Dept of the Admiralty, 1924–; being now (1937) Asst Superintendent, Chart Production and Supplies Branch.

ERNEST CONRAD HAPPOLD. Born 19 Aug. 1899, at Lancaster. S. of Albert Conrad Happold, 9 Rose Bank, Lancaster. Educ. at Royal Grammar School, Lancaster. Adm. 14 Jan. 1918: began res. 9 Oct. 1919. Matric. 21 Oct. 1919. Entrance Exhib., Maths, £30.

> B.A. (2nd Cl. Mech. Sci. Tri., 1922) 1922. Re-elected to Exhib., 1921.
> ✕ 1918–19. 2nd Lieut., R.E. (Signals).
> Engineer.
> Bro. of F. C. Happold (p. 9).

JOHN LEWIS BRADBURY. Born 18 April 1900, at Delph, Saddleworth, Yorks. S. of Buckley Bradbury, Platt Lane, Dobcross, nr Oldham. Educ. at Hulme Grammar School, Oldham. Adm. 14 Jan. 1918: began res. 19 April 1918. Matric. 6 May 1918. Entrance Exhib., Classics, £30.

> B.A. (2nd Cl. Class. Tri. Pt I (N.R.), 1920; 2nd Cl. Engl. Tri. (a), 1921) 1921. M.A. 1927. Re-elected to Exhib., 1920.
> ✕ 1918. Cadet, Cambridge Univ. O.T.C.
> Lecturer, Chester Diocesan Training College for Schoolmasters.

STEPHEN HOWE BAKER. Born 25 April 1900, at Colchester. S. of Edward Percy Baker, Ingram's Well, Sudbury, Suffolk. Educ. at Haileybury College. Adm. 4 April 1918: began res. 19 April 1918. Matric. 6 May 1918.

> Went down after E. 1918.
> ✕ 1918–19. 2nd Lieut., Northumberland Fus.
> Company Director.

RUPERT EBENEZER CLOVER. Born 3 Dec. 1900, at Dedham, Essex. S. of John Percy Clover, The Hall, Dedham. Educ. at Woodbridge School. Adm. 16 July 1918: began res. 5 Oct. 1918. Matric. 21 Oct. 1918.

> B.A. (2nd Cl., 1st Div., Econ. Tri. Pt I, 1920; 2nd Cl., 2nd Div., Pt II, 1921) 1921.
> Was poultry farming in 1931.

DONALD PALMER LINGWOOD. Born 29 Aug. 1900, at Brandon, Suffolk. S. of Harry Lingwood, Astoria, Thetford Road, Brandon. Educ. at Thetford Grammar School. Adm. 18 Aug. 1918: began res. 1 Oct. 1918. Matric. 21 Oct. 1918.

Went down after M. 1918.
⚔ 1918. Cadet, Cambridge Univ. O.T.C.
Engaged in business.

VLADETA POPOVITCH. Born 2 Aug. 1894, at Paratchin, Serbia. S. of Prof. Avram Popovitch, Kosovska Mitrovitza, Serbia. Educ. at Gymnasiums of Nish and Kragujevatz, and Belgrade Univ. Rec. by J. E. Bellows, Administrator, Education Branch, Serbian Relief Fund. Adm. 29 Aug. 1918: began res. 10 Oct. 1918. Matric. 21 Oct. 1918.

B.A. (3rd Cl. Engl. Tri. (*a*), 1920; 3rd Cl. Mod. & Med. Lang. Tri., *f*, 1921) 1921.
⚔ 1914–18. Sergt-Major, Serbian Army. (W.)
Apptd Asst to the Professor of Comparative Literature, Belgrade Univ., 1921. Lecturer in English Language and Literature, Belgrade Univ., 1930–6; and Junior Professor of the same subject there, 1936–.
Ph.D., King's College, London, 1925. Hon. Gen. Sec. of the Belgrade P.E.N. [= Poets, playwrights, essayists, editors and novelists] Club, 1928–31 and 1933–. Hon. Gen. Sec. of the Soc. of Friends of Gt Britain and America in Yugoslavia, 1930–.
Author:
   Shakespeare in Serbia. (*Shakespeare Association. Shakespeare Survey*, 3.) London, 1928.
   Kroz Englesku Književnost. Belgrade, 1928.
   And other works.
Editor, etc.:
   The mountain wreath of P. P. Nyegosh, Prince-Bishop of Montenegro 1830–51; rendered into English by J. W. Wiles; with an introduction by V. Popović. London (1930).

DENIS MᵃᶜCLURE CAMPBELL. Born 26 March 1901, at Cambridge. S. of Edward MᵃᶜClure Campbell, 41 Hills Road, Cambridge. Educ. privately. Adm. 8 Sept. 1918: began res. 11 Oct. 1918. Matric. 21 Oct. 1918.

Went down after L. 1920.
⚔ 1918. Cadet, Cambridge Univ. O.T.C.
Farming in Cambridgeshire.

FALKINER WILLIAM HEWSON. Born 9 Nov. 1900, at Brisbane, Australia. S. of Falkiner Minchin Hewson, Uplands, Sheen Common, S.W. 14. Educ. at Haileybury College. Adm. 3 Oct. 1918: began res. 11 Oct. 1918. Matric. 21 Oct. 1918.

Went down after E. 1919.
Sheep farming in Queensland.

JOHN LONG GROOM. Born 26 Oct. 1900, at Calcutta. S. of John Bax Groom, The Mount, Woodbridge, Suffolk. Educ. at Woodbridge School. Adm. 18 Oct. 1918: began res. 21 Oct. 1918. Matric. 21 Oct. 1918.

B.A. (Ord. degree) 1922.
⚔ 1918. Cadet, Cambridge Univ. O.T.C.
M.R.C.S., L.R.C.P. 1926. In the R.A.F. Medical Service 1928–31, with final rank of Flt Lieut. In private practice at Woodbridge, 1932–.
Bro. of W. H. Groom (p. 81).

ERIC WILLIAM COY. Born 3 July 1901, at Quarrington, Sleaford, Lincs. S. of John William Coy, Caxton House, Grantham Road, Sleaford. Educ. at

Carre's Grammar School, Sleaford. Adm. Jan 1919: began res. 9 Oct. 1919. Matric. 21 Oct. 1919. Entrance Schol., Maths, £60.

B.A. (2ⁿᵈ Cl. Math. Tri. Pt I, 1920; Jun. Opt. Pt II, 1922) 1922. Re-elected to Schol.*, 1921.

PERCY LEONARD LEE. Born 20 June 1901, at Nottingham. S. of Percy William Lee (decᵈ) and Mrs Lee, 35 Stratford Road, West Bridgford, Nottingham. Educ. at Nottingham High School. Adm. Jan 1919: began res. 9 Oct. 1919. Matric. 21 Oct. 1919. Entrance Schol., Nat. Sciences, £60.

B.A. (2ⁿᵈ Cl. Nat. Sci. Tri. Pt I, 1921; 3ʳᵈ Cl. Pt II (Physics), 1922) 1922. M.A. 1927. Re-elected to Schol.*, 1921.
Schoolmaster; with appt. as Asst Master, Queen Mary's School, Basingstoke, 1928–.

ERNEST ALFRED WARDEN. Born 14 May 1901, at Gillingham, Kent. S. of Charles Smith Warden, 108 Rochester Street, Chatham. Educ. at Royal Grammar School, Colchester. Adm. Jan. 1919: began res. 4 Oct. 1919. Matric. 21 Oct. 1919. Entrance Schol., Maths, £50.

B.A. (2ⁿᵈ Cl. Math. Tri. Pt I, 1920; Jun. Opt. Pt II, 1922) 1922. Re-elected to Schol.*, 1921.

GORDON HAROLD TAYLOR. Born 27 Sept. 1900, at Finchfield, Wolverhampton. S. of Albert Taylor, 159 Jeffcock Road, Wolverhampton. Educ. at Wolverhampton Grammar School. Adm. Jan. 1919: began res. 9 Oct. 1919. Matric. 21 Oct. 1919. Entrance Schol., Classics, £50.

B.A., LL.B. (2ⁿᵈ Cl. Class. Tri. Pt I, 1921; 2ⁿᵈ Cl. Law Tri. Pt II, 1922) 1922. M.A. 1927. Re-elected to Schol.*, 1921.
Solicitor (adm. March 1926). After holding other municipal appointments, was Clerk of the Ruislip-Northwood Urban District Council, 1931–3; and has been Town Clerk of Southgate, Middlesex, 1934–.

EDWARD DOUGLAS VAN REST. Born 10 March 1901, at Eastbourne. S. of John Peter van Rest, 19 South Side, Clapham Common, S.W. 4. Educ. at Sir Walter St John's School, Battersea. Adm. Jan. 1919: began res. 8 Oct. 1919. Matric. 21 Oct. 1919. Entrance Schol., Nat. Sciences, £50.

B.A. (3ʳᵈ Cl. Nat. Sci. Tri. Pt I, 1921; 2ⁿᵈ Cl. Pt II (Physics), 1923) 1923. Schol.* of £40, 1921. *Hon. mentioned for Rayleigh Prize*, 1924.
B.Sc., London, 1922. Physics Master, Bancroft's School, Woodford Wells, Essex, 1923–5. In the Forest Products Research Laboratory of the Dept of Scientific and Industrial Research, 1925–; with appt. as Scientific Officer, 1929–.

CORRIE REID SHARMAN. Born 26 April 1900, at Wellingborough, Northants. S. of Hereward Reid Sharman, Lockwood, 30 Kimbolton Road, Bedford. Educ. at Bedford School. Adm. Jan. 1919: began res. 9 Oct. 1919. Matric. 21 Oct. 1919. Entrance Schol., Classics, £40.

B.A., LL.B. (2ⁿᵈ Cl. Class. Tri. Pt I, 1921; 3ʳᵈ Cl. Law Tri. Pt II, 1922) 1922. M.A. 1927. Re-elected to Schol.*, 1921.
Solicitor (adm. Nov. 1925); being partner in Willes, Gladstone & Reid Sharman, 4 Raymond Buildings, Gray's Inn, W.C. 1.

HERBERT BUTTERFIELD, subsequently **Fellow**. Born 7 Oct. 1900, at Oxenhope, nr Keighley, Yorks. S. of Albert Butterfield, 17 Woodhouse Terrace, Oxenhope. Educ. at Keighley Trade and Grammar School. Adm. Jan. 1919: began res. 7 Oct. 1919. Matric. 21 Oct. 1919. Entrance Schol., History, £40.

B.A. (1ˢᵗ Cl., 2ⁿᵈ Div., Hist. Tri. Pt I, 1921; 1ˢᵗ Cl., 1ˢᵗ Div., Pt II, 1922) 1922. M.A. 1926. Schol. of £50, 1920. Schol.* of £60, 1921. Hugo de Balsham Stud. (for research in History), £150, 1922. *Members' Prize (English Essay)*, 1922. *Le Bas Prize*, 1923. Charles Abercrombie Smith Stud. (for research in History), £150, 1923 (but resigned on election to Fellowship). *Prince Consort Prize*, 1924. *Seeley Medal*, 1924. *Jane Eliza Procter Visiting Fellowship, Princeton Univ.*, 1924.

Fellow, 1923 (becoming Research Fellow under the new Statutes in 1926); re-elected Research Fellow, 1929; elected Internal Fellow, 1932; re-elected Internal Fellow, 1937. Librarian, 1925–. Director of Studies in History, 1925–31. Acting Lecturer in History, 1928–9. Lecturer in History, 1930–.

University Lecturer in History, 1930–.

Author:
The historical novel; an essay. (*Le Bas Prize*, 1923.) Cambridge, 1924.
The peace tactics of Napoleon, 1806–8. Cambridge, 1929.
The Whig interpretation of history. London, 1931.

Editor:
Select documents of European history. Vol. 3. 1715–1920. London (1931).

RICHARD DOUGLAS TREVOR HAMILTON. Born 28 Sept. 1900, at Milston, Amesbury, Wilts. S. of Major John Douglas Hamilton, 58 Lancaster Gate, W. 2. Educ. at King William's College, Isle of Man. Adm. Jan. 1919: began res. 1 Oct. 1919. Matric. 21 Oct. 1919. Entrance Exhib., History, £30.

Went down after L. 1921; subsequently became a Non-Coll. Student.

EDWARD MORELAND PARSEY. Born 12 Jan. 1900, at King's Norton, nr Birmingham. S. of Edward William Parsey (Peterhouse, M.A. 1892, M.B. 1894), Glenavon House, King's Norton. Educ. at King Edward's School, Birmingham. Adm. 23 May 1917: began res. 26 April 1919. Matric. 8 May 1919.

B.A. (Ord. degree; all. 2 terms for War serv.) 1921. M.A. 1925.
⚔ 1918–19. Gnr, Royal Marine Artillery.
Called to the Bar, Inner Temple, 28 Jan. 1924. On Oxford circuit; and Asst Chief Clerk, Solicitor's Dept, Board of Trade.

ALFRED WILLIAM MOND. Born 11 Aug. 1901, in London. S. of Emile Schweich Mond, 22 Hyde Park Square, W. 2. Educ. at Charterhouse. Adm. 27 Oct. 1918: began res. 10 Oct. 1919. Matric. 21 Oct. 1919.

B.A. (Ord. degree) 1922.
Was with Brunner, Mond & Co., Ltd (alkali manufacturers). Died 12 Sept. 1928 at Storrington, Sussex.
Bro. of F. L. Mond (p. 16), and first cousin once removed of Sir R. L. Mond (cr. Kt 1932; *Walker*, p. 583).

REGINALD WALTER PERRY. Born 30 Aug. 1898, at Shepherd's Bush, London. S. of Walter Harold Perry, Sunnydale, Cedar Road, Sutton, Surrey. Educ. at Sutton County School. Adm. 23 Nov. 1918: began res. 14 Jan. 1919. Matric. 29 Jan. 1919.

B.A. (Ord. degree; all. 1 term for War serv.) 1921. 2nd Cl. Geog. Tri. Pt II, 1922. M.A. 1927.
Half-Blue: Chess, 1919.
⚔ 1917–18. Lieut., London Regt. (W.)
H.M. Inspector of Taxes, Stourbridge, Worcs.

FREDERICK JOHN WICKS. Born 18 Sept. 1879, at Reading. Of Orwell House, Ranelagh Road, Felixstowe. S. of John Wicks. Educ. at Greyfriars Church School, Reading. Rec. by Lieut.-Col. H. M. Fisher Rowe, Surrey Yeomanry. Adm. 6 Dec. 1918: began res. 14 Jan. 1919. Matric. 29 Jan. 1919.

B.A. (Ord. degree; all. 1 term for War serv.) 1921.
⚔ 1914–19. Lieut., E. Surrey Regt.
Ridley Hall, Cambridge, 1921. Ordained d. 1922, p. 1923 St Edmundsbury and Ipswich. C. of St John Bapt., Ipswich, 1922–3; Warboys, 1923–6; St Paul, Finchley, 1926–7; Clergy Deputation Sec., Church Assoc., 1927–9; R. of Garsdon *w*. Lea and Cleverton, Dio. Bristol, 1929–.

ARTHUR MURRAY MACKINTOSH. Born 14 Aug. 1896, in London. S. of John Charles Mackintosh, Elmbank, Mortlock Road, Kew Gardens, Surrey. Educ. at William Ellis School, Gospel Oak, London. Adm. 20 Dec. 1918: began res. 11 Feb. 1919. Matric. 11 March 1919.

B.A. (2nd Cl., 2nd Div., Econ. Tri. Pt I, 1920; 3rd Cl. Pt II, 1921; all. 2 terms for War serv.) 1921.
⚔ 1915–19. Lieut., E. Surrey Regt. (W.) *M.C.*
Group Sales Manager, Shell-Mex and B.P. Ltd (petroleum products), London.

WILLIAM HARRISON BRINDLEY. Born 20 Oct. 1888, at Glossop, Derby-shire. S. of James Brindley (decd). Educ. at Christ Church Higher Grade School, Southport; and Manchester Univ. Adm. 11 Jan. 1919: began res. 14 Jan. 1919. Matric. 29 Jan. 1919.

B.A. (Ord. degree; all. 4 terms for War serv.) 1920. M.A. 1924.
⚔ 1914–19. Lieut., R.E. (W.) *M.C.*
M.Sc. Tech., Manchester, 1922. Ph.D., Manchester, 1928. A.I.C. 1924. Chemist.
Editor:
    The soul of Manchester. (*Publ. for the Manchester Section of the Soc. of Chemical Industry.*)
    Manchester, 1929.

THAMBAPILLAI RAJENDRA. Born 12 March 1898, at Kuala Lumpur, Malay States. S. of Thambapillai (Interpreter and in charge of a district under the Sultan of Selangor). Educ. at Victoria Institution, Kuala Lumpur. Adm. 14 Jan. 1919: began res. 14 Jan. 1919. Matric. 29 Jan. 1919.

B.A. (Ord. degree) 1921.
Called to the Bar, Middle Temple, 26 Jan. 1923.

NAVAL OFFICERS

On 31 Jan. 1919 thirty junior Naval Officers were received into residence at Peterhouse by arrange-ment with, and on the recommendation of, the Admiralty. They came into residence in order to supplement their previous courses of instruction, which had been interrupted by early mobilization during the Great War. Other Naval Officers were similarly admitted to other Colleges in the University; but their status in the University had not as yet been defined. They did not matriculate, and so did not become members of the University. For these reasons the Peterhouse 'Historical Registers' omit the names of all the Naval Officers who came up to the College in Jan. 1919. They are listed here, however, as a matter of courtesy; and also for the sake of uniformity, since the College 'Historical Registers' contain the names of all other Naval Officers who subsequently entered Peterhouse under the same scheme and who, by matriculation, became members of the University.

The thirty Naval Officers received at Peterhouse on 31 Jan. 1919, and their terms of residence, were as follows:

Sub-Lieut.	Hugh Victor Brodie.	L. and E. 1919.
,,	Sydney Brown.	L. 1919.
,,	Cyril Francis Carpmael.	L. and E. 1919.
,,	Frederick James Chambers.	L. and E. 1919.
,,	Charles Fraser Harrington Churchill.	L. and E. 1919.
,,	Charles Neville Colson.	L. and E. 1919.
,,	John Reginald Hughes D'Aeth.	L. and E. 1919.
,,	Charles Markham David.	L. and E. 1919.
,,	Alec Edward Dodington.	L. and E. 1919.
,,	Ivan Binstead Farrant.	L. and E. 1919.
,,	Roger Henry Charles Fetherstonhaugh-Frampton.	L. and E. 1919.
,,	William Roche Macdonald Fleet.	L. and E. 1919.
,,	Charles Maurice Elton Gifford.	L. and E. 1919.
,,	Jack Marcus Douglas Hunter.	L. and E. 1919.
,,	Robert McLean Lochhead.	L. and E. 1919.
,,	Rupert Harold Nevison Loraine.	L. and E. 1919.
,,	Alastair Neil Macneal.	L. and E. 1919.

Sub-Lieut.	John O'Brien Milner-Barry.	L. and E. 1919.
,,	Oliver Ernest Nicolls.	L. and E. 1919.
,,	Richard Coney Pedder.	L. 1919.
,,	James Douglas Prentice.	L. and E. 1919.
,,	George Lester Roome.	L. and E. 1919.
,,	Frank Schunck.	L. and E. 1919.
,,	Laurence Chase Sharman.	L. and E. 1919.
,,	Edward William Boyd Sim.	L. and E. 1919.
,,	Charles John Percival Small.	L. and E. 1919.
,,	Hubert Benyon Stocken.	L. and E. 1919.
,,	Raymond Maurice Trevelyan Taylor.	L. and E. 1919.
,,	Frederick Francis Orr Vallings.	L. and E. 1919.
,,	Holden Thomas White.	L. and E. 1919.

Midway through the course of instruction undergone by the foregoing Naval Officers, one of the Naval Officers in charge at Cambridge was also received into residence at Peterhouse; and his residence here continued until the termination, nearly four years later, of the Admiralty scheme referred to in the preceding paragraph. This Officer in charge and his terms of residence were:

Eng. Cdr Sydney Philip Start.   E. 1919 to L. 1923 inclusive.

REGINALD WILLIAM GRIFFITHS. Born 13 April 1895, at Tooting, London. S. of Joseph Thomas Griffiths, 11 Denver Road, Stamford Hill, N. 16. Educ. at Central Foundation School, London. Adm. 1 Feb. 1919: began res. 25 April 1919. Matric. 8 May 1919.

B.A., LL.B. (3rd Cl. Hist. Tri. Pt I, 1920; 3rd Cl. Law Tri. Pt II, 1921; all. 2 terms for War serv.) 1921.
⚔ 1914–19. Lieut., Leicestershire Regt; Lieut., R.A.F.
Headmaster of St Cuthbert's School, Kirkcudbright. Capt., T.A. Res. of Officers.
Bro. of P. J. Griffiths (p. 26).

COLIN BATEMAN PEARSON. Born 1 Aug. 1889, at Lightcliffe, Yorks. S. of Rev. Samuel Pearson, 52 Percy Park, Tynemouth. Educ. at Tynemouth School. Adm. 28 Jan. 1919: began res. 9 Oct. 1919. Matric. 21 Oct. 1919.

B.A. (Ord degree; all. 3 terms for War serv.) 1921. M.A. 1926.
⚔ 1915–19. Capt., Durham L.I. (W 2.)
Called to the Bar, Middle Temple, 17 Nov. 1924. Colonial Service, 1928–; with appt. as Chief Police Magistrate, Tonga, S. Pacific, 1928–32; and as Police Magistrate, Gold Coast Colony, 1932–. Capt., Regular Army Res. of Officers.

ROBERT GORDON EVANS. Born 20 Aug. 1899, at Great Barton, Bury St Edmunds. S. of Robert Evans, The Garden House, Great Barton. Educ. at King Edward VI. Grammar School, Bury St Edmunds. Adm. 6 March 1919: began res. 26 April 1919. Matric. 8 May 1919.

B.A. (3rd Cl. Math. Tri. Pt I, 1920; 1st Cl. Geog. Tri. Pt I, 1921; all. 2 terms for War serv.) 1921.
Blue: Cricket, 1921.
⚔ 1918–19. 2nd Lieut., Suffolk Regt.
Asst Master, Dulwich College, 1921–4; and at Wellington College, 1924–. F.R.G.S. 1926.

CYRIL FISHER YOUNGMAN. Born 20 July 1898, at Bury St Edmunds. S. of William Edward Youngman, 83 Guildhall Street, Bury St Edmunds. Educ. at King Edward VI. Grammar School, Bury St Edmunds. Adm. 6 March 1919: began res. 26 April 1919. Matric. 8 May 1919.

B.A. (Ord. degree; all. 2 terms for War serv.) 1921.
⚔ 1916–19. Lieut., Suffolk Regt. (W.) *Died 15 Oct. 1922 at Felixstowe, from consumption due to the effects of War service.*

DAVID HUGHES PARRY. Born 3 Jan. 1893, at Llanaelhaiarn, Carnarvonshire. S. of John Hughes Parry, Penllwyn, Pwllheli, N. Wales. Educ. at Pwllheli County School, and University College of Wales, Aberystwyth (B.A. degree, Wales). Adm. 17 March 1919: began res. 25 April 1919. Matric. 8 May 1919. Aff. Student.

B.A., LL.B. (1ˢᵗ Cl. Law Tri. Pt II, 1920; all. 2 terms for War serv.) 1920. M.A. 1926. LL.M. 1927. ✕ 1916–19. Lieut., R. Welsh Fus. (W.)
Called to the Bar, Inner Temple, 28 June 1922. Lecturer in Law, University College of Wales, Aberystwyth, 1920–4. Lecturer in Law, London School of Economics, 1924–8. Reader in English Law, London Univ., 1928–30. Professor of English Law, and Member of Senate, London Univ., 1930–.
Author:
    The law of succession, testate and intestate. Including the administration of assets and the liability of personal representatives for death duties. London, 1937.
Editor:
    (With Sir B. L. Cherry and J. Chadwick) *Wolstenholme & Cherry's Conveyancing Statutes, &c.* 11th ed. Vol. 2. London, 1927.
    (With J. Cherry) Rt Hon. Sir E. V. Williams' *A treatise on the law of executors and administrators.* 12th ed. 2 vols. London, 1930.
    (With Sir B. L. Cherry and J. R. P. Maxwell) *Wolstenholme & Cherry's Conveyancing Statutes, etc.* 12th ed. 2 vols. London, 1932.

FRANCIS OGILVIE BALFOUR-MELVILLE. Born 31 March 1892, at Geelong, Victoria, Australia. S. of Robert Andrew Agnew Balfour-Melville, Sandringham, Victoria, Australia. Educ. at Brighton Grammar School, Melbourne; and Melbourne Univ. (Ormond College). Adm. 7 April 1919: began res. 24 April 1919. Matric. 8 May 1919.

B.A. (1ˢᵗ Cl. Moral Sci. Tri. Pt I, 1920; all. 5 terms for War Serv.) 1920. ✕ 1916–19. Staff Sergt, Australian Army Medical Corps.
Re-entered Ormond College 1921, and was preparing for the ministry of the Presbyterian Church of Victoria. Killed 6 Feb. 1923 in a driving accident at Sherbrooke, Victoria.

BRUCE LLOYD STOREY. Born 23 Aug. 1898, at Sheffield. S. of Alexander Charles Storey, Yew Villa, Heworth, York. Educ. at Ackworth School, nr Pontefract; and Sheffield Univ. Rec. by P. A. Harverson, M.A. (Peterhouse), and F. Andrews, M.A., Head Master. Adm. 14 April 1919: began res. 26 April 1919. Matric. 8 May 1919.

B.A. (Ord. degree; all. 2 terms for War serv.) 1921. ✕ 1917–19. 2nd Lieut., R.F.A.

Raj Rana FATEHSINGH OF LIMBDI. Born 7 Aug. 1901, at Jamnagar, Kathiawar, India. S. of Dawlat Singh, Thakore Sahib of Limbdi. Educ. at Rajkumar College, Rajkot; Boys' High School, Panchagani; and Fergusson College, Poona. Adm. 27 April 1919: began res. 29 April 1919. Matric. 8 May 1919.

B.A., LL.B. (3ʳᵈ Cl. Hist. Tri. Pt I, 1921; 3ʳᵈ Cl. Law Tri. Pt II, 1922) 1922. M.A. 1926.
Called to the Bar, Inner Temple, 14 May 1924. Chief Minister, Limbdi State. F.R.G.S. 1920.
He matric. as Fateh Sinh LIMBDI.

MICHAIL EFIMOVITCH LUBRZYNSKI. Born 14 June 1899, at Warsaw. S. of Efim Lubrzynski (decᵈ). Educ. at Sixth Gymnasium Petrograd; Petrograd Univ.; and Krakow Univ. Adm. 28 April 1919: began res. 30 April 1919. Matric. 8 May 1919.

Resided till L. 1920 inclusive; thereafter migrated to Christ's College.

CHARLES WILSON BOOTH. Born 4 July 1897, at Dublin. S. of Robert Booth (dec^d) and Mrs Booth, Sunnyside, Wood Road, Hindhead, Surrey. Educ. at Leys School. Adm. 27 Sept. 1916: began res. 9 Oct. 1919. Matric. 21 Oct. 1919.

Went down after E. 1922.
⚔ 1917–19. Lieut., R. Dublin Fus.; attd R. Inniskilling Fus. (W.)
Farming at Warfield, Berks.

LEONARD ALBAN BLAKELOCK. Born 17 May 1897, at Wood Green, Middlesex. S. of Rev. Martin Ogle Blakelock, St Andrew's Vicarage, Muswell Hill, N. 10. Educ. at Felsted School. Adm. 1 Oct. 1916: began res. 9 Oct. 1919. Matric. 21 Oct. 1919.

Went down after E. 1921.
On work in connection with the Church Army during the War, 1917–18.
Actor.

ALBERT EDWARD BRIERLEY. Born 16 Jan. 1901, at Oldham. S. of Abel Brierley, 7 Brompton Street, Oldham. Educ. at Oldham Municipal Secondary School. Adm. 1 June 1918: began res. 7 Oct. 1919. Matric. 21 Oct. 1919.

B.A. (3rd Cl. Hist. Tri. Pt I, 1921; 3rd Cl. Pt II, 1922) 1922. M.A. 1931.
Was Asst Master, Ridley College, St Catharines, Ontario, c. 1932.

THOMAS STUART HAMILTON. Born 27 Feb. 1900, at Cheshunt, Herts. S. of John Robert Hamilton, Colcot, Bycullah Road, Enfield, Middlesex. Educ. at Bishop's Stortford College. Rec. by G. J. Hill, M.A. (Peterhouse). Adm. Feb. 1919: began res. 9 Oct. 1919. Matric. 21 Oct. 1919.

Went down after E. 1920.
Half-Blue: Water Polo, 1920.

HUGH ERNEST WHITWHAM. Born 22 Aug. 1899, at East Barnet, Herts. S. of Frank George Whitwham, 34 Methuen Park, Muswell Hill, N. 10. Educ. at East Finchley Vicarage School. Adm. 1 March 1919: began res. 1 Oct. 1919. Matric. 21 Oct. 1919.

Went down after E. 1920.
Actor Manager.
Bro. of D. A. Whitwham (p. 64).

HEDLEY JOSEPH RICKARDS. Born 9 July 1901, at Clapham, London. S. of Ernest Herbert Rickards, Blythburgh, Grosvenor Avenue, Carshalton, Surrey. Educ. at Whitgift Grammar School, Croydon. Adm. 30 March 1919: began res. 9 Oct. 1919. Matric. 21 Oct. 1919.

B.A., LL.B. (3rd Cl. Law Tri. Pt I, 1921; 3rd Cl. Pt II, 1922) 1922. M.A. 1926. LL.M. 1929.
Solicitor (adm. Oct. 1925); being partner in Carter & Barber, 3 Clement's Inn, Strand, London, W.C. 2.
Bro. of E. S. Rickards (p. 91).

CECIL HUGH WILLIAM PRINCE. Born 19 June 1896, at Salisbury. S. of William John Prince, 66 St Ann's Street, Salisbury. Educ. at Bishop Wordsworth's School, Salisbury; and Winchester Diocesan Training College. Adm. 6 April 1919: began res. 8 Oct. 1919. Matric. 21 Oct. 1919.

B.A. (3rd Cl. Hist. Tri. Pt I, 1921; 3rd Cl. Geog. Tri. Pt I, 1922) 1922. M.A. 1928.
⚔ 1915–19. Lieut., London Regt. (W.) M.
Asst Master, Market Bosworth Grammar School, 1922–3; and at Haberdashers' Aske's Boys' School, Hatcham, S.E. 14, 1923–.

HUBERT MARTIN WILSON. Born 16 June 1900, at Stoke-on-Trent. S. of Herbert Gibson Wilson, 100 Liverpool Road, Birkdale, Southport. Educ. at Willaston School, Nantwich. Adm. 26 April 1919: began res. 8 Oct. 1919. Matric. 21 Oct. 1919.

B.A. (2nd Cl. Class. Tri. Pt I, 1921; 2nd Cl., 1st Div., Hist. Tri. Pt II, 1922) 1922. M.A. 1926. Exhib. of £30, 1920; re-elected, 1922. Adm. Research Stud. as from Oct. 1922.
✗ 1918–19. Pte, The King's (Liverpool Regt).
Studied at Caroline Univ. of Prague, 1923–4. Asst Master, Glasgow Academy, 1924–7. Asst, Lancs County Education Office, 1927–8; and at Kent County Education Office, 1928–9. Deputy Education Sec., N.R. of Yorks County Education Committee, 1929–33. Sec., East Suffolk County Education Committee, 1933–6; and Shropshire County Education Committee, 1936–.

WILLIAM RATNAM SAMUEL SATTHIANADHAN. Born 15 March 1900, at Madras. S. of Dr Samuel Satthianadhan (dec^d) and Mrs Satthianadhan, St Thome, Madras. Educ. privately; then at Presidency College, Madras. Rec. by H. V. Kershaw, B.A., Professor, Presidency College, Madras, and R. M. Statham, B.A. (Peterhouse), Principal, Government College, Kumbakonam. Adm. 26 April 1919: began res. 9 Oct. 1919. Matric. 21 Oct. 1919.

B.A. (2nd Cl. Nat. Sci. Tri. Pt I, 1921; Cert. of Dilig. Study, 1922) 1922.
I.C.S., 1924–; with appt. as Sub-Collector, Madras, 1928–.

HUBERT ERNEST RICKS. Born 18 May 1901, in London. Of 35 Belsize Road, Hampstead, N.W. 6. S. of Ernest Claude Ricks (dec^d). Educ. at University College School. Adm. 1 May 1919: began res. 1 Oct. 1919. Matric. 21 Oct. 1919.

B.A., LL.B. (3rd Cl. Law Tri. Pt I, 1921; 3rd Cl. Pt II, 1922) 1922. M.A. 1926.
Asst Master, Junior Branch, Mill Hill School, 1923–. Called to the Bar, Inner Temple, 17 Nov. 1931.

ALBERT BERESFORD SMITH. Born 20 March 1898, at Cheshunt, Herts. S. of Frederick Ernest Smith (dec^d) and Mrs Smith, Tenby Croft, Cheshunt. Educ. at Ongar School, Essex. Adm. 5 May 1919: began res. 9 Oct. 1919. Matric. 21 Oct. 1919.

Went down after L. 1922. Kitchener Schol., 1919.
✗ 1916–19. Sub-Lieut., R.N.A.S.
Architect and Surveyor.

EDWARD ENOCH JENKINS. Born 8 Feb. 1895, at Cardiff. S. of John William Jenkins, Briar Dene, Whitechurch Road, Cardiff. Educ. at Howard Gardens Municipal Secondary School, Cardiff; and University College of S. Wales and Monmouthshire, Cardiff. Adm. 16 May 1919: began res. 8 Oct. 1919. Matric. 21 Oct. 1919.

B.A., LL.B. (2nd Cl. Law Tri. Pt I, 1921; 2nd Cl. Pt II, 1922) 1922. M.A. 1928.
✗ 1914–19. Corpl, R.E. (Gas Corps); Lieut., R.F.A.
Called to the Bar, Gray's Inn, 14 May 1924. Colonial Service, successively in Nyasaland and N. Rhodesia, 1925–; and with appt. as Solicitor-General, N. Rhodesia, 1936–. F.R.E.S. 1927. F.R.A.I. 1929.

EVAN SILK. Born 22 Feb. 1890, at Blaina, Monmouthshire. S. of William Henry Silk (dec^d) and Mrs Silk, 142 Abertillery Road, Blaina. Educ. at Carmarthen College. Adm. 18 May 1919: began res. 16 Oct. 1919. Matric. 21 Oct. 1919.

B.A., LL.B. (3rd Cl. Hist. Tri. Pt I, 1921; 3rd Cl. Law Tri. Pt II, 1922) 1922. M.A. 1926.
✗ 1915–19. Capt., Welsh Regt. M.
Called to the Bar, Gray's Inn, 17 Nov. 1924. Headmaster, Nantyglo Secondary School, 1924–.

GEORGE WILLIAM BEDELL. Born 28 May 1893, at Didsbury, Manchester. S. of James William Bedell, Glen Wyllin, Burnage Park, Levenshulme, Manchester. Educ. at Manchester Central High School; Manchester P.T. College; and St John's College, Battersea. Adm. 20 May 1919: began res. 9 Oct. 1919. Matric. 21 Oct. 1919.

> B.A., LL.B. (3rd Cl. Math. Tri. Pt I, 1920; 3rd Cl. Law Tri. Pt II, 1921; all. 3 terms for War serv.) 1921. M.A. 1925. LL.M. 1932.
> ✗ 1914–19. Sergt, Middlesex Regt; 2nd Lieut., 66th Punjabis, I.A.; Capt. and Adjt., 2nd Rajputs, I.A.
> Comptroller of Income Tax, States of Jersey, C.I., 1928–39. Apptd Advocate, Royal Court, Jersey, 1939.

VIVIAN JOHN MOORE. Born 4 May 1887, at Flinby, Cumberland. S. of Joseph Moore (dec^d) and Mrs Moore, The Vicarage, Holme St Cuthbert, Maryport, Cumberland. Educ. at Nelson School, Wigton, Cumberland. Adm. 25 May 1919: began res. 9 Oct. 1919. Matric. 21 Oct. 1919.

> B.A., LL.B. (2nd Cl. Math. Tri. Pt I, 1920; 1st Cl. Law Tri. Pt II, 1921; all. 3 terms for War serv.) 1921. M.A. 1926.
> ✗ 1915–18. Capt. and Adjt., R.G.A. *M.C.*
> B.Sc., London, 1911. Asst Master, Fettes College, 1921–2. Asst to Director of Education, Leeds, 1922–5. Director of Education, Walsall, since 1925.

WILLIAM FREDERICK MINDHAM. Born 30 Jan. 1891, at Barnsley, Yorks. S. of William John Mindham, South End, Thorne, nr Doncaster. Educ. at Barnsley and District Holgate Grammar School, and Sheffield Univ. (B.Sc. degree). Adm. 28 May 1919: began res. 16 Oct. 1919. Matric. 21 Oct. 1919.

> Went down during E. 1920.
> ✗ 1917–18. Lieut., Nigeria Regt, W. African Frontier Force.
> Colonial Service: in Survey Dept, Nigeria, 1914–27; and with appt. as Deputy Surveyor-General, Gold Coast, 1927–. F.R.G.S. 1920.

JOHN EDISON CRAWSHAW. Born 29 Aug. 1895, at Burnley, Lancs. S. of Thomas Crawshaw, Glen Rosa, Alan Road, Wellington, Manchester. Educ. at Manchester Grammar School and Manchester Univ. Adm. 3 June 1919: began res. 9 Oct. 1919. Matric. 21 Oct. 1919.

> B.A. (3rd Cl. Mech. Sci. Tri., 1922) 1922.
> ✗ 1914–19. Capt. and Adjt., Manchester Regt.

CHARLES STOWELL MARRIOTT. Born 14 Sept. 1895, at Heaton Moor, Manchester. S. of Joshua Hyde Marriott (dec^d) and Mrs Marriott, St Maybn, Herne Bay, Kent. Educ. at St Columba's College, Rathfarnham, Dublin; and Trinity College, Dublin. Adm. 4 June 1919: began res. 9 Oct. 1919. Matric. 21 Oct. 1919.

> B.A. (Ord. degree; all. 3 terms for War serv.) 1921.
> Blue: Cricket, 1920, 1921.
> ✗ 1915–19. Lieut., Lancashire Fus. (W.)
> Asst Master, Dulwich College, 1921–. Played cricket for Gentlemen *v.* Players, 1921 and 1924; for Lancs county, 1919–22; and has played for Kent county, 1924–.

WILLIAM PERCY WYLIE. Born 18 April 1898, at Newcastle-on-Tyne. S. of Rev. William Samuel Herbert Wylie, 32 Mount Park Crescent, Ealing, W. 5.

Educ. at Westminster School, and King's College, London. Adm. 4 June 1919: began res. 18 Oct. 1919. Matric. 21 Oct. 1919.

B.A. (2ⁿᵈ Cl., 1ˢᵗ Div., Hist. Tri. Pt II, 1921; all. 3 terms for War serv.) 1921. M.A. 1925.
✕ 1917–18. 2nd Lieut., Tank Corps.
Bishops' College, Cheshunt, 1928. Ordained d. 1929, p. 1930 Chelmsford. C. of Hornchurch, 1929–32; Uckfield, 1932–4; St Augustine, W. Bexhill, 1934–5; C. in charge of St Richard, Hayward's Heath, Dio. Chichester, 1935–.

EDMUND JOHN CARTHEW. Born 27 Nov. 1900, at Woodbridge, Suffolk. S. of Colonel Ranulphus John Carthew, Woodbridge Abbey. Educ. at Woodbridge School. Adm. 6 June 1919: began res. 7 Oct. 1919. Matric. 21 Oct. 1919.

B.A., LL.B. (2ⁿᵈ Cl. Law Tri. Pt I, 1921; 1ˢᵗ Cl. Pt II, 1922) 1922. M.A. 1927.
Solicitor (adm. Nov. 1925); practising at 71 Lincoln's Inn Fields, W.C. 2.

PERCIVAL THOMAS ROBINSON. Born 5 Aug. 1892, at Bromsgrove, Worcs. S. of William Robinson, Bournheath, Bromsgrove. Educ. at Bromsgrove Secondary School. Adm. 6 June 1919: began res. 8 Oct. 1919. Matric. 21 Oct. 1919.

B.A. (Ord. degree; all. 2 terms for War serv.) 1921. M.A. 1925.
✕ 1915–19. Lce-Corpl, Worcestershire Regt. (W 3.)
Asst Master, Milton School, Bulawayo, Rhodesia, 1922–9; and subsequently at the Nautical College, Pangbourne, Berks.

DEMETRIUS KONSTANTIN SOUKLERIS. Born 26 Oct. 1881, at Alonistena of Mantinea, Arcadia, Greece. S. of Konstantin Soukleris. Educ. at Athens Univ. (D.Sc. degree). Rec. by General Secretary of the Ministry of Public Education, Athens. Adm. 10 June 1919: began res. 7 July 1919. Matric. 21 Oct. 1919.

Went down after E. 1921.
In the Ministry of Education, Greece.
He matric. as Demetrius Constantin SOUKLERIS.

FREDERICK DANIEL WISEMAN. Born 4 Jan. 1895, at Birmingham. S. of Rev. Frederick Luke Wiseman (Wesleyan Methodist Minister), 33 Routh Road, Wandsworth Common, S.W. 18. Educ. at King Edward's School, Birmingham; and Château de Prangins, Nyon, Vaud, Switzerland. Adm. 20 June 1919: began res. 8 Oct. 1919. Matric. 21 Oct. 1919.

Went down after L. 1920.
✕ 1914–19. 2nd Lieut., Spec. List (Interpreter, etc.); attd R.F.A.; Capt. and Adjt., R.A.S.C. (M.T.). M 2.
Journalist.
Bro. of C. L. Wiseman (p. 6).

EDWARD PRIESTLEY BURDETT. Born 14 March 1896, at Knutsford, Cheshire. S. of Herbert Priestley Burdett, Northfield, Knutsford. Educ. at Rugby School. Adm. 20 June 1919: began res. 1 Oct. 1919. Matric. 21 Oct. 1919.

B.A. (2ⁿᵈ Cl. Mech. Sci. Tri., 1922) 1922. M.A. 1926.
✕ 1915–19. Lieut., S. Lancs Regt; Lieut., R.A.F. (W.)
Engineer. A.M.I.E.E. 1926.

BRYAN WESTGARTH EARLE. Born 4 Sept. 1899, at Hessle, E. Yorks. S. of Ernest Earle, Penguin, Hessle. Educ. at Haileybury College. Adm. 20 June 1919: began res. 9 Oct. 1919. Matric. 21 Oct. 1919.

B.A. (Ord. degree; all. 2 terms for War serv.) 1921. M.A. 1927.
✕ 1918–19. 2nd Lieut., M.G.C.
St Augustine's College, Canterbury, 1922. Ordained d. 1924, p. 1926 Wakefield. C. of St Mary, Barnsley, 1924–6; Batley, 1926–9; R. of Lake Grace, W. Australia, 1929–32; C. of St Matthew, Ashford, Middlesex, 1932–5; Harvey, Dio. Bunbury, W. Australia, 1935–.

STANLEY PARE SIMPSON. Born 17 April 1891, at Christchurch, New Zealand. S. of Alexander Simpson (dec^d) and Mrs Simpson, 153 Bealy Avenue, St Albans, Christchurch, N.Z. Educ. at Sydenham School, Christchurch; Canterbury College School of Art, and Engineering School, Christchurch. Adm. 24 June 1919: began res. 9 Oct. 1919. Matric. 21 Oct. 1919.

> B.A. (Ord. degree) 1922. M.A. 1928.
> ✂. Served in the Great War; but details not found.

HAROLD VIKING GELL KINVIG. Born 20 Oct. 1898, at Castletown, Isle of Man. S. of Thomas Henry Kinvig (dec^d) and Mrs Kinvig, The Parade, Castletown. Educ. at King William's College, Isle of Man. Adm. 25 June 1919: began res. 9 Oct. 1919. Matric. 21 Oct. 1919.

> B.A. (2nd Cl. Class. Tri. Pt I, 1921; 1st Cl. Geog. Tri. Pt I, 1922) 1922. M.A. 1926.
> ✂ 1918-19. 2nd Lieut., R.G.A.
> Asst Master, St Bees School, 1922-7; and at Stowe School, 1927-. F.R.G.S. 1924.

MARCUS STANLEY REUSS BROADBENT. Born 29 July 1899, at Hove, Sussex. S. of Dr Francis Wesley Broadbent (dec^d) and Mrs Broadbent, 20 Orlando Road, Clapham Common, S.W. 4. Educ. at Dulwich College. Adm. 1 July 1919: began res. 2 Oct. 1919. Matric. 21 Oct. 1919.

> B.A. (Ord. degree) 1922. M.A. 1939.
> ✂ 1918-19. Lieut., R.F.A.
> M.R.C.S., L.R.C.P. 1928. Medical Officer, E. African Medical Service, 1929-32. Medical Missionary, C.M.S. Hospital, Ng'ora, Uganda, 1932-.

JOHN MATTHEWS BERKLEY MATTHEWS. Born 20 Aug. 1901, at Hamsterley, parish of Medomsley, Co. Durham. S. of Frederick Berkley Matthews, Westerhall, Langholm, Dumfriesshire. Educ. at Wellington College. Adm. 3 July 1919: began res. 2 Oct. 1919. Matric. 21 Oct. 1919.

> B.A. (Ord. degree) 1923. M.A. 1927.
> Called to the Bar, Gray's Inn, 11 May 1927.

JOHN GARDNER. Born 22 July 1898, at Great Broughton, Cumberland. S. of Thomas Gardner, Bennington Park, Stevenage, Herts. Educ. at Nelson School, Wigton, Cumberland; and King's College, London. Adm. 3 July 1919: began res. 9 Oct. 1919. Matric. 21 Oct. 1919.

> B.A. (2nd Cl. Nat. Sci. Tri. Pt I, 1921) 1922.
> ✂ 1917-19. Lieut., R.G.A.
> Entered the Regular Army, —R. Corps of Signals. 2nd Lieut., 1924 (with seniority of 1918); Lieut., 1924 (with seniority of 1920); Capt., 1929.

VICTOR COATES. Born 13 Sept. 1897, at Belfast. S. of Victor Henry Coates, Grandtully, Strathtay, Perthshire. Educ. at Abbotsholme School, Derbyshire; Heidelberg College, Germany (till 1914); and R.M.A., Woolwich (Oct. 1915 to 1916). Adm. 10 July 1919: began res. 8 Oct. 1919. Matric. 21 Oct. 1919.

> B.A. (3rd Cl. Mod. & Med. Lang. Tri. (I) f, 1921; Spec. Exam. Pol. Econ., 1921; all. 2 terms for War serv.) 1921.
> ✂ 1916-19. Lieut., R.G.A.
> Company Director in Paris.

MATTHEW DOUGLAS MONTEITH DUNN. Born 12 July 1900, at Putney. S. of Matthew Dunn, 51 Mexfield Road, Putney, S.W. 15. Educ. at Sir Walter

St John's School, Battersea. Adm. 10 July 1919: began res. 8 Oct. 1919. Matric. 21 Oct. 1919.

> Went down after E. 1921; subsequently became a Non-Coll. Student.
> ✕ c. 1918. Cadet, R.A.F.

CYRIL ERNEST FISKE. Born 28 June 1892, at Barsham, Suffolk. S. of Samuel Fiske, Staithe Road, Bungay, Suffolk. Educ. at Fauconberge School, Beccles; Bungay Grammar School; and St Mark's College, Chelsea. Adm. 11 July 1919: began res. 13 Oct. 1919. Matric. 19 Nov. 1919.

> B.A. (3rd Cl. Engl. Tri. (a), 1921; 3rd Cl. Geog. Tri. Pt I, 1922) 1922. M.A. 1926.
> ✕ 1914–19. Capt., R.F.A. (W.) *French Croix de Guerre, avec Palme.*
> Headmaster, Katharine Lady Berkeley's Grammar School, Wotton-under-Edge, 1924–. F.R.G.S. 1923.

ARTHUR RAYMOND ELLIS. Born 24 Dec. 1899, at Dewsbury, Yorks. S. of George Ellis, Easthorpe, Mirfield, Yorks. Educ. at Marlborough College. Adm. 15 July 1919: began res. 9 Oct. 1919. Matric. 21 Oct. 1919.

> Went down after M. 1921.
> ✕ 1918–19. Mid., R.N.V.R.

HERBERT JOHN DAVIS. Born 24 Aug. 1900, at Boston, Lincs. S. of John Paxton Davis, 25 Strait Bargate, Boston. Educ. at Boston Grammar School. Adm. 22 July 1919: began res. 8 Oct. 1919. Matric. 21 Oct. 1919.

> B.A. (3rd Cl. Math. Tri. Pt I, 1920; 2nd Cl. Engl. Tri. (a), 1922) 1922. M.A. 1927.
> ✕ 1918–19. Cadet, R.A.F.
> Asst Master, Ripon School, 1922–30; and at Bemrose School, Derby, 1930–4. Head Master, Whitby County School, 1934–.

CHARLES NICHOLAS SPENCER. Born 25 April 1898, at Cardiff. S. of William Spencer, 4 St John's Terrace, Wakefield, Yorks. Educ. at Wakefield Grammar School and Edinburgh Univ. Adm. 28 July 1919: began res. 9 Oct. 1919. Matric. 21 Oct. 1919.

> B.A. (Ord. degree; all. 3 terms for War serv.) 1921.
> ✕ 1915–18. Cadet Lce-Corpl, R. Irish Rifles; Lieut., R.N.V.R. (W 2.)
> Engaged in metallurgical research, 1921–4. At New Scotland Yard, 1925–6. Actor, 1927. Directing the Gate Theatre Studio, London, 1928–.

DONALD RALPH WILLIAM STEVENSON. Born 29 April 1898, at Cambridge. S. of Samuel John Stevenson, 108 Hartington Grove, Cambridge. Educ. at Cambridge and County High School. Adm. 28 July 1919: began res. 9 Oct. 1919. Matric. 21 Oct. 1919.

> B.A. (Ord. degree; all. 2 terms for War serv.) 1921. LL.B. (3rd Cl. Law Tri. Pt II, 1922) 1922. M.A. 1930.
> ✕ 1915–19. Trooper, Suffolk Yeo.; R.A.F.
> Solicitor (adm. Feb. 1925); practising at Cambridge (D. R. W. Stevenson, Squires & Co.).

GEOFFREY LLOYD. Born 21 Sept. 1899, at High Barnet, Herts. S. of Herbert John Lloyd, 26 Marriott Road, High Barnet. Educ. at Gresham's School, Holt. Adm. 1 Aug. 1919: began res. 9 Oct. 1919. Matric. 21 Oct. 1919.

> Went down after M. 1921.
> ✕ 1918–19. 2nd Lieut., King's Royal Rifle Corps.
> In business at Wellington, New Zealand, 1926–31; and subsequently at Merstham, Surrey.
> Bro. of K. Lloyd (p. 12).

EDWARD RUSSELL WELLS. Born 25 May 1898, in London. S. of Dr
(*and later* Sir) Sydney Russell Wells, 16 Lower Seymour Street, Portman Square,
W. 1. Educ. privately. Rec. by W. S. Lilly, LL.M., Hon. Fellow of Peterhouse.
Adm. 2 Aug. 1919: began res. 9 Oct. 1919. Matric. 21 Oct. 1919.

> B.A. (Ord. degree) 1922. M.A. 1927.
> ✗ 1918–19. Lieut., R.G.A. *M.C.*
> Resident Engineer, Jubbulpore Electric Supply Co., Ltd, Jubbulpore, Central Provinces, India.
> A.M.I.Mech.E. 1928.
> He matric. as Edward Russell WELLS.

WILLIAM FRANCIS AYRTON. Born 20 Sept. 1899, at Beccles, Suffolk.
S. of William Ayrton (dec^d) and Mrs Ayrton, The Cliff, Beccles. Educ. at Ipswich
School. Adm. 4 Aug. 1919: began res. 1 Oct. 1919. Matric. 21 Oct. 1919.

> Went down after E. 1922.
> ✗ 1917–19. 2nd Lieut., R.A.F.
> Engaged in business.

CHARLES GASTON BAEHLER. Born 9 Jan. 1897, at Cairo, Egypt. S. of
Charles Albert Baehler, Château Neu-Habsburg, Vorder-Meggen, nr Lucerne.
Educ. at École Nouvelle, Chailly, Lausanne; and Glarisegg, Steckborn, Switzerland.
Adm. 15 Aug. 1919: began res. 9 Oct. 1919. Matric. 21 Oct. 1919.

> Went down after E. 1920.

ALEXANDER SCOTT RUSSELL. Born 5 July 1894, at Selkirk. S. of James
Russell, 34 Upper Hamilton Terrace, N.W. 8. Educ. at George Heriot's School,
Edinburgh; and Edinburgh Univ. Rec. by Alexander Scott, Sc.D. (Peterhouse).
Adm. 1 Sept. 1919: began res. 9 Oct. 1919. Matric. 21 Oct. 1919.

> B.A. (3rd Cl. Nat. Sci. Tri. Pt II (Chemistry), 1921; all. 3 terms for War serv.) 1921. M.A. 1926.
> ✗ 1914–19. Capt., R.G.A. (W.) *M.*
> Ph.D., Sheffield, 1928. Was on the management of the Imperial Tobacco Co., Ltd, Bristol. Died
> 8 April 1939 at Fort William, as the result of an accident on Ben Nevis 7 April 1939.

HUGH LESLIE JOY. Born 19 Feb. 1900, at Duke's Manor, Layer Marney,
Kelvedon, Essex. S. of Cecil Samuel Joy (Peterhouse, B.A. 1884), Flixton, Bungay,
Suffolk. Educ. at Radley College. Adm. 15 Sept. 1919: began res. 9 Oct. 1919.
Matric. 21 Oct. 1919.

> Went down after L. 1920.
> ✗ 1918–19. Cadet, R.A.F.

WALTER GUSTAVO HERTEN. Born 18 April 1901, at Belgrano, Buenos
Aires, Argentine Republic. S. of Gustavo Herten, Calle 11 de Setiembre 1740,
Belgrano, Buenos Aires. Educ. at Belgrano School. Adm. 15 Sept. 1919: began
res. 6 Oct. 1919. Matric. 21 Oct. 1919.

> B.A. (Ord. degree) 1922. M.A. 1926.
> Was a Wool exporter at Buenos Aires. Died 10 March 1931 at Buenos Aires, from complications
> after appendicitis.
> Assumed the surname of HERTEN-GREAVEN on attaining his majority, 18 April 1922.
> Bro. of E. C. Herten, afterwards Herten-Greaven (p. 105).

SHERMAN EWING. Born 26 May 1901, at Yonkers, N.Y. S. of Thomas
Ewing, 45 East 65th Street, New York. Educ. at St Paul's School, Concord, New
Hampshire. Adm. 15 Sept. 1919: began res. 1 Oct. 1919. Matric. 21 Oct. 1919.

> Went down after E. 1920.

KENNETH GORDON SALMON. Born 6 May 1899, at Hampton Bishop, Herefordshire. S. of Harold Masterman Salmon, Marsden House, Whitchurch, Ross-on-Wye, Herefordshire. Educ. at Malvern College. Rec. by Rev. D. O. Thomas, M.A. (Peterhouse), Rector of Whitchurch. Adm. 15 Sept. 1919: began res. 8 Oct. 1919. Matric. 21 Oct. 1919.

> B.A. (Ord. degree) 1922. M.A., M.B., B.Chir. 1926.
> ✕ 1917–19. 2nd Lieut., Grenadier Gds.
> M.R.C.S., L.R.C.P. 1925. In general practice at Cheltenham.

WILLIAM EMERY. Born 29 Jan. 1900, at Ely. S. of George Frederick Emery, Wormley Lodge, Broxbourne, Herts. Educ. at Felsted School. Adm. 20 Sept. 1919: began res. 10 Oct. 1919. Matric. 21 Oct. 1919.

> Went down after E. 1921.
> ✕ 1917–19. 2nd Lieut., R.A.F.
> H.M. Inspector of Taxes.

ROY HULL HOME. Born 15 Sept. 1896, at Bournemouth. S. of A. D. Home, Jinja, Uganda. Educ. at Brighton College. Adm. 24 Sept. 1919: began res. 6 Oct. 1919. Matric. 21 Oct. 1919.

> Went down after L. 1920.
> ✕ 1917 [?]–19. Lieut., King's African Rifles.

ALBERT JOHN LUKE SHEEHAN. Born 18 Oct. 1900, at Calcutta. S. of Frederick Albert Sheehan, 1 Stowre Road, Ballygunge, Calcutta. Educ. at St Joseph's College, Darjeeling. Adm. 24 Sept. 1919: began res. 16 Oct. 1919. Matric. 21 Oct. 1919.

> Went down after E. 1920.

DANIEL AUSTIN LANE. Born 8 Dec. 1894, at St Anne's, Ontario, Canada. S. of John Austin Lane, St Anne's, Ontario. Educ. at High School, Smithville, Ontario; and Victoria College, Toronto Univ. (B.A. degree). Adm. 22 Oct. 1919: began res. 22 Oct. 1919. Matric. 19 Nov. 1919.

> B.A. (1st Cl. Oriental Lang. Tri. Pt I†, and 2nd Cl. Pt II‡, 1921; all. 3 terms for War serv.) 1921.
> ✕ 1916–19. Capt., South Persian Rifles.

GILBERT PALMER CLARIDGE, Sub-Lieut., R.N. Born 8 Jan. 1900, in London. S. of John Gilbert Claridge (dec^d) and Mrs Claridge, 72 Riggindale Road, Streatham, S.W. 16. Educ. at R.N.C. Osborne, Dartmouth and Keyham. Rec. by Admiralty. Adm. 1 Oct. 1919: began res. 11 Oct. 1919. Matric. 21 Oct. 1919.

> Resided M. 1919 and L. 1920.
> ✕ 1915–19. Sub-Lieut., R.N.
> Cdr (1934–), R.N.

PETER WILFRED DIMSDALE, Sub-Lieut., R.N. Born 16 Oct. 1899, at Eastleach, Lechlade, Glos. S. of Robert Dimsdale, Ravenshill, Eastleach, Lechlade. Educ. at R.N.C. Osborne and Dartmouth. Rec. by Admiralty. Adm. 1 Oct. 1919: began res. 11 Oct. 1919. Matric. 21 Oct. 1919.

> Resided M. 1919 and L. 1920.
> ✕ 1916–19. Sub-Lieut., R.N.
> Lieut.-Cdr (1928–), R.N.

RODERICK LATIMER MACKENZIE EDWARDS, Sub-Lieut., R.N. Born 10 July 1900, at Shide, nr Newport, Isle of Wight. S. of Lieut.-Col. Roderick Mackenzie Edwards, C.M.G., The Malt House, Faringdon, Alton, Hants. Educ. at R.N.C. Osborne, Dartmouth and Keyham. Rec. by Admiralty. Adm. 1 Oct. 1919: began res. 13 Oct. 1919. Matric. 21 Oct. 1919.

> Resided M. 1919 and L. 1920.
> ✄ 1916–19. Sub-Lieut., R.N.
> Cdr (1935–), R.N.

JOHN RANULPH DE LA HAULE MARETT, Sub-Lieut., R.N. Born 23 Jan. 1900, at Westbury Lodge, Oxford. S. of Dr Robert Ranulph Marett, Fellow (*and later* Rector) of Exeter College, Oxford, La Haule Manor, Jersey, C.I. Educ. at R.N.C. Osborne and Dartmouth. Rec. by Admiralty. Adm. 1 Oct. 1919: began res. 11 Oct. 1919. Matric. 21 Oct. 1919.

> Resided M. 1919 and L. 1920.
> ✄ 1916–19. Sub-Lieut., R.N.
> Retired from the Navy with rank of Lieut. on 15 Feb. 1923, and subsequently farmed at La Haule Manor, Jersey. Promoted Lieut.-Cdr (ret.) on 15 April 1928. Matric. from Exeter College, Oxford, 14 Oct. 1931. Dipl. in Anthropol., Oxford, 1932. B.Sc., Oxford, 1933. Research Stud. under Oxford Committee for Anthropol., 1934.
> Author:
>> *Race, sex and environment: a study of mineral deficiency in human evolution.* London, 1936 (1935).
> Editor:
>> H. J. C. Molony's *Evolution out of doors: a study of sex differences and animal coloration; edited & with an appendix by J. R. de la H. Marett.* London, 1937.

HUGH DE LAINÉ STANDLEY, Sub-Lieut., R.N. Born 28 Nov. 1899, at Saharunpur, India. S. of Alfred William Standley, Public Works Dept, India. Educ. at R.N.C. Osborne, Dartmouth and Keyham. Rec. by Admiralty. Adm. 1 Oct. 1919: began res. 11 Oct. 1919. Matric. 21 Oct. 1919.

> Resided M. 1919 and L. 1920.
> ✄ 1915–19. Sub-Lieut., R.N.
> Retired from the Navy with rank of Lieut.-Cdr on 1 Dec. 1933.

WILLIAM PATRICK DESMOND VESEY-FITZGERALD, Sub-Lieut., R.N. Born 17 March 1900, at Inchicronan, Co. Kerry. S. of John Vesey Vesey-FitzGerald, K.C., Inchicronan, The Esplanade, Frinton-on-Sea. Educ. at R.N.C. Osborne and Dartmouth. Rec. by Admiralty. Adm. 1 Oct. 1919: began res. 11 Oct. 1919. Matric. 21 Oct. 1919.

> Resided M. 1919 and L. 1920.
> ✄ 1916–19. Sub-Lieut., R.N.
> Promoted Lieut., R.N., 1920. Died 14 Feb. 1923 as the result of an accident, China station.
> He matric. as William Patrick Desmond Vesey FITZGERALD.

GEORGE DUMBA VILLIERS, Sub-Lieut., R.N. Born 6 March 1900, in London. S. of Henry Montagu Villiers, M.V.O., at 49 Hans Place, S.W. 3. Educ. at R.N.C. Osborne and Dartmouth. Rec. by Admiralty. Adm. 1 Oct. 1919: began res. 11 Oct. 1919. Matric. 21 Oct. 1919.

> Resided M. 1919 and L. 1920.
> ✄ 1916–19. Sub-Lieut., R.N.
> Retired from the Navy with rank of Sub-Lieut. (Emergency Officer) on 22 March 1920. Promoted Lieut. (ret.) on 15 Sept. 1921.

PETER KEITH WALLACE, Sub-Lieut., R.N. Born 11 April 1899, at Bracknell, Berks. S. of Major-Gen. (*and later* Sir) Alexander Wallace, C.B., Fleetwood, Wellington College, Berks. Educ. at R.N.C. Osborne, Dartmouth and Keyham. Rec. by Admiralty. Adm. 1 Oct. 1919: began res. 11 Oct. 1919. Matric. 21 Oct. 1919.

Resided M. 1919 and L. 1920.
✕ 1915–19. Sub-Lieut., R.N.
Retired from the Navy with rank of Lieut.-Cdr on 17 Jan. 1933.

Field-Marshal Sir WILLIAM RIDDELL BIRDWOOD, *Bart; Baron* Birdwood, of Anzac and of Totnes, co. Devon, 1938; *G.C.B., G.C.S.I., G.C.M.G., C.I.E., D.S.O.*; subsequently **Master**. Matric. and M.A. 9 May 1931 (originally adm. as Fellow Commoner, 1919–27; 'Order Book', 4 Oct. and 11 Nov. 1919). Hon. LL.D. 1919. **Hon. Fellow**, 1927–31; and again, 1938–. **Master**, 1931–8.

Born 13 Sept. 1865, at Kirkee, India. S. of late Herbert Mills Birdwood, M.A. (1863), LL.D. (1890), C.S.I., I.C.S., formerly Fellow and Hon. Fellow of Peterhouse. Educ. at Clifton College, and R.M.C., Sandhurst.
Lieut., R. Scots Fusiliers, 1883; 12th Lancers, 1885; 11th Bengal Lancers, 1887; Capt., 1896; Major, 1900; Lieut.-Col., 1902; Colonel, 1905; Brig.-Gen., 1909; Major-Gen., 1911; Lieut.-Gen., 1915; Gen., 1917; **Field-Marshal**, 1925.
Adjt., 11th Bengal Lancers, 1889; Adjt., Viceroy's Bodyguard, 1893; Brig.-Major, S. Africa, 1899; D.A.A.G., S. Africa, 1900; Military Sec. to C.-in-C. (General Lord Kitchener), S. Africa, 1902; Asst Military Sec. and Persian Interpreter to C.-in-C., India, 1902; A.A.G., A.H.Q., India, 1904; Military Sec. to C.-in-C. (General Viscount Kitchener), India, 1905; A.D.C. to the King, 1906–11; Brigade Cdr, Kohat Brigade, N.W.F.P., India, 1909; Q.M.G., India, 1912; Sec. to Government of India in Army Dept and Member of Governor-General's Legislative Council, 1912–14; G.O.C., Australian and N.Z. Army Corps, 1914–18, and Australian Imperial Force, 1915–20 (C.-in-C., Mediterranean Expeditionary Force, and commanded Dardanelles Army, 1915–16, for evacuation of Gallipoli Peninsula); General, Commonwealth of Australia Military Forces, 1920, and Field-Marshal, 1920; A.D.C. General to the King, 1917–22; G.O. cmdg.-in-Chief, Northern Army in India, 1920–4; Acting C.-in-C. and Member of Viceroy's Executive Council and Council of State, India, 1924; Member of Executive Council of Governor-General and Member of Council of State of India, 1925; C.-in-C., Army in India, 1925–30.
Grand Officer of the Legion of Honour, and Croix de Guerre, France; Grand Officer of the Crown, and Croix de Guerre, Belgium; Grand Cordon of the Tower and Sword, and Grand Officer of the Military Order of Aviz, Portugal; Order of the Rising Sun, 1st Cl., Japan; Order of the Nile, 2nd Cl.; 1st Cl. Order of Timsa, Persia; American Dist. Serv. Medal.
Colonel of Royal Horse Guards, and Gold Stick, 1933; Colonel of 12th Lancers, 1920; of King Edward's Own Probyn's Horse (11th Bengal Lancers), 1924; of 6th Gurkha Rifles, 1925. Colonel Commandant, 13th Frontier Force Rifles, 1930. Colonel-in-Chief, 1st New Zealand Mounted Rifles (Canterbury Yeomanry Cavalry), 1925. Colonel of 3rd Australian Infantry, and of 16th Australian Light Horse (Hunter River Lancers), 1930.
Knight of Grace, Order of St John of Jerusalem; Freeman of Borough of Totnes, Devon; Trustee, Imperial War Museum.
Hon. LL.D., Melbourne and Sydney, 1920; and Bristol, 1935. Hon. D.C.L., Durham, 1931. Hon. Litt.D., Reading, 1938. Captain of Deal Castle, 1935. President of Clifton College, 1935.
Cr. K.C.M.G. 1914; K.C.S.I. 1915; K.C.B. 1917; G.C.M.G. and 1st **Bart**, of Anzac and of Totnes, co. Devon, 1919; G.C.B. 1923; G.C.S.I. 1930; G.C.V.O. 1937; 1st **Baron** Birdwood, of Anzac and of Totnes, co. Devon, 1938.
The sixth of his family at Peterhouse: for the connections, see *Walker* and pp. 11 and 90 of this Register.

ROY LUBBOCK. Adm. **Fellow**, 30 Oct. 1919. Became Internal Fellow under the new Statutes in 1926; re-elected Internal Fellow, 1930; and again, 1935. M.A. 1920. Director of Studies in Mechanical Sciences, 1920–31. Junior Bursar, 1922–4. Steward, 1922–4 and 1932–. Asst Tutor, 1923–6. Tutorial Bursar, 1924–8.

Lecturer in Mechanical Sciences, 1926–. Senior Bursar, 1929–31. Praelector, 1933–5. Tutor, 1934–.

University Lecturer in Engineering, 1926–.

Born 1 Oct. 1892, at Downe, Kent. S. of Frederic Lubbock, Ide Hill, Kent. Educ. at Eton College K.S.), and King's College (Math. Exhib. and Eton Foundation Schol. for Mech. Sciences; B.A. 1914).

NEVILLE EDWARD SPENCER ALLEN. Born 27 Jan. 1901, at Bournemouth. S. of John Joseph Allen (dec^d) and Mrs Allen, Deene Thorpe, 1 Talbot Avenue, Bournemouth. Educ. at Mill Hill School. Adm. 13 July 1919: began res. 19 Jan. 1920. Matric. 28 Jan. 1920.

B.A. (Ord. degree) 1923.

BERTRAM HERBERT AUSTIN. Born 30 April 1896, at Putney. S. of Herbert Douglas Austin, 15 Clarendon Road, Putney, S.W. 15. Educ. at Childerley Central School, Fulham. Adm. 12 Oct. 1919: began res. 12 Jan. 1920. Matric. 28 Jan. 1920.

B.A. (Ord. degree; all. 4 terms for War serv.) 1921. M.A. 1926.
✗ 1914–19. Lieut., R.F.A.; Staff Capt., G.H.Q., France. (W.) *M.B.E. French Croix de Guerre, avec Étoile en vermeil. Mentioned in French Army Orders.*
Consulting Industrial Engineer.
Author:
(With W. F. Lloyd) *The secret of high wages*... London (1926). [Also publ. in France, Germany, Czechoslovakia, Holland, Norway, Sweden, Spain, U.S.A., Canada and U.S.S.R.]
(With W. F. Lloyd) *Capital for labour*... London, 1927. [Also publ. in U.S.A.]

WILLIAM RICHARDSON FOSTER. Born 22 June 1897, at Darlington. S. of David Foster, Tyneholme, Campbell Road, Gravesend. Educ. at Sir Joseph Williamson's Mathematical School, Rochester; and Gravesend County School. Adm. 10 Nov. 1919: began res. 17 Jan. 1920. Matric. 28 Jan. 1920.

B.A. (2nd Cl. Geog. Tri. Pt I, 1921; 2nd Cl. Pt II, 1922; all. 1 term for War serv.) 1922.
✗ 1915–19. Sapper, R.E.; Lieut., The Buffs (E. Kent Regt).
Engaged in industry.
Bro. of G. A. R. Foster (p. 29).

NORMAN KEITH BARBER. Born 23 Aug. 1894, at Willesden, Middlesex. S. of Thomas Barber (dec^d). Educ. at Latymer Upper School, Hammersmith; and Islington College. Adm. 12 Nov. 1919: began res. 15 Jan. 1920. Matric. 28 Jan. 1920.

B.A., LL.B. (3rd Cl. Math. Tri. Pt I, 1920; 1st Cl. Law Tri. Pt II, 1921; all. 4 terms for War serv.) 1921. M.A. 1926.
✗ 1914–18. Capt., Cheshire Regt. *M.C.*
Mathematical and House Master, Loretto School, 1921–8. Headmaster, Edinburgh Institution (subsequently called Melville College), 1928–.

PIERRE EDMOND BOUILLET. Born 14 Feb. 1903, at Lyons. S. of A. Bouillet (dec^d). Educ. by Pères Maristes, Lyons. Rec. by M. le Directeur de l'Externat Ste Marie, St Barthélemy, Lyons. Adm. 12 Dec. 1919: began res. 15 Jan. 1920. Matric. 28 Jan. 1920.

Went down after L. 1920.
Manager of the Établissements Bouillet Frères et Dufayard (Fabricants de soieries), at Lyons.

KENNETH FREDERICK STARLING. Born 5 Dec. 1901, at Stoke Newington. S. of Percy Frederick Starling, 10 Imperial Road, Wood Green, N. 22. Educ. at Christ's Hospital. Adm. 13 Jan. 1920: began res. 6 Oct. 1920. Matric. 21 Oct. 1920. Entrance Schol., Maths, £70.

B.A. (1st Cl. Math. Tri. Pt I, 1921; 1st Cl. Mech. Sci. Tri., 1923) 1923. Schol.* of £80, 1922.
Mechanical Engineer.

EDGAR JAMES GEATER. Born 27 June 1901, at Newbury, Berks. S. of David Geater, 3 Park View Terrace, Boundary Road, Newbury. Educ. at Christ's Hospital. Adm. 13 Jan. 1920: began res. 5 Oct. 1920. Matric. 21 Oct. 1920. Entrance Schol., Maths, £60.

B.A. (2ⁿᵈ Cl. Math. Tri. Pt I, 1921; Sen. Opt. Pt II, 1923) 1923. M.A. 1927. Re-elected to Schol.*, 1922.
Ridley Hall, Cambridge, 1923. Ordained d. 1924, p. 1925 Exeter. C. of St Andrew, Plymouth, 1924–32; V. of St Boniface, Devonport, Dio. Exeter, 1932–.

ANTHONY ARTHUR EDMUND BECK. Born 26 May 1901, at Wyton Manor, Huntingdon. S. of Arthur Clement Beck, Sandringham, Norfolk. Educ. at Gresham's School, Holt. Adm. 13 Jan. 1920: began res. 4 Oct. 1920. Matric. 21 Oct. 1920. Entrance Schol., Maths, £40.

B.A. (3ʳᵈ Cl. Math. Tri. Pt I, 1921; 3ʳᵈ Cl. Nat. Sci. Tri. Pt I, 1923) 1923.
Initiated the agricultural side of Trinity College (C.M.S.), Kandy, Ceylon, 1923–8. Now (1932) dairy farming in Norfolk.
Bro. of W. O. E. Beck (p. 68).

FRANK ROBERT HUGHES. Born 7 Dec. 1901, at Bedford. S. of Henry Walter Hughes, 31 Honey Hill Road, Bedford. Educ. at Bedford School. Adm. 13 Jan. 1920: began res. 8 Oct. 1920. Matric. 21 Oct. 1920. Entrance Schol., Classics, £40.

B.A. (2ⁿᵈ Cl. Class. Tri. Pt I, 1922; 3ʳᵈ Cl. Econ. Tri. Pt II, 1923) 1923. M.A. 1930. Re-elected to Schol.*, 1922.
Was Asst Master, St John's School, Leatherhead, 1926–33.

ARTHUR KEIGHLEY. Born 13 June 1901, at Idle, Bradford, Yorks. S. of Albert Keighley. Educ. at Bradford Grammar School. Adm. 13 Jan. 1920. Entrance Schol., Nat. Sciences, £40.

Did not matric.

REGINALD ARTHUR WELLDON FINN. Born 14 March 1901, at Sandbach, Cheshire. S. of Sidney Wallace Finn, School House, Sandbach. Educ. at Rossall School. Adm. 13 Jan. 1920: began res. 8 Oct. 1920. Matric. 21 Oct. 1920. Entrance Schol., History, £40.

B.A. (2ⁿᵈ Cl., 1ˢᵗ Div., Hist. Tri. Pt I, 1922; 2ⁿᵈ Cl., 1ˢᵗ Div., Pt II, 1923) 1923. M.A. 1929. Re-elected to Schol.*, 1922.
With William Heinemann, Ltd (publishers), 99 Great Russell Street, London, W.C. 1, 1929–; and is now (1937) Manager of their Educational Dept.
Author:
General knowledge papers for schools. London, 1927.
Cheshire. (Borzoi County Histories.) London, 1928.
Wiltshire. (Borzoi County Histories.) London, 1930.
Do you want a dog? A practical handbook... London (1933).
The pups I bought. London (1933).
Man and his conquest of England. (Beauclerk Books.) London (1936).
The English heritage. London (1937).
Scottish heritage. London (1938).
(With A. J. W. Hill) And so was England born. London (1939).
Editor:
A Galsworthy octave. London, 1932.

ARTHUR BENSLY WHITTINGHAM. Born 10 Oct. 1901, at Weedon, Northants. S. of Ven. Walter Godfrey Whittingham (Peterhouse, M.A. 1909,

Archdeacon of Oakham), Glaston Rectory, Uppingham. Educ. at Oundle School. Adm. 13 Jan. 1920: began res. 7 Oct. 1920. Matric. 21 Oct. 1920. Entrance Exhib., Classics, £30.

B.A. (3rd Cl. Class. Tri. Pt I, 1922; 2nd Cl. Pt II, 1923) 1923. M.A. 1928. Exhib. of £30, 1923.
Architect and Surveyor; practising at Ipswich. A.R.I.B.A. 1930.
Bro. of R. D. Whittingham (p. 112).

WILLIAM PICKARD KEIGHLEY. Born 3 June 1901, at Keighley, Yorks. S. of Smith Keighley, 70 Mannville Road, Keighley. Educ. at Keighley Trade and Grammar School. Adm. 13 Jan. 1920. Entrance Exhib., History, £30.

Did not matric. Died 17 March 1920.

FRANK WILLIAM IVES. Born 9 Dec. 1901, at Lincoln. S. of Stephen Ives (decd) and Mrs Ives, 24 Ashlin Grove, Lincoln. Educ. at Lincoln School. Adm. 13 Jan. 1920: began res. 7 Oct. 1920. Matric. 21 Oct. 1920. Entrance Exhib., History, £30.

B.A. (2nd Cl., 1st Div., Hist. Tri. Pt I, 1922; 1st Cl., 2nd Div., Pt II, 1923) 1923. 2nd Cl. Engl. Tri. (a), 1924. M.A. 1927. Re-elected to Exhib., 1922. Schol.* of £60, 1923.
Asst Master, Leys School, 1924–9; and at Charterhouse, 1929–.

HAROLD CHRISTOPHER WATTS. Born 3 Sept. 1895, at Lenton, Notts. S. of Rev. Alan Hunter Watts, Holy Trinity Vicarage, Brighton. Educ. at Nottingham High School, and University College, Durham. Adm. 2 Jan. 1920: began res. 16 Jan. 1920. Matric. 28 Jan. 1920. Probationer, Indian Forest Service.

B.A. (Dipl. in Forestry, 1921; all. 4 terms for War serv.) 1921.
✕ 1914–19. Capt., Sherwood Foresters (Notts and Derby Regt); Capt., I.A.R.O. (W 2.)
Indian Forest Service, 1921–; with appt. as Deputy Conservator, Central Provinces, 1924–.

AHMED MOHYDEEN. Born 1897. S. of Syed Noorullah Husaini (decd). Educ. at Mohammedan Anglo-Oriental College, Aligarh; and Allahabad Univ. Adm. 4 Jan. 1920: began res. 17 Jan. 1920. Matric. 28 Jan. 1920.

B.A. (2nd Cl., 2nd Div., Econ. Tri. Pt I, 1921; 3rd Cl. Pt II, 1922) 1923.
He matric. as Ahmed Mohy DEEN.

THEODORE HENRY EDGCOME EDWARDS. Born 6 May 1902, at Penzance. S. of Dr Edward Charles Edwards, Trefusis, Penzance. Educ. at Forest School, Walthamstow. Adm. 20 March 1920: began res. 6 Oct. 1920. Matric. 21 Oct. 1920. Organ Scholar.

B.A. (Ord. degree) 1923. M.A. 1935. Re-elected Organ Scholar, 1922.
Solicitor (adm. Nov. 1926); being partner in Tozer, Edwards & McMurtrie, at Teignmouth.
Nephew of late H. J. Edwards, Fellow and Tutor (*Walker*, p. 645).

ROBERT FENTON WILSON. Born 19 Dec. 1894, at Blackburn. S. of William Wilson, 127 Harwood Street, Blackburn. Educ. at C.E. Higher Grade School and Queen Elizabeth's Grammar School, Blackburn; and Municipal Technical School, Blackburn. Adm. 22 March 1919: began res. 23 April 1920. Matric. 5 May 1920.

B.A. (Ord. degree) 1923.
✕ 1916–20. Driver, R.F.A.
Bro. of T. M. Wilson (p. 8).

LAY TEIK GUNN. Born 27 June 1901, at Penang, Straits Settlements. S. of Gunn Tong Eang (dec^d) and Cheah Phaik Suat Neoh, 101 Bishop Street, Penang. Educ. at St Xavier's Institution, Penang. Adm. 13 Jan. 1920: began res. 22 April 1920. Matric. 5 May 1920.

> B.A. (2nd Cl. Nat. Sci. Tri. Pt I, 1923) 1923. M.A. 1926.
> Asst Analyst, Dept of Agriculture, Straits Settlements and F.M.S.

MAURICE DAVENPORT WALKER. Born 8 July 1896, at Cambridge. S. of Rev. Thomas Alfred Walker, LL.D., Fellow and Bursar of Peterhouse. Educ. at Berkhamsted School. Adm. Jan. 1920: began res. 23 April 1920. Matric. 5 May 1920.

> B.A. (2nd Cl. Engl. Tri. (a), 1922; standard of Ord. degree, Sect. B, 1923) 1923. M.A. 1927.
> ✕ 1915–20. 2nd Lieut., R. Berkshire Regt; R.M.C., Sandhurst; Capt., Lancashire Fus. *M.C. M.*
> Westcott House, Cambridge, 1924. Ordained d. 1925, p. 1926 Chelmsford. C. of Romford, 1925–8;
> Minehead, 1928–30; R. of Latimer *w*.Flaunden, 1930–8; St Matthew, Ipswich, Dio. St Edmundsbury
> and Ipswich, 1938–.

ARTHUR EDWARD KEMP. Born 9 Jan. 1899, at Halesworth, Suffolk. S. of John Oddie Kemp, Bank House, Halesworth. Educ. at Bungay Grammar School. Adm. 24 Jan. 1920: began res. 22 April 1920. Matric. 5 May 1920.

> B.A., LL.B. (2nd Cl., 2nd Div., Econ. Tri. Pt I, 1921; 2nd Cl. Law Tri. Pt II, 1922; all. 2 terms for
> War serv.) 1922. M.A. 1934.
> ✕ 1917–19. C.Q.M.S., R. Warwickshire Regt.
> With the Rising Sun Petroleum Co., Ltd., Yokohama, Japan.

ROBERT JAMES HANKINSON. Born 27 June 1900, at Bournemouth. S. of Francis Henry Hankinson, Little Barrs, St Valerie Road, Bournemouth. Educ. at Eastbourne College. Adm. 18 Feb. 1920: began res. 23 April 1920. Matric. 5 May 1920.

> Went down during M. 1921.
> ✕ 1917–19. Pte, R. Sussex Regt; Pte, Hampshire Regt; Pte, London Regt (Artists Rifles).
> Chartered Surveyor and Company Director at Bournemouth. P.A.S.I., F.A.I., M.R.San.I.

WALTER EUGENE SCHOCH. Born 2 Oct. 1899, at Rustenburg, Transvaal. S. of Herman Eugene Schoch, 126 Joubert Street, Sunnyside, Pretoria. Educ. at High School for Boys, Pretoria. Adm. 14 March 1920: began res. 23 April 1920. Matric. 5 May 1920.

> B.A. (3rd Cl. Mech. Sci. Tri., 1923) 1923. M.A. 1926.
> ✕ 1918–20. 2nd Lieut., R.A.F.
> Electrical Engineer at Johannesburg. Associate Member S. African Institute of Electrical Engineers,
> 1928.

STUART BROUGH BAILEY. Born 23 April 1899, at Brisbane, Australia. S. of Edward Bailey (dec^d) and Mrs Bailey (now Mrs McLaughlin), Macedon, Whitehouse, Co. Antrim, Ireland. Educ. at Uppingham School. Adm. 19 March 1920, by *bene discessit* from Selwyn College: began res. 23 April 1920. Matric. 19 Nov. 1919 (from Selwyn College, where he resided M. 1919 and L. 1920).

> B.A. (Ord. degree) 1922. M.A. 1926.
> Ridley Hall, Cambridge, 1922. Ordained d. 1924, p. 1926 Winchester. C. of Egham, 1924–7;
> Perm. to Offic. at St Andrew, Bournemouth, 1927–8; C. of Edgmond, 1928–31; Rugby, 1931–3;
> Perm. to Offic. at Hodnet (in charge of Weston-under-Redcastle), 1933–4; C. of Wem, 1934–7; V. of
> Ash, Dio. Lichfield, 1937–.

BENEDIKT ÖRN BENEDIKTSSON. Born 10 Feb. 1904, at Reykjavik, Iceland. S. of Einar Benediktsson, 5.Juni Plads 5, Copenhagen. Educ. at St Paul's School, London (to 1918); and Benedixen's School, Copenhagen (to 1920). Adm. 26 March 1920: began res. 23 April 1920. Matric. 5 May 1920.

Went down after E. 1921.

FAIRCHILDS LEVANT BENEDICT MacCARTHY. Born 28 May 1896, at Muskegon, Michigan. S. of Rev. Dr Joseph MacCarthy, 68 Lyman Street, Waltham, Mass. Educ. at Waltham High School; Williams College, Williamstown, Mass.; and Colgate Univ., Hamilton, N.Y. Adm. 29 March 1920: began res. 23 April 1920. Matric. 5 May 1920.

B.A. (Ord. degree; all. 2 terms for War serv.) 1922.
✕ 1917–19 [?]. Ambulance Driver, American Field Service; accepted for training as Officer in French Artillery. (W.)
Reported deceased.

FREDERICK WILLIAM COULTAS HEMSLEY. Born 28 July 1896, at West Kirby, Cheshire. S. of Thomas Frederick Hemsley, Collector of Customs and Excise, Harwich. Educ. privately, at Weston-super-Mare. Adm. 15 April 1920: began res. 23 April 1920. Matric. 5 May 1920.

Went down after E. 1920.

CHARLES HAWKEN DRAKE, Sub-Lieut., R.N. Born 26 Aug. 1900, at Plymouth. S. of Eng. Capt. Sidney James Drake, R.N., Maristow, Craneswater Park, Southsea. Educ. at R.N.C. Osborne, Dartmouth and Keyham. Rec. by Admiralty. Adm. 23 April 1920: began res. 23 April 1920. Matric. 5 May 1920.

Resided E. and Long Vac. 1920.
✕ 1916–19. Sub-Lieut., R.N.
Retired from the Navy with rank of Lieut.-Cdr on 15 June 1937.

FRANK GORDON EMLEY, Acting Lieut., R.N. Born 12 June 1897, at Johannesburg, Transvaal. S. of Frank Emley, Rand Club, Johannesburg. Educ. at Charterhouse. Rec. by Admiralty. Adm. 23 April 1920: began res. 23 April 1920. Matric. 5 May 1920.

Resided E. and Long Vac. 1920.
✕ 1916–19. Sub-Lieut., R.N.
Lieut.-Cdr (1927–), R.N.

WILLIAM RICHMOND FELL, Acting Lieut., R.N. Born 31 Jan. 1897, at Wellington, New Zealand. S. of Dr Walter Fell, Mahina, Eastbourne, Wellington, N.Z. Educ. at Wellington College, N.Z.; and R.N.C., Keyham. Rec. by Admiralty. Adm. 23 April 1920: began res. 23 April 1920. Matric. 5 May 1920.

Resided E. and Long Vac. 1920.
✕ 1916–19. Sub-Lieut., R.N.
Lieut.-Cdr (1927–), R.N. O.B.E. 1937.

REVELL CLAYTON HANNAH, Sub-Lieut., R.N. Born 20 Jan. 1900, at Brighton. S. of Walter Rainsford Hannah, 49 Branksome Wood Road, Bournemouth. Educ. at R.N.C. Osborne, Dartmouth and Keyham. Rec. by Admiralty. Adm. 23 April 1920: began res. 23 April 1920. Matric. 5 May 1920.

Resided E. and Long Vac. 1920.
✕ 1916–19. Sub-Lieut., R.N.
Retired from the Navy with rank of Lieut. on 13 Jan. 1923. Promoted Lieut.-Cdr (ret.) on 15 May 1929. Lieut., R.N.V.R.

JOHN KENNETH DOUGLAS HUTCHISON, Sub-Lieut., R.N. Born 25 Aug. 1900, at the R.M.A., Woolwich. S. of Major Kenneth Douglas Hutchison, R.A. Educ. at R.N.C. Osborne, Dartmouth and Keyham. Rec. by Admiralty. Adm. 23 April 1920: began res. 23 April 1920. Matric. 5 May 1920.

> Resided E. and Long Vac. 1920.
> ✗ 1916–19. Sub-Lieut., R.N.
> Retired from the Navy with rank of Lieut. on 22 Aug. 1922. Promoted Lieut.-Cdr (ret.) on 15 Dec. 1928.

GAGE DUNCAN SAFFERY JOHNSON, Sub-Lieut., R.N. Born 12 Sept. 1900, at Sunbury-on-Thames. S. of Gordon Johnson, 28 Philbeach Gardens, Earl's Court, S.W. 5. Educ. at R.N.C. Osborne, Dartmouth and Keyham. Rec. by Admiralty. Adm. 23 April 1920: began res. 23 April 1920. Matric. 5 May 1920.

> Resided E. and Long Vac. 1920.
> ✗ 1916–19. Sub-Lieut., R.N.
> Lieut.-Cdr (1929–), R.N.

PHILIP RUCK KEENE, Acting Lieut., R.N. Born 7 Nov. 1897, at Copford, Essex. S. of Rev. Edmund Ralph Ruck Keene, Copford Rectory, Colchester. Educ. at Haileybury College, and R.N.C., Keyham. Rec. by Admiralty. Adm. 23 April 1920: began res. 23 April 1920. Matric. 5 May 1920.

> Resided E. and Long Vac. 1920.
> ✗ 1916–19. Sub-Lieut., R.N.
> Capt. (1936–), R.N.
> A descendant of Dr Edmund Keene, Master of Peterhouse 1748–54, and Bishop successively of Chester and Ely. For a note on the Keene family, see *Walker*, p. 333.

HUGH MARTYN SIMPSON, Sub-Lieut., R.N. Born 18 Nov. 1897, at Ashton, Preston, Lancs. S. of Martyn Simpson. Educ. at Repton School, and R.N.C., Keyham. Rec. by Admiralty. Adm. 23 April 1920: began res. 23 April 1920. Matric. 5 May 1920.

> Resided E. 1920.
> ✗ 1917–19. Sub-Lieut., R.N.
> Retired from the Navy with rank of Acting Lieut. on 28 May 1920.

JOHN CLARK OGILVIE BURNS. Born 19 Sept. 1901, at Edinburgh. S. of Thomas Burns (dec^d) and Mrs Burns, 138 Newhaven Road, Edinburgh. Educ. at Edinburgh Academy and Edinburgh Univ. Adm. 26 March 1919: began res. 6 Oct. 1920. Matric. 21 Oct. 1920.

> B.A. (Ord. degree) 1923.
> Civil Engineer. F.R.G.S. 1924. Assoc.M.Inst.C.E. 1930.

JOHN BOWEN EDWARDS. Born 30 May 1901, at Folkestone. S. of John Charles Edwards, The Lilacs, 14 Julian Road, Folkestone. Educ. at Tonbridge School; and privately. Adm. 11 May 1919: began res. 5 Oct. 1920. Matric. 21 Oct. 1920.

> Went down during M. 1920.
> Solicitor (adm. March 1926); practising at Weston-super-Mare (John Hodge & Co.).

HAROLD DOUTHWAITE. Born 12 Aug. 1900, at Lancaster. S. of Thomas Douthwaite, 4 Trafalgar Road, Lancaster. Educ. at Royal Grammar School, Lancaster. Adm. 26 May 1919: began res. 1 Oct. 1920. Matric. 21 Oct. 1920.

B.A. (2nd Cl., 2nd Div., Hist. Tri. Pt I, 1922; 3rd Cl. Geog. Tri. Pt I, 1923) 1923.
Blue: Assoc. Football, 1922.
Asst Master, Royal Grammar School, Lancaster, 1923–.

OSWALD FREDERICK SWANBOROUGH. Born 20 Sept. 1900, at Melksham, Wilts. S. of Frederick Thomas Swanborough (dec^d) and Mrs Swanborough, Oakwood, Melksham. Educ. at Clifton College. Adm. 28 Oct. 1919: began res. 5 Oct. 1920. Matric. 21 Oct. 1920.

B.A. (Ord. degree) 1924.

OWEN ROBY JONES. Born 5 Aug. 1901, at Longsight, Manchester. S. of Rev. Daniel Lincoln Jones, Rockford, Sutton Coldfield, Warwickshire. Educ. at King Edward's School, Birmingham. Adm. 22 Nov. 1919: began res. 7 Oct. 1920. Matric. 21 Oct. 1920.

B.A. (2nd Cl. Math. Tri. Pt I, 1921; 2nd Cl., 2nd Div., Hist. Tri. Pt II, 1923) 1923. M.A. 1934.
Asst Master, Glasgow Academy, 1923–9; and at Wellington College, 1930–.

ROBERT JAMES KIRTON. Born 13 July 1901, at Ealing, Middlesex. S. of Albert William Kirton, 23 Carew Road, Ealing, W. 13. Educ. at Merchant Taylors' School. Adm. 14 Jan. 1920: began res. 1 Oct. 1920. Matric. 21 Oct. 1920.

B.A. (2nd Cl. Math. Tri. Pt I, 1921; Sen. Opt. Pt II, 1923) 1923. M.A. 1927. •
Successively Asst Sec. of the London Office, and Asst Actuary (1935–) at the Head Office in Glasgow, of the Scottish Amicable Life Assurance Soc. F.I.A. 1930.

ERIC MICHAEL REED. Born 16 April 1901, at Manchester. S. of Rev. Benjamin Reed, Datchworth Rectory, Stevenage, Herts. Educ. at St Peter's School, York. Adm. 14 Jan. 1920: began res. 8 Oct. 1920. Matric. 21 Oct. 1920.

B.A. (2nd Cl., 1st Div., Hist. Tri. Pt I, 1922; 1st Cl., 2nd Div., Pt II, 1923) 1923. 2nd Cl. Engl. Tri. (a), 1924. Exhib. of £30, 1922. Schol.* of £60, 1923.
Successively with the Asiatic Petroleum Co. (F.M.S.), Ltd, at Kuala Lumpur, F.M.S., and with the Shell Co. of Portugal, Ltd, at Lisbon.

PEDRO PARRA Y DE LOS REYES. Born 23 Sept. 1899, at Santo Domingo, W. Indies. S. of Juan Parra Alba, Villa Ozama, Avenida de San Sebastián, Sevilla. Educ. at Fettes College, Edinburgh; Instituto Católico de Artes é Industrias, Madrid; and Escuela Central de Ingenieros Industriales, Madrid. Adm. 14 Jan. 1920: began res. 11 Oct. 1920. Matric. 21 Oct. 1920.

Resided till E. 1923 inclusive. B.A. (Ord. degree) 1925.
Was a Cable Engineer in Spain in 1931.

DONALD ADRIAN WALLACE THESIGER. Born 28 Oct. 1901, at Bombay. S. of the Hon. Percy Mansfield Thesiger, M.B.E., 25 Cranley Gardens, S.W. 7. Educ. at Winchester College. Adm. 24 Jan. 1920: began res. 4 Oct. 1920. Matric. 21 Oct. 1920.

Went down after L. 1923.

DOUGLAS MACRAE TAYLOR. Born 5 Oct. 1901, at Batley, Yorks. S. of Arthur William Taylor, Oakwood House, Batley. Educ. at Mill Hill School; and privately. Rec. by N. B. G. James, M.A., House Master, Mill Hill School; and Rev. E. R. Borthwick, M.A. (Peterhouse), Stuston Rectory, Scole, Norfolk. Adm. 27 Jan. 1920: began res. 1 Oct. 1920. Matric. 21 Oct. 1920.

>B.A. (Ord. degree) 1923. M.A. 1933.
>Dipl. of the École des Sciences Politiques, section diplomatique, Paris, 1927. Writer, resident at Cagnes-sur-Mer, A.M., France; also of Dominica, B.W.I., where he engages in ethnological field work.

EDWARD GREY JONES. Born 16 June 1899, at Prenton, Birkenhead. S. of Arthur Grey Jones, 12 Beresford Road, Oxton, Birkenhead. Educ. at Uppingham School. Adm. 28 Jan. 1920: began res. 1 Oct. 1920. Matric. 21 Oct. 1920.

>B.A. (Ord. degree; all. 3 terms for War serv.) 1922.
>✕ 1917–19. Lieut., R.A.F.

SENG CHIN CHAN. Born 25 April 1900, at Malacca, Straits Settlements. S. of Chan Kang Swi. Educ. at High School, Malacca; and privately. Adm. 7 March 1920: began res. 1 Oct. 1920. Matric. 21 Oct. 1920.

>B.A. (Ord. degree) 1923. M.A. 1927.

NORMAN ERNEST JACOB. Born 9 July 1901, at Carnarvon. S. of Frederick Ernest Gibson Jacob, Hillside, Penarth. Educ. at Tonbridge School. Adm. 30 March 1920: began res. 4 Oct. 1920. Matric. 21 Oct. 1920.

>Went down during L. 1922.
>Was at one time with Insurance companies in S. Wales.

RICHARD WILLIAM BURNS COX. Born 27 Nov. 1895, at Acton, Middlesex. S. of Thomas Burns Cox, 60 Lady Margaret Road, Southall, Middlesex. Educ. at Featherstone Road Council School, Southall; and Ordination Test School, Knutsford. Adm. 3 April 1920: began res. 6 Oct. 1920. Matric. 21 Oct. 1920.

>B.A. (Ord. degree; all. 3 terms for War serv.) 1922. M.A. 1927.
>✕ 1915–19. Pte, R.A.M.C.; Rfn, King's Royal Rifle Corps.
>Wycliffe Hall, Oxford, 1923. Ordained d. 1924, p. 1925 Chelmsford. C. of Prittlewell, 1924–7; Leyton (in charge of St Edward), 1927–9; St Michael and All Angels, Sunninghill, 1929–33; V. of Fletching, Dio. Chichester, 1933–.

ROY ALAN LEWIS. Born 6 Jan. 1890, at Pinetown, Durban, Natal. S. of Charles Lewis, 9 Eagle Mansions, London, N. 16. Educ. at Merton Road School, Southfields, London; and Ordination Test School, Knutsford. Adm. 3 April 1920: began res. 6 Oct. 1920. Matric. 21 Oct. 1920.

>B.A. (Ord. degree; all. 3 terms for War serv.) 1922. M.A. 1926.
>✕ 1914–18. Trooper, 1st Life Gds. (W.) (P.) D.C.M.
>Wells Theol. Coll., 1923. Ordained d. 1924 Canterbury. C. of St George, Ramsgate, 1924–7.

SYED ASHRAF AHMED. Born April 1900, at Delhi. S. of Syed Mohammed Meer. Educ. at Mohammedan Anglo-Oriental School, Aligarh. Adm. 7 May 1920: began res. 8 Oct. 1920. Matric. 23 Nov. 1920.

>Went down after E. 1921.

JOHN JOSEPH DARLISON. Born 1 Nov. 1890, at Victoria Park, London. S. of Joseph John Darlison (dec^d) and Mrs Darlison, Springfield Avenue, Muswell

54 PETERHOUSE REGISTER [1920

Hill, N. 10. Educ. at Coopers' Company's School, Bow, E. 3. Adm. 12 May 1920: began res. 1 Oct. 1920. Matric. 21 Oct. 1920.

B.A. (Ord. degree) 1923. M.A. 1927.
✕ (after previous rejections) 1917–19. Lieut., R.F.A. (W.)
Studied anatomy and physiology at Univ. of the Witwatersrand, S. Africa; then lectured on various nature subjects, etc.
D.O. (Eng.) 1934,—from the British School of Osteopathy; in practice at 62 Brook Street, Mayfair, W. 1; and has lectured and demonstrated at the British School of Osteopathy. Instigator, founder member, and first Hon. Sec. of the British Institute of Osteopathic Research.
Author:
   The new art of healing: osteopathy. Some popular questions answered. London (1936).

JOHN HUNTER LINDSAY. Born 11 Feb. 1902, at Belfast. S. of David Johnston Lindsay, Ashburn, Strandtown, Belfast. Educ. at Malvern College. Adm. 15 May 1920: began res. 1 Oct. 1920. Matric. 21 Oct. 1920.

B.A. (Ord. degree) 1923.
Cousin of R. L. G. Lindsay (p. 13).

IAN HARRINGTON HOWELL. Born 26 Nov. 1901, at Tientsin, China. S. of William May Howell, 25 Barton Avenue, Southend-on-Sea. Educ. at Marlborough College. Adm. 20 May 1920: began res. 6 Oct. 1920. Matric. 21 Oct. 1920.

B.A., LL.B. (3rd Cl. Econ. Tri. Pt I, 1922; 2nd Cl., 2nd Div., Law Tri. Pt II, 1923) 1923.
Merchant at Tientsin, China.

WALTER HENRY BERNARD MOORE. Born 4 March 1902, at Wednesbury, Staffs. S. of Dr Hubert Andrew David Moore, 32 Rawmarsh Hill, Parkgate, nr Rotherham, Yorks. Educ. at King Edward VII. School, Sheffield. Adm. 20 May 1920: began res. 1 Oct. 1920. Matric. 21 Oct. 1920.

Went down after E. 1923.
M.B., Ch.B., Sheffield, 1930. In practice at Wellingborough, Northants.

SUDHENDRA NATH MOZUMDAR. Born 9 Nov. 1896, at Patna, Bihar and Orissa, India. S. of Bhupendra Nath Mozumdar (decᵈ). Educ. at Canning College, Lucknow (B.Sc. degree, Allahabad Univ.). Rec. by Sir Joseph Henry Stone, C.I.E., India Office, Whitehall. Adm. 1 June 1920: began res. 7 Oct. 1920. Matric. 21 Oct. 1920. Probationer, I.C.S.

Resided till end of E. 1921.
I.C.S. 1921–; with appt. as officiating Deputy Commissioner, Orissa, 1932–.

ARCADIUS (ARKASHA) SKIDELSKY. Born 29 Oct. 1901, at Vladivostok. S. of Jacob Labovitch Skidelsky. Educ. at Tonbridge School. Adm. 2 June 1920: began res. 1 Oct. 1920. Matric. 21 Oct. 1920.

B.A. (3rd Cl. Econ. Tri. Pt I, 1922; 2nd Cl., 2nd Div., Pt II, 1923) 1923. M.A. 1937.
He matric. as Arcadius SKIDELSKY.

THOMAS JOSEPH SAVAGE. Born 5 Feb. 1900, at Leytonstone, Essex. S. of Samuel Joseph Savage (decᵈ) and Mrs Savage (now Mrs Johnston), Amberley, 34 Plough Lane, Purley, Surrey. Educ. at Highgate School. Adm. 5 June 1920: began res. 7 Oct. 1920. Matric. 21 Oct. 1920.

B.A. (2nd Cl. Mech. Sci. Tri., 1923) 1923. M.A. 1935.
✕ 1918–19. Cadet, R.A.F.
College of the Resurrection, Mirfield, 1924. Ordained d. 1926, p. 1927 Southwark. C. of St John Evang. w. All Saints, Waterloo Road, Lambeth, 1926–8; Chaplain, S. African Church Railway Mission, Dio. Pretoria, 1928–31; C. of All Hallows, Barking, London, 1932–5; Chaplain, Toc H. Headquarters and Transvaal Area, and Lic. to Offic. Dio. Johannesburg, 1935–7; R. of Springs, Dio. Johannesburg, 1937–.

MARTIUS REDWORTH WILES FISON. Born 6 Jan. 1903, at Ipswich. S. of William Martius Wiles Fison, Sudbury, Suffolk. Educ. at Leys School. Adm. 24 June 1920: began res. 4 Oct. 1920. Matric. 21 Oct. 1920.

Went down after M. 1920.
Solicitor (adm. Feb. 1929); practising at Ipswich and Felixstowe (Fison & Co.).
Bro. of R. A. P. Fison (p. 87).

THOMAS LESLIE GRIFFITHS. Born 27 Dec. 1901, at West Didsbury, Manchester. S. of Thomas Percy Griffiths, Westover, West Didsbury. Educ. at Manchester Grammar School. Adm. 24 June 1920: began res. 5 Oct. 1920. Matric. 21 Oct. 1920.

B.A. (Ord. degree) 1923. M.A. 1934.
M.R.C.S., L.R.C.P. 1926. In practice at Yarm, Yorks.

ARTHUR HARROLD MEUX. Born 10 Oct. 1898, at New Cross, London. S. of Henry Edward Meux, 169 Drakefell Road, Brockley, S.E. 4. Educ. at Roan School, Greenwich. Rec. by J. E. G. de Montmorency, M.A., LL.B. (Peterhouse). Adm. 24 June 1920: began res. 9 Oct. 1920. Matric. 21 Oct. 1920.

B.A. (2nd Cl., 2nd Div., Hist. Tri. Pt I, 1922; 2nd Cl. Geog. Tri. Pt I, 1923) 1923. Dipl. in Geog. 1923. M.A. 1927.
✕ 1917–19. 1st Cl. Air Mechanic, R.A.F.
Asst Master, Battersea Grammar School, 1924–30; (as House Master) at Forest Hill School, Dawes Road, London, S.E. 23, 1930–2; and (as Head of Geography Dept and 6th Form Master) at Brockley County School, 1932–.

EDWARD JAMES LATIMER ROSS. Born 24 Feb. 1902, at Harlesden, Middlesex. S. of James Ross, 2 Firs Avenue, Muswell Hill, N. 10. Educ. at City of London School. Adm. 25 June 1920: began res. 7 Oct. 1920. Matric. 21 Oct. 1920.

B.A. (Ord. degree) 1923.
Woollen Merchant.
Bro. of R. G. W. Ross (p. 111).

PHILIP JOHN STROHMENGER. Born 11 Dec. 1901, at Windsor. S. of (later Sir) Ernest John Strohmenger, C.B., 19 Porchester Terrace, W. 2. Educ. at Malvern College. Adm. 25 June 1920: began res. 7 Oct. 1920. Matric. 21 Oct. 1920.

Went down after E. 1921.
With Shell-Mex and B.P., Ltd (petroleum products).

EDWARD CHARLES BUTTER ASHFORD. Born 27 June 1901, at Bath. S. of Edwin Charles Ashford, The Moorlands, Englishcombe Lane, Bath. Educ. at Malvern College. Adm. 26 June 1920: began res. 7 Oct. 1920. Matric. 21 Oct. 1920.

B.A. (Ord. degree) 1923.
Solicitor (adm. May 1929); practising at Malmesbury, Wilts.

ROLAND JEFFERY. Born 25 Oct. 1901, at Houghton-le-Spring, Co. Durham. S. of Albert John Jeffery, Claremont, W. Stanley, Co. Durham. Educ. at Consett Secondary School. Adm. 27 June 1920: began res. 6 Oct. 1920. Matric. 21 Oct. 1920.

B.A. (2nd Cl. Nat. Sci. Tri. Pt I, 1922; Spec. Exam. Geol., 1923) 1923. 2nd Cl. Nat. Sci. Tri. Pt II (Mineral.), 1924. M.A. 1927.
Senior Chemical Master, Barnard Castle School, 1925–8; and at The Cedars School Leighton Buzzard, 1928–.

AKBAR HUSAIN. Born 7 Oct. 1896, at Bara Banki, United Provinces, India. S. of Sarfarez-Hasan. Educ. at Canning College, Lucknow (B.A. degree, Allahabad Univ.). Rec. by Sir Joseph Henry Stone, C.I.E., India Office, Whitehall. Adm. 1 July 1920: began res. 7 Oct. 1920. Matric. 21 Oct. 1920. Probationer, I.C.S.

Resided till end of E. 1921.
I.C.S., 1921–; with appt. as District and Sessions Judge, United Provinces, 1930–.
Nephew of C. M. Husain (or Husein; *Walker*, p. 659).

FREDERICK JULIUS ABBOTT. Born 25 Nov. 1901, at Wellington, New Zealand. S. of Albert James Abbott, 25 Jewin Crescent, London, E.C. 1. Educ. at Malvern College. Adm. 13 July 1920: began res. 4 Oct. 1920. Matric. 23 Nov. 1920.

Went down after E. 1922.
Shipping Agent: Abbott, Oram & Co., Ltd, 25 Jewin Crescent, London, E.C. 1.

MAURICE HANNAGAN. Born 18 Dec. 1899, at Calcutta. S. of Maurice Hannagan, Queen's Courts, 20 Macleod Street, Calcutta. Educ. at La Martinière, Calcutta. Rec. by W. R. C. Adcock, M.A., LL.B. (Peterhouse), Principal. Adm. 29 July 1920: began res. 1 Oct. 1920. Matric. 21 Oct. 1920.

B.A. (2nd Cl., 2nd Div., Hist. Tri. Pt I, 1922; 3rd Cl. Pt II, 1923) 1923.
Reported to have been at one time in the Egyptian Educational Service.

MAUNG TUN TIN. Born 24 April 1897, at Thonzé, Burma. S. of Maung Po Saih. Educ. at Rangoon College. Adm. 31 July 1920: began res. 4 Oct. 1920. Matric. 21 Oct. 1920.

Went down after E. 1921.

DANIEL DAWSON. Born 14 Oct. 1896, at Cullingworth, Bingley, Yorks. S. of William Dawson, 80 Long Lane, Harden, Bingley. Educ. at Bingley Grammar School and Leeds Univ. (B.A. degree). Adm. 9 Aug. 1920: began res. 7 Oct. 1920. Matric. (as Research Stud.) 25 Feb. 1921.

Resided M. 1920, M. 1921, L. and E. 1922. M.Litt. 1926. Research Stud. of the College (in History), £100, 1922.
✕ 1915–19. Sergt, W. Yorks Regt. (W 2.)
Lecturer in History, St David's College, Lampeter, 1923–.
Author:
    The Mexican adventure. London, 1935.

THOMAS GUY LUCAS. Born 6 May 1888, at Chelmsford, Essex. S. of Thomas Lucas (decd). Educ. at Handsworth Grammar School, Staffs. Adm. 16 Aug. 1920: began res. 1 Oct. 1920. Matric. 21 Oct. 1920.

B.A. (Ord. degree; all. 4 terms for War work) 1922. M.A. 1927.
On production work in England during the War, 1915–19.
Organist and Choirmaster, St John's Church, Lafayette Square, Washington, D.C.

WILLIAM CLIFFORD THOMAS. Born 22 March 1900, at Cwmaman, Aberdare. S. of Charles Thomas, 1 Oakwood Row, Pontrhydyfen, Port Talbot, Glam. Educ. at Port Talbot County School. Adm. 1 Sept. 1920: began res. 7 Oct. 1920. Matric. 21 Oct. 1920.

B.A. (3rd Cl. Math. Tri. Pt I, 1922; 2nd Cl. Geog. Tri. Pt I, 1923) 1923. M.A. 1927.
✕ 1918–19. 2nd Air Craftman, R.A.F.
Asst Master, Queen Mary's School, Walsall, 1923–6; and at Liverpool College, 1926–. F.R.G.S. 1923.

RONALD WILKINSON KENYON. Born 27 July 1902, at York. S. of Arthur Edward Kenyon, Thorpe-on-the-Hill, nr Lincoln. Educ. at Lincoln School. Adm. 11 Sept. 1920: began res. 5 Oct. 1920. Matric. 21 Oct. 1920.

> B.A. (2nd Cl. Mod. & Med. Lang. Tri., f, 1922; 3rd Cl. Engl. Tri. (a), 1923) 1923. M.A. 1927.
> Asst Master, Orme Boys' School, Newcastle-under-Lyme, 1924–5; and Senior Mod. Lang. Master, Collyer's School, Horsham, Sussex, 1925–.

EDWARD ANDREW GARLAND. Born 10 May 1898, at Leamington Spa. S. of Colonel Ernest Alfred Crowder Garland, D.S.O., The White Cottage, Budleigh Salterton, Devon. Educ. at Sherborne School. Rec. by Forestry Dept, School of Agriculture. Adm. 21 Sept. 1920: began res. 21 Oct. 1920. Matric. 23 Nov. 1920. Probationer, Indian Forest Service.

> B.A. (Dipl. in Forestry, 1922; all. 3 terms for War serv. and 1 for Forestry work) 1922. M.A. 1933.
> ✕ 1917–20. 2nd Lieut., Worcestershire Regt.
> Indian Forest Service, 1922–; with appt. as Deputy Conservator, Bombay, 1925–.

GEOFFREY WILLIAM MARSHALL. Born 19 Aug. 1900, at Beckenham, Kent. S. of William Marshall, 14 Vermont Road, Upper Norwood, S.E. 19. Educ. at Dulwich College. Adm. 28 Sept. 1920: began res. 7 Oct. 1920. Matric. 21 Oct. 1920.

> B.A. (Ord. degree) 1923. M.A. 1927.
> Engineer. A.M.I.Mech.E. 1933.
> Cousin of J. W. Marshall (p. 96).

TERENCE JAMES HAMILTON BLACK. Born 10 Sept. 1901, at Edgbaston, Birmingham. S. of Rev. James Black, R.N. (dec^d) and Mrs Black (now Mrs Paling), 19 Duke Street, St James's, S.W. 1. Educ. at Sedbergh School. Adm. 6 Oct. 1920: began res. 8 Oct. 1920. Matric. 21 Oct. 1920.

> B.A. (3rd Cl. Econ. Tri. Pt I, 1922; 2nd Cl., 2nd Div., Hist. Tri. Pt II, 1923) 1923.
> With the Shell Co. of Egypt, Ltd (petroleum), at Cairo.

HUCK LIM ONG. Born 10 Nov. 1901, at Penang, Straits Settlements. S. of Ong Hun Lien. Educ. at Free School, Penang. Adm. 8 Oct. 1920: began res. 10 Oct. 1920. Matric. 21 Oct. 1920.

> Resided till M. 1923 inclusive. B.A. (3rd Cl. Law Tri. Pt I, 1922; Spec. Exam. Law, 1921 and 1923; [Grace 11 in *Acta* of 15 Oct. 1938]) 1938.
> Advocate and Solicitor at Penang.

WALTER ERNEST HIGHAM, Acting Lieut., R.N. Born 25 Nov. 1897, in London. S. of Ernest John Higham, D. Dudley Mansions, 29 Abbey Road, N.W. 8. Educ. at Harrow School, and R.N.C., Keyham. Rec. by Admiralty. Adm. 1 Oct. 1920: began res. 8 Oct. 1920. Matric. 21 Oct. 1920.

> Resided M. 1920 and L. 1921.
> ✕ 1916–19. Sub-Lieut., R.N.
> Lieut.-Cdr (1927–), R.N.

CECIL NORMAN ADAMS, Sub-Lieut., R.N. Born 29 Oct. 1899, at Penang, Straits Settlements. S. of Arthur Adams, Rockleigh, Swanage. Educ. at Sherborne School and H.M.S. Conway. Rec. by Admiralty. Adm. 1 Oct. 1920: began res. 11 Oct. 1920. Matric. 21 Oct. 1920.

> Resided M. 1920 and L. 1921.
> ✕ 1917–19. Acting Sub-Lieut., R.N.
> Retired from the Navy with rank of Lieut. on 5 Oct. 1922. Promoted Lieut.-Cdr (ret.) on 15 Sept. 1929.

JOHN WILLIAM JOSSELYN, Sub-Lieut., R.N. Born 13 Nov. 1900, at Madras. S. of Colonel John Josselyn, C.M.G., D.S.O., O.B.E. Educ. at R.N.C. Osborne and Dartmouth. Rec. by Admiralty. Adm. 1 Oct. 1920: began res. 8 Oct. 1920. Matric. 21 Oct. 1920.

> Resided M. 1920 and L. 1921.
> ✕ 1917–19. Acting Sub-Lieut., R.N.
> Cdr (1933–), R.N.

EDMUND LAWRANCE DEBONNAIRE MOORE, Sub-Lieut., R.N. Born 1 Oct. 1900, at Fu-Chow, China. S. of Charles Spurgeon Moore, Stanhope, The Avenue, New Bushey, Herts. Educ. at R.N.C. Osborne and Dartmouth. Rec. by Admiralty. Adm. 1 Oct. 1920: began res. 8 Oct. 1920. Matric. 21 Oct. 1920.

> Resided M. 1920 and L. 1921.
> Half-Blue: Fencing (Sabre), 1921.
> ✕ 1917–19. Sub-Lieut., R.N.
> Promoted Lieut., R.N., 1921. Killed 3 Aug. 1928 in an aeroplane accident at Edgware, Middlesex.

ERIC STANLEY OATLEY, Sub-Lieut., R.N. Born 6 April 1899, at East Farleigh, Kent. S. of Thomas Oatley, Laurel Villas, 145 Union Street, Maidstone. Educ. at Maidstone Grammar School, and R.N.C., Keyham. Rec. by Admiralty. Adm. 1 Oct. 1920: began res. 8 Oct. 1920. Matric. 21 Oct. 1920.

> Resided M. 1920 and L. 1921.
> ✕ 1917–19. Sub-Lieut., R.N.
> Lieut.-Cdr (1928–), R.N. A.M.I.E.E. 1931.

JAMES REGINALD POCOCK, Sub-Lieut., R.N. Born 27 April 1899, at Lewisham. S. of Capt. James Charles Pocock, O.B.E., Evercreech House, Evercreech, Somerset. Educ. at Cheltenham College. Rec. by Admiralty. Adm. 1 Oct. 1920: began res. 12 Oct. 1920. Matric. 21 Oct. 1920.

> Resided M. 1920 and L. 1921.
> ✕ 1917–19. Mid., R.N.
> Retired from the Navy with rank of Acting Lieut. on 10 May 1922.

CHRISTOPHER FRANCIS BOYD POWELL, Sub-Lieut., R.N. Born 20 Oct. 1898, at Colombo, Ceylon. S. of Edwin Evans Powell, Langarron, Barnstaple, N. Devon. Educ. at Charterhouse. Rec. by Admiralty. Adm. 1 Oct. 1920: began res. 8 Oct. 1920. Matric. 21 Oct. 1920.

> Resided M. 1920 and L. 1921.
> ✕ 1917–19. Mid., R.N.
> Retired from the Navy with rank of Lieut.-Cdr on 13 Oct. 1934.

GEOFFREY HOWARD STEVENS, Sub-Lieut., R.N. Born 19 Feb. 1899, in London. S. of Edward Stevens, Creswell Cottage, Wormley, Broxbourne, Herts. Educ. at Gresham's School, Holt; and R.N.C., Keyham. Rec. by Admiralty. Adm. 1 Oct. 1920: began res. 8 Oct. 1920. Matric. 21 Oct. 1920.

> Resided M. 1920 and L. 1921.
> ✕ 1917–19. Mid., R.N.
> Retired from the Navy with rank of Lieut. on 7 Jan. 1923. Promoted Lieut.-Cdr (ret.) on 15 Feb. 1929.

ROBERT ARTHUR DAVIS WATSON, Capt., R.E. Born 23 June 1896, at Dalhousie, India. S. of Major-Gen. Sir Harry Davis Watson, K.B.E., C.B.,

C.M.G., C.I.E., M.V.O., I.A. Educ. at Wellington College; R.M.A., Woolwich; and S.M.E., Chatham. Rec. by War Office. Adm. 1 Oct. 1920: began res. 7 Oct. 1920. Matric. 21 Oct. 1920.

Resided M. 1920, L. E. and Long Vac. 1921.
⚔ 1915–19. Capt., R.E. *M. And* Afghanistan, N.W. Frontier 1919.
Major (1930–), R.E.

WILLIAM FREKE HASTED, Lieut., R.E. Born 28 Sept. 1897, at Waltair, Vizagapatam, Madras. S. of William Anderson Hasted, Director of Survey, Madras Presidency. Educ. at Cheltenham College; R.M.A., Woolwich; and S.M.E., Chatham. Rec. by War Office. Adm. 1 Oct. 1920: began res. 7 Oct. 1920. Matric. 21 Oct. 1920.

Resided till E. 1921 inclusive; thereafter migrated to Non-Coll. Students.
⚔ 1915–19. Lieut., R.E. *M.C.*

RICHARD FRANCIS O'DONNELL GAGE, Lieut., R.E. Born 29 Nov. 1897, at Dublin. S. of Capt. Richard Stewart Gage (dec^d), Rathlin Island, Co. Antrim. Educ. at Wellington College, and R.M.A., Woolwich. Rec. by War Office. Adm. 1 Oct. 1920: began res. 7 Oct. 1920. Matric. 21 Oct. 1920.

Resided M. 1920, L. E. and Long Vac. 1921.
⚔ 1915–19. Lieut., R.E. (W.) *M.C.*
Major (1932–), R.E.

Sir CHRISTOPHER JOSEPH QUINTIN BRAND, *K.B.E.*, Flt Lieut., R.A.F. Born 25 May 1893, at Beaconsfield, nr Kimberley, S. Africa. S. of Edward Christoffel Joseph Brand, c/o Union Club, Johannesburg. Educ. at Marist Brothers' College, Johannesburg. Rec. by Air Ministry. Adm. 1 Oct. 1920: began res. 1 Oct. 1920. Matric. 21 Oct. 1920.

Resided till end of E. 1922.
⚔ 1914–19. 2nd Lieut., Witwatersrand Rifles, Union of S. Africa Defence Force; Sqdn Ldr, R.A.F. (W 2.) *D.S.O. M.C. D.F.C. M.*
Destroyed a Gotha in the last air raid on England, night of 19/20 May 1918. Made the pioneer flight from London to Cape Town in 1920 with Colonel Sir H. A. Van Ryneveld, K.B.E., D.S.O., M.C., and was cr. K.B.E. in recognition thereof.
Group Capt. (1935–), R.A.F. Director General of Aviation, Egypt, 1932–6. Deputy Director of Maintenance and Repair, Air Ministry, 1936–7; and Director, 1937–.

Rt Hon. Baron CHALMERS (*Sir* Robert Chalmers), of Northiam, co. Sussex, *P.C.*, *G.C.B.*, subsequently **Master**. Matric. 21 Oct. 1920; and incorp. M.A. (from Oriel College, Oxford), 4 Dec. 1920. Hon. LL.D. 1924. **Master**, 1924–31. **Hon. Fellow**, 1935–8.

Born 18 Aug. 1858, at Hornsey, Middlesex. S. of John Chalmers (dec^d), of Aberdeen. Educ. at City of London School, and Oriel College, Oxford (Class. Schol.; B.A. 1881; M.A. 1908; Hon. Fellow, 1918).
Entered Treasury, 1882; Asst Sec., 1903–7; Chairman, Board of Inland Revenue, 1907–11; Permanent Sec. to Treasury and Auditor of Civil List, 1911–13. Governor of Ceylon, 1913–16. Under-Sec. to Lord Lieutenant of Ireland, 1916; and Joint Permanent Sec. to Treasury, 1916–19.
Hon. Member, Chartered Surveyors' Institution, 1910. Member of Royal Commission on Oxford and Cambridge Universities, 1920. President, Royal Asiatic Soc., 1922–5. Trustee, British Museum, 1924–31. F.B.A. 1927. President, International Congress of Orientalists, Oxford, 1928.
Hon. LL.D., Glasgow, 1913; and St Andrews, 1930. Hon. D.Litt., Oxford, 1923.
Cr. C.B. 1900; K.C.B. 1908; G.C.B. 1916; 1st **Baron** Chalmers, of Northiam, co. Sussex, 1919. P.C. (Ireland) 1916.
Died 17 Nov. 1938 at Oxford.
Father of R. Chalmers (*Walker*, p. 679) and uncle of W. H. L. Crauford (*Walker*, p. 673).

Author:
A history of currency in the British Colonies. London (1893).
Editor, translator:
The Jātaka, or Stories of the Buddha's former births. Translated from the Pāli by various hands, under the general editorship of E. B. Cowell. Vol. 1. Translated by R. Chalmers. Cambridge, 1895.
The Majjhima-Nikāya. Edited by R. Chalmers [in continuation of the edition of V. Trenckner, vol. 1, 1888]. Vols. 2 & 3. (Pali Text Soc.) London (1896–1902).
Further dialogues of the Buddha; translated from the Pali of the Majjhima-Nikāya by Lord Chalmers. 2 vols. (Sacred Books of the Buddhists, 5 & 6.) London, 1926–7.
Buddha's Teachings, being the Sutta-Nipāta...edited in the original Pali text with an English version...by Lord Chalmers. (Harvard Oriental Ser., 37.) Cambridge, Mass., 1932.

DONALD ROSE PATERSON. Born 30 April 1902, at Cardiff. S. of Dr Donald Rose Paterson, 15 St Andrew's Crescent, Cardiff. Educ. at Marlborough College. Adm. 20 Dec. 1920: began res. 14 Jan. 1921. Matric. 27 Jan. 1921.

B.A. (3rd Cl. Geog. Tri. Pt I, 1922; standard of Ord. degree, Pt II, 1923) 1923. M.A. 1928.
Entered the Regular Army,—R. Corps of Signals. 2nd Lieut., 1924 (with seniority of 1923); Lieut., 1925; Capt., 1934. F.R.G.S. 1922. A.M.I.E.E. 1937.
Was a member of the expedition led by Major R. A. Bagnold into the Libyan Desert, 1932.

VERNON CYRIL PRINS. Born 14 Aug. 1900, at Rangoon. S. of Philip Anstruther Cyril Prins, 117 Ripon Street, Calcutta. Educ. at La Martinière, Calcutta. Rec. by W. R. C. Adcock, M.A., LL.B. (Peterhouse), Principal. Adm. 16 Dec. 1920: began res. 15 April 1921. Matric. 3 May 1921.

B.A. (2nd Cl., 2nd Div., Hist. Tri. Pt I, 1923; 2nd Cl., 2nd Div., Pt II, 1924) 1924. M.A. 1928.
History Master, Victoria School, Kurseong, India.

NAZIR AHMAD. Born 1 June 1898, at Lahore. S. of Malik Miran Bakhsh, Kakhezian Lane, Lahore. Educ. at Mohammedan Anglo-Oriental College, Aligarh; and Allahabad Univ. (B.Sc. degree). Rec. by Dr C. Wali-Mohammad, M.A. (Peterhouse), and Prof. A. S. Hemmy. Adm. 8 Jan. 1921: began res. 14 Jan. 1921. Matric. 21 Jan. 1921. Research Stud.

M.Sc. 1924. Ph.D. 1925.
Head of Science Dept, Islamia College, Lahore, 1925–9. Asst Director and then Acting Director, Technological Laboratory, Matunga, Bombay, 1929–31; and Director, 1931–.
Fellow of Punjab Univ., 1927–9. Member of Punjab Research Council, 1929–.
Author of various publications on cottons.

JAMES GRAHAM, Acting Lieut., R.N. Born 18 Dec. 1898, at Singapore. S. of James Graham, Hollingden, Woldingham, Surrey. Educ. at Charterhouse, and R.N.C., Keyham. Rec. by Admiralty. Adm. 2 May 1921: began res. 2 May 1921. Matric. 3 May 1921.

Resided E. and Long Vac. 1921.
✕ 1917–19. Sub-Lieut., R.N.
Retired from the Navy with rank of Lieut.-Cdr on 20 April 1931. Now (1934) fruit farming at Elgin, Cape Province, S. Africa.

ALARIC TREVOR HORTON, Sub-Lieut., R.N. Born 29 June 1900, at Godalming, Surrey. S. of Percy Henry Horton, Trehunsey Vean, Mawnan, nr Falmouth. Educ. at R.N.C. Osborne and Dartmouth. Rec. by Admiralty. Adm. 2 May 1921: began res. 2 May 1921. Matric. 3 May 1921.

Resided E. and Long Vac. 1921.
✕ 1917–19. Acting Sub-Lieut., R.N.
Retired from the Navy with rank of Lieut. on 31 March 1923. Promoted Lieut.-Cdr (ret.) on 15 Sept. 1929. After retirement from Navy was a Depôt Superintendent with the British Petroleum Co., Ltd, till 1932; thereafter was Resident Inspector at Aylesbury of the Norwich Union Life Insurance Society till 1934. Died 17 June 1934 in London.

GERALD DE ORELLANA BERWICK LAURENCE, Acting Sub-Lieut., R.N.
Born 22 Aug. 1901, at Norwood Green, Middlesex. S. of George Herbert Laurence,
40 Brunswick Square, Hove, Sussex. Educ. at R.N.C. Osborne and Dartmouth.
Rec. by Admiralty. Adm. 2 May 1921: began res. 2 May 1921. Matric. 3 May 1921.

> Resided E. and Long Vac. 1921.
> ✕ 1917–19. Mid., R.N.
> Retired from the Navy with rank of Lieut. on 4 Aug. 1927.

CHRISTOPHER PLEYDELL-BOUVERIE, Acting Sub-Lieut., R.N. Born
4 Nov. 1901, in London. S. of Lieut.-Col. the Hon. Stuart Pleydell-Bouverie,
D.S.O., High Barn, Godalming, Surrey. Educ. at R.N.C. Osborne and Dartmouth.
Rec. by Admiralty. Adm. 4 May 1921: began res. 4 May 1921. Matric. 25 May
1921.

> Resided E. and Long. Vac. 1921.
> ✕ 1917–19. Mid., R.N.
> Retired from the Navy with rank of Sub-Lieut. on 9 Dec. 1922. Promoted Lieut. (ret.) on 15 Sept.
> 1924.
> Author:
>   The cosmic awakening. London, 1934.
>   Objective evolution. London (1936).

ROBERT HEDLEY SELBORNE RODGER, Acting Sub-Lieut., R.N. Born
24 Oct. 1901, at Yetholm, Kelso, N.B. S. of Alexander Rodger, Yetholm. Educ.
at R.N.C. Osborne and Dartmouth. Rec. by Admiralty. Adm. 2 May 1921:
began res. 2 May 1921. Matric. 3 May 1921.

> Resided E. and Long Vac. 1921.
> ✕ 1917–19. Mid., R.N.
> Lieut.-Cdr (1931–), R.N.

RICHARD GRAHAM STEWART, Acting Sub-Lieut., R.N. Born 5 Aug.
1901, at Wemyss Bay, Renfrewshire. S. of Ninian Bannatyne Stewart, Dunloe,
Wemyss Bay. Educ. at R.N.C. Osborne and Dartmouth. Rec. by Admiralty.
Adm. 2 May 1921: began res. 2 May 1921. Matric. 3 May 1921.

> Resided E. and Long Vac. 1921.
> ✕ 1917–19. Mid., R.N.
> Lieut.-Cdr (1931–), R.N.

OWEN FRANCIS MACTIER WETHERED, Sub-Lieut., R.N. Born 20 April
1900, at Maidenhead. S. of Lieut.-Col. Francis Owen Wethered, C.M.G., Meadside,
Marlow, Bucks. Educ. at R.N.C. Osborne and Dartmouth. Rec. by Admiralty.
Adm. 2 May 1921: began res. 2 May 1921. Matric. 3 May 1921.

> Resided E. and Long Vac. 1921.
> ✕ 1917–19. Acting Sub-Lieut., R.N.
> Cdr (1936–), R.N.

LEONARD WILLIAM SIDNEY WRIGHT, Sub-Lieut., R.N. Born 23 May
1900, at Southsea. S. of Paymaster Capt. Sidney William Wright, R.N., 11 Worthing
Road, Southsea. Educ. at R.N.C. Osborne and Dartmouth. Rec. by Admiralty.
Adm. 2 May 1921: began res. 2 May 1921. Matric. 3 May 1921.

> Resided E. and Long Vac. 1921.
> ✕ 1917–19. Acting Sub-Lieut., R.N.
> Retired from the Navy with rank of Lieut. on 31 March 1923. Promoted Lieut.-Cdr (ret.) on
> 15 Aug. 1929. Now (1931) in Colonial Service, with appt. as District Officer, British Solomon Islands
> Protectorate.

LESLIE WALTER ALLAM AHRENDT. Born 16 Sept. 1903, at Witham, Essex. S. of Walter Frank Ahrendt, 55 Warren Road, Reigate, Surrey. Educ. at Reigate Grammar School. Adm. 12 Jan. 1921: began res. 5 Oct. 1921. Matric. 21 Oct. 1921. Entrance Schol., Maths, £60.

B.A. (1st Cl. Math. Tri. Pt I, 1922; Wrang. Pt II, 1924) 1924. Re-elected to Schol.*, 1923. M.A. 1928.

St Stephen's House, Oxford, 1924. Ordained d. 1926, p. 1927 Southwark. C. of St Saviour w. St Peter, Southwark (in charge of St Peter from 1927), and Acting Asst Chaplain, Guy's Hospital, 1926–31; Priest Vicar of Southwark Cathedral, 1929–31; Chaplain, King's College Hospital, Denmark Hill, 1931–4; C. of St Anne's, Soho, Dio. London, 1934–.

WILLIAM ALFRED WOOSTER. Born 18 Aug. 1903, in London. S. of Ernest Alfred Wooster, 225 Oundle Road, Peterborough. Educ. at Deacon's School, Peterborough. Adm. 12 Jan. 1921: began res. 5 Oct. 1921. Matric. 21 Oct. 1921. Entrance Schol., Nat. Sciences, £60.

B.A. (1st Cl. Nat. Sci. Tri. Pt I, 1923; 1st Cl. Pt II (Physics), 1924) 1924. Ph.D. 1927. M.A. 1928. Schol.* of £70, 1923. J. M. Dodds Stud., £100, and Hugo de Balsham Stud., £50 (both for research in Physics), 1924. Adm. Research Stud. as from Oct. 1924. Charles Abercrombie Smith Stud. (for research in Physics), £150, 1925 (held for 2 years).

College Director of Studies in Natural Sciences, 1928–30.

University Demonstrator in Mineralogy, 1927–35. University Lecturer in Mineralogy and Petrology, 1935–.

Author:

A textbook on crystal physics. Cambridge, 1938.

WILLIAM HERBERT PEAREY. Born 8 March 1903, at Tynemouth. S. of William Pearey, Flüelen, Tynemouth. Educ. at Ipswich School. Adm. 12 Jan. 1921: began res. 6 Oct. 1921. Matric. 21 Oct. 1921. Entrance Schol., Maths (allowed in 1922 to change to Economics), £40.

B.A. (2nd Cl. Math. Tri. Pt I, 1922; 2nd Cl. Econ. Tri. Pt II, 1924) 1924. Re-elected to Schol.*, 1923. Chartered Accountant. A.C.A. 1927. Lieut. (1929–), R. Northumberland Fus. (T.A.).

PERCY JOHN McALLISTER. Born 10 Aug. 1902, at Abergavenny, Monmouthshire. S. of John George Love McAllister, 124 St Awdry's Road, Barking, Essex. Educ. at Palmer's School, Grays, Essex. Adm. 12 Jan. 1921: began res. 5 Oct. 1921. Matric. 21 Oct. 1921. Entrance Schol., Maths, £40.

B.A. (2nd Cl. Math. Tri. Pt I, 1922; Sen. Opt. Pt II, 1924) 1924. Re-elected to Schol.*, 1923. Asst Master, Mill Hill School, 1926–.

ALAN VYVYAN SYMONS. Born 22 Nov. 1902, at Bradford, Yorks. S. of William Wallace Symons, 7 Farcliffe Terrace, Bradford. Educ. at Bradford Grammar School. Adm. 12 Jan. 1921: began res. 6 Oct. 1921. Matric. 21 Oct. 1921. Entrance Schol., Classics, £40.

B.A. (2nd Cl. Class. Tri. Pt I, 1923; 2nd Cl. Pt II, 1924) 1924. M.A. 1939. Re-elected to Schol.*, 1923.

With Tootal Broadhurst Lee Co., Ltd (cotton spinners and manufacturers), Manchester.

JOHN THORNE THORNE. Born 27 Nov. 1902, in London. S. of Leslie Thorne Thorne, 19 Pembridge Square, W. 2. Educ. at St Paul's School. Adm. 12 Jan. 1921: began res. 5 Oct. 1921. Matric. 21 Oct. 1921. Entrance Schol., Classics, £40.

B.A. (3rd Cl. Class. Tri. Pt I, 1923; 3rd Cl. Pt II, 1924) 1924. M.A. 1928.

Westcott House, Cambridge, 1925. Ordained d. 1926, p. 1927 Southwark. C. of St John Evang., Caterham Valley, 1926–9; S.P.G. Mission, Cawnpore, 1929–32; Additional Curates Soc. Chaplain, Moradabad, 1932–3; Allahabad, 1933–4; V. of Stillingfleet, 1934–7; C. of Benhilton, 1937–8; S.P.G. Mission, Moradabad, Dio. Lucknow, 1938–.

FRANK ALFRED BENEDICTUS. Born 7 March 1903, in London. S. of Isaac Henry Benedictus, Lansallos, 59 Christchurch Avenue, N.W. 6. Educ. at Merchant Taylors' School. Adm. 12 Jan. 1921: began res. 5 Oct. 1921. Matric. 21 Oct. 1921. Entrance Schol., Nat. Sciences, £40.

B.A. (3rd Cl. Nat. Sci. Tri. Pt I, 1923; 3rd Cl. Pt II (Chemistry), 1924) 1924.

WILLIAM GORDON EAST. Born 10 Nov. 1902, at Battersea. S. of George Richard East (dec^d) and Mrs East (now Mrs Waight), 5 Margaretta Terrace, Chelsea, S.W. 3. Educ. at Sloane School, Chelsea. Adm. 12 Jan. 1921: began res. 5 Oct. 1921. Matric. 21 Oct. 1921. Entrance Schol., History, £40.

B.A. (2nd Cl., 1st Div., Hist. Tri. Pt I, 1923; 1st Cl., 2nd Div., Pt II, 1924) 1924. M.A. 1928. Re-elected to Schol.*, 1923. Hugo de Balsham Stud. (for research in History), £100, 1924. *Grant of £40 from Worts Fund*, 1925. *Thirlwall Prize*, 1927.
Asst Lecturer in Historical Geography, London School of Economics, 1927–33; and Lecturer, 1933–.
Author:
    The union of Moldavia and Wallachia, 1859; an episode in diplomatic history. (*Thirlwall Prize*, 1927.) Cambridge, 1929.
    An historical geography of Europe. London (1935).

HAROLD RICHARD ALDRIDGE. Born 20 July 1902, in London. S. of Richard Aldridge, 3 Osterley Road, Stoke Newington, N. 16. Educ. at Owen's School, Islington. Adm. 12 Jan. 1921: began res. 5 Oct. 1921. Matric. 21 Oct. 1921. Entrance Schol., History, £40.

B.A. (2nd Cl., 1st Div., Hist. Tri. Pt I, 1923; 1st Cl., 2nd Div., Pt II, 1924) 1924. M.A. 1928. Re-elected to Schol.*, 1923. Schol.* of £60, 1924.
In the Dept of Manuscripts, British Museum, 1926–; with appt. as Asst Keeper (1st Class), 1935–. Adm. a student at the Middle Temple, Oct. 1931.
Author:
    (With Sir P. H.-S. Hartley) *Johannes de Mirfeld of St Bartholomew's, Smithfield; his life and works.* Cambridge, 1936.
    And contributor to *The British Museum Quarterly.*

CYRIL GEORGE CHALLENGER. Born 8 May 1902, at Leeds. S. of William George Challenger, 27 Howard Place, Carlisle. Educ. at Carlisle Grammar School. Adm. 12 Jan. 1921: began res. 5 Oct. 1921. Matric. 21 Oct. 1921. Entrance Exhib., Classics, £30.

B.A. (1st Cl. Class. Tri. Pt I, 1923; 2nd Cl. Pt II, 1924) 1924. 2nd Cl. Theol. Tri. Pt II (e), 1926. M.A. 1928. Schol.* of £40, 1922; and of £60, 1923. Lady Kay Divinity Scholar, Jesus College, 1924. *Hulsean Prize*, 1927.
Ripon Hall, Oxford, 1926. Ordained d. 1927, p. 1928 Southwark. C. of St Bartholomew, Sydenham, 1927–30; Caversham (in charge of St Barnabas, Emmer Green), 1930–2; V. of Hill St James, Dio. Birmingham, 1932–.
Author:
    The excellence of revealed religion: an enquiry into the meaning of revelation. (*Hulsean Prize*, 1927). Cambridge, 1928.

GARETH AIMERS EASON. Born 21 Nov. 1902, at Dublin. S. of William Waugh Eason (dec^d) and Mrs Eason (now Mrs J. Hill Tulloch), 10 Bushey Park Road, Rathgar, Dublin. Educ. at Shrewsbury School. Adm. 12 Jan. 1921: began res. 3 Oct. 1921. Matric. 21 Oct. 1921. Entrance Exhib., Nat. Sciences, £30.

B.A. (3rd Cl. Nat. Sci. Tri. Pt I, 1924) 1924. M.A., M.B., B.Chir. 1930. Re-elected to Exhib., 1923. M.R.C.S., L.R.C.P. 1927. M.R.C.P. 1929. In practice at Wimbledon Common.

JAMES LATIMER. Born 1 Jan. 1902, at Liverpool. S. of James Latimer, Golf Links Hotel, Port Erin, Isle of Man. Educ. at King William's College, Isle of Man. Adm. 12 Jan. 1921 : began res. 6 Oct. 1921. Matric. 21 Oct. 1921. Entrance Exhib., History, £30.

B.A. (2nd Cl., 2nd Div., Hist. Tri. Pt I, 1923; 2nd Cl., 1st Div., Pt II, 1924) 1924. Re-elected to Exhib., 1923.
With Macneill & Co. (East India merchants), Calcutta.

WALTER ELLIOTT WINSTANLEY. Born 11 June 1902, at Whitchurch, Salop. S. of William Jordan Winstanley [decd?] and Mrs Winstanley, Highbury, Southlands Avenue, Wolstanton, Staffs. Educ. at Newcastle-under-Lyme High School. Adm. 12 Jan. 1921: began res. 5 Oct. 1921. Matric. 21 Oct. 1921. Entrance Exhib., History, £30.

B.A. (2nd Cl., 2nd Div., Hist. Tri. Pt I, 1923; 2nd Cl., 2nd Div., Pt II, 1924) 1924. M.A. 1935. Re-elected to Exhib., 1923.
Asst Master, Framlingham College, 1925–.

DUDLEY ARTHUR WHITWHAM. Born 15 April 1901, at New Barnet, Herts. S. of Frank George Whitwham, 34 Methuen Park, Muswell Hill, N. 10. Educ. at East Finchley Vicarage School. Adm. 25 Oct. 1919: began res. 6 Oct. 1921. Matric. 21 Oct. 1921.

B.A. (Ord. degree) 1924. M.A. 1934.
Westcott House, Cambridge, 1924. Ordained d. 1926, p. 1927 London. C. of St Alban, Acton Green, 1926–9; Asst Director, London Diocesan Council for Youth, 1929–35; and Director, 1935–; C. of St Margaret, Lothbury, City and Dio. London, 1929–.
Bro. of H. E. Whitwham (p. 36).

GEORGE JOHN HINNELL. Born 28 April 1903, at Bury St Edmunds. S. of Dr Joseph Squier Hinnell, O.B.E., 62 Garland Street, Bury St Edmunds. Educ. at King Edward VI. Grammar School, Bury St Edmunds. Adm. 24 Sept. 1920: began res. 5 Oct. 1921. Matric. 21 Oct. 1921.

B.A. (Ord. degree) 1925.
Was studying medicine at St Thomas's Hospital, London. Died 19 Dec. 1928 at Felbrigge, Norfolk, from phthisis following scarlet fever with broncho-pneumonia.

EDWARD CECIL DUFFETT. Born 31 March 1903, at Sidcup, Kent. S. of Henry Allcroft Duffett, Withy Holt, Sidcup. Educ. at Brighton College. Adm. 28 Sept. 1920: began res. 5 Oct. 1921. Matric. 21 Oct. 1921.

B.A. (Ord. degree) 1925.
M.R.C.S., L.R.C.P. 1928. In practice at Plymouth; and Medical Officer to Trinity House Lighthouse Establishments there.

JOSEPH SANKEY BLOMFIELD. Born 21 March 1903, at Halstead, Essex. S. of Alfred Blomfield, Maplestead Hall, Halstead. Educ. at Bishop's Stortford College. Adm. 6 Oct. 1920: began res. 6 Oct. 1921. Matric. 21 Oct. 1921.

Went down after E. 1923.
Farming at Halstead.

HUBERT ALLEN BROWNING. Born 17 Dec. 1902, at Stratford St Mary, Suffolk. S. of Rev. Berthold Alexander Browning, The Rectory, Stratford St Mary. Educ. at R.N.C. Osborne and Dartmouth. Adm. 26 Jan. 1921: began res. 5 Oct. 1921. Matric. 21 Oct. 1921.

B.A. (Ord. degree) 1924.
Went to New Zealand in 1925, and took up farming there at Maraekakaho Valley, Hastings, Hawkes Bay.

THOMAS ESMOND KINGSLEY COOPER. Born 4 March 1903, at St Albans. S. of Thomas Cooper (Peterhouse, M.A. 1893), Spring Valley, St Albans. Educ. at Marlborough College. Adm. 5 Feb. 1921: began res. 5 Oct. 1921. Matric. 21 Oct. 1921.

B.A. (3rd Cl. Hist. Tri. Pt I, 1923; all. Ord. degree, Geog. Tri. Pt I, 1924) 1924. M.A. 1928.
Asst Master, St Neots (a preparatory school), Eversley, Hants, 1924–31; and joint Head Master there, 1931–.

HAROLD ERIC HARTLEY GOLDFINCH. Born 3 Aug. 1902, at Stratford, Essex. S. of Harold Willie Goldfinch, 3 Skelton Road, Forest Gate, E. 7. Educ. at West Ham Municipal Central Secondary School. Adm. 9 Feb. 1921: began res. 4 Oct. 1921. Matric. 21 Oct. 1921.

B.A. (3rd Cl. Math. Tri. Pt I, 1922; 2nd Cl. Nat. Sci. Tri. Pt II (Physics), 1924) 1924. M.A. 1928.
B.Sc., London, 1924. Asst Master, Barking Abbey School, Essex, 1925–30; and at Plaistow Secondary School, London, E. 13, 1930–. A.R.C.M. 1930.

FREDERICK RALPH PATTISON. Born 28 May 1903, at Tow Law, Co. Durham. S. of Frederick Ralph Pattison, 117 Dan's Castle, Tow Law. Educ. at Wolsingham Grammar School. Adm. 8 March 1921: began res. 5 Oct. 1921. Matric. 21 Oct. 1921.

B.A. (3rd Cl. Math. Tri. Pt I, 1922; Jun. Opt. Pt II, 1924) 1924. M.A. 1928.
Was Asst Master, Bishop's College School, Lennoxville, Quebec, in 1932.

EDWARD CLAYTON-JONES. Born 28 May 1903, at Ilfracombe. S. of Owen Clayton Jones, Silverton House, Silverton, Devon. Educ. at Exeter School. Adm. 4 April 1921: began res. 5 Oct. 1921. Matric. 21 Oct. 1921.

Resided till E. 1924 inclusive. M.B., B.Chir. 1929.
L.M.S.S.A., M.R.C.S., L.R.C.P. 1927. In general practice, 1929–37. Sub-editor of The Lancet, 1938–.

RICHARD HENNIS OLPHERTS CORYTON. Born 3 Sept. 1902, at Bankipur, India. S. of Richard Wybrands Coryton, Government House, Calcutta. Educ. at Clifton College. Adm. 10 April 1921: began res. 5 Oct. 1921. Matric. 21 Oct. 1921.

B.A. (Ord. degree) 1924.
Entered the Regular Army,—R. Corps of Signals. 2nd Lieut., 1925 (with seniority of 1923); Lieut., 1925; Capt., 1934. G.S.O. 3, War Office, 1937–.

WILLIAM EDWARD MILLER. Born 5 June 1902, in London. S. of Arthur William Miller, 52 Ramsden Road, Balham, S.W. 12. Educ. at Sir Walter St John's School, Battersea. Adm. 11 April 1921: began res. 5 Oct. 1921. Matric. 21 Oct. 1921.

B.A. (3rd Cl. Nat. Sci. Tri. Pt I, 1923; 3rd Cl. Pt II (Physics), 1924) 1924.
Technical Editor of The wireless and gramophone trader.

WILLIAM WRAY THORNTON. Born 10 May 1903, at Rotherham, Yorks. S. of William Thornton, The Woodlands, Thorpe, Derbyshire. Educ. at South Shields High School. Adm. 26 April 1921: began res. 5 Oct. 1921. Matric. 21 Oct. 1921.

Died 11 June 1924, whilst still in residence, as the result of a motor accident.

JOHN RONALD STUART WEBB. Born 9 March 1902, at New Quay, Cardigan-shire. S. of William John Webb, Traethgwyn, New Quay. Educ. at Dean Close School, Cheltenham. Adm. 29 April 1921: began res. 3 Oct. 1921. Matric. 21 Oct. 1921.

B.A. (Ord. degree) 1924. M.A., M.B., B.Chir. 1930.
M.R.C.S., L.R.C.P. 1927. In practice at Carmarthen, S. Wales.

LIONEL WALTER DUNSTERVILLE. Born 9 Sept. 1902, at Tientsin, China. S. of Major-Gen. Lionel Charles Dunsterville, C.B., C.S.I., The Cronk, Port St Mary, Isle of Man. Educ. at Clayesmore School, Winchester. Adm. 25 May 1921: began res. 5 Oct. 1921. Matric. 21 Oct. 1921.

B.A. (Ord. degree) 1924. M.A. 1932.
Accountant Clerk to Gibbs & Co. (shipping agents), Antofagasta, Chile, 1925–7. Asst Master, Antofagasta British School, Chile, 1927–; and interim Headmaster, 1928–9.

IAN CHARLES BENDALL. Born 21 May 1902, at Leckhampton, nr Chelten-ham. S. of John David Bendall, Home Orchard, Leckhampton. Educ. at Cheltenham Grammar School. Adm. 28 May 1921: began res. 5 Oct. 1921. Matric. 21 Oct. 1921.

B.A. (Ord. degree) 1924.
Asst Master, St John's School, Leatherhead, 1925–7; at King's School, Canterbury, 1927–8; at St Bees School, 1929–38 (House Master, 1931–8); and at St Peter's School, York, 1938–.

HAROLD BERWICK GOODRIDGE. Born 23 Feb. 1901, at St John's, New-foundland. S. of John Richard Goodridge (dec[d]), St John's, Newfoundland. Educ. at Bedford School. Adm. 15 July 1921: began res. 4 Oct. 1921. Matric. 21 Oct. 1921.

B.A. (2nd Cl., 2nd Div., Hist. Tri. Pt I, 1923; 2nd Cl. Geog. Tri. Pt I, 1924) 1924. M.A. 1928.
Asst Master, Mount House (a preparatory school), Hartley, Plymouth, 1925–9; at Berkhamsted School, 1929–33; and at Daly College, Indore, Central India, 1934–. F.R.G.S. 1924.

ERNEST HENRY WETTON BIGGS. Born 9 July 1903, at Finsbury Park, London. S. of John Clewin Biggs, 23 Belsize Avenue, Hampstead, N.W. 3. Educ. at University College School; and privately, with J. Jenkins, M.A., Hazelcroft, 3 Grove Park Road, Weston-super-Mare. Adm. 26 Aug. 1921: began res. 3 Oct. 1921. Matric. 21 Oct. 1921.

B.A. (Ord. degree) 1925.
Obtained an appointment with the Antwerp branch of General Motors Ltd, in 1927.

GEORGE PEARSON COOKE. Born 17 April 1902, at Keighley, Yorks. S. of George Cook, 87 Ashleigh Street, Keighley. Educ. at Keighley Trade and Grammar School. Adm. 13 Sept. 1921: began res. 1 Oct. 1921. Matric. 21 Oct. 1921.

B.A. (2nd Cl. Mech. Sci. Tri., 1924) 1924. Schol.* for Mech. Sciences, £40, 1922.
Engineer.

CHARLES ROBERT DOUGALL. Born 16 Oct. 1897, at Glasgow. S. of Charles Shirra Dougall, Dollar Academy, Scotland. Educ. at Dollar Academy. Adm. 16 Sept. 1921: began res. 4 Oct. 1921. Matric. 21 Oct. 1921.

B.A., LL.B. (2nd Cl., 2nd Div., Econ. Tri. Pt I, 1923; 2nd Cl., 2nd Div., Law Tri. Pt II, 1924) 1924.
⚔ 1915–19. Lieut., Argyll and Sutherland Highlanders; Lieut., R.A.F. (W 2.) (P.)
Asst Commissioner, National Savings Committee.

WILLIAM JAMES BUXTON. Born 15 Aug. 1902, at Tynemouth. S. of William Bolam Buxton, 27 Albury Park Road, Tynemouth. Educ. at Sedbergh School. Adm. 24 Sept. 1921: began res. 7 Oct. 1921. Matric. 21 Oct. 1921.

Went down after M. 1924.
Died 17 Feb. 1934 of ill health.

SYED MUHAMMED HADI. Born 12 Aug. 1898, at Hyderabad, Deccan, India. S. of Capt. Syed Mohamed (dec^d). Educ. at Nizam's College, Hyderabad. Adm. 28 Sept. 1921: began res. 7 Oct. 1921. Matric. 21 Oct. 1921. Aff. Stud.

B.A. (3rd Cl. Econ. Tri. Pt I, 1923; all. Ord. degree, Pt II, 1924) 1924. M.A. 1929.
Blue: Lawn Tennis, 1922, 1923, 1924. Represented Cambridge v. Oxford at Table Tennis, 1923.
Represented India at Lawn Tennis in the Davis Cup, 1923, 1924, 1925; and in the Olympic Games at Paris, 1924. Also played Lawn Tennis for Oxford and Cambridge v. Harvard and Yale, 1924; and has played Cricket for India v. Australia.
Studied physical education training at Pennsylvania Univ., U.S.A., 1925. In the service of H.E.H. The Nizam of Hyderabad as Director of Physical Education, 1926–.
He matric. as Syud Mohammed HADI.
Bro. of S. A. Akbar (p. 9).

RICHARD MAXWELL JACK. Born 18 March 1900, at Pretoria, Transvaal. S. of John Jack, 949 Church Street, Arcadia, Pretoria. Educ. at King Edward VII. School, Johannesburg; and Royal Technical College, Glasgow. Adm. 4 Oct. 1921: began res. 7 Oct. 1921. Matric. 21 Oct. 1921.

B.A. (Ord. degree) 1924.
✂ 1918–19. Cadet, R.M.A., Woolwich.
With the Asiatic Petroleum Co., Ltd, at Hongkong, 1924–.

OWEN MEYRICK. Born 18 Dec. 1901, at Marlborough. S. of Edward Meyrick, Thornhanger, Marlborough. Educ. privately, by his father. Adm. 5 Oct. 1921: began res. 7 Oct. 1921. Matric. 21 Oct. 1921.

B.A. (2nd Cl. Class. Tri. Pt I, 1923; 3rd Cl. Pt II, 1924) 1924.

ARTHUR LESLIE MORTON. Born 4 July 1903, at Hengrave, nr Bury St Edmunds. S. of Arthur Spence Morton, Stanchils', Hengrave. Educ. at Eastbourne College. Adm. 7 Oct. 1921: began res. 7 Oct. 1921. Matric. 21 Oct. 1921.

B.A. (3rd Cl. Hist. Tri. Pt I, 1923; 3rd Cl. Engl. Tri. (a), 1924) 1924.
Bro. of M. L. Morton (p. 110).

GEORGE DOUGLAS MURRAY. Born 17 Nov. 1901, at Dunedin, New Zealand. S. of William Murray, Sishes End, Stevenage, Herts. Educ. at Wanganui College, N.Z.; Christ's College, Christchurch, N.Z.; and privately, with Rev. A. H. Gardner, M.A. Adm. 7 Oct. 1921: began res. 7 Oct. 1921. Matric. 21 Oct. 1921.

Went down after E. 1924.
Went to S. Africa for fruit farming.

NOEL WILKIN. Born 30 Dec. 1902, at South Shields. S. of Alfred Benjamin Wilkin [dec^d?] and Mrs Wilkin, Keri, Beechcroft Avenue, Golders Green, N.W. 4. Educ. at Leys School; and privately. Rec. by E. T. Garnier, M.A., private tutor. Adm. 7 Oct. 1921: began res. Oct. 1921. Matric. 21 Oct. 1921.

B.A. (Ord. degree) 1924.
Was a Company Secretary in 1931.

WILLIAM OLIVER ERNEST BECK. Born 3 Jan. 1904, at Sandringham, Norfolk. S. of Arthur Clement Beck, Sandringham. Educ. at Gresham's School, Holt. Adm. 8 Oct. 1921: began res. 7 Oct. 1921. Matric. 21 Oct. 1921.

> B.A. (Ord. degree) 1924.
> Sub-Agent on the Sandringham Estate.
> Bro. of A. A. E. Beck (p. 47).

TREVOR GEORGE NESBITT. Born 21 June 1903, at Bridgnorth, Salop. S. of Rev. George Richard Nesbitt, The Rectory, High Ongar, Essex. Educ. at Haileybury College. Rec. by Rev. W. R. Lloyd, M.A. (Peterhouse), Housemaster. Adm. 10 Oct. 1921: began res. 7 Oct. 1921. Matric. 21 Oct. 1921.

> Went down after E. 1922.
> Was with the Anglo-American Oil Co., Ltd. Died 19 Dec. 1930 at High Ongar, from septicaemia and pneumonia following a chill.

ROGER FREDERICK, Sub-Lieut., R.N. Born 5 Sept. 1900, at Burgh Hall, Burgh Castle, Great Yarmouth. S. of Henry Penrice Frederick, Burgh Hall, Burgh Castle. Educ. at R.N.C. Osborne and Dartmouth. Rec. by Admiralty. Adm. 7 Oct. 1921: began res. 7 Oct. 1921. Matric. 21 Oct. 1921.

> Resided M. 1921 and L. 1922.
> ✕ 1917–19. Mid., R.N.
> Lieut.-Cdr (1930–), R.N.

RICHARD CECIL DUDLEY GRIMES, Acting Lieut., R.N. Born 3 July 1899, at Derby. S. of Ernest William Grimes, 11 Wilmot Street, Derby. Educ. at Derby School, and R.N.C., Keyham. Rec. by Admiralty. Adm. 7 Oct. 1921: began res. 7 Oct. 1921. Matric. 21 Oct. 1921.

> Resided M. 1921 and L. 1922.
> ✕ 1918–19. Mid., R.N.
> Lieut.-Cdr (1929–), R.N.

ERIC GEORGE McGREGOR, Sub-Lieut., R.N. Born 23 Jan. 1901, at South Queensferry, Scotland. S. of George McGregor, 2 Brading Avenue, Eastern Parade, Southsea. Educ. at R.N.C. Osborne and Dartmouth. Rec. by Admiralty. Adm. 7 Oct. 1921: began res. 7 Oct. 1921. Matric. 21 Oct. 1921.

> Resided M. 1921 and L. 1922.
> ✕ 1917–19. Mid., R.N.
> Cdr (1936–), R.N.

HERCULES BRADSHAW FORBES MOORHEAD, Sub-Lieut., R.N. Born 10 Feb. 1901, at Cheltenham. S. of John Hercules Murray Moorhead, Hong Kong and Shanghai Bank, 9 Gracechurch Street, E.C. 3. Educ. at R.N.C. Osborne and Dartmouth. Rec. by Admiralty. Adm. 7 Oct. 1921: began res. 7 Oct. 1921. Matric. 21 Oct. 1921.

> Resided M. 1921 and L. 1922.
> ✕ 1917–19. Mid., R.N.
> Retired from the Navy with rank of Lieut.-Cdr on 6 Jan. 1932. Colonial Service, with appt. as Director of Government Meteorological Station, St Georges, Bermuda, 1932–.

CHARLES FREDERICK NOCK, Acting Lieut., R.N. Born 12 Sept. 1899, in London. S. of Charles William Nock (dec^d) and Mrs Nock, 32 Plympton Road,

Brondesbury, N.W. 6. Educ. at St Lawrence College, Ramsgate; and R.N.C., Keyham. Rec. by Admiralty. Adm. 7 Oct. 1921: began res. 7 Oct. 1921. Matric. 21 Oct. 1921.

Resided M. 1921 and L. 1922.
✕ 1918–19. Mid., R.N.
Retired from the Navy with rank of Lieut. on 31 March 1923. Promoted Lieut.-Cdr (ret.) on 15 July 1929. Now (1935) Electrical Engineer, with Hopkinson Induction Motors, N. Acton, London, W. 3.

EDWARD PITCAIRN GAMBIER SANDWITH, Acting Lieut., R.N. Born 21 Jan. 1899, at Harworth Vicarage, Notts. S. of Rev. Edward Pitcairn Sandwith (dec^d) and Mrs Sandwith, 26 Canynge Square, Clifton, Bristol. Educ. at Clifton College, and R.N.C., Keyham. Rec. by Admiralty. Adm. 7 Oct. 1921: began res. 7 Oct. 1921. Matric. 21 Oct. 1921.

Resided M. 1921 and L. 1922.
✕ 1918–19. Mid., R.N.
Retired from the Navy with rank of Lieut. on 15 Feb. 1923. Promoted Lieut.-Cdr (ret.) on 15 July 1929. On retirement from the Navy he took up farming at Chilanga, N. Rhodesia; now (1934) has a Government appointment at Luanshya, N. Rhodesia.

WILLIAM HARRY BINCKES WALLACE, Sub-Lieut., R.N. Born 18 Aug. 1900, at King's Lynn. S. of William Harry Binckes Wallace, St Edmund's Lodge, Greevegate Road, Hunstanton. Educ. at H.M.S. Conway, and R.N.C., Dartmouth. Rec. by Admiralty. Adm. 7 Oct. 1921: began res. 7 Oct. 1921. Matric. 21 Oct. 1921.

Resided M. 1921 and L. 1922.
✕ 1917–19. Mid., R.N.
Lieut.-Cdr (1930–), R.N.

JOHN GUY DOUGLAS WETHERFIELD, Sub-Lieut., R.N. Born 18 Feb. 1901, at Lewknor, Oxon. S. of Rev. Samuel Wetherfield, Buckland Rectory, Betchworth, Surrey. Educ. at R.N.C., Dartmouth. Rec. by Admiralty. Adm. 7 Oct. 1921: began res. 7 Oct. 1921. Matric. 21 Oct. 1921.

Resided M. 1921 and L. 1922.
✕ 1917–19. Mid., R.N.
Lieut.-Cdr (1931–), R.N.

CHARLES FAIRBRIDGE AUGUSTIN BIRD, Lieut., R.E. Born 13 May 1898, at Pietermaritzburg, Natal. S. of Christopher John Bird, C.M.G., Scottsville, Pietermaritzburg. Educ. at Bedford School, and R.M.A., Woolwich. Rec. by War Office. Adm. 4 Oct. 1921: began res. 4 Oct. 1921. Matric. 21 Oct. 1921.

Resided M. 1921, L. E. and Long Vac. 1922.
✕ 1916–19. Lieut., R.E. *And* Afghanistan, N.W. Frontier 1919.
Retired from the Army with rank of Capt. on 7 Nov. 1928, on account of ill health.

WALTER HERBERT BLAGDEN, Lieut., R.E. Born 8 Oct. 1896, at Plumstead, London. S. of Walter John Blagden, 5 St Margaret's Terrace, Plumstead, S.E. 18. Educ. at Bancroft's School, Woodford Wells, Essex; and R.M.A., Woolwich. Rec. by War Office. Adm. 4 Oct. 1921: began res. 4 Oct. 1921. Matric. 21 Oct. 1921.

Resided M. 1921, L. E. and Long Vac. 1922.
✕ 1916–19. Lieut., R.E. (W.)
Major (1935–), R.E.

REGINALD GILBERT GODSON, Lieut., R.E. Born 7 May 1897, at Pieter-maritzburg, Natal. S. of Colonel Gilbert Godson-Godson, D.S.O., 53 Roslyn Apartments, Osborne Street, Winnipeg, Manitoba. Educ. at High School, Van-couver; and R.M.C., Kingston, Ontario. Rec. by War Office. Adm. 4 Oct. 1921: began res. 4 Oct. 1921. Matric. 21 Oct. 1921.

>   Resided M. 1921, L. E. and Long Vac. 1922.
>   ✕ 1916–19. Lieut., R.E.
>   Retired from the Army with rank of Capt. on 30 May 1928, on account of ill health contracted on active service.

FRANK FOWLER, Flt Lieut., R.A.F. Born 28 May 1897, at Duleek, Co. Meath. S. of George Hurst Fowler, Eureka, Kells, Co. Meath. Educ. at Repton School. Rec. by Air Ministry. Adm. 4 Oct. 1921: began res. 4 Oct. 1921. Matric. 30 Nov. 1921.

>   B.A. (Ord. degree; all. 3 terms as Commiss. Off.) 1923.
>   ✕ 1915–19. Major, R.A.F. (W.) *D.S.C. A.F.C. French Croix de Guerre.*
>   Retired from the R.A.F. with rank of Wing Cdr on 20 June 1934.

HORACE GORDON-DEAN, Sqdn Ldr, R.A.F. Born 3 Dec. 1890, in London. S. of George Frederick Dean, 3 The Bishop's Avenue, N. 2. Educ. at King's College School. Rec. by Air Ministry. Adm. 5 Oct. 1921: began res. 5 Oct. 1921. Matric. 21 Oct. 1921.

>   B.A. (3rd Cl. Mech. Sci. Tri., 1923; all. 3 terms as Commiss. Off.) 1923.
>   ✕ 1914–19. Lce-Corpl, H.A.C.; Lieut., York and Lancaster Regt; Major, R.A.F. *A.F.C.*
>   Dipl. in Aeronautics, Imperial College of Science and Technology, London, 1925. Retired from the R.A.F. with rank of Group Capt. on 16 May 1938. Operation Officer, Directorate of Operational Services and Intelligence, Air Ministry, 1938–.

FRANCIS SINCLAIR THOMPSON, Lieut., R.C. of S. Born 23 July 1897, at Bideford, Devon. S. of Charles Sinclair Thompson (decᵈ) and Mrs Thompson, Ashfield, Ashford, nr Barnstaple. Educ. at Blundell's School, and R.M.A., Wool-wich. Rec. by War Office. Adm. 6 Oct. 1921: began res. 6 Oct. 1921. Matric. 21 Oct. 1921.

>   B.A. (Ord. degree; all. 3 terms as Commiss. Off.) 1923.
>   ✕ 1916–19. Lieut., R.E.
>   Retired from the Army with rank of Major on 4 Feb. 1937.

CHRISTOPHER HAMILTON FRANCE-HAYHURST. Born 8 April 1902, at Hartford, Cheshire. S. of Walter France-Hayhurst (decᵈ) and Mrs France-Hayhurst, Hartford House, Hartford. Educ. at Shrewsbury School. Adm. Dec. 1921: began res. 11 Jan. 1922. Matric. 28 Jan. 1922.

>   B.A. (3rd Cl. Hist. Tri. Pt I, 1923; 3rd Cl. Pt II, 1924) 1924.

HENRY JAMES SHOLTO DOUGLAS. Born 14 Jan. 1903, at Hove, Sussex. S. of Lieut.-Col. Henry Mitchell Sholto Douglas, Hemingford Abbots, St Ives, Hunts. Educ. at Harrow School. Adm. Dec. 1921: began res. 11 Jan. 1922. Matric. 8 March 1922.

>   B.A. (Ord. degree) 1924.
>   Entered the Regular Army: 2nd Lieut., 1st King's Dragoon Gds, 1925 (with seniority of 1924); Lieut., 1926; transferred to Scots Gds, 1930.

STEPHEN ROMER ASCHERSON, Sub-Lieut., R.N. Born 11 June 1901, in London. S. of Charles Stephen Ascherson, Stede Court, Harrietsham, Kent. Educ. at R.N.C. Osborne and Dartmouth. Rec. by Admiralty. Adm. 19 April 1922: began res. 19 April 1922. Matric. 4 May 1922.

Resided E. and Long Vac. 1922.
⚔ 1917–19. Mid., R.N.
Retired from the Navy with rank of Lieut.-Cdr on 11 Jan. 1934.

EDMUND GILES BURROWS, Sub-Lieut., R.N. Born 5 April 1901, at Galle, Ceylon. S. of Rev. Montagu John Burrows, Colombo, Ceylon. Guardian (uncle): Bp of Chichester, The Palace, Chichester. Educ. at R.N.C. Osborne and Dartmouth. Rec. by Admiralty. Adm. 19 April 1922: began res. 19 April 1922. Matric. 4 May 1922.

Resided E. and Long Vac. 1922.
⚔ 1917–19. Mid., R.N.
Promoted Lieut., R.N., 1923. Killed 16 Sept. 1924 in a motor accident near Quebec.

RICHARD ELLIS BUTLER, Sub-Lieut., R.N. Born 6 March 1901, at Blackheath, London. S. of Alfred George Butler, 2 Eliot Vale, Blackheath, S.E. 3. Educ. at R.N.C. Osborne and Dartmouth. Rec. by Admiralty. Adm. 19 April 1922: began res. 19 April 1922. Matric. 4 May 1922.

Resided E. and Long Vac. 1922.
⚔ 1917–19. Mid., R.N.
Lieut.-Cdr (1931–), R.N.

MILES AMBROSE GREGORY CHILD, Sub-Lieut., R.N. Born 8 May 1901, at Cobham, Surrey. S. of Stephen Ambrose Child, The Crossways, Cobham. Educ. at R.N.C. Osborne and Dartmouth. Rec. by Admiralty. Adm. 19 April 1922: began res. 19 April 1922. Matric. 4 May 1922.

Resided E. and Long Vac. 1922.
⚔ 1917–19. Mid., R.N.
Lieut.-Cdr (1930–), R.N.

HAROLD SPENCER COOPER, Sub-Lieut., R.N. Born 2 June 1901, in London. S. of Henry Spencer, 18 Portman Street, W. 1. Educ. at R.N.C. Osborne and Dartmouth. Rec. by Admiralty. Adm. 19 April 1922: began res. 19 April 1922. Matric. 4 May 1922.

Resided E. and Long Vac. 1922.
⚔ 1917–19. Mid., R.N.
Retired from the Navy with rank of Lieut. on 22 April 1929. Promoted Lieut.-Cdr (ret.) on 15 Oct. 1930.

CHARLES RICHARD GARRETT, Sub-Lieut., R.N. Born 13 March 1901, at Chandernagore, India. S. of Abraham Garrett, Calcutta. Educ. at R.N.C. Osborne and Dartmouth. Rec. by Admiralty. Adm. 19 April 1922: began res. 19 April 1922. Matric. 4 May 1922.

Resided E. and Long Vac. 1922.
⚔ 1917–19. Mid., R.N.
Retired from the Navy with rank of Lieut.-Cdr on 31 Jan. 1934.

RICHARD MOORE, Acting Sub-Lieut., R.N. Born 13 March 1902, at Southsea. S. of Paymaster-in-Chief Richard Edwin Moore (decᵈ), R.N. Educ. at R.N.C.

Osborne and Dartmouth. Rec. by Admiralty. Adm. 19 April 1922: began res. 19 April 1922. Matric. 4 May 1922.

> Resided E. and Long Vac. 1922.
> ✕ 1918–19. Mid., R.N.
> Lieut.-Cdr (1931–), R.N.

SAMUEL HENRY TAYLOR, Sub-Lieut., R.N. Born 13 June 1900, at Clifton, Bristol. S. of John Mathews Taylor, 22 Royal York Crescent, Clifton. Educ. at R.N.C. Osborne and Dartmouth. Rec. by Admiralty. Adm. 19 April 1922: began res. 19 April 1922. Matric. 4 May 1922.

> Resided E. and Long Vac. 1922.
> ✕ 1917–19. Mid., R.N.
> Retired from the Navy with rank of Lieut. on 22 March 1926. Promoted Lieut.-Cdr (ret.) on 15 Oct. 1930. Now (1931) an Investment Banker.

VINCENT ELLIS DAVIES. Born 3 June 1903, at Old Colwyn, Denbighshire. S. of Rev. Ellis Davies, Whitford Vicarage, Holywell, Flints. Educ. at St John's School, Leatherhead. Adm. 13 Dec. 1921: began res. 10 Oct. 1922. Matric. 23 Oct. 1922. Entrance Schol., History, £80.

> B.A. (2nd Cl., 1st Div., Hist. Tri. Pt I, 1924; 2nd Cl., 1st Div., Pt II, 1925) 1925. M.A. 1932. Schol.* of £40, 1924. Probationer, I.C.S., M. 1925 to E. 1926.
> I.C.S., 1926–; with appt. as officiating Magistrate and Collector, Bihar, 1933–.

CHARLES MILLINGTON. Born 19 Sept. 1904, at Southwark. S. of Joseph John Millington, 66 Newcomen Street, Southwark, S.E. 1. Educ. at St Olave's and St Saviour's Grammar School, Bermondsey. Adm. 13 Dec. 1921: began res. 10 Oct. 1922. Matric. 23 Oct. 1922. Entrance Schol., Classics, £60.

> B.A. (1st Cl. Class. Tri. Pt I, 1924; aegr. Pt II, 1925) 1925. 3rd Cl. Theol. Tri. Pt I, 1926. M.A. 1930. Schol.* of £70, 1924. Lady Kay Divinity Scholar, Jesus College, 1925.
> Ely Theol. Coll., 1926. Ordained d. 1927 Southwell, p. 1928 Derby. C. of St Bartholomew, Clay Cross, 1927–9; Missioner, Clare College Mission, Rotherhithe, 1929–33; Member of the Community of the Resurrection, Mirfield, 1935–.

LESLIE HAROLD ROBINSON. Born 19 Oct. 1903, in London. S. of George Robinson, Avon Lodge, 189 Richmond Road, Kingston-on-Thames. Educ. at Owen's School, Islington. Adm. 13 Dec. 1921: began res. 10 Oct. 1922. Matric. 23 Oct. 1922. Entrance Schol., History, £60.

> B.A. (2nd Cl., 1st Div., Hist. Tri. Pt I, 1924; 2nd Cl., 2nd Div., Pt II, 1925) 1925. M.A. 1932. Schol.* of £40, 1924.
> Asst Master, Warwick School, 1927–.

WILLIAM ARNOLD JOHNSON. Born 21 June 1903, at Whitby, Yorks. S. of John William Johnson, Second Avenue, Bradford Moor, Bradford, Yorks. Educ. at Bradford Grammar School. Adm. 13 Dec. 1921: began res. 10 Oct. 1922. Matric. 23 Oct. 1922. Entrance Schol., Maths, £40.

> B.A. (3rd Cl. Math. Tri. Pt I, 1923; 2nd Cl. Mech. Sci. Tri., 1925) 1925. M.A. 1929. Exhib. for Mech. Sciences, £30, 1924. *John Bernard Seely Prize*, 1924.
> Railway Officer with the London, Midland and Scottish Railway Co.; in 1931 at Chief General Superintendent's Dept, Derby. Assoc. M.Inst.C.E. 1929. A.M.I.Mech.E. 1930.

FREDERICK FRANCIS PERCIVAL SMITH. Born 5 Nov. 1903, at Keighley, Yorks. S. of Evan Francis Smith, 41 Rawling Street, Keighley. Educ. at Keighley

Trade and Grammar School. Adm. 13 Dec. 1921: began res. 10 Oct. 1922. Matric. 23 Oct. 1922. Entrance Schol., Nat. Sciences, £40.

B.A. (1st Cl. Nat. Sci. Tri. Pt I, 1924; 1st Cl. Pt II (Chemistry), 1925) 1925. Ph.D. 1928. Schol. of £60, 1923. Schol.* of £70, 1924; and of £60, 1925. Adm. Research Stud. as from Oct. 1925. J. M. Dodds Stud. (for research in Chemistry), £50, 1926. Charles Abercrombie Smith Stud. (for research in Chemistry), £150, 1927 (but resigned June 1928). *Gordon Wigan Prize* (aeq.), 1927.
Industrial Chemist; with Imperial Chemical Industries Ltd, 1928–.

GEORGE WILLIAM GREENAWAY. Born 7 Jan. 1903, at Wargrave, Berks. S. of George Henry Greenaway, 3 Whitehall Place, S.W. 1. Educ. at Emanuel School, Wandsworth Common. Adm. 13 Dec. 1921: began res. 10 Oct. 1922. Matric. 23 Oct. 1922. Entrance Schol., History, £40.

B.A. (1st Cl., 2nd Div., Hist. Tri. Pt I, 1924; 1st Cl., 2nd Div., Pt II, 1925) 1925. M.A. 1929. Schol.* of £60, 1924; re-elected, 1925. *Deserving of Commendation for Lightfoot Schol.*, 1926. *Lightfoot Schol.*, 1927. Hugo de Balsham Stud. (for research in History), £75, 1927. *Prince Consort Prize*, 1930. *Gladstone Memorial Prize*, 1930.
Gladstone Research Stud., St Deiniol's Library, Hawarden, 1928–9. Asst Lecturer in History, University College of the South West of England, Exeter, 1930–6; and Lecturer in Mediaeval History, 1936–.
Author:
    Arnold of Brescia. (*Prince Consort and Gladstone Memorial Prizes*, 1930.) Cambridge, 1931.

LESLIE ADAMS JONES. Born 29 March 1903, at Wolverhampton. S. of Ernest Adams Jones, Iffley, Woodfield Avenue, Penn, Wolverhampton. Educ. at Wolverhampton Grammar School. Adm. 13 Dec. 1921: began res. 10 Oct. 1922. Matric. 23 Oct. 1922. Entrance Exhib., Classics, £30.

B.A. (2nd Cl. Class. Tri. Pt I, 1924; 2nd Cl. Pt II, 1925) 1925. M.A. 1929. Exhib. of £40, 1924.
Asst Master, Crypt Grammar School, Gloucester, 1926–8; at Dorking High School, 1928–31; and at Sutton County School, Surrey, 1931–.

WALTER JOHN ROBERTS. Born 7 Jan. 1904, at Merton, Surrey. S. of John Henry Roberts, Brampton, Hunts. Educ. at Huntingdon Grammar School. Adm. 13 Dec. 1921: began res. 10 Oct. 1922. Matric. 23 Oct. 1922. Entrance Exhib., History, £30; and Miller Exhib.

B.A. (2nd Cl., 1st Div., Hist. Tri. Pt I, 1924; 2nd Cl., 1st Div., Pt II, 1925) 1925. M.A. 1929. Exhib. of £40, 1924. Re-elected to Miller Exhib., 1924.
Asst Master, Drax Grammar School, Selby, 1926–7; and at Stockton Grammar School, 1927–.

JOHN RASHLEIGH LOWE. Born 31 May 1900, at Wansford, Northants. S. of John Edward Lowe (decd) and Mrs Lowe (now Mrs Cobbold), The Drift House, Stamford, Lincs. Educ. at St Edmund's School, Canterbury; and Ordination Test School, Knutsford. Adm. 1921: began res. 10 Oct. 1922. Matric. 23 Oct. 1922.

B.A. (2nd Cl., 1st Div., Hist. Tri. Pt I, 1924; 3rd Cl. Theol. Tri. Pt I, Sec. A, 1925) 1925. M.A. 1929.
Westcott House, Cambridge, 1925. Ordained d. 1926, p. 1927 Southwark. C. of St George, Camberwell (Trinity College Mission), 1926–30; Shrivenham w. Watchfield, 1930–2; V. of St Philip and All Saints, N. Sheen, 1932–4; R. of Quenington w. Coln St Aldwyn and Hatherop, Dio. Gloucester, 1934–. Rural Dean of Fairford, 1936–. Chaplain to the Forces, 4th Class, R.A.C.D. (T.A.), 1937–.

WHINFIELD BOLTON. Born 25 Aug. 1904, at Barrow-in-Furness. S. of Wilfred Bolton, 73 Holker Street, Barrow-in-Furness. Educ. at Barrow Municipal Secondary School. Adm. 24 Nov. 1921: began res. 10 Oct. 1922. Matric. 23 Oct. 1922.

B.A. (2nd Cl. Mod. & Med. Lang. Tri., f, 1924; 3rd Cl. Engl. Tri. (a), 1925) 1925. M.A. 1929.
Asst Master, Chesterfield Grammar School, 1926–.

ALANSON WORK WILLCOX. Born 30 July 1901, at Akron, Ohio. S. of
Prof. Walter Francis Willcox, 3 South Avenue, Ithaca, N.Y. Educ. at Cornell
Univ., Ithaca (A.B. degree). Adm. 4 March 1922: began res. 10 Oct. 1922. Matric
23 Oct. 1922.

Went down after E. 1923.
LL.B., Harvard, 1926. Member of the firm Schurman, Wiley and Willcox (lawyers), 49 Wall Street,
New York, 1929–.

SYDNEY FREDERICK TURNER. Born 28 Feb. 1904, at Mansfield, Notts.
S. of Arthur Joseph Turner (dec^d) and Mrs Turner, 105 Rosemary Street, Mansfield.
Educ. at Queen Elizabeth's Grammar School, Mansfield. Rec. by J. B. D. Godfrey,
M.A. (Peterhouse), Head Master. Adm. 13 March 1922: began res. 10 Oct. 1922.
Matric. 23 Oct. 1922.

B.A. (3rd Cl. Math. Tri. Pt I, 1923; 2nd Cl. Geog. Tri. Pt I, 1924; 2nd Cl. Pt II, 1925) 1925. M.A.
1932.
Colonial Service: in Survey Dept, N. Rhodesia, 1925–; and now (1931) with appt. as District Surveyor there.

ULRICH SCOTT TRUNINGER. Born 12 Aug. 1902, at Buenos Aires,
Argentine Republic. S. of U. B. Truninger, San Diego, Estación Rocamora,
Entre Ríos, Argentine Republic. Educ. at Marlborough College. Rec. by Rev.
E. R. Borthwick, M.A. (Peterhouse); and W. A. Knight, M.A., D.Sc., Asst Master,
Marlborough College. Adm. 28 March 1922: began res. 10 Oct. 1922. Matric.
23 Oct. 1922.

Went down after E. 1923.

WILLIAM JOSEPH MOFFAT. Born 4 June 1905, at Stafford. S. of William
Moffat, 191 Corporation Street, Stafford. Educ. at King Edward VI. Grammar
School, Stafford. Adm. 11 April 1922: began res. 10 Oct. 1922. Matric. 23 Oct.
1922.

B.A. (Ord. degree) 1926.
M.R.C.S., L.R.C.P. 1929. In practice at Stafford.

DONALD KEANE INGLE. Born 30 April 1904, at Bombay. S. of Frederick
Arthur Ingle, c/o Messrs King, King & Co., P.O. Box 110, Bombay. Educ. at
Perse School, Cambridge. Adm. 6 June 1922: began res. 10 Oct. 1922. Matric.
23 Oct. 1922.

B.A. (2nd Cl., 1st Div., Hist. Tri. Pt I, 1924; 2nd Cl., 1st Div., Law Tri. Pt II, 1925) 1925. M.A. 1931.
North Borneo Civil Service, 1926–.

JOHN EDWARD BLAKENEY. Born 2 Dec. 1901, at Sheffield. S. of Rev.
Edward Purdon Blakeney, St Matthias' Vicarage, Sheffield. Educ. at Trent College.
Adm. 8 July 1922: began res. 10 Oct. 1922. Matric. 23 Oct. 1922.

B.A. (Ord. degree) 1925. M.A. 1930.
Asst Master, Sunnydown (a preparatory school), Hog's Back, Guildford, 1925–30. Headmaster,
Merton Court (also preparatory), Foots Cray, Kent, 1931–.

CHRISTOPHER BRADSHAW GARNETT. Born 14 Nov. 1903, at Warrington,
Lancs. S. of Philip Carlisle Garnett (dec^d) and Mrs Garnett, Haynes, Southbourne
Cliff Drive, Bournemouth. Educ. at Clayesmore School, Winchester. Adm. 8 July
1922: began res. 10 Oct. 1922. Matric. 23 Oct. 1922.

B.A. (Ord. degree) 1925. M.A. 1929.
Colonial Service, with appt. as District Agricultural Officer, Tanganyika Territory, 1926–.

WILFRED VIVIAN HOWELLS. Born 7 June 1903, at Trimsaran, nr Llanelly. S. of John Howells, 18 Northampton Place, Swansea. Educ. at Mill Hill School. Adm. 8 July 1922: began res. 10 Oct. 1922. Matric. 23 Oct. 1922.

> B.A. (Ord. degree) 1925. M.A. 1929. M.B., B.Chir. 1931.
> M.R.C.S., L.R.C.P. 1929. In practice at Swansea.

LEWIS EDWARD VAN MOPPES. Born 22 Sept. 1904, at Muswell Hill, Middlesex. S. of Meyer Louis Van Moppes, St Ronans, Church End, Finchley, N. 3. Educ. at Mill Hill School. Adm. 8 July 1922: began res. 10 Oct. 1922. Matric. 23 Oct. 1922.

> B.A. (Ord. degree) 1925.
> Industrial Diamond Merchant.

CLARENCE ROBINSON. Born 18 May 1903, at Flushing, Long Island, U.S.A. S. of Clarence Robinson (dec^d) and Mrs Robinson, Brooklands, Jersey, C.I. Educ. at Marlborough College. Adm. 17 July 1922: began res. 10 Oct. 1922. Matric. 23 Oct. 1922.

> B.A. (Ord. degree) 1925. M.A. 1930.
> Was engaged in aviation in U.S.A. F.R.G.S. 1927. Killed 27 Aug. 1937 in a flying accident in U.S.A. Bro. of K. Robinson (p. 93).

THOMAS ANTHONY ENSOR. Born 24 May 1903, at Dorchester. S. of Thomas Henry Ensor, Clandon, Prince of Wales Road, Dorchester. Educ. at Marlborough College; and privately, with Rev. L. G. Harrison, B.A. Adm. 21 July 1922: began res. 10 Oct. 1922. Matric. 23 Oct. 1922.

> Went down after L. 1924.
> Died 9 May 1925 at Dorchester, after an illness lasting nearly a year.

NAI SAWAT SVETATISHA. Born 22 April 1898, at Bangkok, Siam. Educ. at Chulalongkorn Univ., Siam; and privately, with P. Hope, M.A., Craighurst, Southwold. Adm. 21 July 1922: began res. 10 Oct. 1922. Matric. 23 Oct. 1922.

> B.A. (Ord. degree) 1925.
> Went into the Custom House, Bangkok, in 1926.
> He matric. as Sawat SVETATISHA.

WILLIAM FRANCIS FORSTER GRACE. Born 10 Sept. 1899, at Huyton, Lancs. S. of William Grace, Thornfield, Rupert Road, Huyton. Educ. at St Francis Xavier's College, Liverpool; and Liverpool Univ. (B.A. degree). Adm. 21 July 1922: began res. 6 Oct. 1922. Matric. (as Research Stud.) 23 Oct. 1922. Charles Abercrombie Smith Stud. (for research in History), £150, 1922.

> Ph.D. 1925.
> ✕ 1917–18. Pte, Welsh Regt.
> M.A., Liverpool, 1925. Senior History Master, St Francis Xavier's College, Liverpool, 1924–.
> F.R.Hist.Soc. 1929.

YASUO ARAI. Born 27 June 1902, at Tokyo, Japan. S. of T. Arai, Tokyo. Educ. at 1st Middle School, Sendai, Japan; and privately with A. H. Peart, LL.M. (Peterhouse). Rec. by A. H. Peart. Adm. 1 Aug. 1922: began res. 10 Oct. 1922. Matric. 23 Oct. 1922.

> B.A. (Ord. degree) 1925.

ROWLAND MARCUS WOODMAN. Born 26 Nov. 1899, at Leeds. S. of Wallace Woodman, 72 Lady Pit Lane, Leeds. Educ. at Leeds Univ. (M.Sc. degree). Adm. 8 Aug. 1922: began res. 9 Oct. 1922. Matric. 23 Oct. 1922. Research Stud.

Ph.D. 1925.
✗ 1917–19. Pte, Leicestershire Regt.
Physical Chemist, Horticultural Research Station, School of Agriculture, Cambridge, 1922–; and Lecturer at the School of Agriculture. F.I.C. 1927. A.Inst.P. 1927.
County Councillor for Waterbeach Division of Cambs. Vice-President, Cambs Liberal Assoc. Member of numerous Cambs Committees and Sub-Committees.
Author or joint author of some seventy papers on physical, colloid and dispersoid chemistry, vegetable nutrition, etc.

CHINUBHAI CHAMAULAL JAVERI. Born 26 June 1902, at Ahmedabad, Bombay Presidency. S. of Chamaulal Vadilal Javeri, Chowpatty, Bombay. Guardian: Kastoorbhai Manibhai Nagersheth, Cuff Parade, Colaba, Bombay. Educ. at Elphinstone High School, Bombay. Adm. 16 Aug. 1922: began res. 10 Oct. 1922. Matric. 23 Oct. 1922.

B.A. (Ord. degree) 1925. M.A. 1929.
In business at Bombay.
Cousin of P. K. Nagersheth (p. 114).

JOHN BURLEY PICTON. Born 4 Feb. 1905, at Church Hulme, Cheshire. S. of Lionel James Picton, O.B.E., Holmes Chapel, Cheshire. Educ. at St Bees School. Adm. 17 Aug. 1922: began res. 10 Oct. 1922. Matric. 23 Oct. 1922.

B.A. (Ord. degree) 1925.

WALTER LLEWELLYN OWEN. Born 11 June 1888, at Ealing, Middlesex. S. of William Price Owen, Watertown, Umberleigh, N. Devon. Educ. at Leys School. Adm. 17 Aug. 1922: began res. 10 Oct. 1922. Matric. 23 Oct. 1922.

Went down after E. 1924.
✗ 1914–19. Bt Major, The King's (Liverpool Regt); Lieut.-Col., S. Lancs Regt; Lieut.-Col., The Queen's (R.W. Surrey Regt). (W 2.) D.S.O. M.C. M 2.

ALAN CREE. Born 25 April 1904, at Chopwell, Co. Durham. S. of John Cree, Burnbrae, Rookhope, Eastgate, Co. Durham. Educ. at Wolsingham Grammar School. Adm. 1922: began res. 10 Oct. 1922. Matric. 23 Oct. 1922.

B.A. (3ʳᵈ Cl. Nat. Sci. Tri. Pt I, 1925) 1925. M.A. 1929.
Asst Master, Ardingly College, 1925–.

EDWIN VERNON RHYS. Born 3 April 1902, at Williamsburg, Iowa. S. of Rev. Thomas Devey Rhys, 695 Chester Road, Erdington, Birmingham. Educ. at Ordination Test School, Knutsford. Adm. 1922: began res. 10 Oct. 1922. Matric. 23 Oct. 1922.

B.A. (Ord. degree) 1926. M.A. 1930.
Lincoln Theol. Coll., 1926. Ordained d. 1928, p. 1929 Birmingham. C. of St Francis, Bourneville, 1928–32; Chaplain of Erdington House and Homes, 1932–7; V. of St Mary, Aston Brook, Dio. Birmingham, 1937–.

CYRIL UNDERWOOD. Born 30 Nov. 1904, at Oldham, Lancs. S. of Thomas Underwood, 33 Gainsborough Avenue, Oldham. Educ. at Hulme Grammar School, Oldham. Adm. 2 Oct. 1922: began res. 10 Oct. 1922. Matric. 23 Oct. 1922.

B.A. (2ⁿᵈ Cl. Math. Tri. Pt I, 1923; 1ˢᵗ Cl. Nat. Sci. Tri. Pt II (Physics), 1925) 1925. M.A. 1929.
Research Physicist, British Cotton Industry Research Assoc., Manchester.

JOHN RAVENOR KNOWLES. Born 14 Oct. 1904, at Tientsin, China. S. of George Stanley Knowles, Tientsin. Educ. at Reading School; and privately. Adm. 4 Oct. 1922: began res. 10 Oct. 1922. Matric. 23 Oct. 1922.

B.A. (Ord. degree) 1925.
Engineer.

MALIK MOHAMMED ASLAM KHAN. Born 26 Aug. 1905, at Pindi Baha-ud-in, Punjab, India. S. of Malik Mohammed Din, Baha-ud-in, Punjab. Educ. at Woodbridge School. Adm. 10 Oct. 1922: began res. 10 Oct. 1922. Matric. 23 Oct. 1922.

B.A. (Ord. degree) 1925. M.A. 1929.
Called to the Bar, Inner Temple, 27 Jan. 1930. Advocate of the High Court, Lahore. Director of the International Trading Corporation, Ltd, Lahore.
Has translated into Urdu various works of D. H. Lawrence, N. Evreinov and A. Chekhov.

MICHAEL JOHN PAGET BAXTER. Born 4 Aug. 1902, at Islington. S. of Michael Paget Baxter, 1 Hove Seaside Villas, Hove, Sussex. Educ. at Brighton College; and privately. Adm. 10 Oct. 1922: began res. 10 Oct. 1922. Matric. 23 Oct. 1922.

Went down after L. 1923.

KENNETH WALTER MUSSEN CAMPBELL. Born 2 Oct. 1902, at Benares, India. S. of Major William Kenneth Hamilton Campbell, I.A. (dec^d), and Mrs Campbell, The Grange, Bishop's Stortford, Herts. Educ. privately, with Rev. J. R. C. Forrest, M.A., Swanbourne Vicarage, Winslow, Bucks. Adm. 10 Oct. 1922: began res. 10 Oct. 1922. Matric. 23 Oct. 1922.

Went down after E. 1924.
Engaged in experimental electro-medical work with Vapozol, Ltd, London, 1924–6. Rubber planting in Negri Sembilan, F.M.S., 1926–8. Tin mining in Perak, F.M.S., 1928–31. Living independently in Cameron Highlands, Pahang, F.M.S., 1931–.

JOSEPH LANGDON JEKYLL. Born 27 July 1903, at Leytonstone, Essex. S. of Lewis Nugent Jekyll, Gainsborough House, Leytonstone. Educ. at Forest School, Walthamstow. Adm. 10 Oct. 1922: began res. 10 Oct. 1922. Matric. 23 Oct. 1922.

Resided till M. 1925 inclusive. B.A. (Ord. degree) 1927.
M.R.C.S., L.R.C.P. 1930. In practice at Leytonstone.
Bro. of N. D. Jekyll (p. 102).

ASHTON CECIL LISTER. Born 31 Jan. 1905, at Dursley, Glos. S. of Charles Ashton Lister, C.B.E., Stinchcombe Hill House, Dursley. Educ. at Clifton College. Adm. 10 Oct. 1922: began res. 10 Oct. 1922. Matric. 23 Oct. 1922.

Went down after E. 1923.
Apptd Sales Manager in 1924, and Director in 1929, of R. A. Lister & Co., Ltd (engineers), Dursley.

JOHN JAMES KENWORTHY RHODES. Born 21 July 1903, at Blackpool. S. of Oliver Arnold Rhodes, Vaude Vista, Bolton-le-Sands, Lancs. Educ. at Royal Grammar School, Lancaster. Adm. 10 Oct. 1922: began res. 10 Oct. 1922. Matric. 23 Oct. 1922.

B.A. (Ord. degree) 1925.
Industrial Physicist.

HERBERT GRIMLEY ROWLAND. Born 10 Feb. 1905, at Birmingham. S. of Frank Rowland, 40 Bristol Road, Birmingham. Educ. at Nautical College, Pangbourne. Adm. 10 Oct. 1922: began res. 10 Oct. 1922. Matric. 23 Oct. 1922.

Went down after L. 1924.
Called to the Bar, Gray's Inn, 26 Jan. 1928.

ALFRED JOHN ELLIOTT TAYLOR. Born 19 May 1904, in London. S. of John Vining Elliott Taylor, Vinings, Church Road, Hayward's Heath, Sussex. Educ. at Clifton College. Adm. 10 Oct. 1922: began res. 10 Oct. 1922. Matric. 23 Oct. 1922.

B.A. (3rd Cl. Econ. Tri. Pt I, 1924; 3rd Cl. Pt II, 1925) 1925. M.A. 1932.
Chartered Accountant. Now (1933) an Advertising Agent, with R. Anderson & Co., 14 King William Street, Strand, London, W.C. 2.

EDWARD THORNTON (*Count of Cassilhas*, of the Kingdom of Portugal), Flt Lieut., R.A.F. Born 27 Oct. 1893, at Woodhurst, Crawley, Sussex. S. of Edward Thornton (decᵈ) and Mrs Thornton, Beedingwood, Horsham, Sussex. Educ. at Eton College. Rec. by Air Ministry. Adm. 1922: began res. 6 Oct. 1922. Matric. 21 Oct. 1912 (from Trinity College, where he resided M. 1912 to E. 1914 inclusive).

Resided till end of E. 1923.
✗ 1914–19. Lieut., R. Fusiliers; attd R.E. (Signals); Capt., R.A.F.
Wing Cdr (1937–), R.A.F.
Succeeded his grandfather as 3rd Count of Cassilhas, of the Kingdom of Portugal, 1906.

HUGH WHELER BUSH, Lieut., R.E. Born 23 July 1898, at Bath. S. of Rev. Herbert Wheler Bush, Bathford Vicarage, Bath. Educ. at Cheltenham College, and R.M.A., Woolwich. Rec. by War Office. Adm. 1922: began res. 10 Oct. 1922. Matric. 23 Oct. 1922.

Resided till end of E. 1923.
✗ 1917–19. Lieut., R.E. *M. And* Iraq Operations 1919–20; Waziristan 1919–21; and N.W. Frontier of India 1930–1.
Major (1937–), R.E.

ROBERT PHILIP AUGUSTUS DOUGLAS LITHGOW, Lieut., R.E. Born 18 July 1898, at Farnborough, Hants. S. of Dr Robert Alexander Douglas Lithgow (decᵈ). Educ. at Charterhouse, and R.M.A., Woolwich. Rec. by War Office. Adm. 1922: began res. 10 Oct. 1922. Matric. 23 Oct. 1922.

Resided till end of E. 1923.
✗ 1917–19. Lieut., R.E. *And* Afghanistan, N.W. Frontier 1919.
Major (1936–), R.E.

DENYS REDWOOD VACHELL, Lieut., R.E. Born 7 May 1898, at Cleeve, nr Bristol. S. of Alfred Redwood Vachell, Cleeve. Educ. at Clifton College, and R.M.A., Woolwich. Rec. by War Office. Adm. 1922: began res. 10 Oct. 1922. Matric. 23 Oct. 1922.

B.A. (2nd Cl. Mech. Sci. Tri., 1924; all. 3 terms as Commiss. Off.) 1924.
✗ 1917–19. Lieut., R.E. *M.C. and Bar*.
Retired from the Army with rank of Capt. on 12 Aug. 1935.

GEOFFREY LOUIS BODOANO, Sub-Lieut., R.N. Born 3 June 1901, at Withington, Manchester. S. of Francis Henry Bodoano, 9 Stanley Road, Whalley

Range, Manchester. Educ. at R.N.C. Osborne and Dartmouth. Rec. by Admiralty. Adm. 1922: began res. 10 Oct. 1922. Matric. 23 Oct. 1922.

> Resided M. 1922 and L. 1923.
> ✕ 1917–19. Mid., R.N.
> Lieut.-Cdr (1930–), R.N.
> He matric. as Geoffrey Lewis BODOANO.

RICHARD PASTON MACK, Sub-Lieut., R.N. Born 15 June 1901, at Lammas, Norfolk. S. of Rev. Edgar Shepheard Paston Mack, Donnigers, Swanmore, Hants. Educ. at R.N.C. Osborne and Dartmouth. Rec. by Admiralty. Adm. 1922: began res. 10 Oct. 1922. Matric. 23 Oct. 1922.

> Resided M. 1922 and L. 1923.
> ✕ 1917–19. Mid., R.N.
> Lieut.-Cdr (1930–), R.N. M.V.O. 1934.

WALTER GARDEN BLAIKIE MACKENZIE, Sub-Lieut., R.N. Born 7 April 1900, at Swatow, China. S. of Rev. Murdo Campbell Mackenzie, Swatow, China. Educ. at Fettes College, and R.N.C., Keyham. Rec. by Admiralty. Adm. 1922: began res. 10 Oct. 1922. Matric. 23 Oct. 1922.

> Resided M. 1922 and L. 1923.
> Blue: Rugby Football, 1922.
> ✕ 1918–19. Mid., R.N.
> Lieut.-Cdr (1930–), R.N.

GUY ROBERT PILCHER, Sub-Lieut., R.N. Born 19 June 1901, at Basing, nr Basingstoke. S. of Alexander Munsey Warton Pilcher, Hook, Basingstoke. Educ. at R.N.C. Osborne and Dartmouth. Rec. by Admiralty. Adm. 1922: began res. 10 Oct. 1922. Matric. 23 Oct. 1922.

> Resided M. 1922 and L. 1923.
> ✕ 1917–19. Mid., R.N.
> Lieut.-Cdr (1931–), R.N.

ERIC ALONZO STOCKER, Sub-Lieut., R.N. Born 17 April 1900, at St Austell, Cornwall. S. of Frederick Alonzo Stocker, Penleigh, St Austell. Educ. at Christ's Hospital, and R.N.C., Keyham. Rec. by Admiralty. Adm. 1922: began res. 10 Oct. 1922. Matric. 23 Oct. 1922.

> Resided M. 1922 and L. 1923.
> ✕ 1918–19. Mid., R.N.
> Lieut.-Cdr (1930–), R.N.

CLIVE GORDON TRENCHAM, Sub-Lieut., R.N. Born 10 April 1901, at Snodland, Kent. S. of Adolphus Octavius Trencham, 52 Elsworthy Road, Hampstead, N.W. 3. Educ. at R.N.C. Osborne and Dartmouth. Rec. by Admiralty. Adm. 1922: began res. 10 Oct. 1922. Matric. 23 Oct. 1922.

> Resided M. 1922 and L. 1923.
> ✕ 1917–19. Mid., R.N.
> Retired from the Navy with rank of Lieut. on 30 May 1931. Promoted Lieut.-Cdr (ret.) on 15 June 1931. Now (1935) an officer in the Colombian Navy.

GUY STANLEY WINDEYER, Sub-Lieut., R.N. Born 13 Dec. 1900, at Pymble, Willoughby at St Leonards, New South Wales, Australia. S. of Richard

Windeyer, K.C., Sydney, Australia. Educ. at R.N.C. Osborne and Dartmouth. Rec. by Admiralty. Adm. 1922: began res. 10 Oct. 1922. Matric. 23 Oct. 1922.

Resided M. 1922 and L. 1923.
✕ 1917–19. Mid., R.N.
Retired from the Navy with rank of Lieut.-Cdr on 19 May 1933.

EDWARD CAREY FRANCIS. Adm. **Fellow**, 30 Oct. 1922. Fellow, 1922–30 (becoming Internal Fellow under the new Statutes in 1926). *Rayleigh Prize*, 1923. M.A. 1925. Director of Studies in Mathematics, 1922–8. Lecturer in Mathematics, 1922–8. Librarian, 1924–5. Senior Bursar, 1924–8.
Governor of Huntingdon Grammar School, 1924–8.
University Lecturer in Mathematics, 1926–7.

Born 13 Sept. 1897, in London. S. of Edward James Pocock Francis, 182 Sutherland Avenue, Maida Hill, W. 9. Educ. at William Ellis School, Gospel Oak, London; and Trinity College (Math. Schol.; B.A. 1921).
✕ 1916–19. Lieut., R.F.A. (Spec. Res.); attd H.A.C. *M.*
Lay Missionary (C.M.S.), Kenya Colony, 1928–; with appt. from that date as Principal, Maseno School, P.O. Luanda.
Bro. of D. N. Francis (p. 99).

Rev. CHARLES SCOTT GILLETT. Adm. **Fellow**, 6 Dec. 1922. Matric. 7 Dec. 1922; and incorp. M.A. (from Queen's College, Oxford), 19 Jan. 1923. Fellow, 1922–32 (becoming Internal Fellow under the new Statutes in 1926). Dean and Chaplain, 1922–32. Director of Studies in Theology, 1922–32; and in Moral Sciences, 1925–8. Praelector, 1923–6. Junior Bursar, 1924–32. Catechist, 1925–32. Steward, 1926–32.
Pro-Proctor, 1925–6. Junior Proctor, 1926–7.

Born 12 Dec. 1880, at Woolsthorpe-by-Belvoir, Lincs. S. of Rev. Edward Alfred Gillett, St Edward's, Islip, Oxon. Educ. at St Edward's School, Oxford; and Queen's College, Oxford (Class. Schol.; B.A. 1904; M.A. 1921).
Asst Master, St Edward's School, Oxford, 1905–10. Ordained d. 1913 Southwark, p. 1914 Worcester. Asst C., Halesowen, 1913–14; Chaplain, Liddon House, South Audley Street, 1914–21, and Asst C., Grosvenor Chapel, South Audley Street, 1915–21; Vice-Principal, Westcott House, Cambridge, 1921–2.
Apptd Principal, Chichester Theol. Coll., 1933. Select Preacher, Cambridge, 1923, 1932, 1936; and at Oxford, 1927–8. Examining Chaplain to Bp of Southwell, 1924–7; to Bp of Derby, 1927–35; and to Bp of Brechin, 1935–. Fellow of Woodard Corporation, 1924–. Governor of St Edward's School, Oxford, 1926–; and of Chichester High School for Girls, 1938–.

IAN ARNOT GIBSON. Born 8 Nov. 1904, at Glasgow. S. of John Craigie Gibson, Box 325, Cape Town, S. Africa. Educ. at Sherborne School. Adm. 9 Nov. 1922: began res. 15 Jan. 1923. Matric. 29 Jan. 1923.

B.A. (Ord. degree) 1925.
Adm. into the Soc. of Accountants, Edinburgh, 1929. With J. & A. Churchill (medical publishers), 40 Gloucester Place, Portman Square, London, W. 1, 1933–.

MUSHTAQ AHMED KHAN. Born 8 April 1904, at Jullundur, Punjab, India. S. of Fakhruddin Ahmed Khan, Hyderabad, Deccan. Educ. at Mohammedan Anglo-Oriental School, Aligarh; and Muslim Univ., Aligarh. Rec. by E. A. Seaton, M.A., Oxford. Adm. 1922: began res. 20 April 1923. Matric. 4 May 1923.

B.A. (3rd Cl. Econ. Tri. Pt I, 1925; 3rd Cl. Pt II, 1926) 1926. M.A. 1932.
With H.E.H. The Nizam's State Railway, Secunderabad, 1928–; apptd Asst Commercial Manager, 1931. G.Inst.T. 1933.

DONALD BROACKES. Born 2 April 1904, at Abercarn, Monmouthshire. S. of Major James George Broackes, The Cottage, Abercarn. Educ. at Repton School. Adm. 1922: began res. 20 April 1923. Matric. 4 May 1923.

> B.A. (Ord. degree) 1926. M.A. 1930.
> Solicitor (adm. Feb. 1931); practising at Bingley, Yorks (Weatherhead & Butcher).

WILLIAM HERBERT GROOM. Born 27 Aug. 1902, at Calcutta. S. of John Bax Groom, The Mount, Woodbridge, Suffolk. Educ. at Woodbridge School, and R.M.C., Sandhurst. Adm. 1923: began res. 20 April 1923. Matric. 4 May 1923.

> B.A. (Ord. degree) 1926. M.A. 1930.
> Winner, with S. M. White (1st Trinity B.C.), of the Lowe Double Sculls, 1925.
> Rubber Planter, New Rompin Rubber Estate, Rompin, Negri Sembilan, F.M.S., 1927-38. Ridley Hall, Cambridge, 1939.
> Bro. of J. L. Groom (p. 30).

JAMES GEOFFERY SEDDON BROWN. Born 15 Feb. 1905, at Wigan, Lancs. S. of Lieut.-Col. (*and later* Sir) Norman Seddon Brown, Parkfield, 28 Trafalgar Road, Birkdale, Lancs. Educ. at Haileybury College. Adm. 1922: began res. 20 April 1923. Matric. 4 May 1923.

> Went down after M. 1924.
> Half-Blue: Boxing, 1924.
> Continental Manager with Horrockses, Crewdson & Co., Ltd (cotton spinners and manufacturers), Manchester.

WALTER ALEXANDER RIMINGTON. Born 31 Oct. 1903, at Khandala, India. S. of Frank Cartwright Rimington, Villa Herakleid, Monaco. Educ. at Uppingham School. Adm. 1922: began res. 16 Jan. 1923. Matric. 29 Jan. 1923.

> B.A. (Ord. degree) 1926.
> Asst Master in preparatory schools successively at Hindhead and Broadstairs, 1926-31. Partner at Shrewsbury House (also preparatory), Ditton Hill, Surbiton, Surrey, 1931-.

FRANK LOVELL SMITH. Born 15 Sept. 1904, at Cambridge. S. of Thomas Smith, 9 Chedworth Street, Cambridge. Educ. at Perse School, Cambridge. Adm. 13 Dec. 1921: began res. 12 Oct. 1923. Matric. 22 Oct. 1923. Entrance Schol. (1922), History, £60.

> B.A. (2nd Cl., 1st Div., Hist. Tri. Pt I, 1925; 2nd Cl., 1st Div., Pt II, 1926) 1926. Schol.* of £50, 1925. Probationer, I.C.S., M. 1926 and L. 1927.
> I.C.S., 1927-; with appt. as officiating additional District and Sessions Judge, United Provinces, 1935-.

LEONARD OSWALD REGAN. Born 24 Jan. 1904, at Wimbledon. S. of William James Regan, 95 Woodside, Wimbledon, S.W. 19. Educ. at St Paul's School. Adm. 16 Dec. 1922: began res. 12 Oct. 1923. Matric. 22 Oct. 1923. Entrance Schol., Classics, £80.

> B.A. (2nd Cl. Class. Tri. Pt I, 1925; 2nd Cl. Pt II, 1926) 1926. Schol.* of £50, 1925.
> With the Architectural Press Ltd, 9 Queen Anne's Gate, London, S.W. 1.
> Bro. of E. C. Regan (p. 24).

CHARLES JOHN RAPHAEL BARNEWALL STEWART. Born 17 July 1904, in London. S. of Dr Kenneth Trevor Stewart, 52 Wimpole Street, W. 1. Educ. at Ampleforth College. Adm. 16 Dec. 1922: began res. 12 Oct. 1923. Matric. 22 Oct. 1923. Entrance Schol., Maths, £60.

> B.A. (2nd Cl. Math. Tri. Pt I, 1924; 3rd Cl. Mech. Sci. Tri., 1926) 1926. Schol.* for Mech. Sciences, £40, 1925.
> Civil Engineer.

HUBERT DENYS EDDOWES ROKEBY. Born 19 Dec. 1903, at Bombay. S. of Samuel Rokeby (dec^d) and Mrs Rokeby, Fulshaw Lodge, Cheltenham. Educ. at Winchester College. Adm. 16 Dec. 1922: began res. 12 Oct. 1923. Matric. 22 Oct. 1923. Entrance Schol., Maths, £40.

B.A. (3rd Cl. Math. Tri. Pt I, 1924; 3rd Cl. Econ. Tri. Pt II, 1926) 1926. M.A. 1931.
St Stephen's House, Oxford, 1926. Ordained d. 1928, p. 1929 Peterborough. C. of St Mary Virg., Kettering, 1928–32; Clewer St Stephen, 1932–3; All Saints, Twickenham, Dio. London, 1933–.

BASIL CHRISTIAN ALTHAM HARTLEY. Born 30 May 1904, at Cleeve Vicarage, nr Bristol. S. of Rev. Christian Hartley, Cleeve Vicarage. Educ. at Rossall School. Adm. 16 Dec. 1922: began res. 12 Oct. 1923. Matric. 22 Oct. 1923. Entrance Schol., Classics, £40.

B.A. (3rd Cl. Class. Tri. Pt I, 1925; 1st Cl. Pt II, 1926) 1926. M.A. 1930. Exhib. of £30, 1925. Schol.* of £60, 1926.
Schoolmaster; with appt. as Asst Master, St John's School, Leatherhead, 1932, and subsequently at Shirley House (a preparatory school), Watford.

JOHN PERCIVAL BIDDULPH. Born 15 Feb. 1904, at Sproughton, nr Ipswich. S. of Brig.-Gen. George Warren Biddulph, The Cottage, Brandon, Suffolk. Educ. at Oundle School. Adm. 16 Dec. 1922: began res. 12 Oct. 1923. Matric. 22 Oct. 1923. Entrance Schol., History, £40.

B.A. (2nd Cl., 1st Div., Hist. Tri. Pt I, 1925; 2nd Cl., 1st Div., Pt II, 1926) 1926. Re-elected to Schol.*, 1925.
Malayan Civil Service, 1926–; in the Chinese Protectorate Dept.

PERCY BROOKSBANK WALKER. Born 25 Aug. 1903, at Soothill, Batley, Yorks. S. of John William Walker, Chidswell Farm, Dewsbury, Yorks. Educ. at Wheelwright Grammar School, Dewsbury. Adm. 16'Dec. 1922: began res. 12 Oct. 1923. Matric. 22 Oct. 1923. Entrance Exhib., Maths, £30.

B.A. (2nd Cl. Math. Tri. Pt I, 1924; 2nd Cl. Mech. Sci. Tri., 1926) 1926. M.A., Ph.D. 1931. Exhib. for Mech. Sciences, £30, 1925. Adm. Research Stud. as from Oct. 1926. *Busk Studentship in Aero-nautics*, 1926; *re-elected*, 1927. J. M. Dodds Stud. (for research in Aeronautics), £50, 1927; re-elected, 1928. Armourers' and Brasiers' Company's Research Fellowship in Aeronautics, 1928 (held for 2 years). On the design staff of Sir W. G. Armstrong Whitworth Aircraft Ltd, Coventry, 1930–. A.F.R.Ae.S. 1932.
Author:
    Growth of circulation about a wing, and an apparatus for measuring fluid motion. (*Air Ministry. Aeronautical Research Committee: Reports and Memoranda, no.* 1402.) London, 1932.

KENNETH FRANCIS FOWLER RANKEN. Born 26 May 1904, at South Walsham, Norwich. S. of Rev. Francis Smith Ranken, South Walsham Rectory. Educ. at Marlborough College. Adm. 16 Dec. 1922: began res. 12 Oct. 1923. Matric. 22 Oct. 1923. Entrance Exhib., Classics, £30.

B.A. (3rd Cl. Class. Tri. Pt I, 1925; 3rd Cl. Geog. Tri. Pt I, 1926) 1926.

WILLIAM SIDNEY WINSCOM. Born 2 May 1903, at Keighley, Yorks. S. of Charles Arthur Winscom, Lynwood, Thwaites Brow, Keighley. Educ. at Keighley Trade and Grammar School. Adm. 16 Dec. 1922: began res. 12 Oct. 1923. Matric. 22 Oct. 1923. Entrance Exhib., Nat. Sciences, £30.

B.A. (2nd Cl. Nat. Sci. Tri. Pt I, 1926) 1926. M.A. 1933. Re-elected to Exhib., 1925; and again, 1926.
With Lever Brothers, Ltd (soap manufacturers), Port Sunlight, Cheshire, 1928–30. Sectional Chemist, British Industrial Solvents Ltd, Hull, 1930–.

RALPH ANDERSON JACKSON. Born 1 April 1904, at Lincoln. S. of William Henry Jackson, 44 Oakfield Grove, Manningham, Bradford. Educ. at Bradford Grammar School. Adm. 16 Dec. 1922: began res. 12 Oct. 1923. Matric. 22 Oct. 1923. Entrance Exhib., Nat. Sciences, £30.

B.A. (2nd Cl. Nat. Sci. Tri. Pt I, 1925; 2nd Cl. Pt II (Chemistry), 1926) 1926. M.A. 1930. Schol.* of £40, 1924.
Works Manager with Hudson, Scott & Sons, Ltd (colour printers and metal box makers), Carlisle.

HUBERT GREENWOOD. Born 17 June 1904, at Keighley, Yorks. S. of Arthur Greenwood, 12 Nares Street, Keighley. Educ. at Keighley Trade and Grammar School. Adm. 16 Dec. 1922: began res. 12 Oct. 1923. Matric. 22 Oct. 1923. Entrance Exhib., History, £30.

B.A. (1st Cl., 2nd Div., Hist. Tri. Pt I, 1925; 2nd Cl., 1st Div., Pt II, 1926) 1926. M.A. 1930. Schol.* of £50, 1925.
Asst Master, Sir Joseph Williamson's Mathematical School, Rochester, 1927–9; and at Tollington School, Muswell Hill, London, N. 10, 1929–.

CHARLTON NICHOLLS. Born 8 Aug. 1904, at Meerbrook Vicarage, nr Leek, Staffs. S. of Rev. Walter Charlton Nicholls, St George's Vicarage, Wellington, Salop. Educ. at Denstone College. Adm. 16 Dec. 1922: began res. 12 Oct. 1923. Matric. 22 Oct. 1923. Entrance Exhib., History, £30.

B.A. (2nd Cl., 1st Div., Hist. Tri. Pt I, 1925; 2nd Cl., 1st Div., Pt II, 1926) 1926. Exhib. of £40, 1925.
Sudan Political Service, 1926–.

CHARLES MURRAY ACWORTH GAYER. Born 27 July 1904, at Chart Sutton, Kent. S. of Rev. Arthur Cecil Stopford Gayer (decd) and Mrs Gayer, 2 Park Road, Redhill, Surrey. Educ. at Marlborough College. Adm. 16 Dec. 1922: began res. 12 Oct. 1923. Matric. 22 Oct. 1923. Entrance Exhib., History, £30.

B.A. (2nd Cl., 2nd Div., Hist. Tri. Pt I, 1925; 2nd Cl., 1st Div., Pt II, 1926) 1926. M.A. 1932. Re-elected to Exhib., 1925.
Colonial Service, Uganda, 1926–; now (1931) with appt. as District Officer.

CUTHBERT COLLIN DAVIES. Born 16 April 1896, at Narbeth, Pembroke-shire. S. of David Collins Davies, Mathias and Co., Narbeth. Educ. at University College of Wales, Aberystwyth (B.A. degree, Wales). Adm. 2 Jan. 1923: began res. 12 Oct. 1923. Matric. (as Research Stud.) 22 Oct. 1923.

Ph.D. 1926.
⚔ 1915–22. Lieut., W. Yorks Regt; Capt., 1st K.G.O. Gurkha Rifles, I.A. (W 2.) (Service included Afghanistan, N.W. Frontier, 1919 (Third Afghan War); and Waziristan, 1921–2.)
History Master, Regent Street Polytechnic, London, 1927–9. Lecturer in Indian History, School of Oriental Studies, London Univ., 1929–36 (and Supervisor of I.C.S. Probationers there, 1932–6). University Reader in Indian History, Oxford, 1936–. M.A. (by Decree), Oxford, 6 Oct. 1936; and matric. from Balliol College, 20 Oct. 1936. F.R.Hist.Soc. 1933.
Author:
  The problem of the North-West Frontier, 1890–1908, with a survey of policy since 1849. Cambridge, 1932.

CHARLES MAURICE HUDSON. Born 8 Nov. 1904, at Littleborough, Lancs. S. of James Arthur Hudson, Hillside, Littleborough. Educ. at Radley College. Adm. 19 Jan. 1923: began res. 12 Oct. 1923. Matric. 22 Oct. 1923.

B.A. (2nd Cl., 2nd Div., Law Tri. Pt I, 1925; 3rd Cl. Pt II, 1926) 1926. M.A. 1930.
Solicitor (adm. Jan. 1930); being partner in Brierley & Hudson, at Rochdale and Littleborough, Lancs.

CHARLES RICHARD HALL. Born 16 Sept. 1903, at York. S. of Charles
Rhodes Hall (dec^d) and Mrs Hall, Clarence Croft, New Earswick, York. Educ. at
Loretto School. Adm. 13 March 1923: began res. 12 Oct. 1923. Matric. 22 Oct.
1923. Organ Scholar.

Went down after E. 1924.
Organist and Choirmaster, Hook Memorial Church, Leeds, 1924–6. Wycliffe Hall, Oxford, 1926.
Ordained d. 1926, p. 1928 Ripon. C. of Leeds, 1926–33; V. of Bardsey, Dio. Ripon, 1933–6.

JACK MYDDLETON HORNSBY. Born 10 May 1905, in London. S. of
Frederick Myddleton Hornsby, 3 Whitehall Court, S.W. 1. Educ. at Westminster
School. Adm. 4 April 1923: began res. 12 Oct. 1923. Matric. 22 Oct. 1923.

Went down after E. 1926.
Asst Surveyor with Knight, Frank & Rutley (estate agents), 20 Hanover Square, London, W. 1,
1927–31. Now (1933) Sec. to Whitehall Court Ltd, Whitehall, S.W. 1.

ARTHUR THOMAS CARROLL. Born 1 March 1905, at Vancouver. S. of
John T. Carroll (dec^d) and Mrs Carroll, 37 Queen's Gate Gardens, S.W. 7. Educ.
at Loretto School. Adm. 14 April 1923: began res. 12 Oct. 1923. Matric. 22 Oct.
1923.

B.A. (Ord. degree) 1926.
Adm. a Solicitor and called to the Bar, Vancouver, British Columbia, Oct. 1929; and in practice
there with the firm of Walsh, Bull, Housser, Tupper & Ray (Barristers and Solicitors).

JOSEPH HELLMANN KIRKLAND. Born 3 Oct. 1904, at Johannesburg,
Transvaal. S. of John Wilkinson Kirkland, Crown House, Aldwych, W.C. 2.
Educ. at Houghton Preparatory College, Johannesburg. Rec. by G. M. Clark
(Peterhouse, B.A. 1890; Sidney Sussex College, M.A. 1899), Johannesburg. Adm.
26 April 1923: began res. 12 Oct. 1923. Matric. 22 Oct. 1923.

B.A. (Ord. degree) 1927.
Managing Director of J. W. Kirkland & Son (Pty), Ltd (engineers and importers), Johannesburg.

WILLIAM CHAMBERS PARKE. Born 28 June 1901, at Decatur, Illinois.
S. of Guy James Parke, 621 North Main Street, Decatur. Educ. at Hotchkiss
School, Lakeville, Conn.; and Yale Univ. (Yale College, B.A. degree). Adm.
26 April 1923: began res. 24 Oct. 1923. Matric. 30 Nov. 1923. Research Stud.

Went down after E. 1924.
Banker. With Schlubach, Thiemer & Co., Hamburg, 1925; with J. Henry Schröder & Co., London,
1926; with the Bankers Trust Co., New York, 1927–30; and with the Continental Illinois National
Bank and Trust Co., Chicago, 1931–.

ROBERT TUNSTILL. Born 6 June 1903, at Reedley Hallows, Lancs. S. of
Robert Tunstill (dec^d) and Mrs Tunstill, Broughton Bank, Grange-over-Sands,
Lancs. Educ. at Bilton Grange, nr Rugby; and privately. Adm. 6 June 1923:
began res. 12 Oct. 1923. Matric. 22 Oct. 1923.

B.A. (2nd Cl., 2nd Div., Hist. Tri. Pt I, 1925; 2nd Cl., 2nd Div., Engl. Tri. (a), 1927) 1927.
Joined the staff of *The London Mercury* in 1928.

EMERSON BLAUVELT QUAILE. Born 11 March 1900, in Staten Island,
N.Y. S. of Rev. G. E. Quaile, Salisbury School, Salisbury, Conn. Educ. at Yale
Univ. (Yale College, B.A. degree). Adm. 11 June 1923: began res. 12 Oct. 1923.
Matric. 22 Oct. 1923.

Went down after E. 1924.
✕ 1918. United States Army.
Was a master at Hotchkiss School, Lakeville, Conn., in 1931.

IAN ALEXANDER MATASON MUIR. Born 8 March 1905, at Troon, Ayrshire. S. of Alexander Muir, St Monenna, Troon. Educ. at Uppingham School. Adm. 2 July 1923: began res. 12 Oct. 1923. Matric. 22 Oct. 1923.

B.A. (Ord. degree) 1927.
Engineering Asst, Metropolitan Water Board, 1926–9. Works Agent and Asst Outside Manager, Matthew Muir & Co., Ltd (engineering and public works contractors), Kilmarnock, 1929–32. Works Engineer, D. G. Somerville & Co., Ltd (engineering contractors), 35 Grosvenor Place, London, S.W. 1, 1932–.
Cousin of J. M. Muir (p. 128).

LESLIE WALSTON BLOUNT. Born 10 Oct. 1898, at Derby. S. of Albert Edwin Blount, 31 Walbrook Road, Derby. Educ. at Ordination Test School, Knutsford. Adm. 17 July 1923: began res. 12 Oct. 1923. Matric. 22 Oct. 1923.

B.A. (Ord. degree) 1926. M.A. 1930.
✂ 1918–19. Signaller, R.G.A.
Lincoln Theol. Coll., 1926. Ordained d. 1927, p. 1928 Norwich. C. of St James, Great Yarmouth, 1927–32; Royston, Yorks, 1932–4; C. in charge of St Peter, Galley Common, Dio. Coventry, 1934–.

LESLIE GRUNDELL FORREST. Born 19 July 1905, at Bridlington, Yorks. S. of Alfred Forrest (dec^d). Guardian: David Flather, Banner Cross Hall, Sheffield. Educ. at Repton School. Adm. 17 July 1923: began res. 12 Oct. 1923. Matric. 22 Oct. 1923.

B.A. (Ord. degree) 1926. M.A. 1935.
Westcott House, Cambridge, 1926. Ordained d. 1928, p. 1929 Sheffield. C. of St Mary, Sheffield, 1928–30; St Luke, Battersea, 1930–4; Soham, 1934–5; Chaplain, Missions to Seamen, Hamburg, 1935–.

NARAYANASAMI CUMARASAMI. Born 14 Feb. 1903, at Kuala Lumpur, Malay States. S. of Cumarasami, 2 Maxwell Road, Kuala Lumpur. Educ. at Victoria Institution, Kuala Lumpur. Adm. 17 July 1923: began res. 12 Oct. 1923. Matric. 22 Oct. 1923.

B.A. (3rd Cl. Law Tri. Pt I, 1925; 3rd Cl. Pt II, 1926) 1926.
Called to the Bar, Lincoln's Inn, 2 May 1928.

JOHN REGINALD COLLETT STOCK. Born 5 June 1900, at Worsborough, nr Barnsley, Yorks. S. of Rev. Frederick Cecil Stock, Worsborough Vicarage. Educ. at St Edward's School, Oxford; and privately. Adm. 17 July 1923: began res. 12 Oct. 1923. Matric. 22 Oct. 1923.

B.A. (Ord. degree) 1926. M.A. 1930.
Surveyor, first with Keffi Consolidated Tin Mines Co., Ltd, Jos, Northern Nigeria, then with Associated Tin Mines of Nigeria, Ltd, 1926–32. Asst Manager, Sokoto (Nigeria) Gold Mines, Ltd, 1933–.

REGINALD PITT STEWART TAYLOR. Born 30 July 1904, in London. S. of Colonel Francis Pitt Stewart Taylor, C.M.G., Old Court, Bray, Co. Wicklow. Educ. at Marlborough College. Adm. 17 July 1923: began res. 12 Oct. 1923. Matric. 22 Oct. 1923.

Went down during L. 1924.

WILFRID ERNEST THOROWGOOD. Born 15 Oct. 1904, in London. S. of Alfred Ernest Thorowgood, Thorlands, Farnham Lane, Haslemere, Surrey. Educ. at Wrekin College, Wellington, Salop; and privately. Adm. 17 July 1923: began res. 12 Oct. 1923. Matric. 22 Oct. 1923.

B.A. (Ord. degree) 1926. M.A. 1930.
Civil Engineer. Assoc.M.Inst.C.E. 1930.

ASHLEY IRWIN ROACH. Born 28 May 1905, at Sandown, Isle of Wight. S. of Surgeon Cdr Sidney Roach, R.N., Priory Cottage, Brading, I.O.W. Educ. at Marlborough College. Adm. 25 July 1923: began res. 12 Oct. 1923. Matric. 22 Oct. 1923.

B.A. (Ord. degree) 1926. M.A. 1930. Probationer, Colonial Service, M. 1929 to E. 1930.
Was in the Colonial Service, Kenya Colony, 1930–4, with final appt. as District Officer. Died 29 Oct. 1934 at Lodwar, Turkana Province, Kenya, from cerebral malaria.

ENRIQUE PIDAL. Born 3 May 1904, at Mieres, Spain. S. of Marqués de Villaviciosa de Asturias, Calle de Castellana 8, Madrid. Educ. privately. Rec. by Luis Lirio y Santos de Lamadrid, Madrid. Adm. 9 Aug. 1923: began res. 12 Oct. 1923. Matric. 22 Oct. 1923.

B.A. (Ord. degree) 1926.
In 1937 was fighting for the Insurgent forces in the Spanish Civil War.

HENRY ELLIS WARD. Born 3 Dec. 1900, at Swindon, Wilts. S. of Frederick Joseph Ward, 4 Southbrook Street, Swindon. Educ. at Ordination Test School, Knutsford. Adm. 7 Sept. 1923: began res. 12 Oct. 1923. Matric. 22 Oct. 1923.

B.A. (2nd Cl., 2nd Div., Hist. Tri. Pt I, 1925; 3rd Cl. Pt II, 1926) 1926. M.A. 1931.
Matric. from Wadham College, Oxford, 19 Oct. 1926; B.A., Oxford, 1928. Ripon Hall, Oxford, 1926. Ordained d. 1928, p. 1929 Southwark. C. of St Paul, Kingston Hill, 1928–30; C. in charge of Ramsbury w. Axford, 1930–1; C. of Hawkhurst (in charge of All Saints), Dio. Canterbury, 1931–.

WILLIAM HOMER WHITE. Born 21 Oct. 1900, at Salem, Illinois. S. of Rev. William Dean White, Atlanta, Texas. Educ. at Yale Univ. (Yale College, B.A. degree). Adm. 21 Sept. 1923: began res. 12 Oct. 1923. Matric. 22 Oct. 1923.

Went down after E. 1924.
Since going down was at one time writing plays in Spain.

HERBERT WILLIAM BARRITT. Born 12 Feb. 1904, at Crosshills, nr Keighley, Yorks. S. of William Barritt, St Andrew's Terrace, Crosshills. Educ. at Keighley Trade and Grammar School. Adm. 29 Sept. 1923: began res. 12 Oct. 1923. Matric. 22 Oct. 1923.

B.A. (2nd Cl. Nat. Sci. Tri. Pt I, 1926) 1926. 2nd Cl. Nat. Sci. Tri. Pt II (Chemistry), 1927. M.A. 1930.
Asst Master, Wellingborough School, 1927–.

DANIEL AUGUSTINE METCALF. Born 22 April 1904, in London. S. of Thomas John Metcalf, Moorings, Overcliffe, Gravesend, Kent. Educ. at Stony-hurst College. Adm. 2 Oct. 1923: began res. 12 Oct. 1923. Matric. 22 Oct. 1923.

B.A. (Ord. degree) 1926. M.A., M.B., B.Chir. 1936.
M.R.C.S., L.R.C.P. 1929. In practice at Westcliff-on-Sea.
Bro. of J. Metcalf (p. 108).

HARRY LISMER SHORT. Born 12 July 1906, at Crewe. S. of Rev. Henry Fisher Short, 41 Oxford Road, Bootle, Liverpool. Educ. at Bootle Secondary School. Adm. 2 Oct. 1923: began res. 12 Oct. 1923. Matric. 22 Oct. 1923.

B.A. (2nd Cl., 1st Div., Hist. Tri. Pt I, 1925; 1st Cl., 2nd Div., Pt II, 1926) 1926. M.A. 1930. Schol.* for History, £40, 1924.
Manchester College, Oxford, 1926–9 (Arlosh Schol.). Dr Daniel Williams Divinity Schol., 1927–9. Hibbert Schol., Harvard Univ., 1929–30. Unitarian Minister: at Rochdale, 1930–5; and at Brixton, London, 1935–.

HERBERT NICHOLS PEARSON. Born 12 Aug. 1899, at Manchester. S. of Edmund Curtis Pearson, Pendleton, Kilner Park, Ulverston. Educ. at Victoria Grammar School, Ulverston. Adm. 6 Oct. 1923: began res. 12 Oct. 1923. Matric. 22 Oct. 1923.

Went down after L. 1924.

WILLIAM LANCELOT DAWES. Born 16 March 1904, at Kemsdale House, nr Faversham, Kent. S. of William Charles Dawes (dec^d) and Mrs Dawes, Mount Ephraim, Faversham. Educ. privately. Adm. 6 Oct. 1923: began res. 12 Oct. 1923. Matric. 22 Oct. 1923.

Went down after L. 1924.

RUSSELL WILLIAM ABEL. Born 8 July 1905, at Kwato, Papua. S. of Rev. Charles William Abel, 87 Worple Road, Wimbledon, S.W. 19. Educ. privately. Rec. by W. N. Marcy, 22 Chancery Lane, W.C. 2. Adm. 8 Oct. 1923: began res. 12 Oct. 1923. Matric. 22 Oct. 1923.

B.A. (3rd Cl. Engl. Tri. (a), 1925; 3rd Cl. Anthropol. Tri., 1926) 1926. M.A. 1931.
Lay Missionary, Kwato Mission of Papua, 1926–.
Author:
    Charles W. Abel of Kwato: forty years in dark Papua... New York (1934).

RUPERT AMBROSE PERCY FISON. Born 25 Sept. 1905, at Beeston Regis, Norfolk. S. of William Martius Wiles Fison, Sudbury, Suffolk. Educ. at Sudbury Grammar School. Adm. 8 Oct. 1923: began res. 12 Oct. 1923. Matric. 22 Oct. 1923.

B.A. (Ord. degree) 1927. M.A. 1930.
Solicitor (adm. Dec. 1930); practising at Felixstowe and Ipswich (Fison & Co.).
Bro. of M. R. W. Fison (p. 55).

JUAN MODESTO DE VENGOECHEA. Born 18 June 1904, at Bogotá, Colombia. S. of Carlos Arturo de Vengoechea, O.B.E., Apartado 118, Bogotá. Educ. at Herne Bay College, Kent. Adm. 9 Oct. 1923: began res. 12 Oct. 1923. Matric. 22 Oct. 1923.

B.A. (Ord. degree) 1927.
Owner and manager of a coffee plantation in Colombia.

JUSTINIAN HEDLEY BARTLETT. Born 29 Aug. 1904, at Saffron Walden, Essex. S. of Hedley Coward Bartlett, Saffron Walden. Educ. at Epsom College. Adm. 10 Oct. 1923: began res. 12 Oct. 1923. Matric. 22 Oct. 1923.

B.A. (Ord. degree) 1926.
M.R.C.S., L.R.C.P. 1930. In practice at Saffron Walden.

KHWAJA SARWAR HASAN. Born 18 Oct. 1902, at Panipat, Punjab, India. S. of Khwaja Anwar Hasan, Sarfabad, Hyderabad, Deccan. Educ. at Nizam's College, Hyderabad; and Muslim Univ., Aligarh (B.A. degree, Allahabad Univ.). Adm. 11 Oct. 1923: began res. 12 Oct. 1923. Matric. 22 Oct. 1923. Aff. Stud.

B.A., LL.B. (3rd Cl. Law Tri. Pt I, 1924; aegr. Pt II, 1925) 1925. M.A. 1932.
Called to the Bar, Middle Temple, 26 Jan. 1927. Lecturer in Law, Delhi Univ., 1930–.

WILLIAM ARTHUR BROWN. Born 13 Aug. 1903, at Dolphinholme, nr Lancaster. S. of Arthur Knighton Brown, Dolphinholme. Educ. at Royal Grammar

School, Lancaster. Adm. 11 Oct. 1923: began res. 12 Oct. 1923. Matric. 22 Oct. 1923.

B.A. (Ord. degree) 1926.
B. ès L., Paris. Was a Schoolmaster in 1929.

REGINALD HALL BENNETT. Born 8 Jan. 1889, at Lewisham. S. of Robert Charles Bennett, Branscombe House, Ravensbourne Park, Catford, S.E. 6. Educ. at St Dunstan's College, Catford. Rec. by Colonel I. Curtis, M.A. (Peterhouse), Air Ministry. Adm. 12 Oct. 1923: began res. 12 Oct. 1923. Matric. 22 Oct. 1923.

B.A. (Ord. degree) 1926. M.A. 1930.
Half-Blue: Lacrosse, 1924, 1925, 1926.
Indian Police, 1908–22, with final appt. as District Superintendent (Local Major). Education Officer, R.A.F., 1923–.

CLARENCE EDWARD WILLIAMS LOCKYER, Flt Lieut., R.A.F. Born 22 Aug. 1892, at Poona, India. S. of James Edward Lockyer (dec^d). Educ. at Horsham Grammar School, and University College, London (B.Sc. degree). Rec. by Air Ministry. Adm. 6 July 1923; began res. 12 Oct. 1923. Matric. 22 Oct. 1923.

B.A. (2nd Cl. Mech. Sci. Tri., 1925; all. 3 terms as Commiss. Off.) 1925. M.A. 1936. J. M. Dodds Stud. (for research in Aeronautics), £50, 1925. *John Bernard Seely Prize*, 1925.
✕ 1914–19. Lieut., R.F.A.; Capt., R.A.F. M 2. *Order of the Nile, 4th Class (Egypt)*.
Wing Cdr (1936–), R.A.F. Chief Instructor, Cambridge Univ. Air Squadron, 1936–.
Author:
   (With B. M. Jones and W. S. Farren) *Preliminary experiments on two-dimensional flow round bodies moving through a stationary fluid*. (*Air Ministry. Aeronautical Research Committee: Reports and Memoranda, no. 1065.*) London, 1927.
   (With H. M. Garner) *The aerodynamics of a simple servo-rubber system*. (*Air Ministry. Aeronautical Research Committee: Reports and Memoranda, no. 1105.*) London, 1928.

RICHARD LUKE HANSARD, Lieut., R.C. of S. Born 2 Aug. 1898, at Timsbury Manor, Hants. S. of Henry Luke Tite Hansard (dec^d) and Mrs Hansard, Preston Cross, Bookham, Surrey. Educ. at Cheltenham College, and R.M.A., Woolwich. Rec. by War Office. Adm. 9 July 1923: began res. 12 Oct. 1923. Matric. 22 Oct. 1923.

B.A. (Ord. degree; all. 3 terms as Commiss. Off.) 1925. M.A. 1931.
✕ 1916–19. Lieut., R.F.A. (W.)
Retired from the Army with rank of Lieut. on 17 Sept. 1927. Took up farming at N'joro, Kenya Colony, in 1927. Died 12 May 1938 in London, following an operation.

COLQUHOUN LLOYD FOX, Lieut., R.E. Born 15 July 1898, at Edinburgh. S. of Herbert Lloyd Fox (dec^d). Educ. at Christ's Hospital, and R.M.A., Woolwich. Rec. by War Office. Adm. 23 July 1923: began res. 12 Oct. 1923. Matric. 22 Oct. 1923.

Resided till end of E. 1924.
✕ 1918–19. 2nd Lieut., R.E.
Major (1938–), R.E.

REGINALD STILLINGFLEET, Lieut., R.E. Born 5 April 1897, at Beckwithshaw, Harrogate. S. of James Thomas Stillingfleet [dec^d?] and Mrs Stillingfleet, Beckwithshaw. Educ. at R.M.A., Woolwich. Rec. by War Office. Adm. 23 July 1923: began res. 12 Oct. 1923. Matric. 22 Oct. 1923.

B.A. (2nd Cl. Mech. Sci. Tri., 1925; all. 3 terms as Commiss. Off.) 1925. Exhib. for Mech. Sciences, £40, 1924.
✕ 1917–19. Lieut., R.E. *And* Iraq Operations 1919–20; Waziristan 1919–21; and Waziristan 1921–4.
Major (1937–), R.E. A.M.I.E.E. 1928.

RALPH PUNG WHEELER, Lieut., R.E. Born 21 Nov. 1898, in London. S. of Charles William Wheeler, Morven, Lyttleton Road, Stechford, nr Birmingham. Educ. at Owen's School, Islington; privately; and at R.M.A., Woolwich. Rec. by War Office. Adm. 23 July 1923: began res. 12 Oct. 1923. Matric. 22 Oct. 1923.

Resided till end of E. 1924.
⚔ 1917–19. Lieut., R.E.
Major (1937–), R.E.

HAROLD ALFRED HAINES, Flg. Off., R.A.F. Born 22 Nov. 1899, at Ilford, Essex. S. of Alfred Thomas Haines, The Old Vicarage, Bradford Road, Seven Kings, Essex. Educ. at City of London School. Rec. by Air Ministry. Adm. 11 Sept. 1923: began res. 12 Oct. 1923. Matric. 22 Oct. 1923.

B.A. (Ord. degree; all. 3 terms as Commiss. Off.) 1925.
⚔ 1917–19. Probationary Flt Off., R.N.A.S.; Lieut., R.A.F. *D.F.C.*
Wing Cdr (1939–), R.A.F.

BERTRAND LESLIE HALLWARD. Adm. **Fellow**, 29 Oct. 1923. Fellow, 1923–39 (becoming Internal Fellow under the new Statutes in 1926; re-elected, 1929; and again, 1934). M.A. 1926. Lecturer in Classics, 1923–39. Director of Studies in Classics, 1924–31. Steward, 1924–6. Praelector, 1926–33 and 1935–9. Tutor, 1934–9.

Governor of Hertford Grammar School, 1926–39; of Huntingdon Grammar School, 1928–39; and of Letchworth Grammar School, 1930–9.

University Lecturer in Classics, 1926–39. Deputy Orator, 1930–1. Pro-Proctor, 1933–4. Senior Proctor, 1934–5. Additional Pro-Proctor, 1935–6.

Born 24 May 1901, at Hove, Sussex. S. of Norman Leslie Hallward, Westcote, Dunsfold, Godalming, Surrey. Educ. at Haileybury College, and King's College (Class. Schol.; B.A. 1922). *Studentship of British School at Athens*, 1922.
Asst Master, Harrow School, 1923. Apptd Head Master, Clifton College, 1939.
Contributor to:
    The Cambridge Ancient History, vol. 8. Cambridge, 1930.

ERIC MALLIE LING-MALLISON. Born 22 Aug. 1905, in London. S. of George Mallison, 57 Promenade des Anglais, Nice, France. Educ. at Clifton College; and Collège de Normandie. Adm. 17 Oct. 1923: began res. 14 Jan. 1924. Matric. 28 Jan. 1924.

Went down during L. 1924.
B.Sc., Lille. Called to the Bar, Middle Temple, 17 Nov. 1927. On Midland circuit.
Author:
    Law relating to women. London, 1930.
    The law relating to advertising. London, 1931.
He matric. as Eric Mallie Ling MALLISON.

ROBERT ALEXANDER WEBB. Born 26 July 1891, at Charleston, South Carolina. S. of Rev. Prof. Robert Alexander Webb (dec^d), Louisville, Kentucky. Educ. at Southwestern Univ. (A.B. degree); and Johns Hopkins Univ., Baltimore (M.D. degree). Adm. Jan. 1924: began res. 14 Jan. 1924. Matric. 23 Oct. 1922 (as Research Stud. from Gonville and Caius College, where he resided M. 1922 to M. 1923 inclusive). Charles Abercrombie Smith Stud. (for research in Pathology), £150, 1924.

Ph.D. 1925.
⚔ 1917–19. Civilian medical practitioner, attd R.A.M.C.; Capt., Medical Corps, United States Army, attd R.A.M.C. Invalided.
In private practice (Pathology) at Cincinnati, Ohio, 1919–20. Research post in Pathology at the

Bland Sutton Institute, Middlesex Hospital, 1920. M.R.C.S., L.R.C.P. 1921. Demonstrator in Pathology, Manchester Univ., 1921–2. Research (on behalf of Medical Research Council) in Dept of Pathology, Cambridge, 1922–6. University Demonstrator in Pathology, Cambridge, 1926–9; and Lecturer, 1929–33. Professor of Pathology, London Univ., London (Royal Free Hospital) School of Medicine for Women, 1933–.

ARTHUR SMALLWOOD WINDER. Born 22 March 1905, at Nether Staveley, Westmorland. S. of William Smallwood Winder (dec^d). Guardian (uncle): John Smallwood Winder, Heathfield, Kendal. Educ. at Rugby School and Edinburgh College of Art. Adm. 17 Jan. 1923: began res. 22 April 1924. Matric. 31 May 1924.

Resided E. 1924 to E. 1926, and L. and E. 1933. B.A. (3rd Cl. Engl. Tri. (a), 1926; 1st Cl. First Exam. in Architect. Studies, 1933) 1933.
Engaged in architectural studies.

IAN SCOTT HAMMOND. Born 1 Oct. 1904, at Amsterdam, Transvaal. S. of Robert Woodward Hammond (Peterhouse, M.A. 1911), Head Master of Plumtree School, S. Rhodesia. Educ. at Plumtree School, S. Rhodesia. Adm. 4 Dec. 1923: began res. 22 April 1924. Matric. 27 May 1924.

B.A. (3rd Cl. Geog. Tri. Pt I, 1925; 3rd Cl. Pt II, 1927) 1928.
In the Geological Dept of the Anglo-Persian Oil Co., Ltd, 1927–8. Asst Master, successively at Bedford School and at the Royal Grammar School, Newcastle-on-Tyne, 1928–9. Sarawak Civil Service, 1930–; with appt. as Land Settlement Officer, 1935–.
Bro. of J. M. Hammond (p. 138).

RICHARD DOUGLAS DAVIS BIRDWOOD. Born 5 Jan. 1905, at Agra, India. S. of Gordon Travers Birdwood (Peterhouse, M.D. 1896), 26 The Beach, Walmer, Kent. Educ. at Clifton College. Adm. 11 Feb. 1921: began res. 10 Oct. 1924. Matric. 21 Oct. 1924.

B.A. (3rd Cl. Nat. Sci. Tri. Pt I, 1927) 1927. M.A. 1932. Colonial Office Course, M. 1927 and L. 1928.
Colonial Service, with appt. as Cadet in the Administrative Service of Nigeria, 1928–32. Then studied medicine at St Thomas's Hospital, London. M.R.C.S., L.R.C.P. 1937. Entered the I.M.S.: Lieut., 1937; Capt., 1938.
The seventh of his family at Peterhouse: for the connections, see *Walker* and pp. 11 and 45 of this Register.

NOEL ALBERT CHRISTOPHER. Born 14 Dec. 1905, at Rangoon. S. of Sydney Albert Christopher, Advocate of the High Court of Burma, Churchill House, Churchill Road, Rangoon. Educ. at St Joseph's College, Darjeeling. Adm. 2 Oct. 1922: began res. 10 Oct. 1924. Matric. 21 Oct. 1924.

B.A. (Ord. degree) 1927.
Called to the Bar, Lincoln's Inn, 18 Nov. 1929.

JOHN JAMES HANNING. Born 26 Nov. 1906, at Stoke Newington. S. of William Hanning (dec^d) and Mrs Hanning, 1 Rue Édouard-Fournier, Paris. Educ. at Clifton College. Rec. by R. P. Keigwin, M.A. (Peterhouse), House Master. Adm. 2 March 1923: began res. 10 Oct. 1924. Matric. 21 Oct. 1924.

Went down after L. 1925.
Engineer: Director of Maison Hanning, 17 Rue de Maubeuge, Paris, 9me.

GORDON NELSON DOCK. Born 21 May 1906, at Port Elizabeth, S. Africa. S. of John Dock, Port Elizabeth Club, Port Elizabeth. Educ. at Clifton College. Rec. by R. P. Keigwin, M.A. (Peterhouse), House Master. Adm. 23 May 1923: began res. 10 Oct. 1924. Matric. 21 Oct. 1924.

B.A. (3rd Cl. Law Tri. Pt I, 1926; standard for Ord. degree, Pt II, 1927) 1927. M.A. 1931.
Called to the Bar, Inner Temple, 19 Nov. 1928. Advocate of Supreme Court, S. Africa, 1932–.

WILLIAM ARMITAGE FORBES. Born 31 May 1905, at Clevedon, Somerset. S. of Barré Robert Machray Forbes, 9 Beaufort Road, Clifton. Educ. at Clifton College. Adm. 29 Oct. 1923: began res. 10 Oct. 1924. Matric. 21 Oct. 1924.

> B.A. (3rd Cl. Law Tri. Pt I, 1926; standard for Ord. degree, Pt II, 1927) 1927. Colonial Office Course, L. and E. 1928.
> Colonial Service, Tanganyika Territory, 1928–; now (1932) with appt. as Asst District Officer.
> Bro. of D. B. Forbes (p. 136) and cousin of J. C. Gurney (p. 8).

ERNEST STANLEY RICKARDS. Born 25 May 1907, at Carshalton, Surrey. S. of Ernest Herbert Rickards, Blythburgh, Grosvenor Avenue, Carshalton. Educ. at University School, Hastings. Adm. 25 Nov. 1923: began res. 10 Oct. 1924. Matric. 21 Oct. 1924.

> B.A. (3rd Cl. Law Tri. Pt I, 1926; 3rd Cl. Pt II, 1927) 1927.
> Solicitor (adm. Oct. 1930); practising at Taunton.
> Bro. of H. J. Rickards (p. 36).

WALTER ERIC WOLFF. Born 25 June 1905, in London. S. of Henry Wolff, 3 Lyndhurst Gardens, Hampstead, N.W. 3. Educ. at St Paul's School. Adm. 18 Dec. 1923: began res. 10 Oct. 1924. Matric. 21 Oct. 1924. Entrance Schol., History, £80.

> B.A. (2nd Cl., 1st Div., Hist. Tri. Pt I, 1926; 1st Cl., 2nd Div., Law Tri. Pt II, 1927) 1927. Schol.* of £40, 1926.
> Solicitor (adm. Nov. 1930); practising with Herbert Oppenheimer, Nathan, Vandyk & Mackay, at 1 & 2 Finsbury Square, London, E.C. 2.

ALEXANDER JOHN KNOTT. Born 25 July 1905, at Cambridge. S. of Hammett Charles Knott (Peterhouse, M.A. 1887), Fellow and Bursar of Selwyn College, 8 Cranmer Road, Cambridge. Educ. at Perse School, Cambridge. Adm. 18 Dec. 1923: began res. 10 Oct. 1924. Matric. 21 Oct. 1924. Entrance Schol., Classics, £60.

> B.A. (2nd Cl. Class. Tri. Pt I, 1926; 2nd Cl. Pt II, 1927) 1927. M.A. 1932. Schol.* of £40, 1926. Colonial Office Course, M. 1927 and L. 1928.
> Colonial Service, Nigeria, 1928–; now (1933) with appt. as Asst District Officer.
> Bro. of C. S. Knott (p. 26).

BRIAN THOMAS FLANAGAN. Born 20 Jan. 1905, at Westminster. S. of Patrick Flanagan, 36 Sneyd Road, Cricklewood, N.W. 2. Educ. at William Ellis School, Gospel Oak, London. Adm. 18 Dec. 1923: began res. 10 Oct. 1924. Matric. 21 Oct. 1924. Entrance Schol., Maths, £60.

> B.A. (1st Cl. Math. Tri. Pt I, 1925; Jun. Opt. Pt II; 1927) 1927. Re-elected to Schol.*, 1926.

MICHAEL HERBERT SWINBURNE HANCOCK. Born 15 April 1905, at Kensington. S. of Rev. Herbert Hancock, Stokesby Rectory, Great Yarmouth. Educ. at Marlborough College. Adm. 18 Dec. 1923: began res. 10 Oct. 1924. Matric. 21 Oct. 1924. Entrance Schol., Maths, £60.

> B.A. (2nd Cl. Math. Tri. Pt I, 1925; 3rd Cl. Theol. Tri. Pt I, Sec. A, 1927) 1927. M.A. 1931.
> Cuddesdon Theol. Coll., 1927. Ordained d. 1928, p. 1929 Southwark. C. of Lewisham, 1928–34; Perm. to Offic. at St Peter, Eaton Square, 1934–5; C. of Wimbledon (in charge of St John Bapt.), 1935–6; R. of Stokesby w. Herringby, Dio. Norwich, 1936–.

WILLIAM GERALD WORMAL. Born 20 June 1906, at Lincoln. S. of William Nathan Wormal, Westholme, Church Lane, Lincoln. Educ. at Lincoln School.

Adm. 18 Dec. 1923: began res. 10 Oct. 1924. Matric. 21 Oct. 1924. Entrance Schol., History, £60.

B.A. (2ⁿᵈ Cl., 1ˢᵗ Div., Hist. Tri. Pt I, 1926; 2ⁿᵈ Cl., 1ˢᵗ Div., Pt II, 1927) 1927. Schol.* of £40, 1926. Colonial Office Course, L. and E. 1928.
Colonial Service, Nigeria, 1928–; with appt. in the Administrative Service.

JOSEPH WILLIAM HUNT. Born 21 May 1905, at Islington. S. of Joseph Hunt, 113 Lothair Road, Finsbury Park, N. 4. Educ. at Owen's School, Islington. Adm. 18 Dec. 1923: began res. 10 Oct. 1924. Matric. 21 Oct. 1924. Entrance Schol., History, £40.

B.A. (2ⁿᵈ Cl., 1ˢᵗ Div., Hist. Tri. Pt I, 1926; 1ˢᵗ Cl., 2ⁿᵈ Div., Pt II, 1927) 1927. M.A. 1931. Re-elected to Schol.*, 1926. Schol.†, 1927.
Asst Master, Tollington School, Muswell Hill, 1928–9; and at Latymer Upper School, Hammersmith, 1929–.

HENRY WILSON SMITH. Born 30 Dec. 1904, at Newcastle-on-Tyne. S. of John Wilson Smith, 27 Simonburn Avenue, Newcastle. Educ. at Royal Grammar School, Newcastle. Adm. 18 Dec. 1923: began res. 10 Oct. 1924. Matric. 21 Oct. 1924. Entrance Schol., History, £40.

B.A. (1ˢᵗ Cl., 1ˢᵗ Div., Hist. Tri. Pt I, 1926; 1ˢᵗ Cl., 1ˢᵗ Div., Pt II, 1927) 1927. Schol. of £50, 1925. Schol.* of £70, 1926.
Asst Principal, Post Office, 1927–30. Transferred to the Treasury, 1930; and is now (1932) Asst Private Sec. to the Chancellor of the Exchequer.

CYRIL KENNETH SANSBURY. Born 21 Jan. 1905, at Streatham, London. S. of Cyril Jackson Sansbury, 69 Mount Nod Road, Streatham, S.W. 16. Educ. at St Paul's School. Adm. 18 Dec. 1923: began res. 10 Oct. 1924. Matric. 21 Oct. 1924. Entrance Exhib., Classics, £30.

B.A. (2ⁿᵈ Cl. Class. Tri. Pt I, 1926; 1ˢᵗ Cl. Theol. Tri. Pt I, Sec. A, 1927) 1927. 1ˢᵗ Cl. Theol. Tri. Pt II (b), 1928. M.A. 1931. Re-elected to Exhib., 1926. Schol.†, 1927.
Westcott House, Cambridge, 1927. Ordained d. 1928, p. 1929 Southwark. C. of St Peter, Dulwich Common, 1928–31; Perm. to Offic. at Wimbledon, 1931–2; S.P.G. Mission at Numazu (in charge of Kofu, 1933–4), Japan, 1932–4; Lecturer at the Central Theological College, and British Chaplain of St Andrew, City and Dio. Tokyo, 1934–; Examining Chaplain to Bp in S. Tokyo, 1935–; and Chaplain to the British Embassy, Tokyo, 1938–.
Bro. of G. R. Sansbury (p. 132).

HERBERT BLUETT COURCHÉE. Born 2 Feb. 1905, at Clapton, London. S. of Herbert Courchée, Army Audit Office, Cairo, Egypt. Educ. Merchant Taylors' School. Adm. 18 Dec. 1923: began res. 10 Oct. 1924. Matric. 21 Oct. 1924. Entrance Exhib., Maths, £30.

B.A. (1ˢᵗ Cl. Math. Tri. Pt I, 1925; Sen. Opt. Pt II, 1927) 1927. Schol.* of £40, 1925; re-elected, 1926.
B.Sc., London, 1927. Asst Master, King's School, Canterbury, 1927–9; and at Merchant Taylors' School, Crosby, 1929–.

JOHN MCVEAN LUARD. Born 2 March 1906, at Eastby, parish of Embsay, Northallerton. S. of Major Hugh Bixby Luard, I.M.S. (ret.), Woodlands, Little Baddow, Chelmsford. Educ. at Malvern College. Adm. 21 Jan. 1924: began res. 10 Oct. 1924. Matric. 21 Oct. 1924.

B.A. (3ʳᵈ Cl. Mod. & Med. Lang. Tri. Pt I, s, 1926; 3ʳᵈ Cl. Pt II, 1927) 1927.
With the British Petroleum Co., Ltd, 1927–9; and with the Anglo-Persian Oil Co., Ltd, in Teheran, 1929–.

THOMAS CLEGG TURNER. Born 9 July 1904, at Batley, Yorks. S. of Richard Turner, Bunkers Lane, Staincliffe, Batley. Educ. at Wheelwright Grammar School, Dewsbury. Adm. 5 Feb. 1924: began res. 10 Oct. 1924. Matric. 21 Oct. 1924.

B.A. (3rd Cl. Math. Tri. Pt I, 1925; 2nd Cl. Geog. Tri. Pt I, 1926; 1st Cl. Geog. Tri. Pt II (1), 1927) 1927. M.A. 1931. In E. 1927 given title of Scholar for 1926–7.
Asst Master, Churcher's College, Petersfield, Hants, 1927–. F.R.G.S. 1927.

HAROLD LEONARD PETAVEL. Born 26 April 1900, in London. S. of Capt. James William Petavel, R.E. (ret.), Lecturer at Calcutta Univ. Educ. at King's School, Canterbury. Adm. 21 Feb. 1924: began res. 10 Oct. 1924. Matric. 21 Oct. 1924.

B.A. (3rd Cl. Nat. Sci. Tri. Pt I, 1927) 1927.
✗ 1918–20. Pte, The Queen's (R.W. Surrey Regt); Sergt, Military Intelligence, Cologne. Merchant.

MARIE HENRY EDWARD DEVAUX. Born 29 Nov. 1905, at Castries, St Lucia, B.W.I. S. of John Devaux, Chief Clerk and Estate Owner, Colonial Bank, St Lucia. Educ. at St Mary's College, St Lucia. Adm. 4 March 1924: began res. 10 Oct. 1924. Matric. 21 Oct. 1924.

B.A. (3rd Cl. Law Tri. Pt I, 1926; 3rd Cl. Pt II, 1927) 1927. M.A. 1934. Tropical African Services Course, L. and E. 1929.
Called to the Bar, Lincoln's Inn, 19 Nov. 1928. Colonial Service, Gold Coast Colony, 1929–; now (1931) with appt. as Asst District Commissioner.

KENT ROBINSON. Born 16 Oct. 1907, at Flushing, Long Island, U.S.A. S. of Clarence Robinson (decd) and Mrs Robinson, Brooklands, Jersey, C.I. Educ. at Marlborough College. Adm. 25 March 1924: began res. 10 Oct. 1924. Matric. 21 Oct. 1924.

B.A. (Ord. degree) 1927.
Engaged in aviation in U.S.A.
Bro. of C. Robinson (p. 75).

NORMAN SPENCER DEEKS. Born 4 March 1906, in London. S. of William Charles Deeks, 24 Honeywell Road, S.W. 11. Educ. at Emanuel School, Wandsworth Common. Adm. 12 April 1924: began res. 10 Oct. 1924. Matric. 21 Oct. 1924.

B.A. (2nd Cl. Math. Tri. Pt I, 1925; 3rd Cl. Nat. Sci. Tri. Pt II (Physics), 1927) 1927. M.A. 1935.
B.Sc., London, 1927. Mathematical and Science Master, Loretto School, 1928–33. Working with the C.M.S. as Asst Master, St Andrew's College, Oyo, Nigeria, 1933–.

HAROLD WILLIAM FAIRLIE. Born 30 Oct. 1905, at Acton, Middlesex. S. of James Fairlie, 17 Mayfield Road, Acton, W. 3. Educ. at St Paul's School. Adm. 28 April 1924: began res. 10 Oct. 1924. Matric. 21 Oct. 1924.

B.A. (3rd Cl. Class. Tri. Pt I, 1926; 3rd Cl. Pt II, 1927) 1927.
Clerk with N. M. Rothschild & Sons (merchants and bankers), New Court, St Swithin's Lane, London, E.C. 4.

HUGH MALCOLM BRODIE. Born 31 Dec. 1899, at Coventry. S. of Rev. Frank Malcolm Brodie, 76 St Helen's Road, Hastings. Educ. at King Edward's School, Birmingham; City of London School; and University College, London. Adm. 18 May 1924: began res. 10 Oct. 1924. Matric. 21 Oct. 1924.

B.A. (2nd Cl., 2nd Div., Engl. Tri. (a), 1926; Cert. of Dilig. Study, 1927) 1927. M.A. 1931.
✗ 1918–19. 2nd Lieut., R.A.F.
St Stephen's House, Oxford, 1927. Ordained d. 1928, p. 1929 London. C. of St Mary, Somers Town, and Magdalen College (Oxford) Missioner, 1928–30; Asst Master, Radley College, 1930– (and Chaplain, 1933–); Lic. to Offic. Dio. Oxford, 1931–.

REX WELLER HARTLEY. Born 15 June 1905, at Anerley, Kent. S. of John William Hartley (dec[d]) and Mrs Hartley, Abingdon House, Bromley, Kent. Educ. at Westminster School. Adm. 19 May 1924: began res. 10 Oct. 1924. Matric. 28 Nov. 1924.

Went down after M. 1925.
Half-Blue: Golf, 1925, 1926. (Captain for the year 1925–6.)

CLARENCE EDWARD ARNOLD. Born 15 Feb. 1902, at Streatham, London. S. of Fred Arnold, Stonehills, College Road, Dulwich. Educ. at Dulwich College. Adm. 23 June 1924: began res. 10 Oct. 1924. Matric. 21 Oct. 1924.

B.A. (3rd Cl. Nat. Sci. Tri. Pt I, 1926; Cert. of Dilig. Study, 1927) 1927. M.A. 1931.
Coffee and general produce merchant, 1920–4. Ridley Hall, Cambridge, 1927. Ordained d. 1927, p. 1929 London. C. of St Mary, Islington, 1927–30; C.M.S. Mission, Dio. Egypt, 1930–.

CYRIL HAROLD FRY. Born 22 Oct. 1905, in London. S. of Emile George Edward Fry, 239 Burrage Road, Plumstead, S.E. 18. Educ. at Herne Bay College, Kent. Adm. 26 June 1924: began res. 10 Oct. 1924. Matric. 21 Oct. 1924.

B.A. (Ord. degree) 1927.
Architect and Surveyor.

JORGE AUGUSTIN SEGURA. Born 23 Sept. 1904, at Buenos Aires, Argentine Republic. S. of Dr Eliseo V. Segura, 1070 Carlos Pellegrini, Buenos Aires. Educ. at Colegio Nacional, Buenos Aires; and privately, with W. N. Marcy, 22 Chancery Lane, W.C. 2. Adm. 26 June 1924: began res. 10 Oct. 1924. Matric. 21 Oct. 1924.

Went down after E. 1925.
Engaged successively in farming, and now (1933) in business with Philips South American Export Co., Buenos Aires.

OSCAR STANLEY WIGHT. Born 10 Sept. 1906, at Georgetown, Demerara, British Guiana. S. of Percy C. Wight, 50 Main Street, Georgetown, Demerara. Educ. at Herne Bay College, Kent. Adm. 26 June 1924: began res. 10 Oct. 1924. Matric. 21 Oct. 1924.

Went down during M. 1925.
In business at Georgetown, Demerara.

MASTERSHIP OF
THE RT HON
BARON CHALMERS, OF NORTHIAM,

P.C., G.C.B., M.A., Hon. LL.D. (Cambridge, Glasgow and
St Andrews), Hon. D.Litt. (Oxford), F.B.A.

MASTER, 1924–31

(Adm. Master, 5 July 1924)

HARRY VAN ALST BROWER. Born 24 April 1904, at New York. S. of
Harry Van Alst Brower, 10 East 53 Street, New York. Educ. at St Bernard's,
Groton; Pomfret School, Conn.; and Princeton Univ. Adm. 17 July 1924: began
res. 10 Oct. 1924. Matric. 21 Oct. 1924.

Went down after L. 1926.
Was with the Bankers Trust Co., Place Vendôme, Paris, in 1926.

NOEL GERARD KENNARD. Born 27 Dec. 1905, at Estancia Marabú, Santa
Eleodora, F.C.P., Argentine Republic. S. of Capt. Vivian George Kennard, Frith,
Stalbridge, Dorset. Educ. at Cheltenham College. Adm. 18 July 1924: began
res. 10 Oct. 1924. Matric. 21 Oct. 1924.

Went down after E. 1926.
Fruit growing in the Argentine Republic.

IAN BEGBIE. Born 8 July 1905, at Bombay. S. of Sir James Begbie, The
Croft, Prideaux Road, Eastbourne. Educ. at Malvern College. Adm. 21 July
1924: began res. 10 Oct. 1924. Matric. 21 Oct. 1924.

B.A. (Ord. degree) 1927.
Forest Asst with the Bombay Burmah Trading Corporation, Ltd, in Burma, 1927–.

ARTHUR JOHN EVANS. Born 15 Aug. 1903, at Bakewell, Derbyshire. S. of
Charles Walter Evans, Matlock House, Bakewell. Educ. at Bradfield College.
Adm. 23 July 1924: began res. 10 Oct. 1924. Matric. 21 Oct. 1924.

B.A. (3rd Cl. Nat. Sci. Tri. Pt I, 1926; Cert. of Dilig. Study, 1927) 1927. M.A. 1931.
Asst Master, St John's College, Jaffna, Ceylon, 1927–30. Westcott House, Cambridge, 1930. Ordained
d. 1932, p. 1933 Southwell. C. of St Peter, Mansfield, 1932–5; C. in charge of St James district,
Porchester, Dio. Southwell, 1935–.

FRANK MIDDLETON DUNWELL. Born 25 Oct. 1904, at Bradford, Yorks.
S. of Richard Middleton Dunwell, 17 Coleridge Road, Bradford. Educ. at Bradford
Grammar School. Adm. 25 July 1924: began res. 10 Oct. 1924. Matric. 21 Oct. 1924.

B.A. (3rd Cl. Nat. Sci. Tri. Pt I, 1927) 1927. 3rd Cl. Law Tri. Pt II, 1928. M.A. 1936.
Solicitor (adm. June 1932); practising at Lewes, Sussex.

CHARLES REGINALD SANDERSON. Born 2 Jan. 1906, at Hessle, E. Yorks. S. of Charles Herbert Sanderson, Southfield, Hessle. Educ. at Haileybury College. Adm. 29 July 1924: began res. 10 Oct. 1924. Matric. 21 Oct. 1924.

B.A. (3rd Cl. Engl. Tri. (a), 1926; standard for Ord. degree, Law Tri. Pt II, 1927) 1927.
Successively Asst Master, Hymer's College, Hull, and now (1933) Asst Educational Representative with Messrs Blackie & Son, Ltd (publishers).

GEORGE BAILLIE. Born 6 Dec. 1904, at Claydon, Suffolk. S. of Major George Baillie (decd) and Mrs Baillie, Meonstoke, Bishop's Waltham, Hants. Educ. at Cheltenham College and Bristol Univ. Adm. 30 July 1924: began res. 10 Oct. 1924. Matric. 21 Oct. 1924.

Went down after L. 1925.
Engineer.

JOHN WILMOTT MARSHALL. Born 8 Jan. 1905, at Simla, India. S. of Sir John Hubert Marshall, C.I.E., Director-General of Archaeology, India. Educ. at Haileybury College; and privately. Adm. 31 July 1924: began res. 10 Oct. 1924. Matric. 28 Nov. 1924.

B.A. (Ord. degree) 1928.
Asst Transportation Officer, Bengal Nagpur Railway, 1928–31. With Amherst Villiers Superchargers Ltd, London, 1931–2. Now (1934) Internal Combustion Engineer: Marshall Superchargers, 22 Pembridge Crescent, London, W. 11.
Cousin of G. W. Marshall (p. 57).

LESLIE MASON RILEY. Born 11 March 1906, at Bootle, Liverpool. S. of Frederick William Riley, 97 Linacre Lane, Bootle. Educ. at Bootle Secondary School. Adm. 5 Sept. 1924: began res. 10 Oct. 1924. Matric. 21 Oct. 1924.

B.A. (2nd Cl., 1st Div., Hist. Tri. Pt I, 1926; 1st Cl., 2nd Div., Pt II, 1927) 1927. 3rd Cl. Geog. Tri. Pt I, 1928. M.A. 1931. Exhib. of £30, 1926. Schol.†, 1927.
Schoolmaster, 1929–36. Education Officer, R.A.F., 1937–.

HARRY VICTOR BEARMAN. Born 31 Dec. 1905, at Wanstead, Essex. S. of Frank Charles Bearman, The Hill House, Stanmore, Middlesex. Educ. at Harrow School. Adm. 9 Sept. 1924: began res. 10 Oct. 1924. Matric. 21 Oct. 1924.

Went down after M. 1925.
Dealer in antiques and works of art.

WILLIAM KENNETH PROCTER. Born 25 Nov. 1905, at Penang, Straits Settlements. S. of William Dilcock Procter, Eastern Extension Telegraph Co., Peking, China. Educ. at Dulwich College. Adm. 11 Sept. 1924: began res. 10 Oct. 1924. Matric. 21 Oct. 1924.

B.A. (3rd Cl. Econ. Tri. Pt I, 1926; 3rd Cl. Pt II, 1927) 1927.
Insurance Broker.
Bro. of L. R. Procter (p. 111).

WYNDHAM STANLEY COX. Born 16 June 1903, at Streatham, London. S. of Charles Willoughby Cox, 7 Eden Road, Croydon. Educ. at Whitgift Grammar School, Croydon. Adm. 17 Sept. 1924: began res. 10 Oct. 1924. Matric. 21 Oct. 1924.

B.A. (Ord. degree) 1927.
Ridley Hall, Cambridge, 1927. Ordained d. 1928 Dover for Canterbury, p. 1929 Canterbury. C. of St George Mart., Deal, 1928–30; Holy Trinity, Ramsgate, 1930–2; St Luke, Camberwell, Dio. Southwark, 1932–; St Michael Royal w. St Martin Vintry and All Hallows the Great and the Less, London, 1933–5.
He altered the order of his names to Stanley Wyndham Cox in 1927.

Daniel Charles Sturge MOORE. Born 5 Nov. 1905, in London. S. of Thomas Sturge Moore, Hillcroft, Steep, Petersfield, Hants. Educ. at Bedales School. Adm. 21 Sept. 1924: began res. 10 Oct. 1924. Matric. 21 Oct. 1924.

Went down after E. 1926.
Farming in Australia, 1927–30. Leader for the Workers' Travel Assoc., in Paris, 1931.
Editor:
   (With T. Sturge Moore) *Works and days, from the Journal of Michael Field* [*i.e. Katherine Bradley and Edith Cooper*]. London (1933).

Alden HOLM-SMITH. Born 10 June 1903, at Mason City, Iowa. S. of Clifford Pabody Smith, 236 Huntington Avenue, Boston, Mass. Educ. at Princeton Univ. Adm. 2 Oct. 1924: began res. 10 Oct. 1924. Matric. 21 Oct. 1924.

Went down after E. 1925.
Half-Blue: Lawn Tennis, 1925.
Was engaged in business successively with C. D. Jackson & Co. (marble importers), New York, and with the Bankers Trust Co., New York. Died 12 Feb. 1929 at Phoenix, Arizona.

William Geoffrey MEGGITT, Flt Lieut., R.A.F. Born 8 April 1894, at Mansfield, Notts. S. of George Teale Meggitt, The Cliff, Eveswell Park, Newport, Monmouthshire. Educ. at Newport (Mon.) High School. Rec. by Air Ministry. Adm. 14 July 1924: began res. 10 Oct. 1924. Matric. 21 Oct. 1924.

B.A. (Ord. degree; all. 3 terms as Commiss. Off.) 1926.
✗ 1915–19. Lieut., Welsh Regt; Lieut., R.A.F. (P.) *M.C.*
Killed 28 Jan. 1927 in an aeroplane accident at Norbury, Surrey; being then still Flt Lieut., R.A.F.

David Arthur RENDLE, Lieut., R.E. Born 8 Jan. 1899, at Sutton, Surrey. S. of Dr Alfred Barton Rendle, F.R.S., 28 Holmbush Road, Putney, S.W. 15. Educ. at King's College School; and R.M.A., Woolwich. Rec. by War Office. Adm. 10 Aug. 1924: began res. 10 Oct. 1924. Matric. 21 Oct. 1924.

Resided till end of E. 1925.
✗ 1918–19. 2nd Lieut., R.E.
Capt. (1929–), R.E.

Cecil Herbert HARRISON, Flg. Off., R.A.F. Born 27 Oct. 1896, at Harrogate. S. of Alfred Harrison (dec^d). Educ. at Horst College, Pannal, Yorks; Harrogate Secondary School; and Harrogate Art School. Rec. by Air Ministry. Adm. 20 Aug. 1924: began res. 10 Oct. 1924. Matric. 21 Oct. 1924.

B.A. (3rd Cl. Mech. Sci. Tri., 1926; all. 3 terms as Commiss. Off.) 1926.
✗ 1915–19. Lieut., King's Own (Yorkshire L.I.); Lieut., R.A.F.
Dipl. in Aeronautics, Imperial College of Science and Technology, London, 1927. Promoted Flt Lieut., R.A.F., 1925; and Sqdn Ldr, 1935. Died 6 Jan. 1936 at the Home Aircraft Depôt, Henlow, Beds.

Basil John Wade COXETER. Born 3 Feb. 1906, at Oxford. S. of John Wade Coxeter, Kinloss, Woodside, nr Abingdon. Educ. at Clifton College. Adm. 17 Dec. 1924: began res. 12 Jan. 1925. Matric. 28 Jan. 1925.

Went down after E. 1926.

George Theodore ENNIS. Born 24 Nov. 1905, at Entebbe, Uganda. S. of George Francis Macdaniel Ennis, Justice of Supreme Court, Ceylon. Educ. at King's School, Canterbury. Adm. 18 Dec. 1924: began res. 12 Jan. 1925. Matric. 28 Jan. 1925.

Went down after L. 1926.
Reported deceased.

ERIC WESTBURY. Born 8 Feb. 1906, in London. S. of Claude Frederick Westbury, 163 King's Avenue, S.W. 12. Educ. at Dulwich College. Adm. 18 Dec. 1924: began res. 12 Jan. 1925. Matric. 28 Jan. 1925.

B.A. (3rd Cl. Econ. Tri. Pt I, 1926; 3rd Cl. Pt II, 1927) 1927. M.A. 1934.
East India Importer.

HEM SINGH PRUTHI. Born Feb. 1897, at Begowalo (Sialkote), Punjab, India. S. of Dr Bhagat Singh Pruthi, Police and Jail Hospital, Gujranwala, Punjab. Educ. at Government College, Lahore (M.Sc. degree, Punjab Univ.). Adm. 28 July 1924: began res. 9 Oct. 1924. Matric. 24 Oct. 1922 (as Non-Coll. Research Stud., residing as such M. 1922 to E. 1924 inclusive). Charles Abercrombie Smith Stud. (for research in Zoology), £100, 1924.

Ph.D. 1924. Resided at Peterhouse M. 1924 to E. 1925 inclusive. *Nominated by the Special Board for Biol. and Geol. to use the Univ. Table at the Zoological Station at Naples for 1 month from 1 June 1925. Nominated by the same Board to occupy the Univ. Table at the Laboratory of the Marine Biological Assoc. at Plymouth for 3 months from 15 April 1926. Fellowship of the International Education Board (Rockefeller Foundation), 1925.*
Asst Superintendent, Zoological Survey of India, Indian Museum, Calcutta.
Author of numerous papers on insects.

JAMES ALBERT LOVATT WENGER. Born 21 June 1905, at Basford, Staffs. S. of Adolph Henry Charles Wenger, Trentham Priory, nr Stoke-on-Trent. Educ. at Repton School; and privately. Adm. 25 March 1925: began res. 20 April 1925. Matric. 4 May 1925.

B.A. (Ord. degree) 1929. M.A. 1932.
With Wengers Ltd (potters' colour manufacturers), Etruria, Stoke-on-Trent.

EDWARD HENRY WOOLF. Born 11 May 1904, at Sandbach, Cheshire. S. of Edward Samuel Woolf (decd) and Mrs Woolf, The White House, Ashley, Market Drayton, Staffs. Educ. at Malvern College. Adm. 25 March 1925: began res. 20 April 1925. Matric. 4 May 1925.

Went down after E. 1926.
Farming at Ferney Castle, Reston, Berwickshire.
Bro. of J. L. Woolf (p. 106).

GEORGE VALENTINE MERVYN HEAP. Born 14 Feb. 1906, at Shenfield, Essex. S. of Rev. Harry Hubert Heap, Littlehempston Rectory, Totnes, S. Devon. Educ. privately. Adm. 25 May 1925, by *bene discessit* from Selwyn College: began res. 13 Oct. 1925. Matric. 22 Oct. 1924 (from Selwyn College, where he resided M. 1924, L. and E. 1925).

B.A. (1st Cl. Class. Tri. Pt I, 1926; adm. to degree without further exam.) 1927. Dipl. in Class. Archaeology, 1929. M.A. 1931. Schol.* of £70, 1926. Schol.†, 1927. *Evans Prize,* 1928.
Asst Lecturer in Classics, University College of the South West of England, Exeter, 1930–6; Lecturer, 1936–; and Acting Head of Dept of Classics, 1938–.

HECTOR JAMES McCURRACH. Born 11 March 1907, at Perth. S. of James McCurrach, Duntanlich, Kinnoull, Perth. Educ. at Leys School. Adm. 24 June 1924: began res. 9 Oct. 1925. Matric. 21 Oct. 1925. Organ Scholar.

B.A. (Ord. degree) 1928. Mus.B. 1930. M.A. 1932. Re-elected Organ Scholar, 1927; and again (Bernard Hale), 1928. *John Stewart of Rannoch Schol. in Sacred Music,* 1928. Leaf Grant, 1929.
Sir James Caird Travelling Schol. (Senior) in Music, 1930. Organist and Music Master, Sedbergh School, 1931–.

DAVID NOEL FRANCIS. Born 13 July 1904, at Hampstead. S. of Edward
James Pocock Francis (dec^d) and Mrs Francis, 182 Sutherland Avenue, W. 9. Educ.
at William Ellis School, Gospel Oak, London. Adm. 18 Oct. 1924: began res.
10 Oct. 1925. Matric. 21 Oct. 1925.

B.A. (2ⁿᵈ Cl., 1ˢᵗ Div., Econ. Tri. Pt I, 1927; 2ⁿᵈ Cl., 1ˢᵗ Div., Archaeol. & Anthropol. Tri., Sec. A,
1928) 1928. 2ⁿᵈ Cl. Theol. Tri. Pt I, Sec. A, 1930. M.A. 1932. Exhib. for Economics, £30, 1926;
re-elected, 1927.
Wesley House, Cambridge, 1928. Methodist Minister: Missionary Soc., London, 1930–3; Hyderabad
district, India, 1933–.
Bro. of E. C. Francis, Fellow (p. 80).

MAURICE BARLOW DANIELS. Born 1 April 1906, at Farnley Tyas, nr
Huddersfield. S. of William Oliver Daniels, 22 Rigby Lane, Bradshaw, nr Bolton.
Educ. at Bolton Municipal Secondary School. Adm. 17 Dec. 1924: began res.
10 Oct. 1925. Matric. 21 Oct. 1925. Entrance Schol., Maths, £60.

B.A. (1ˢᵗ Cl. Math. Tri. Pt I, 1926; Sen. Opt. Pt II, 1928) 1928. M.A. 1935. Schol.†, 1927. Goldsmiths' Co.'s Exhib., 1927. Kitchener Schol., 1927.
With Thomson McLintock & Co. (Chartered Accountants); at their Manchester office, 1929–32;
and at their London one, 1932–.

CHARLES CECIL EAGLESFIELD. Born 28 June 1906, at Swansea. S. of
Charles John Eaglesfield, 52 Stanley Road, Hoylake, Cheshire. Educ. at Clifton
College. Adm. 17 Dec. 1924: began res. 10 Oct. 1925. Matric. 21 Oct. 1925.
Entrance Schol., Maths, £60.

B.A. (1ˢᵗ Cl. Math. Tri. Pt I, 1926; 2ⁿᵈ Cl. Mech. Sci. Tri., 1928) 1928. Schol.† for Mech. Sciences,
1927.

DAVID FISH.WICK. Born 29 April 1906, at Keighley, Yorks. S. of Thomas
Fishwick, Burnwell House, Thackley, Bradford, Yorks. Educ. at Bradford Grammar
School. Adm. 17 Dec. 1924: began res. 10 Oct. 1925. Matric. 21 Oct. 1925.
Entrance Schol., Classics, £60.

B.A. (1ˢᵗ Cl. Class. Tri. Pt I, 1927; 1ˢᵗ Cl. Pt II, 1928) 1928. Goldsmiths' Co.'s Exhib., 1926
(held for 2 years). Schol.†, 1927. Probationer, I.C.S., M. 1928 to E. 1929.
I.C.S., with appt. as Asst Commissioner, Burma, 1929–.

PHILIP CHARLES ROMANS. Born 8 March 1906, at Gloucester. S. of
Arthur Ernest Romans, 2 Grafton Villas, Calton Road, Gloucester. Educ. at
Crypt Grammar School, Gloucester. Adm. 17 Dec. 1924: began res. 10 Oct. 1925.
Matric. 21 Oct. 1925. Entrance Schol., History, £60.

B.A. (2ⁿᵈ Cl., 2ⁿᵈ Div., Hist. Tri. Pt I, 1927; 2ⁿᵈ Cl., 2ⁿᵈ Div., Engl. Tri., Sec. A, 1928) 1928.
M.A. 1932. Exhib., 1927.
Professor of English, Baroda College, India, 1932–.

ARTHUR RONALD BIELBY. Born 9 Dec. 1906, at Thornaby-on-Tees. S. of
Arthur Bielby, 3 Westfield Way, Dormanstown, Redcar, Yorks. Educ. at Sir William
Turner's School, Coatham, Redcar. Adm. 17 Dec. 1924: began res. 10 Oct. 1925.
Matric. 21 Oct. 1925. Entrance Schol., Maths, £40.

B.A. (1ˢᵗ Cl. Math. Tri. Pt I, 1926; Wrang. Pt II, 1928) 1928. M.A. 1932. Schol.* of £50, 1926.
Schol.†, 1927.
Asst Master, Heversham Grammar School, 1928–9; and at Taunton's School, Southampton, 1929–.

GEORGE THOMSON PARTRIDGE. Born 18 May 1906, at Carmarthen. S. of Thomas Teil Partridge, 134 Foxhall Road, Nottingham. Educ. at Nottingham High School. Adm. 17 Dec. 1924: began res. 5 Oct. 1925. Matric. 21 Oct. 1925. Entrance Schol., Classics (all. to change to Nat. Sciences and M.B. Exams), £40.

B.A. (Ord. degree) 1928. M.A., M.B., B.Chir. 1933. Exhib., 1927.
M.R.C.S., L.R.C.P. 1931. F.R.C.S. 1934. In consulting practice as an Orthopaedic Surgeon in Chester. Hon. Orthopaedic Surgeon, Chester Royal Infirmary; and Surgical Registrar to the Robert Jones and Agnes Hunt Orthopaedic Hospital, Oswestry.

PHILIP HERBERT BRIGSTOCK TRASLER. Born 11 Feb. 1906, at Northampton. S. of Herbert Brigstock Trasler, 37 York Road, Northampton. Educ. at Northampton Town and County School. Adm. 17 Dec. 1924: began res. 10 Oct. 1925. Matric. 21 Oct. 1925. Entrance Schol., Nat. Sciences, £40.

B.A. (2nd Cl. Nat. Sci. Tri. Pt I, 1927; 3rd Cl. Pt II (Geol.), 1928) 1928. Schol.†, 1927.
Chemist, with Trinidad Leaseholders Ltd, Trinidad, 1928–.

LAURENCE DUVALL GILLIAM. Born 4 March 1907, at Fulham. S. of Ernest William Gilliam, 20 Bolton Gardens, Teddington, Middlesex. Educ. at City of London School. Adm. 17 March 1924: began res. 10 Oct. 1925. Matric. 21 Oct. 1925. Entrance Schol., History, £40.

B.A. (2nd Cl., 1st Div., Hist. Tri. Pt I, 1927; 2nd Cl., 2nd Div., Pt II, 1928) 1928. Schol.†, 1927.
With the Gramophone Co., Ltd, London, 1928–31. Stage and journalistic work, 1931–2. Joined editorial staff of *The Radio Times*, April 1932; transferred to Productions Dept (as Special Programme Producer), B.B.C., Oct. 1932.

WILLIAM EVAN WILLIAMS. Born 26 April 1906, at Liverpool. S. of William Hugh Williams, 9 Frederick Avenue, Penkhull, Stoke-on-Trent. Educ. at Newcastle-under-Lyme High School. Adm. 17 Dec. 1924: began res. 10 Oct. 1925. Matric. 21 Oct. 1925. Entrance Schol., History, £40.

B.A. (1st Cl., 1st Div., Hist. Tri. Pt I, 1927; 1st Cl., 1st Div., Pt II, 1928) 1928. M.A. 1932. Schol. of £50, 1926. Schol.†, 1927. Goldsmiths' Co.'s Exhib., 1926 (held for 2 years); and their Senior Studentship, 1928 (held for 2 years). Hugo de Balsham Stud. (for research in History), £100, 1928. *Prince Consort Prize*, 1932.
Asst Master, Birkenhead Institute, 1930–.
Author:
     The rise of Gladstone to the leadership of the Liberal Party, 1859 to 1868. (*Prince Consort Prize*, 1932.) Cambridge, 1934.

JACK ROBERT BURT. Born 31 March 1907, at Battersea. S. of Robert George Burt, 79 Sugden Road, S.W. 11. Educ. at Emanuel School, Wandsworth Common. Adm. 17 Dec. 1924: began res. 10 Oct. 1925. Matric. 21 Oct. 1925. Entrance Schol., History, £40.

B.A. (2nd Cl., 2nd Div., Hist. Tri. Pt I, 1927; 2nd Cl. Theol. Tri. Pt II (c), 1928) 1928. Exhib., 1927.
Westcott House, Cambridge, 1931.

CYRIL FRANK GENGE. Born 9 Aug. 1906, at Upton St Leonards, Glos. S. of Frank Genge, School House, Upton St Leonards. Educ. at Crypt Grammar School, Gloucester. Adm. 17 Dec. 1924: began res. 10 Oct. 1925. Matric. 21 Oct. 1925. Entrance Exhib., Classics, £30.

B.A. (3rd Cl. Class. Tri. Pt I, 1927; P.S. Exam. Economics, 1928) 1928.
Asst Master, Wem Grammar School, Salop, 1929–30; at Chard School, Somerset, 1931–3; and at St Anselm's School, Park Lane, Croydon, Surrey, 1933–.

WILLIAM LIONEL KELLY. Born 2 Jan. 1906, at Peel, Isle of Man. S. of Frederick John Taubman Kelly, 12 Douglas Street, Peel. Educ. at King William's College, Isle of Man. Adm. 17 Dec. 1924: began res. 10 Oct. 1925. Matric. 21 Oct. 1925. Entrance Exhib., Classics, £30.

B.A. (2ⁿᵈ Cl. Class. Tri. Pt I, 1927; 2ⁿᵈ Cl. Pt II, 1928) 1928. Exhib., 1927.
With the London and North Eastern Railway Co., 1928–; being Asst to District Passenger Manager, Manchester, 1933–.

OLIVER HENRY LIONEL COHEN. Born 29 Aug. 1904, in S. Africa. S. of Walter Samuel Cohen, Amersfort, Berkhamsted, Herts. Educ. at Clifton College. Adm. 17 Jan. 1925: began res. 9 Oct. 1925. Matric. 21 Oct. 1925.

B.A. (3ʳᵈ Cl. Hist. Tri. Pt I, 1927; 3ʳᵈ Cl. Pt II, 1928) 1928.

WILLIAM PHILIP GABRIEL TAYLOR. Born 24 July 1906, at Ootacamund, Madras. S. of Herbert Douglas Taylor (Peterhouse, adm. 1883; decᵈ) and Mrs Taylor, Woodside, Pyrford Heath, nr Woking, Surrey. Educ. at Marlborough College. Adm. 19 Jan. 1925: began res. 10 Oct. 1925. Matric. 21 Oct. 1925.

B.A. (3ʳᵈ Cl. Intercoll. Exam. in Nat. Sci., 1927; adm. to degree without further exam.) 1928. M.A. 1932.
For his father and grandfather (J. W. Taylor, Fellow), see *Walker*.

STANLEY GEORGE LEWIS. Born 25 Sept. 1905, at Lincoln. S. of John Thomas Lewis, 9 Arboretum Avenue, Lincoln. Educ. at Lincoln School. Adm. 14 Feb. 1925: began res. 10 Oct. 1925. Matric. 21 Oct. 1925.

B.A. (3ʳᵈ Cl. Math. Tri. Pt I, 1927; 2ⁿᵈ Cl. Geog. Tri. Pt I, 1928) 1928. M.A. 1932.
Asst Master, Bedford Modern School, 1929–. Lieut. (1932–), Bedford Modern School O.T.C. (T.A.).

CHARLES MARSHAL BEAVIS. Born 1 Aug. 1907, at Wick, nr Bristol. S. of Dr Charles Beavis, Naishcombe House, Wick. Educ. at Clifton College. Adm. 16 March 1925: began res. 9 Oct. 1925. Matric. 21 Oct. 1925.

B.A. (Ord. degree) 1928.

WILLIAM ROBERT FRANCIS ELLIS. Born 11 Dec. 1906, at Stanmore, Middlesex. S. of Henry Reginald Ellis, Medical Office, Lagos, Nigeria. Educ. at Cheltenham College. Rec. by H. H. Hardy, M.B.E., M.A., Head Master; and R. Geoffrey Ellis, M.P., M.A. (Peterhouse). Adm. 17 March 1925: began res. 10 Oct. 1925. Matric. 21 Oct. 1925.

B.A. (3ʳᵈ Cl. Nat. Sci. Tri. Pt I, 1928) 1928. M.A. 1932.
Asst Master, Downside School, 1928–.
Nephew of Sir R. G. Geoffrey Ellis, Bart (cr. Bart 1932; *Walker*, p. 622), and cousin of C. E. F. Ellis (p. 119) and G. M. E. Paulson (p. 115).

CHARLES JOHN RADCLIFFE HUSBAND. Born 9 May 1907, at Ripon. S. of Lieut.-Col. John Charles Radclyffe Husband, M.D., 1 The Crescent, Ripon. Educ. at Cheltenham College. Adm. 17 March 1925: began res. 10 Oct. 1925. Matric. 21 Oct. 1925.

B.A. (2ⁿᵈ Cl., 1ˢᵗ Div., Law Tri. Pt I, 1927; 2ⁿᵈ Cl., 1ˢᵗ Div., Pt II, 1928) 1928. LL.B. 1930. M.A. 1934. Exhib. for Law, £30, 1926; re-elected, 1927.
Solicitor (adm. Oct. 1931); practising at Bridgwater and Highbridge, Somerset (J. Ruscombe Poole & Son). Also a Notary-Public (adm. Feb. 1934) and a Company Director.
He matric. as Charles John Radclyffe HUSBAND.

ANDREW BARTLEY GORDON MEIN. Born 31 July 1906, at Cardiff. S. of Thomas Gordon Mein, 9 Springfield Avenue, Harrogate. Educ. at Brighton College. Adm. 17 March 1925: began res. 5 Oct. 1925. Matric. 21 Oct. 1925.

Went down after E. 1926.
M.R.C.S., L.R.C.P. 1935. In practice at Cornholme, Todmorden, Yorks.

NUGENT DAVY JEKYLL. Born 8 March 1907, at Leytonstone, Essex. S. of Lewis Nugent Jekyll, Gainsborough House, Leytonstone. Educ. at Forest School, Walthamstow. Adm. 20 March 1925: began res. 5 Oct. 1925. Matric. 21 Oct. 1925.

B.A. (Ord. degree) 1929. M.A., M.B., B.Chir. 1937.
M.R.C.S., L.R.C.P. 1932. Entered the I.M.S.: Lieut., 1938 (with seniority of 1937); Capt., 1938.
Bro. of J. L. Jekyll (p. 77).

ERIC BRICKNELL SMITH. Born 11 May 1906, at Gloucester. S. of George James Smith, 2 Furlong Road, Gloucester. Educ. at Crypt Grammar School, Gloucester. Adm. 29 March 1925: began res. 10 Oct. 1925. Matric. 21 Oct. 1925.

B.A. (3rd Cl. Math. Tri. Pt I, 1926; 2nd Cl., 2nd Div., Law Tri. Pt II, 1928) 1928. M.A. 1932.
Schoolmaster.

PRASIDDHI SMITASIRI. Born 13 April 1906, at Bangkok, Siam. Guardian: Phya Bharata, Superintendent Siamese Government Students, 51 Barkston Gardens, S.W. 5. Educ. privately, with Rev. C. E. Green, B.A., Lichborough Rectory, Weedon, Northants. Adm. 6 April 1925: began res. 10 Oct. 1925. Matric. 21 Oct. 1925.

Went down after E. 1926.

Baron BRADBURY (*Sir* John Swanwick Bradbury), of Winsford, co. Chester, *G.C.B.* Adm. by invitation of the Master and Fellows ('Order Book', 19 May 1925) on his admission as Hon. LL.D. 9 June 1925.

Born 23 Sept. 1872, at Winsford, Cheshire. S. of John Bradbury (dec^d), of Winsford. Educ. at King's School, Chester; Manchester Grammar School; and Brasenose College, Oxford (Class. Schol. and Senior Hulme Exhib.; B.A. 1895; M.A. 1926; Hon. Fellow, 1926).
Entered Colonial Office, 1896; transferred to Treasury, 1897. Under-Treasurer of Natal, 1904–5. Private Sec. to Chancellor of the Exchequer (Rt Hon. H. H. Asquith, M.P.), 1905–8. Principal Clerk in Treasury, 1908–13; and First Treasury Officer of Accounts, 1908–11. Insurance Commissioner and Member of National Insurance Joint Committee, 1911–13. Joint Permanent Sec. to Treasury, 1913–19.
Principal British Delegate on Reparations Commission, Paris, 1919–25. Government Director of Anglo-Persian Oil Co., Ltd, 1925–7. Chairman, National Food Council, 1925–9. Chairman of Bankers' Clearing House Committee and President of British Bankers' Assoc., 1929–30; and again, 1935–6.
Hon. LL.D., Manchester, 1925.
Cr. C.B. 1909; K.C.B. 1913; G.C.B. 1920; 1st **Baron** Bradbury, of Winsford, co. Chester, 1925.

Rt Hon. Viscount CAVE (*Sir* George Cave), of Richmond, co. Surrey, *P.C.*, *G.C.M.G.* Adm. by invitation of the Master and Fellows ('Order Book', 19 May 1925) on his admission as Hon. LL.D. 9 June 1925.

Born 23 Feb. 1856, in London. S. of late Thomas Cave (Sheriff of London, 1863–4; M.P. for Barnstaple, 1865–80), of Richmond, Surrey. Educ. at Merchant Taylors' School, and St John's College, Oxford (Class. Schol.; B.A. 1878; M.A. 1912; Hon. Fellow, 1916; D.C.L. 1925).
Called to the Bar, Inner Temple, 9 June 1880; K.C. 1904; Bencher, 1912. Chairman, Surrey Quarter Sessions, 1894–1911. Recorder of Guildford, 1904–15. M.P., Kingston Division, 1906–18. Standing Counsel to Oxford Univ., 1913–15. Attorney-General to the Prince of Wales, 1914–15. Solicitor-General, 1915–16. Home Secretary, 1916–19. Lord High Chancellor, Oct. 1922–Jan. 1924; and again, Nov. 1924–March 1928. Counsellor of State during the King's absence abroad, 1925.
Chairman of Contraband Committee, 1915; of S. Rhodesia Commission, 1919–20; of Munitions

Enquiry Tribunal, 1921; of Voluntary Hospitals Committee, 1921; of Committee on Trade Boards, 1921–2; and of British Empire Cancer Campaign, 1924. Apptd a Lord of Appeal, 1919; and a Trustee, Beit Memorial Fellowships for Medical Research, 1925. Chancellor of Oxford Univ., 1925–8.

D.L. and Vice-Lieut., Surrey. Hon. Freeman of Boroughs of Kingston-on-Thames, Guildford and Richmond, Surrey. Hon. Freeman of the Merchant Taylors' Co. and of the Armourers' and Brasiers' Co.

Hon. D.C.L., Oxford, 1924.

Cr. Kt, 1915; 1st **Viscount** Cave, of Richmond, co. Surrey, 1918; G.C.M.G. 1921. P.C. 1915.

Died 29 March 1928 at Burnham-on-Sea, Somerset.

WILLIAM ANTHONY HEWLETT. Born 21 Feb. 1889, at Briton Ferry, Glam. S. of Daniel Hewlett (dec[d]). Educ. at Neath Road Elementary School, Briton Ferry; University Tutorial Classes; and Ruskin College, Oxford. Rec. by Board of Extra-Mural Studies. Adm. 18 June 1925: began res. 10 Oct. 1925. Matric. 21 Oct. 1925. Extra-Mural Stud.

Resided till end of E. 1927.

Engaged during 1914–19 on work of national importance in the Iron and Steel Trade.

Organiser for the Mid-Glamorgan Area of the Workers' Educational Assoc., and Tutor of the One Year Class at Neath, Glam.

JOHN ALDER CRIPPS BLUMER. Born 4 Nov. 1904, at Stafford. S. of Frederick Milnes Blumer, The Mount, Stafford. Educ. at Malvern College and St Bartholomew's Hospital. Adm. 23 June 1925: began res. 10 Oct. 1925. Matric. 21 Oct. 1925.

B.A. (Ord. degree) 1928. M.A. 1934.

Colonial Service, with appt. as Superintendent of Education, Tanganyika Territory, 1928–.

Bro. of G. F. Blumer (p. 136).

JOHN GROVE DUNNING. Born 12 Nov. 1906, at Barrow-in-Furness. S. of Elisha Dunning, 18 Milford Terrace, Hartington Street, Derby. Educ. at Derby Municipal Secondary School. Adm. 23 June 1925: began res. 10 Oct. 1925. Matric. 21 Oct. 1925.

B.A. (2nd Cl., 2nd Div., Hist. Tri. Pt I, 1927; 2nd Cl. Geog. Tri. Pt I, 1928) 1928. M.A. 1932.

Asst Master, Ulster Provincial School (Friends' School), Lisburn, 1928–32; and at Wellingborough Grammar School, 1932–. F.R.G.S. 1928.

Bro. of N. G. Dunning (p. 21).

CHARLES THOMAS STROUD. Born 5 April 1907, at Binsted, Alton, Hants. S. of Thomas Francis Augustine Stroud, Hazel Bank, Rowledge, Farnham, Surrey. Educ. at Farnham Grammar School. Adm. 23 June 1925: began res. 10 Oct. 1925. Matric. 21 Oct. 1925.

B.A. (2nd Cl. Math. Tri. Pt I, 1926; Jun. Opt. Pt II, 1928) 1928. M.A. 1932.

Asst Master, Holborn Estate Grammar School, Du Cane Road, London, W. 12, 1930–.

CHARLES ARTHUR TYLER ELLIS. Born 24 Oct. 1906, at Market Lavington, Wilts. S. of Arthur Tyler Ellis, 47 Wick Road, Brislington, Bristol. Educ. at Bristol Grammar School. Adm. 10 July 1925: began res. 10 Oct. 1925. Matric. 21 Oct. 1925.

B.A. (2nd Cl. Math. Tri. Pt I, 1926; Sen. Opt. Pt II, 1928) 1928. Kitchener Schol., 1926 (held for 2 years).

With Harrods Ltd (departmental store), Knightsbridge, London, S.W. 1, 1928–9. Afterwards engaged in advertising.

GILDART EDGAR PEMBERTON JACKSON. Born 27 July 1906, at High Legh, Cheshire. S. of Rev. Gildart Arthur Jackson (Peterhouse, M.A. 1893), St Paul's Vicarage, 8 Adamson Road, South Hampstead, N.W. 3. Educ. at Aldenham School. Adm. 13 July 1925: began res. 10 Oct. 1925. Matric. 21 Oct. 1925.

B.A. (Ord. degree) 1928.
Architect; being partner in Beresford Pite, Jackson & Partners, 1 & 2 Gray's Inn Place, Gray's Inn, W.C. 1. A.R.I.B.A. 1932.

ARTHUR CECIL HARPER. Born 17 Oct. 1905, at Stowmarket, Suffolk. S. of Henry Cecil Harper, Gower Lodge, Cedar Road, Sutton, Surrey. Educ. at Malvern College. Adm. 20 July 1925: began res. 10 Oct. 1925. Matric. 21 Oct. 1925.

B.A. (Ord. degree) 1928. M.A. 1932.
Unauthorised Clerk, London Stock Exchange; being with Atchley & Heron, 265 Gresham House, Old Broad Street, London, E.C. 2, 1934–.

JOHN CECIL LAWSON. Born 1 Feb. 1905, at Bradford, Yorks. S. of Andrew Moir Lawson, 28 Park Drive, Bradford. Educ. at Bradford Grammar School. Adm. 20 July 1925: began res. 5 Oct. 1925. Matric. 21 Oct. 1925.

B.A. (Ord. degree) 1928.
Engineer: with Douglas, Lawson & Co., Ltd (engineers and ironfounders), Birstall, nr Leeds.

HUGH RIDLEY ORMEROD. Born 7 Oct. 1906, at Wimborne, Dorset. S. of Dr Ernest William Ormerod, Beauchamp Lodge, Wimborne. Educ. at Bradfield College. Adm. 20 July 1925: began res. 5 Oct. 1925. Matric. 21 Oct. 1925.

Went down after M. 1926.
Went to S. Africa in 1927. In British S. African Police, 1928–.

JOHN HENRY PAUL PENNINGTON. Born 13 June 1906, at Stockton-on-Tees. S. of Rev. Charles George Trenchard Sale Pennington, The Vicarage, Kirkby Stephen, Westmorland. Educ. at Lincoln School. Adm. 20 July 1925: began res. 9 Oct. 1925. Matric. 21 Oct. 1925.

B.A. (2nd Cl., 2nd Div., Hist. Tri. Pt I, 1927; 2nd Cl., 1st Div., Pt II, 1928) 1928.
Asst Master, City of Oxford School, 1928–9; and at Dulwich College, 1929–.

GEOFFREY NEVEY SOUTHERDEN. Born 20 Oct. 1906, at Exeter. S. of Frank Southerden, 11 Gordon Road, Exeter. Educ. at Exeter School. Adm. 20 July 1925: began res. 5 Oct. 1925. Matric. 21 Oct. 1925.

B.A. (2nd Cl. Intercoll. Exam. in Mech. Sci., 1927; adm. to degree without further exam.) 1928. M.A. 1932. Exhib. for Mech. Sciences, £30, 1926; re-elected, 1927.
Railway Clerk with the Great Western Railway Co., 1928–. A.M.Inst.T. 1936.

GEORGE TRYPANIS. Born 13 Feb. 1907, at Alexandria, Egypt. S. of Emmanuel Trypanis (dec^d). Guardian: Alexander Milne, University School, Hastings. Educ. at University School, Hastings. Adm. 20 July 1925: began res. 4 Oct. 1925. Matric. 21 Oct. 1925.

B.A. (3rd Cl. Mech. Sci. Tri., 1928) 1928.
Asst Engineer, Electric Transport Co., Athens.

WILFRID ISAAC DAVID. Born 2 Oct. 1907, at Bombay. S. of Isaac David, I. David and Co., Ltd, Fort, Bombay. Educ. at Cathedral and John Connon High

School, Bombay; and privately, with U. Gilder, M.A., c/o Cathedral High School, Bombay. Adm. 11 Aug. 1925: began res. 9 Oct. 1925. Matric. 21 Oct. 1925.

B.A. (3rd Cl. Econ. Tri. Pt I, 1927; standard for Ord. degree, Hist. Tri. Pt II, 1928) 1928.
Novelist and journalist.
Author:
    Monsoon; a novel. London (1933).

HUGH GRAHAM SOULSBY. Born 22 Dec. 1904, at Gateshead-on-Tyne. S. of Rev. Joseph Graham Soulsby, Bourne House, Burnopfield, Co. Durham. Educ. at Armstrong College, Newcastle-on-Tyne (B.A. degree, Durham Univ.). Adm. 17 Aug. 1925: began res. 10 Oct. 1925. Matric. 21 Oct. 1925. Aff. Stud.

B.A. (1st Cl., 2nd Div., Hist. Tri. Pt II, 1926; Cert. of Dilig. Study, 1927) 1927. Schol.* of £60, 1926. *Commonwealth Fund Fellowship, Johns Hopkins Univ.*, 1928. Probationer, Colonial Service, M. 1932 to E. 1933.
Ph.D., Johns Hopkins Univ., 1931. Colonial Service, Uganda, 1932–; now (1936) with appt. as Asst District Officer.
Author:
    The right of search and the slave trade in Anglo-American relations, 1814–62. (Johns Hopkins Univ. Studies in Hist. and Polit. Science, 51, ii.) Baltimore, 1933.

EDGAR CLARENCE HERTEN. Born 11 June 1906, at Buenos Aires, Argentine Republic. S. of Gustavo Herten, Villanueva 1348, Belgrano, Buenos Aires. Educ. at Belgrano School. Adm. 4 Sept. 1925: began res. 10 Oct. 1925. Matric. 21 Oct. 1925.

B.A. (Ord. degree) 1929. M.A. 1932. B.Chir. 1934. M.B. 1937.
M.R.C.S., L.R.C.P. 1933. Supervisor of Out Patient Surgery, London Hospital, in 1938.
Assumed the surname of HERTEN-GREAVEN on attaining his majority, 11 June 1927.
Bro. of W. G. Herten, afterwards Herten-Greaven (p. 42).

CHURCHILL SATTERLEE. Born 25 May 1904, at Lenox, Mass. S. of Churchill Satterlee (decd) and Mrs Satterlee, Lenox, Mass. Educ. at St Paul's School, Concord, New Hampshire; and Harvard Univ. (Harvard College). Adm. 14 Sept. 1925: began res. 10 Oct. 1925. Matric. 21 Oct. 1925.

Went down during E. 1926.
A.B., Harvard, 1926.
Was with the New York Guaranteed Mortgage Protection Corporation, New York, in 1935.

JOHN HARVARD-WATTS. Born 8 March 1907, at Hurstpierpoint, Sussex. S. of Rev. Samuel Harvard Harvard-Watts, Blickling Rectory, Aylsham, Norfolk. Educ. at St Edward's School, Oxford; and privately. Adm. 8 Oct. 1925: began res. 12 Oct. 1925. Matric. 21 Oct. 1925.

Went down after E. 1927.
Schoolmaster.

LAURENCE NANSON HENDERSON. Born 24 May 1907, at Rio de Janeiro, Brazil. S. of Charles Henderson, 295 Cosme Velho, Aguas Férreas, Rio de Janeiro. Educ. at Haileybury College. Adm. 8 Oct. 1925: began res. 10 Oct. 1925. Matric. 21 Oct. 1925.

Went down after E. 1928.

AUSTIN ROBERT MILLER. Born 15 Nov. 1906, at Isleworth, Middlesex. S. of Thomas Hugh Miller (Peterhouse, B.A. 1878), Lansdowne, Nairn. Educ.

at St Paul's School. Adm. 8 Oct. 1925: began res. 10 Oct. 1925. Matric. 21 Oct. 1925.

> Died 12 Nov. 1926, whilst still in residence, from meningitis.
> Trial Cap for Rowing, 1925.

CECIL ANDRÉ POLLARD. Born 13 Dec. 1902, at Bridgwater, Somerset. S. of Henry William Pollard [dec^d?] and Mrs Pollard, Oakfield, Wembdon, Bridgwater. Educ. privately. Rec. by J. Jenkins, M.A., Weston-super-Mare; and Major S. A. Hughes, Holt, Norfolk. Adm. 8 Oct. 1925: began res. 10 Oct. 1925. Matric. 21 Oct. 1925.

> B.A. (3rd Cl. Engl. Tri. (a), 1927; P.S. Exam. French, 1929) 1929. M.A. 1933.

CHARLES WILFRED ROBBINS. Born 27 May 1907, at New Barnet, Herts. S. of William Joseph Robbins, Holmwood, Hadley Wood, Middlesex. Educ. at Aldenham School. Adm. 8 Oct. 1925: began res. 10 Oct. 1925. Matric. 21 Oct. 1925.

> B.A. (Ord. degree) 1928. M.A. 1932.
> Solicitor (adm. June 1932); being partner in Robbins, Olivey & Lake, 218 Strand, London, W.C. 2, and Hadley Wood.

HENRY KENDALL ROBINSON. Born 15 Sept. 1906, at Penrith, Cumberland. S. of Jonathan William Robinson (dec^d). Guardian: Dr Daniel Charles Edington, Birbeck House, Penrith. Educ. at St Bees School. Adm. 8 Oct. 1925: began res. 10 Oct. 1925. Matric. 21 Oct. 1925.

> B.A. (3rd Cl. Hist. Tri. Pt I, 1927; standard for Ord. degree, Law Tri. Pt II, 1928) 1928. Tropical African Services Course, M. 1928 to E. 1929.
> Colonial Service, Nigeria, 1929–; now (1934) with appt. as Asst District Officer.

STANHOPE PETER ALEXANDER SANDBERG. Born 12 June 1906, at Limpsfield, Surrey. S. of Christer Peter Sandberg, C.B.E., Lewins, Crockham Hill, Kent. Educ. at Harrow School; and privately. Adm. 8 Oct. 1925: began res. 11 Oct. 1925. Matric. 21 Oct. 1925.

> B.A. (Ord. degree) 1928.
> Metallurgical Engineer with Messrs Sandberg, 40 Grosvenor Gardens, London, S.W. 1.

GEORGE RAYMOND WEBSTER. Born 21 March 1907, at Porth, Glam. S. of George Webster, Bryngarw, Porth. Educ. at Dean Close School, Cheltenham. Adm. 8 Oct. 1925: began res. 10 Oct. 1925. Matric. 21 Oct. 1925.

> B.A. (Ord. degree) 1928. M.A. 1932.
> Cuddesdon Theol. Coll., 1929. Ordained d. 1930, p. 1931 Oxford. C. of St Mary Virg. (in charge of St Saviour, 1935–), Reading, Dio. Oxford, 1930–.

JOHN LAWRENCE WOOLF. Born 20 Aug. 1906, at Sandbach, Cheshire. S. of Edward Samuel Woolf (dec^d) and Mrs Woolf, The White House, Ashley, Market Drayton, Staffs. Educ. at Malvern College; and privately. Adm. 8 Oct. 1925: began res. 10 Oct. 1925. Matric. 21 Oct. 1925.

> B.A. (Ord. degree) 1928.
> Entered the Regular Army: 2nd Lieut., The Welch Regt, 1929: resigned, 1931. Cotton planting with the Sudan Plantations Syndicate, Ltd, 1931–3.
> He matric. as John Laurence WOOLF.
> Bro. of E. H. Woolf (p. 98).

LOUDOUN JAMES MACLEAN, Flt Lieut., R.A.F. Born 1 Feb. 1893, at Acton, Middlesex. S. of Loudoun Francis MacLean, C.I.E. (dec^d), and Mrs MacLean, 9 Longfield Road, Ealing, W. 5. Educ. at Fettes College, and R.M.A., Woolwich. Rec. by Air Ministry. Adm. 21 July 1925: began res. 5 Oct. 1925. Matric. 21 Oct. 1925.

B.A. (Ord. degree; all. 3 terms as Commiss. Off.) 1928.
⚔ 1914–19. Capt., R.E.; attd R.F.C.; Hon. Major, R.A.F. (W.) *M.C. and Bar. M.*
Retired from the R.A.F. with rank of Sqdn Ldr on 1 April 1935.

CHARLES EDMUND MAITLAND, Flt Lieut., R.A.F. Born 3 July 1899, at Southsea. S. of Surgeon Capt. Percy Edmund Maitland, R.N., 3 Victoria Park Road, Heavitree, Exeter. Educ. at Felsted School, and R.M.A., Woolwich. Rec. by Air Ministry. Adm. 21 July 1925: began res. 5 Oct. 1925. Matric. 21 Oct. 1925.

B.A. (2nd Cl. Mech. Sci. Tri., 1927; all. 3 terms as Commiss. Off.) 1928. *John Bernard Seely Prize,* 1927.
⚔ 1917–19. Lieut., R.A.F. *D.F.C.*
Wing Cdr (1937–), R.A.F. A.F.C. 1932.

DAVID BERNARD KENNEDY YOUNG, 2nd Lieut., R.E. Born 22 May 1905, at Murree, Punjab, India. S. of Lieut.-Col. David Coley Young, I.A. (dec^d), and Mrs Young, Luxor House, Sands Road, Paignton, Devon. Educ. at Wellington College; R.M.A., Woolwich; and S.M.E., Chatham. Rec. by War Office. Adm. 7 Aug. 1925: began res. 5 Oct. 1925. Matric. 21 Oct. 1925.

Resided till end of E. 1926.
Promoted Lieut., R.E. 1927. Died 13 Feb. 1928 at Roorkee, United Provinces, India, as the result of an accident.

RAJ NARAIN BHATIA. Born 28 Dec. 1907, at Jaunpur, United Provinces, India. S. of Prof. Ram Narain Bhatia, Radice Road, Butlerganj, Lucknow. Educ. at Lucknow Christian College. Rec. by S. L. Bhatia, M.D. (Peterhouse), Prof. of Physiology and Dean of Grant Medical College, Bombay. Adm. 29 March 1926: began res. 20 April 1926. Matric. 4 May 1926.

B.A. (Ord. degree) 1929.
M.R.C.S., L.R.C.P. 1932. In practice at Lucknow.
Nephew of his recommender, S. L. Bhatia (*Walker*, p. 676).

JAMES MACK GERSTLEY. Born 11 Nov. 1907, in London. S. of James Gerstley, 61 Great Cumberland Place, W. 1. Educ. at Cheltenham College. Adm. 4 Sept. 1925: began res. 9 Oct. 1926. Matric. 21 Oct. 1926.

2nd Cl., 2nd Div., Mod. & Med. Lang. Tri. Pt I, *f, g*, 1927; 2nd Cl., 1st Div., Hist. Tri. Pt II, 1928. Went down after E. 1928.
Was with the Great Western Electro-Chemical Co., San Francisco, California, in 1931.

WILLIAM ECCLESTON WELLS. Born 9 Nov. 1906, at Bilston, Staffs. S. of John Wells, Wellington House, Bilston. Educ. at Ellesmere College; and privately. Adm. 7 Oct. 1925: began res. 4 Oct. 1926. Matric. 21 Oct. 1926.

B.A. (Ord. degree) 1930. M.A., B.Chir. 1934. M.B. 1937.
In practice at Bilston.

FREDERICK JAMES PORTER. Born 22 Jan. 1908, at Lytham, Lancs. S. of John Porter, 3 Bazley Road, Ansdell, Lytham. Educ. at King Edward VII. School, Lytham. Adm. 9 Nov. 1925: began res. 9 Oct. 1926. Matric. 21 Oct. 1926.

B.A. (2nd Cl., 2nd Div., Hist. Tri. Pt I, 1928; 2nd Cl. Geog. Tri. Pt I, 1929) 1929. M.A. 1933.
Asst Master, Allhallows School, Honiton, 1929–34; and at Wallasey Grammar School, 1934–.

CHANDLER BRAGDON. Born 15 Dec. 1907, at Rochester, N.Y. S. of Claude Bragdon, The Shelton, 49th Street and Lexington Avenue, New York. Educ. at Kent School, Conn.; and Princeton Univ. Adm. 2 Dec. 1925: began res. 8 Oct. 1926. Matric. 21 Oct. 1926.

B.A. (2nd Cl., 1st Div., Hist. Tri. Pt I, 1928; 2nd Cl., 2nd Div., Pt II, 1929) 1929. M.A. 1934.
History Master, Kent School, Conn., 1929–30. Private Tutor, Rochester, N.Y., 1930–3. Instructor in English and English History, Berry College, Mt Berry, Georgia, 1934.

BURTON STACEY HAWKE. Born 5 June 1906, at Leyton, Essex. S. of Burton Hawke, 8 Lyndhurst Drive, Leyton, E. 10. Educ. at Forest School, Walthamstow; and King's College, London (B.A. degree). Rec. by Prof. F. J. C. Hearnshaw, M.A., LL.M. (Peterhouse), King's College, London. Adm. 7 Dec. 1925: began res. 9 Oct. 1926. Matric. 21 Oct. 1926. Aff. Stud.

B.A. (2nd Cl., 1st Div., Hist. Tri. Pt I, 1927; 2nd Cl., 1st Div., Pt II, 1928) 1928. M.A. 1933.
Asst Master, Ryde Grammar School, Isle of Wight, 1928–30; and at Coatham School, Redcar, 1930–.

JAMES METCALF. Born 23 Oct. 1907, in London. S. of Thomas John Metcalf, St Helens, Thorpe Bay Gardens, Thorpe Bay, Essex. Educ. at Stonyhurst College. Adm. 7 Dec. 1925: began res. 5 Oct. 1926. Matric. 21 Oct. 1926.

B.A. (3rd Cl. Nat. Sci. Tri. Pt I, 1928; 3rd Cl. Pt II (Pathol.), 1929) 1929. M.A., M.B., B.Chir. 1934. M.R.C.S., L.R.C.P. 1932. In practice at Wimbledon.
Bro. of D. A. Metcalf (p. 86).

CHRISTOPHER WOODFORDE. Born 29 Nov. 1907, at Ashwell, Baldock, Herts. S. of Robert Edmond Heighes Woodforde, Ashwell, Baldock. Educ. at King's School, Bruton. Adm. 19 Dec. 1925: began res. 9 Oct. 1926. Matric. 21 Oct. 1926.

B.A. (2nd Cl., 2nd Div., Hist. Tri. Pt I, 1928; P.S. Exam. Bible, 1929) 1929. M.A. 1933.
Wells Theol. Coll., 1929. Ordained d. 1930 St Edmundsbury and Ipswich for Norwich, p. 1932 Lincoln. C. of St Margaret w. St Nicholas, King's Lynn, 1930–2; Louth w. Welton le Wolde, 1932–4; Drayton w. Hellesdon, 1934–6; R. of Exford, Dio. Bath and Wells, 1936–. F.S.A. 1937.
Author:
A guide to the medieval glass in Lincoln Cathedral. London (1933).
The medieval glass of St. Peter Mancroft, Norwich. Norwich [1935].
Stained and painted glass in England. (*Pages from the Past.*) London (1937).

FRANK ETHERINGTON POOL. Born 21 April 1907, at Cheltenham. S. of Frederick William Pool, Homelea, Camelsdale, Haslemere, Surrey. Educ. at Farnham Grammar School. Adm. 22 Dec. 1925: began res. 11 Oct. 1926. Matric. 21 Oct. 1926. Entrance Schol., Maths, £80.

B.A. (1st Cl. Math. Tri. Pt I, 1927; standard of Ord. degree, Pt II, 1929) 1929.

GODFREY LOUIS BARBER. Born 1 Nov. 1906, at 32 Gunter Grove, S.W. 10. S. of Henry Albert Barber, 36 Fernshaw Road, S.W. 10. Educ. at City of London School. Adm. 22 Dec. 1925: began res. 9 Oct. 1926. Matric. 21 Oct. 1926. Entrance Schol., Classics, £60.

B.A. (1st Cl. Class. Tri. Pt I (g, l), 1928; 1st Cl. Pt II, 1929) 1929. M.A. 1933. Lady Mary Ramsey Schol., 1928. Leaf Stud., £50, 1929. *Prince Consort Prize*, 1934.
Asst Master, Westminster School, 1929–.
Author:
The historian Ephorus. (*Prince Consort Prize*, 1934.) Cambridge, 1935.

DEREK ROLAND WIGRAM. Born 18 March 1908, at Bromley, Kent. S. of Roland Lewis Wigram (dec^d) and Mrs Wigram, 16 Porchester Square, W. 2. Educ. at Marlborough College. Adm. 22 Dec. 1925: began res. 9 Oct. 1926. Matric. 21 Oct. 1926. Entrance Schol., Classics, £60.

B.A. (2nd Cl. Class. Tri. Pt I, 1928; 1st Cl. Pt II, 1929) 1929. M.A. 1933. Exhib., 1928. Re-elected to title of Scholar, 1929.
Asst Master, Whitgift School, Croydon, 1929–.

WILLIAM EWART MATTHEWS. Born 29 Aug. 1907, at Brondesbury, Middlesex. S. of William Henry Ewart Matthews, 41 Westbury Road, Wembley. Educ. at Harrow County School. Adm. 22 Dec. 1925: began res. 10 Oct. 1926. Matric. 21 Oct. 1926. Entrance Schol., Nat. Sciences, £60.

B.A. (1st Cl. Nat. Sci. Tri. Pt I, 1928; 1st Cl. Pt II (Physics), 1929) 1929. M.A. 1936. Kitchener Schol., 1926 (held for 3 years). Gisborne Schol., 1928.
Asst Master, Weymouth College, 1929; and at Shrewsbury School, 1930–.

ALFRED ERIC ECCLESTONE. Born 2 April 1908, at Alsager, Cheshire. S. of Alfred Ecclestone, Lancaster Road, Newcastle, Staffs. Educ. at Newcastle-under-Lyme High School. Adm. 22 Dec. 1925: began res: 9 Oct. 1926. Matric. 21 Oct. 1926. Entrance Schol. (Lady Ward), History, £60.

B.A. (1st Cl., 2nd Div., Hist. Tri. Pt I, 1928; 1st Cl., 2nd Div., Pt II, 1929) 1929. 2nd Cl., 1st Div., Engl. Tri. Pt I, 1930. M.A. 1937. Re-elected to Lady Ward Schol., 1928; and again, 1929. Leaf Stud., £25, 1929.
Asst Master, Chesterfield Grammar School, 1931–4; and at Whitgift Middle School, Croydon, 1934–.

LESLIE LEWIS JAMES DREW. Born 19 Jan. 1907, in London. S. of Lewis James Drew, 52 Marville Road, Fulham, S.W. 6. Educ. at Sloane School, Chelsea. Adm. 22 Dec. 1925: began res. 9 Oct. 1926. Matric. 21 Oct. 1926. Entrance Schol., History, £60.

B.A. (1st Cl., 2nd Div., Hist. Tri. Pt I, 1928; 1st Cl., 2nd Div., Pt II, 1929) 1929. M.A. 1933. Cosin Schol., 1928.
Asst Master, Corinth College, Cheltenham, 1929–31. Lecturer in History, Saltley College, Birmingham, 1931–.

ARTHUR CYRIL PAGET. Born 3 Sept. 1907, at Witcombe, nr Gloucester. S. of Harry Paget, Witcombe. Educ. at Crypt Grammar School, Gloucester. Adm. 22 Dec. 1925: began res. 9 Oct. 1926. Matric. 21 Oct. 1926. Entrance Exhib., Maths, £40.

B.A. (1st Cl. Math. Tri. Pt I, 1927; Sen. Opt. Pt II, 1929) 1929. Ironmongers' Co.'s Exhib., 1927 (held for 2 years). Schol.†, 1927. Blyth Schol., 1928.
Asst Master, Edinburgh Institution, 1929–30; and at Crypt Grammar School, Gloucester, 1930–.

NORMAN LESLIE VINCENT BECK. Born 31 May 1907, at Northampton. S. of Albert Edward Beck, 25 Ardington Road, Northampton. Educ. at Northampton Town and County School. Adm. 22 Dec. 1925: began res. 8 Oct. 1926. Matric. 21 Oct. 1926. Entrance Exhib., Maths, £40.

B.A. (1st Cl. Math. Tri. Pt I, 1927; Sen. Opt. Pt II, 1929) 1929. Schol.†, 1927. Exhib., 1928.
H.M. Inspector of Taxes.

RONALD PATRICK RICHARDS. Born 17 March 1908, at Santos, Brazil. S. of Arthur Richards, Caixa 752, Santos. Educ. at Weymouth College. Adm.

22 Dec. 1925: began res. 9 Oct. 1926. Matric. 21 Oct. 1926. Entrance Exhib., Classics, £40.

B.A. (2nd Cl. Class. Tri. Pt I, 1928; 2nd Cl. Pt II, 1929) 1929. Exhib., 1928.

ROBERT ARTHUR HUMPHREYS. Born 6 June 1907, at Lincoln. S. of Robert Humphreys, School House, Rosemary Lane, Lincoln. Educ. at Lincoln School. Adm. 22 Dec. 1925: began res. 9 Oct. 1926. Matric. 21 Oct. 1926. Entrance Exhib., History, £40.

B.A. (1st Cl., 2nd Div., Hist. Tri. Pt I, 1928; 1st Cl., 2nd Div., Pt II, 1929) 1929. Ph.D. 1932. M.A. 1933. Schol.†, 1927. Whitgift Schol., 1928. Leaf Stud., £25, 1929. Hugo de Balsham Grant (for research in History), £60, 1929. Adm. Research Stud. as from Oct. 1929. *Commonwealth Fund Fellowship, Michigan Univ.*, 1930.
Asst Lecturer in American History, University College, London, 1932–5; and Lecturer, 1935–. F.R.Hist.Soc. 1938.

GEORGE HENRY BRINKWORTH. Born 12 April 1907, at Ramsey, Isle of Man. S. of George Arthur Brinkworth, 25 Park Road, Nailsworth, Glos. Educ. at Strand School, Brixton Hill, S.W. 2. Adm. 20 Jan. 1926: began res. 9 Oct. 1926. Matric. 21 Oct. 1926.

B.A. (2nd Cl., 1st Div., Hist. Tri. Pt I, 1928; 2nd Cl. Geog. Tri. Pt I, 1929) 1929. Dipl. in Geog. 1929. Leaf Grant, 1929.
Asst Master, Bishop Wordsworth's School, Salisbury, 1930; at Hastings Grammar School, 1930–4; and at Holt School, Liverpool, 1934–.

MAX LAMPRAY MORTON. Born 31 March 1907, at Hengrave, nr Bury St Edmunds. S. of Arthur Spence Morton, 170 Woodbridge Road, Ipswich. Educ. at Ipswich School. Adm. 2 Feb. 1926: began res. 10 Oct. 1926. Matric. 21 Oct. 1926.

B.A. (2nd Cl., 2nd Div., Hist. Tri. Pt I, 1928; 2nd Cl., 2nd Div., Pt II, 1929) 1929.
Asst Master, St Christopher School, Letchworth, 1929–.
Bro. of A. L. Morton (p. 67).

JOHN BERNARD KENYON. Born 6 April 1907, at Stockport. S. of Harold James Kenyon, The Croft, Bramhall Park Road, Bramhall, Cheshire. Educ. at Manchester Grammar School. Adm. 25 Feb. 1926: began res. 9 Oct. 1926. Matric. 21 Oct. 1926.

B.A. (2nd Cl. Class. Tri. Pt I, 1928; 3rd Cl. Pt II, 1929) 1929. M.A. 1933.
Asst Master, Taunton School, 1929–.

FREDERIK MAY STUART TEGNER. Born 8 March 1908, at Yokohama. S. of Frederik May Tegner (decd) and Mrs Tegner, Tangley, Underhill Park Road, Reigate. Educ. at Clifton College. Adm. 26 Feb. 1926: began res. 10 Oct. 1926. Matric. 21 Oct. 1926.

B.A. (Ord. degree) 1929.
With the Ethyl Export Corporation, London, 1931–.

GEOFFREY GOODGAMES ARMSTRONG. Born 23 Sept. 1907, at Eynesbury, St Neots, Hunts. S. of Thomas Armstrong, 31 Kimbolton Road, Bedford. Educ. at Bedford Modern School. Adm. 26 March 1926: began res. 9 Oct. 1926. Matric. 21 Oct. 1926.

B.A. (2nd Cl., 2nd Div., Hist. Tri. Pt I, 1928; 3rd Cl. Geog. Tri. Pt I, 1929) 1929. M.A. 1935.
Asst Master, King's School, Ely, 1929–30; and at Harrow County School, 1931–.

GEORGE FREDERIC CHESTER DOUGHTY. Born 7 Sept. 1908, at Poringland Rectory, Norwich. S. of Rev. Frederic Ernest Doughty (Peterhouse, M.A. 1893), Martlesham Rectory, Woodbridge, Suffolk. Educ. at Repton School. Adm. 26 March 1926: began res. 9 Oct. 1926. Matric. 21 Oct. 1926.

Went down after M. 1926.
Was in the Merchant Service, 1927–32.

JOHN CAMPIN PEEKE NEWMAN. Born 5 June 1906, at Bishop's Stortford. S. of John Campin Newman, Thorley House, Bishop's Stortford. Educ. at Leys School. Adm. 26 March 1926: began res. 11 Oct. 1926. Matric. 21 Oct. 1926.

Went down after E. 1927.
On the London Stock Exchange, 1929–.

RICHARD GEORGE WARWICK ROSS. Born 25 May 1908, at Hornsey, Middlesex. S. of James Ross, 2 Firs Avenue, Muswell Hill, N. 10. Educ. at City of London School. Adm. 26 March 1926: began res. 9 Oct. 1926. Matric. 21 Oct. 1926.

B.A. (3rd Cl. Law Tri. Pt I, 1928; standard for Ord. degree, Pt II, 1929) 1929. M.A. 1935.
Solicitor (adm. Jan. 1933); being partner in Kingsley Wood, Williams & Murphy, 15 Walbrook, E.C. 4, etc., London.
Bro. of E. J. L. Ross (p. 55).

CHARLES EDGAR WARE. Born 26 Oct. 1908, at Exeter. S. of Edgar Felix Ware, 4 Baring Place, Exeter. Educ. at Exeter School. Adm. 26 March 1926: began res. 9 Oct. 1926. Matric. 21 Oct. 1926.

B.A. (3rd Cl. Nat. Sci. Tri. Pt I, 1929) 1929. M.A. 1933.
Chartered Surveyor: Charles E. Ware & Son, 18 Bedford Circus, Exeter. P.A.S.I., A.A.I.

JOHN CHARLES BUCKLEY. Born 30 June 1907, at Nottingham. S. of Dr James Charles Buckley, Southfields, Bramcote, Notts. Educ. at Eastbourne College. Adm. 29 March 1926: began res. 4 Oct. 1926. Matric. 21 Oct. 1926.

B.A. (Ord. degree) 1929.
M.R.C.S., L.R.C.P. 1934. In practice in London. Capt. (1938–), R.A.M.C. (T.A.).

PETER GLANVILLE NOTLEY. Born 30 May 1908, at Little Common, nr Bexhill, Sussex. S. of Lewis Glanville Notley, 2 Riverside, Barrackpore, India. Guardian in England: Arthur Hunter, Sardinia House, 52 Lincoln's Inn Fields, W.C. 2. Educ. at Clifton College. Rec. by N. Whately, M.A., Head Master, and R. P. Keigwin, M.A. (Peterhouse), House Master. Adm. 29 March 1926: began res. 10 Oct. 1926. Matric. 21 Oct. 1926.

Went down after E. 1928.

ANDREW PAUL. Born 19 Jan. 1907, at Helensburgh, Dumbartonshire. S. of Henry Stoddart Paul, Levenford Works, Dumbarton. Educ. at Trinity College, Glenalmond. Adm. 29 March 1926: began res. 9 Oct. 1926. Matric. 21 Oct. 1926.

B.A. (2nd Cl., 2nd Div., Hist. Tri. Pt I, 1928; 2nd Cl., 2nd Div., Pt II, 1929) 1929.
Sudan Political Service, 1929–.

LESLIE ROBERT PROCTER. Born 24 July 1907, at Penang, Straits Settlements. S. of William Dilcock Procter, Eastern Extension Telegraph Co., Peking,

China. Educ. at Dulwich College. Adm. 29 March 1926: began res. 9 Oct. 1926. Matric. 21 Oct. 1926.

> B.A. (3rd Cl. Hist. Tri. Pt I, 1928; 3rd Cl. Law Tri. Pt II, 1929) 1929.
> Was with C. R. Andrews (Motors) Ltd, 50 Berkeley Street, London, W. 1, 1929–31.
> Bro. of W. K. Procter (p. 96).

JOHN FERGUSON SANDERSON. Born 24 Jan. 1908, at Kilmacolm, Renfrewshire. S. of John Martin Sanderson, Linthill, Lilliesleaf, Roxburghshire. Educ. at Loretto School. Rec. by N. K. Barber, M.C., B.A., LL.B. (Peterhouse), Asst Master. Adm. 29 March 1926: began res. 8 Oct. 1926. Matric. 21 Oct. 1926.

> B.A. (Ord. degree) 1929. M.A. 1934.
> Company Director in Glasgow. 2nd Lieut., T.A. Res. of Officers.

ROBERT DAVIE WHITTINGHAM. Born 26 Dec. 1907, at Knighton Vicarage, Leicester. S. of Rt Rev. Lord Bishop of St Edmundsbury and Ipswich (Peterhouse, D.D. 1923), The Bishop's House, Ipswich. Educ. at Oundle School. Adm. 29 March 1926: began res. 9 Oct. 1926. Matric. 21 Oct. 1926.

> B.A. (2nd Cl. Math. Tri. Pt I, 1927; 2nd Cl., 2nd Div., Engl. Tri. Pt I, 1929) 1929.
> Solicitor (adm. Feb. 1933); practising at Newport, Isle of Wight.
> Bro. of A. B. Whittingham (p. 47).

RICHARD EDWARD BLACK, 2nd Lieut., R.E. Born 3 Nov. 1906, at Calcutta. S. of Colonel James Alexander Black, M.B.E., I.M.S. (dec᷊d), and Mrs Black, M.B.E., 4 Albyn Terrace, Aberdeen. Educ. at R.N.C. Osborne and Dartmouth; and R.M.A., Woolwich. Rec. by War Office. Adm. 21 April 1926: began res. 24 Oct. 1926. Matric. 26 Nov. 1926.

> B.A. (3rd Cl. Mech. Sci. Tri., 1928; all 3 terms as Commiss. Off.) 1928.
> Capt. (1937–), R.E.

ALLEN EDWARD WHITING. Born 18 Nov. 1904, at Philadelphia, Pa. S. of Allen Edward Whiting, 320 North 13th Street, Philadelphia. Educ. at St Paul's School, Concord, New Hampshire; and Yale Univ. (Yale College, Ph.B. degree). Adm. 23 April 1926: began res. 9 Oct. 1926. Matric. 21 Oct. 1926. Aff. Stud.

> B.A. (3rd Cl. Engl. Tri. Pt I, 1928) 1928.
> Half-Blue: Swimming, 1927, 1928. Represented Cambridge v. Oxford at Ice Hockey, 1926, 1927 (and was Captain, 1927–8).
> Killed 4 July 1929 in a motor accident at Radnor, Pa.
> Bro. of W. Whiting (p. 145).

JOHN GRAHAME DOUGLAS CLARK, subsequently **Bye-Fellow**. Born 28 July 1907, at Shortlands, Kent. S. of Charles Douglas Clark (dec᷊d) and Mrs Clark, The Veranda, Seaford, Sussex. Educ. at Marlborough College. Adm. 22 May 1926: began res. 9 Oct. 1926. Matric. 21 Oct. 1926.

> B.A. (2nd Cl., 1st Div., Hist. Tri. Pt I, 1928; 1st Cl. Archaeol. & Anthropol. Tri., Sec. A, 1930) 1930.
> M.A., Ph.D. 1933. Adm. Research Stud. as from Oct. 1930. Hugo de Balsham Stud. (for research in Archaeology), £100, 1930; re-elected, £80, 1931.
> **Bye-Fellow**, 1932–5.
> Asst Lecturer in Faculty of Archaeology and Anthropology, 1936–. F.S.A. 1933.
> Author:
>> *The Mesolithic age in Britain.* Cambridge, 1932.
>> *The Mesolithic settlement of northern Europe: a study of the food-gathering peoples of northern Europe during the early post-glacial period.* Cambridge, 1936.
>> And contributor to vol. 1 of 'Cambridgeshire and the Isle of Ely' in *The Victoria History of the Counties of England.* London, 1938.
> Editor (1935–):
>> *Proceedings of the Prehistoric Society.* Cambridge.

ALLAN FREDERICK REYNOLDS CARLING. Born 15 March 1907, at Stevenage, Herts. S. of Frederick Reynolds Carling, Bedwell Croft, Stevenage. Educ. at Aldenham School. Adm. 22 June 1926: began res. 10 Oct. 1926. Matric. 21 Oct. 1926.

B.A. (3rd Cl. Engl. Tri. Pt I, 1928; 3rd Cl. Econ. Tri. Pt II, 1930) 1930. M.A. 1933.
Editor of *The Granta*, E. and M. 1929.
With the Southdown Motor Services Ltd. A.M.Inst.T. 1938.

RONALD RADCLIFFE. Born 21 April 1906, at Liverpool. S. of Harold Radcliffe, 8 St John's Road, Wallasey, Cheshire. Educ. at Liscard High School, Wallasey, and Liverpool Univ. (B.Sc. degree). Rec. by Prof. J. C. Burkill, M.A., Liverpool Univ. (*later* Fellow and Tutor of Peterhouse). Adm. 26 June 1926: began res. 9 Oct. 1926. Matric. 21 Oct. 1926. Aff. Stud.

B.A. (Sen. Opt. Math. Tri. Pt II (*b*), 1927; Cert. of Dilig. Study, 1928) 1928.

HENDRICK DENNIS CHIGNELL. Born 14 May 1907, at Chester. S. of Rev. Hendrick Chignell, Northenden Rectory, Manchester. Educ. at St John's School, Leatherhead. Adm. 2 July 1926: began res. 9 Oct. 1926. Matric. 21 Oct. 1926.

B.A. (3rd Cl. Hist. Tri. Pt I, 1928; 3rd Cl. Pt II, 1929) 1929. Probationer, Colonial Service, M. 1929 to E. 1930.
Colonial Service, Uganda, 1930–; now (1935) with appt. as Asst District Officer.

FREDERICK GEORGE FRANK DRAKE. Born 22 May 1908, at Heavitree, Devon. S. of Wilfred Drake, 1 Holland Park Road, Kensington, W. 14. Educ. at Southgate County School. Adm. 2 July 1926: began res. 9 Oct. 1926. Matric. 21 Oct. 1926.

B.A. (2nd Cl., 2nd Div., Econ. Tri. Pt I, 1928; 3rd Cl. Pt II, 1929) 1929.
Chartered Accountant; being with Price, Waterhouse & Co., 3 Frederick's Place, Old Jewry, London, E.C. 2. A.C.A. 1933.

PERCY HALFORD GENT. Born 7 Aug. 1908, at Newcastle-on-Tyne. S. of Henry Gent, 20 Queen's Road, Harrogate. Educ. at Clifton College. Adm. 2 July 1926: began res. 8 Oct. 1926. Matric. 21 Oct. 1926.

B.A. (3rd Cl. Law Tri. Pt I, 1928; standard for Ord. degree, Pt II, 1929) 1929. LL.B. 1930.
With the London and North Eastern Railway Co. (Traffic Dept), 1932–.

WHITFIELD AVA AYNSLEY GREENWELL. Born 8 Aug. 1907, at Stanner's Hill Manor, Chobham, Surrey. S. of Major Aynsley Eyre Greenwell, Summers Place, Billingshurst, Sussex. Educ. at Harrow School. Adm. 2 July 1926: began res. 10 Oct. 1926. Matric. 21 Oct. 1926.

Went down after E. 1929.
Insurance Broker, with Sedgwick, Collins & Co., Ltd, 7 Gracechurch Street, London, E.C. 3, 1929–; also Managing Director of Caledonian Romana (Insurance Co.), Calea Victorici 2, Bucharest.

GORDON WILFRED PINK. Born 6 Nov. 1906, at Brockley, London. S. of Rev. Arthur Penrhyn Stanley Pink, The Rectory, Woodchester, Stroud, Glos. Educ. at St John's School, Leatherhead. Adm. 2 July 1926: began res. 10 Oct. 1926. Matric. 21 Oct. 1926.

B.A. (3rd Cl. Hist. Tri. Pt I, 1928; 3rd Cl. Geog. Tri. Pt I, 1929) 1929. M.A. 1935.

JAMES BREMNER DOW. Born 6 Oct. 1905, at Edinburgh. S. of James Dow, 10 Queen's Crescent, Edinburgh. Educ. at George Watson's College, Edinburgh; and Edinburgh Univ. (M.A. degree). Adm. 12 Aug. 1926: began res. 8 Oct. 1926. Matric. 21 Oct. 1926. Aff. Stud.

B.A. (Sen. Opt. Math. Tri. Pt II, 1928) 1928. Schol.† for Maths, 1927.
Engaged in actuarial work.

GERALD HOCKEN KNIGHT. Born 27 July 1908, at Glencoe, Par Station, Cornwall. S. of Alwyne Knight, Wyngarvey, Par Station. Educ. at Truro Cathedral School. Rec. by Rt Rev. Lord Bishop of Truro, and H. S. Middleton, M.A., Mus.B. (Peterhouse). Adm. 17 Aug. 1926: began res. 8 Oct. 1926. Matric. 21 Oct. 1926.

B.A. (3rd Cl. Engl. Tri. Pt I, 1928; Mus.B. Exam. Pt I, 1930) 1930. Mus.B. 1932. M.A. 1933. *John Stewart of Rannoch Schol. in Sacred Music*, 1927.
Asst Organist, Truro Cathedral, 1922–6. Student at College of St Nicolas (School of English Church Music), Chislehurst, Kent, 1930–2; and Tutor, 1932–. Organist and Choirmaster, St Augustine's Church, Queen's Gate, S. Kensington, S.W. 7, 1931–6. Organist and Master of the Choristers, Canterbury Cathedral, 1936–. A.R.C.O. 1929. F.R.C.O. 1935.

PRIYAMITRE KASTOORBHAI NAGERSHETH. Born 5 July 1908, at Ahmedabad, Bombay Presidency. S. of Kastoorbhai Manibhai Nagersheth, Wanda Villa, Ahmedabad. Educ. at Bishop Cotton School, Simla; and Cathedral and John Connon High School, Bombay. Adm. 4 Oct. 1926: began res. 10 Oct. 1926. Matric. 21 Oct. 1926.

B.A. (3rd Cl. Law Tri. Pt I, 1928; 3rd Cl. Pt II, 1929) 1929. M.A. 1933.
Called to the Bar, Inner Temple, 26 Jan. 1933.
Cousin of C. C. Javeri (p. 76).

EDWARD VINCENT BOXER. Born 14 March 1908, at Johannesburg, Transvaal. S. of Arthur Edward Boxer, Union Club, 52 Avenue de la Toison d'Or, Brussels. Educ. at Charterhouse. Adm. 8 Oct. 1926: began res. 11 Oct. 1926. Matric. 21 Oct. 1926.

B.A. (Ord. degree) 1929.
Manager, Boxer Radio Co., Ltd, 8 Seymour Place, London, W. 1.

Dom ANTONIO D'ALMEIDA. Born 15 Oct. 1907, at Cintra, Lisbon. S. of Count Lavradio, 15 Montague Road, Richmond, Surrey. Educ. at Stonyhurst College. Adm. 12 Oct. 1926: began res. 10 Oct. 1926. Matric. 21 Oct. 1926.

Went down after M. 1927.
Civil Engineer. With Benguela Railway Co., West Africa, 1929–30; with Pauling & Co., Ltd (of 26 Victoria Street, London, S.W. 1) on Mombasa Harbour Works, Kenya Colony, 1930–1, and on Beira Harbour Works, East Africa, 1931–2; with Benguela Railway Co. again, 1932–4; and with Beralt Tin and Wolfram, Ltd (tin mines), Portugal, 1934–.
His father is Dom Antonio d'Almeida, Conde do Lavradio, Acting Equerry to the exiled Queen Amelia of Portugal.

LESLIE ALFRED PINFOLD. Born 5 April 1907, at Wimbledon. S. of William John Pinfold, 28 Netherhall Gardens, Hampstead, N.W. 3. Educ. at Highgate School. Adm. 18 Dec. 1926, by *bene discessit* from Non-Coll. Board: began res. 14 Jan. 1927. Matric. 22 Oct. 1926 (as Non-Coll. Student, residing as such M. 1926).

B.A. (Ord. degree) 1929.

HORACE BUSHNELL LEARNED. Born 5 July 1904, at New Haven, Conn. S. of Prof. Henry Barrett Learned, 2123 Bancroft Place, Washington, D.C. Educ. at Thacher School, Ojai, California; and Yale Univ. (Yale College). Adm. 17 June 1926: began res. 14 Jan. 1927. Matric. 28 Jan. 1927.

Went down after L. 1928.
Asst Manager, Manufacturing division, Cheney Brothers (silk manufacturers), South Manchester, Conn.

FRANK WILLCOX. Born 23 Jan. 1908, in London. S. of Frank Pierce Willcox, Seamore Court, Seamore Place, Park Lane, W. 1. Educ. at Cheltenham College. Adm. 22 Dec. 1926: began res. 13 Jan. 1927. Matric. 28 Jan. 1927.

Went down after E. 1927.
Asst Master, Trinity College School, Port Hope, Ontario, 1927–8. With George A. Touche & Co. (Chartered Accountants), first at Toronto and subsequently at Montreal, 1928–. Also a Director of mining companies.

GEOFFREY ANTHONY EDWARD DREW WRIGHT. Born 26 June 1908, at Croydon, Surrey. S. of Thomas Reuben Wright (decd) and Mrs Wright, Burwood, 4 Radcliffe Road, E. Croydon. Educ. at Marlborough College. Adm. 6 Jan. 1927: began res. 13 Jan. 1927. Matric. 28 Jan. 1927.

Went down after E. 1928.
With Meredith & Drew Ltd (biscuit manufacturers), 158–174 Shadwell High Street, London, E. 1.

GODFREY MARTIN ELLIS PAULSON. Born 6 July 1908, at Alderley Edge, Cheshire. S. of Lieut.-Col. Peter Paulson, O.B.E., 29 East Drive, Queen's Park, Brighton. Educ. at Westminster School. Rec. by R. Geoffrey Ellis, M.P., M.A. (Peterhouse); and B. F. Hardy, M.A., House Master. Adm. 25 March 1925: began res. 5 Oct. 1927. Matric. 1 Nov. 1927.

B.A. (2nd Cl., 2nd Div., Hist. Tri. Pt I, 1929; 2nd Cl., 1st Div., Pt II, 1930) 1930. Probationer, Colonial Service, M. 1930 to E. 1931.
Colonial Service, with appt. as Asst District Commissioner, Gold Coast Colony, 1931–2. Solicitor (adm. Feb. 1936); being partner in Stones, Morris & Stone, 41 Moorgate, London, E.C. 2.
Nephew of Sir R. Geoffrey Ellis, Bart (cr. Bart 1932; Walker, p. 622), and cousin of W. R. F. Ellis (p. 101) and C. E. F. Ellis (p. 119).

PATRICK CHARLES MOLLER BEILBY. Born 4 Dec. 1908, at Edinburgh. S. of Eric Moller Beilby, 23 Ravelston Park, Edinburgh. Educ. at Loretto School. Adm. 18 Dec. 1926: began res. 5 Oct. 1927. Matric. 1 Nov. 1927.

B.A. (Ord. degree) 1930. M.A. 1934.
With William McEwan & Co., Ltd (brewers), Edinburgh, 1930–.

EDWIN CYRIL BLACKMAN. Born 6 June 1908, at Portsmouth. S. of Edwin Cecil Martin Blackman, 37 Carnarvon Road, Buckland, Portsmouth. Educ. at Portsmouth Grammar School. Adm. 21 Dec. 1926: began res. 5 Oct. 1927. Matric. 1 Nov. 1927. Entrance Major Schol., Classics.

B.A. (1st Cl. Class. Tri. Pt I, 1929; 2nd Cl. Pt II, 1930) 1930. M.A. 1934. Kitchener Schol., 1927 (held for 3 years). Robert Slade Schol., 1929. Members' Prize (Latin Essay), 1929.
Manchester College, Oxford, 1930–3. Marburg Univ., 1933–4. Congregational Minister: Resident Tutor, Cheshunt College, Cambridge, 1934–.

DOUGLAS DAKIN. Born 13 July 1907, at Highnam, nr Gloucester. S. of Frederick Griffiths Dakin, School House, Deerhurst, nr Tewkesbury. Educ. at

Rendcomb College, Cirencester. Adm. 21 Dec. 1926: began res. 5 Oct. 1927. Matric. 1 Nov. 1927. Entrance Minor Schol., History.

B.A. (1ˢᵗ Cl., 2ⁿᵈ Div., Hist. Tri. Pt I, 1929; 1ˢᵗ Cl., 2ⁿᵈ Div., Pt II, 1930) 1930. M.A. 1934. Goldsmiths' Co.'s Exhib., 1929. John Cosin Schol., 1929; re-elected (Honorary), 1930. Leaf Grant, 1930.
Ph.D., London, 1936. Asst Master, Haberdashers' Aske's Hampstead School, 1931–5. Lecturer in History, Birkbeck College (London Univ.), 1935–.
Author:
    Turgot and the 'ancien régime' in France. London (1939).

JAMES TAYLOR GARRUS. Born 4 May 1908, at Orlando, Florida. S. of H. P. N. Garrus (decᵈ) and Mrs Garrus, 9 Clarendon Avenue, Leamington Spa. Educ. at Marlborough College. Adm. 21 Dec. 1926: began res. 5 Oct. 1927. Matric. 1 Nov. 1927. Entrance Exhib., Mod Languages (all. to change to Law).

B.A. (3ʳᵈ Cl. Law Tri. Pt I, 1929; 3ʳᵈ Cl. Pt II, 1930) 1930. M.A. 1934.
Went to Chicago in 1931, with the intention of being admitted to the Illinois Bar.

FREDERICK VICTOR HARRISON. Born 23 May 1908, at Penkhull, Stoke-on-Trent. S. of Joseph Herbert Harrison, 333 Princes Road, Penkhull. Educ. at Newcastle-under-Lyme High School. Adm. 21 Dec. 1926: began res. 5 Oct. 1927. Matric. 1 Nov. 1927. Entrance Exhib., History.

Exhib., 1929. Went down after M. 1929.

HUGH FRANCIS HODGE. Born 6 March 1908, at Deptford. S. of Herbert Hodge, 5 Streatham Place, S.W. 2. Educ. at Weymouth College. Adm. 21 Dec. 1926: began res. 5 Oct. 1927. Matric. 1 Nov. 1927. Entrance Exhib., History.

B.A. (2ⁿᵈ Cl., 2ⁿᵈ Div., Hist. Tri. Pt I, 1929; 3ʳᵈ Cl. Engl. Tri. Pt I, 1930) 1930. M.A. 1934. Exhib., 1929.
Lay Missionary (C.M.S.), teaching at Maseno School, Kenya Colony, 1930–3. Wycliffe Hall, Oxford, 1934. Ordained d. 1934 Lichfield for Mombasa, p. 1936 Mombasa. Asst Master, Alliance High School, Kikuyu, Dio. Mombasa, 1934–.

KENNETH ALBERT MATTHEWS. Born 21 May 1908, at Luton, Beds. S. of Rev. Albert James Matthews, 12 Prince's Avenue, Grimsby. Educ. at Kingswood School, Bath. Adm. 21 Dec. 1926: began res. 5 Oct. 1927. Matric. 1 Nov. 1927. Entrance Major Schol., Classics.

B.A. (1ˢᵗ Cl. Class. Tri. Pt I, 1929; 2ⁿᵈ Cl. Moral Sci. Tri. Pt II (a), 1931) 1933. Lady Mary Ramsey Schol., 1929; re-elected, 1930. Leaf Stud., £50, 1930.
Asst Master, Spetsae School (Gulf of Nauplia, Greece), 1931–2. Subsequently author and journalist.
Author:
    Aleko. [*A novel.*] London (1934).
    Greek salad: an autobiography of Greek travel. London, 1935.
    Celia employed. [*A novel.*] London (1937).
Translator:
    Lysis, a dialogue of Plato. Fulcrum Press (Strand on the Green, W. 4, 1930).

JOSEPH PEDOE. Born 31 Jan. 1908, in London. S. of Simon Cohen, 88ᶜ Pelham Street, E. 1. Educ. at Central Foundation School, London; and East London College. Adm. 21 Dec. 1926: began res. 5 Oct. 1927. Matric. 1 Nov. 1927. Entrance Major Schol., Maths.

B.A. (1ˢᵗ Cl. Math. Tri. Pt I, 1928; Sen. Opt. Pt II, 1930) 1930. M.A. 1934. Francis Gisborne Schol., 1929.
B.Sc., London, 1929. Apptd Senior Math. Lecturer, College of Technology, Rugby, 1939.
His surname was changed by deed poll from COHEN to PEDOE before his admission.

NORMAN STAFFORD PRICE. Born 16 Jan. 1908, at Stafford. S. of John Price, 14 New Garden Street, Stafford. Educ. at King Edward VI. Grammar School, Stafford. Adm. 21 Dec. 1926: began res. 5 Oct. 1927. Matric. 1 Nov. 1927. Entrance Minor Schol., Maths.

B.A. (2nd Cl. Math. Tri. Pt I, 1928; Jun. Opt. Pt II, 1930) 1930. Schol.†, 1929.
H.M. Inspector of Taxes.

HARRY ARNOLD ROBINSON. Born 10 Aug. 1908, at Clayton, nr Bradford, Yorks. S. of Arnold Robinson [decd?] and Mrs Robinson, 4 Alton Grove, Heaton, Bradford. Educ. at Bradford Grammar School. Adm. 21 Dec. 1926: began res. 5 Oct. 1927. Matric. 1 Nov. 1927. Entrance Minor Schol., Classics.

B.A. (2nd Cl. Class. Tri. Pt I (g, l), 1929; 2nd Cl. Pt II, 1930) 1930. Schol.†, 1929.

JOHN QUERIPEL WOOD. Born 8 April 1908, at Worthing. S. of William Willoughby Wood, Hartswell House, Wiveliscombe, Somerset. Educ. at Wellington College. Adm. 21 Dec. 1926: began res. 5 Oct. 1927. Matric. 1 Nov. 1927. Entrance Minor Schol., Classics.

B.A. (1st Cl. Class. Tri. Pt I (g, l), 1929; 1st Cl. Pt II, 1930) 1930. Edward Lord North Schol., 1929.
Mercantile Asst with the Bombay Burmah Trading Corporation, Ltd, in Burma, 1930–.

ARNOLD GEOFFROY DE MONTMORENCY. Born 27 July 1908, at Greenwich. S. of Prof. James Edward Geoffrey de Montmorency (Peterhouse, M.A. 1907, LL.B. 1890), 31 Lee Terrace, Blackheath, S.E. 3. Educ. at Westminster School. Adm. 22 Dec. 1926: began res. 5 Oct. 1927. Matric. 1 Nov. 1927.

B.A. (2nd Cl., 2nd Div., Hist. Tri. Pt I, 1929; 2nd Cl., 2nd Div., Law Tri. Pt II, 1930) 1930. LL.B. 1931. M.A. 1934.
Harmsworth Law Schol. (£200 a year for 3 years), 1931. Called to the Bar, Middle Temple, 17 Nov. 1932. On S. Eastern circuit.

HORACE DUDLEY McDONOGH ELLIS. Born 5 July 1908, at Kensington. S. of Dr William McDonogh Ellis, Greenbanks, Woldingham, Surrey. Educ. at Eastbourne College. Adm. 22 Dec. 1926: began res. 5 Oct. 1927. Matric. 1 Nov. 1927.

B.A. (2nd Cl. Mech. Sci. Tri., 1930) 1930. M.A. 1934. Exhib. for Mech. Sciences, 1928; re-elected, 1929.
Research for Signals Experimental Establishment (War Office), Engineering Laboratory, Oxford, 1930–2. Radio research with Murphy Radio Ltd, 1932–. G.I.E.E. 1933.

VINCENT STRUAN ROBERTSON. Born 10 May 1908, at Enfield Chase, Middlesex. S. of Walter Knyvett Robertson, South Lodge, Enfield Chase. Educ. at Aldenham School. Adm. 22 Dec. 1926: began res. 5 Oct. 1927. Matric. 1 Nov. 1927.

B.A. (3rd Cl. Class. Tri. Pt I, 1929; 3rd Cl. Theol. Tri. Pt I, Sec. A, 1931) 1931. M.A. 1938.
Westcott House, Cambridge, 1930. Ordained d. 1932, p. 1933 London. C. of St Mary, Twickenham, 1932–4; R. of All Saints, Langholm, 1934–6; V. of Doulting w. E. and W. Cranmore and Downhead, Dio. Bath and Wells, 1936–.

FRANCIS BRIAN ANTHONY RUNDALL. Born 11 Sept. 1908, at Gillingham, Kent. S. of Lieut.-Col. Charles Frank Rundall, C.M.G., D.S.O., The Chestnuts, Needham Market, Suffolk. Educ. at Marlborough College. Adm. 22 Dec. 1926: began res. 5 Oct. 1927. Matric. 1 Nov. 1927.

B.A. (2nd Cl., 1st Div., Mod. & Med. Lang. Tri. Pt I, French, 1928; 2nd Cl., 2nd Div., Pt I, German, 1928; 2nd Cl., 1st Div., Pt II, 1930) 1930. Exhib., 1929. Leaf Grant, 1929; and again, 1930.
H.M. Consular Service, 1930–; served 1930–5 successively in Antwerp, Colón (Republic of Panama) and Panama; and has been Acting Consul-General, Boston, Mass., 1935–.

NIGEL MARLIN BALCHIN. Born 3 Dec. 1908, at Potterne, Wilts. S. of William Edwin Balchin, High Street, West Lavington, Wilts. Educ. at Dauntsey School, West Lavington. Adm. 5 Jan. 1927: began res. 5 Oct. 1927. Matric. 1 Nov. 1927.

B.A. (2ⁿᵈ Cl. Nat. Sci. Tri. Pt I, 1929; Cert. of Dilig. Study, 1930) 1930. Exhib. for Nat. Sciences, 1928; re-elected, 1929. Leaf Grant, 1930.
Investigator, National Institute of Industrial Psychology, 1930–5. Marketing executive with Rowntree & Co., Ltd (chocolate manufacturers), 1935–.
Author:
   No sky. [*A novel.*] London (1934).
   Simple life. [*A novel.*] London (1935).
   Income and outcome: a study of personal finance. London (1936).
   Lightbody on liberty. [*A novel.*] London, 1936.
And under the pseudonym 'Mark Spade':
   How to run a bassoon factory: or, Business explained. London (1934).
   Business for pleasure. London (1935).
   Fun and games: how to win at almost anything. London (1936).
Also a regular contributor to *Punch.*

KEITH SOMERVILLE LAURIE. Born 6 Oct. 1908, at Rangoon. S. of Maxwell Laurie (Peterhouse, adm. 1887), M.V.O., I.C.S. (ret.), The Cottage, St Ives, Cornwall. Educ. at Shrewsbury School. Adm. 5 Jan. 1927: began res. 5 Oct. 1927. Matric. 1 Nov. 1927.

B.A. (1ˢᵗ Cl. Class. Tri. Pt I (*G, l*), 1929; 2ⁿᵈ Cl., 2ⁿᵈ Div., Hist. Tri. Pt II, 1930) 1930. M.A. 1935. Exhib. for Classics, 1928. Thomas Parke Schol., 1929.
With the Burmah Oil Co., Ltd, 1930–.

ARTHUR TILLOTSON. Born 30 April 1908, at Aireside, Farnhill, Yorks. S. of John Henry Tillotson, 10 Ermysted Street, Skipton, Yorks. Educ. at Keighley Trade and Grammar School. Adm. 7 Jan. 1927: began res. 5 Oct. 1927. Matric. 1 Nov. 1927.

B.A. (2ⁿᵈ Cl., 1ˢᵗ Div., Hist. Tri. Pt I, 1929; 1ˢᵗ Cl., 2ⁿᵈ Div., Pt II, 1930) 1930. 2ⁿᵈ Cl., 1ˢᵗ Div., Engl. Tri. Pt II, 1931. M.A. 1934. Alistair Bevington Schol., 1930.
Matric. from Merton College, Oxford, 14 Oct. 1931; incorp. B.A., 13 Feb. 1932; and res. till end of Hilary Term 1934. Asst Under-Librarian, University Library, Cambridge, 1934–.

DAVID LEWIS THOMSON. Born 22 Nov. 1908, at Slough, Bucks. S. of Harold Thomson, Southwold, Slough. Educ. at Leys School. Rec. by Rev. H. Bisseker, M.A., Head Master, and F. W. Ives, M.A. (Peterhouse), Asst Master. Adm. 22 Jan. 1927: began res. 5 Oct. 1927. Matric. 1 Nov. 1927.

B.A. (1ˢᵗ Cl., 2ⁿᵈ Div., Hist. Tri. Pt I, 1929; 1ˢᵗ Cl. Engl. Tri. Pt I, 1931) 1931. M.A. 1936. John Whitgift Schol., 1929; re-elected, 1930. Leaf Grant, 1930.
Asst Master, Ottershaw College, Chertsey, Surrey, 1932–.

CHARLES ATKINSON. Born 15 Aug. 1908, at Eastbourne. S. of Charles Edward Atkinson (decᵈ). Guardian (aunt): Miss C. F. Symington, 1 Chatsworth Gardens, Eastbourne. Educ. at Monkton Combe School. Rec. by Rev. E. Hayward, M.A., Head Master; and R. A. Gordon, K.C., M.A., LL.M. (Peterhouse). Adm. 22 March 1927: began res. 5 Oct. 1927. Matric. 1 Nov. 1927.

3ʳᵈ Cl. Mod. & Med. Lang. Tri. Pt I, French, 1928. Went down after E. 1929.
Cousin of G. H. Atkinson (*Walker*, p. 672).

GODFREY BOWER. Born 21 Jan. 1908, at Farnborough, Kent. S. of Theodore Herbert Bower (dec^d). Guardian (aunt): Miss Lucy Anne Rowe, Willow Cottage, St Michael's Road, Headingley, Leeds. Educ. at Radley College; and privately, with Rev. A. Browning, B.A., Penn Street Vicarage, Amersham, Bucks. Adm. 22 March 1927: began res. 5 Oct. 1927. Matric. 1 Nov. 1927.

B.A. (3rd Cl. Hist. Tri. Pt I, 1929; standard for Ord. degree, Theol. Tri. Pt I, 1931) 1931.
St Stephen's House, Oxford, 1932. Ordained d. 1932, p. 1933 Rochester. C. of St Luke, Bromley Common, 1932–6; St Andrew, Ham, Dio. Southwark, 1936–8; Chaplain, R.N., 1938–.

CHARLES EDWIN FRANCIS ELLIS. Born 19 Nov. 1907, in London. S. of Lieut.-Col. William Francis Ellis, O.B.E. (late R.A.M.C.), Tangier, Morocco. Educ. at Bradfield College; and privately, with H. M. Vizard, M.A. (Peterhouse), 60 Denmark Villas, Hove, Sussex. Rec. by Rev. R. D. Beloe, M.A., Head Master of Bradfield College; and R. Geoffrey Ellis, M.P., M.A. (Peterhouse). Adm. 22 March 1927: began res. 5 Oct. 1927. Matric. 1 Nov. 1927.

B.A. (Ord. degree) 1930.
Student of art and writing.
Nephew of Sir R. Geoffrey Ellis, Bart (cr. Bart 1932; *Walker*, p. 622), and cousin of W. R. F. Ellis (p. 101) and G. M. E. Paulson (p. 115).

CLAUDE KENNETH HAILEY. Born 21 May 1908, at Llandaff North, Glam. S. of Claude Percival Hailey, Petherton, Llandaff, Glam. Educ. at Mill Hill School. Adm. 22 March 1927: began res. 5 Oct. 1927. Matric. 1 Nov. 1927.

B.A. (3rd Cl. Econ. Tri. Pt I, 1929; 3rd Cl. Pt II, 1930) 1930.
With the Anglo-Continental Guano Works Ltd, 9 Fenchurch Avenue, London, E.C. 3, 1930–; now (1935) Asst Manager in their Export office.

RICHARD CHARLES ROY MORRELL. Born 2 April 1908, at Highgate. S. of Richard Turner Morrell, 44 Cholmeley Park, Highgate, N. 6. Educ. at Highgate School. Adm. 22 March 1927: began res. 5 Oct. 1927. Matric. 1 Nov. 1927.

B.A. (1st Cl. Engl. Tri. Pt I, 1929; 2nd Cl., 1st Div., Pt II, 1931) 1931. M.A. 1934. Andrew Perne Schol., 1929; re-elected, 1930.
Lecturer in English Language, Helsingfors Univ., 1931–4. Temporary Lecturer in English Literature, Raffles College, Singapore, 1934–.

HUGH JOHN VIVIAN MORTON. Born 10 Oct. 1909, at Stafford. S. of Hugh Lloyd Morton, 48 Tixall Road, Stafford. Educ. at King Edward VI. Grammar School, Stafford. Adm. 22 March 1927: began res. 5 Oct. 1927. Matric. 1 Nov. 1927.

B.A. (Ord. degree) 1930. M.A., M.B., B.Chir. 1935.
M.R.C.S., L.R.C.P. 1933. In practice at Witney, Oxon.

JOHN BUCKLEY RODERICK. Born 29 Oct. 1908, at Cambridge. S. of Dr Henry Buckley Roderick, O.B.E., 17 Trumpington Street, Cambridge. Educ. at Malvern College. Adm. 22 March 1927: began res. 5 Oct. 1927. Matric. 1 Nov. 1927.

Went down after L. 1928.

ERNEST ALFRED THOMPSON. Born 23 Feb. 1908, at Manchester. S. of Alfred John Thompson, 8 Seventh Avenue, Broadway, Blackpool. Educ. at King

Edward VII. School, Lytham. Adm. 22 March 1927: began res. 5 Oct. 1927. Matric. 1 Nov. 1927.

> B.A. (2nd Cl. Nat. Sci. Tri. Pt I, 1930) 1930.
> Was H.M. Inspector of Taxes at Keighley, Yorks, 1930–2.

GORDON TURNER. Born 3 Oct. 1909, at Rochdale. S. of Harold Rupert Turner, Thrum Hall, Rochdale. Educ. at Malvern College. Adm. 22 March 1927: began res. 5 Oct. 1927. Matric. 1 Nov. 1927.

> B.A. (2nd Cl., 2nd Div., Econ. Tri. Pt I, 1929; Cert. of Dilig. Study, 1930) 1930. M.A. 1934.
> With Turner & Newall, Ltd (manufacturers of asbestos, magnesia and allied products), Rochdale, 1931–; now (1935) with a subsidiary Co., Keasbey & Mattison Co., Ambler, Pa.

RICHARD GRAHAM HARRINGTON. Born 3 June 1909, at St John's, Newfoundland. S. of Samuel Talbot Harrington, P.O. Box 95, St John's, Newfoundland. Educ. at Leys School. Adm. 23 March 1927: began res. 5 Oct. 1927. Matric. 1 Nov. 1927.

> B.A. (3rd Cl. Law Tri. Pt I, 1929; 3rd Cl. Pt II, 1930) 1930.
> With the Asiatic Petroleum Co., Ltd, at Nairobi, Kenya Colony, 1930–4. Sec., The Motor House, Malvern, 1935–.

CECIL CUTHBERT PARROTT. Born 29 Jan. 1909, at Plymouth. S. of Eng. Capt. Jasper William Alfred Parrott, R.N. (ret.), Denham, Northchurch, Berkhamsted, Herts. Educ. at Berkhamsted School. Adm. 29 March 1927: began res. 5 Oct. 1927. Matric. 1 Nov. 1927.

> B.A. (2nd Cl. Class. Tri. Pt I, 1928; 2nd Cl., 2nd Div., Engl. Tri. Pt I, 1930) 1930. Kitchener Schol., 1927 (held for 3 years). *Prox. acc. for Members' Prize (English Essay)*, 1928. 2nd *Winchester Reading Prize (aeq.)*, 1930. Leaf Grant, 1930.
> Asst Master, Christ's Hospital, 1931; and at Edinburgh Academy, 1931–4. English Tutor to H.R.H. the Crown Prince (now H.M. King Peter) of Yugoslavia, Belgrade, 1934–.

ERNEST DAVID TOWLE JOURDAIN. Born 24 July 1908, at Silchar, Assam, India. S. of Rev. Reginald Towle Jourdain, Woodham Vicarage, Woking. Educ. at St Edward's School, Oxford. Adm. 8 April 1927: began res. 5 Oct. 1927. Matric. 1 Nov. 1927.

> B.A. (2nd Cl. Math. Tri. Pt I, 1928; 3rd Cl. Nat. Sci. Tri. Pt II (Physics), 1930) 1930.
> Asst Examiner, Patent Office, 1930–5; and Examiner, 1935–.
> Bro. of R. T. Jourdain (p. 150).

ALFRED GARRATT FOSTER-BARHAM, 2nd Lieut., R.E. Born 25 Aug. 1906, at Wimbledon. S. of Hugh Garratt Foster-Barham, The Pines, Queen's Road, Nelson, New Zealand. Educ. at Oundle School; R.M.A., Woolwich; and S.M.E., Chatham. Rec. by War Office. Adm. 6 June 1927: began res. 1 Oct. 1927. Matric. 1 Nov. 1927.

> B.A. (3rd Cl. Intercoll. Exam. in Mech. Sci., 1928; adm. to degree without further exam.; all. 3 terms as Commiss. Off.) 1929.
> Promoted Lieut., R.E., 1929. Died 16 Feb. 1930 at the Royal Military Hospital, Aldershot, as the result of a riding accident.

LAURENCE HARRY MILNER GULLAND. Born 24 March 1908, at Partick, Glasgow. S. of James Dugald Gulland, Bourne Hall, Bushey, Herts. Educ. at Haileybury College. Adm. 20 April 1927: began res. 5 Oct. 1927. Matric. 1 Nov. 1927.

> B.A. (2nd Cl. Class. Tri. Pt I (g, L), 1929; 3rd Cl. Pt II, 1930) 1930. M.A. 1934. *Hon. mentioned for Porson Prize*, 1929.
> Asst Master, Junior Branch, Mill Hill School, 1930–.

REGINALD CARNEGIE BARNES. Born 27 Feb. 1909, at Southampton. S. of Reginald Speke Barnes (dec^d) and Mrs Barnes, The Cottage, Stratton, N. Cornwall. Educ. at Blundell's School. Adm. 11 July 1927: began res. 5 Oct. 1927. Matric. 1 Nov. 1927.

  B.A. (3rd Cl. Hist. Tri. Pt I, 1929; P.S. Exam. Latin, 1931) 1931.

PETER BURTON. Born 4 May 1908, at Southampton. S. of Herbert Burton, Meadowhead, Bassett, Southampton. Educ. at Eastbourne College. Adm. 11 July 1927: began res. 5 Oct. 1927. Matric. 1 Nov. 1927.

  B.A. (Ord. degree) 1930.
  Architect.

ANDREW CROOKSTON. Born 6 Dec. 1908, at Mauchline, Ayrshire. S. of Andrew White Crookston, 38 Grosvenor Gardens, S.W. 1. Educ. at Charterhouse. Adm. 11 July 1927: began res. 5 Oct. 1927. Matric. 1 Nov. 1927.

  Went down after E. 1930.
  Mining engineer in Egypt and phosphate merchant in London. Director of the Egyptian Phosphate Co., Ltd, and of Crookston Bros, Ltd (phosphate of lime merchants).

JOHN DENNIS FOWLER GREEN. Born 9 May 1909, at Stroud, Glos. S. of Henry Green, The Manor, Chedworth, Glos. Educ. at Cheltenham College. Adm. 11 July 1927: began res. 5 Oct. 1927. Matric. 1 Nov. 1927.

  B.A. (2nd Cl., 2nd Div., Hist. Tri. Pt I, 1929; 3rd Cl. Law Tri. Pt II, 1931) 1931.
  Represented Cambridge v. Oxford in Rélay Races (Hurdles), 1927, 1928. President of Union Soc., L. 1931.
  Entrance Schol. (200 guineas a year for 3 years), Inner Temple, 1930. Called to the Bar, Inner Temple, 17 Nov. 1933. On Oxford circuit.
  Grandson of J. F. Green (*Walker*, p. 487).
  Author:
    Mr. Baldwin: a study in post-War Conservatism. London (1933).

EDWARD CLARK HASLAM. Born 17 June 1908, at Gateshead, Co. Durham. S. of Henry Augustus Haslam, The Gables, Durham Road, Low Fell, Gateshead. Educ. at Mill Hill School. Adm. 11 July 1927: began res. 5 Oct. 1927. Matric. 1 Nov. 1927.

  B.A. (3rd Cl. Econ. Tri. Pt I, 1929; standard of Ord. degree, Pt II, 1930) 1930. M.A. 1935.
  Shipbroker, with E. R. Newbigin Ltd, Newcastle-on-Tyne, 1930–; being a Director of the firm, 1933–.

GEOFFREY VYVYAN ARUNDELL SECCOMBE-HETT. Born 5 March 1909, in London. S. of Geoffrey Seccombe Hett, 86 Brook Street, Grosvenor Square, W. 1. Educ. at Harrow School. Adm. 11 July 1927: began res. 5 Oct. 1927. Matric. 1 Nov. 1927.

  B.A. (Ord. degree) 1931. M.A. 1935.
  Half-Blue: Fencing (Foils), 1929, 1930. (Captain, 1930.)
  Represented Great Britain at Fencing (Foils) in the European Championships at Vienna in 1931, and at Budapest in 1933; v. U.S.A. at New York, 1934; and in the Olympic Games at Berlin, 1936.
  Journalist, with the Amalgamated Press Ltd (Sir John Hammerton's Dept), 1935–. Special Correspondent of *The Field* in Korea, 1935.
  Nephew of C. E. S. C. Donnithorne (*Walker*, p. 647), and cousin of R. S. A. Donnithorne (p. 146).

ARTHUR LLEWELLYN JONES. Born 18 Dec. 1908, at Prestwich, Lancs. S. of William Llewellyn Jones, Bewdley, Alderley Edge, Cheshire. Educ. at

Clifton College. Adm. 11 July 1927: began res. 5 Oct. 1927. Matric. 1 Nov. 1927.

B.A. (3ʳᵈ Cl. Math. Tri. Pt I, 1929; 3ʳᵈ Cl. Econ. Tri. Pt II, 1930) 1930. M.A. 1934.
In management of Lloyd's Packing Warehouses Ltd, Manchester.

THOMAS MARTIN. Born 31 Aug. 1909, at Hamburg. S. of Walter Martin (decᵈ) and Mrs Martin, The Grange, Winchester Road, Bassett, Southampton. Educ. at Cheltenham College. Adm. 11 July 1927: began res. 5 Oct. 1927. Matric. 1 Nov. 1927.

B.A. (Ord. degree) 1930.
Underwriter at Lloyd's, Leadenhall Street, London, E.C. 3.

WILLIAM GARVIN MORWOOD. Born 28 June 1909, at Mussoori, United Provinces, India. S. of Lieut.-Col. James Morwood, I.M.S. (ret.), Air-Lawn, Malone Park, Belfast. Educ. at Royal Academical Institution, Belfast. Adm. 11 July 1927: began res. 5 Oct. 1927. Matric. 1 Nov. 1927.

B.A. (3ʳᵈ Cl. Hist. Tri. Pt I, 1929; standard of Ord. degree, Law Tri. Pt II, 1930) 1930. M.A. 1934.
Has been in U.S.A. since 1930. Studied at Univ. of California, 1930–1. Journalist, 1931–2. Advertising copy writer, 1932. Schoolmaster, 1933–4. Theatrical director, 1934–.

ROBERT OWEN MOSSOP. Born 1 Sept. 1909, at Woking. S. of Robert Mossop, Oak Bank, Guildford Road, Woking. Educ. at Eastbourne College. Adm. 11 July 1927: began res. 5 Oct. 1927. Matric. 1 Nov. 1927.

B.A. (Exempted through illness from Hist. Tri. Pt I, 1929; 3ʳᵈ Cl. Pt II, 1930) 1930. M.A. 1935.
Westcott House, Cambridge, 1932. Ordained d. 1933, p. 1934 Oxford. C. of Earley, Dio. Oxford, 1933–.

LANCELOT PURTON SAMUELS. Born 8 Aug. 1909, at Manchester. S. of Lawrence Lancelot Samuels, Quarry Bank, Styal, nr Manchester. Educ. at Bradfield College. Adm. 11 July 1927: began res. 5 Oct. 1927. Matric. 1 Nov. 1927.

B.A. (Ord. degree) 1930. M.A. 1934.
Chartered Accountant; being with Jones, Crewdson & Youatt, 7 Norfolk Street, Manchester. A.C.A. 1934.

ARTHUR HENRY SEYMOUR-LUCAS. Born 30 May 1908, at Bushey, Herts. S. of Sydney Charles Seymour-Lucas, 64 Falconer Road, Bushey. Educ. at Aldenham School. Adm. 11 July 1927: began res. 5 Oct. 1927. Matric. 1 Nov. 1927.

B.A. (3ʳᵈ Cl. Engl. Tri. Pt I, 1929; 2ⁿᵈ Cl., 2ⁿᵈ Div., Mod. & Med. Lang. Tri. Pt I, French, 1930) 1930.
Entered the R.A.F.: Flg. Off., 1931; Flt Lieut., 1935; Sqdn Ldr, 1938.

CARMALT HARDEMAN SMITH. Born 2 April 1909, at Solihull, Warwickshire. S. of Frank Hardeman Smith, Blythehurst, Copt Heath, Solihull. Educ. at Uppingham School. Adm. 11 July 1927: began res. 5 Oct. 1927. Matric. 1 Nov. 1927.

B.A. (Ord. degree) 1930. M.A. 1934.
Chartered Accountant; being with F. H. Frost, 25 Bennett's Hill, Birmingham. A.C.A. 1934.

JOHN FRASER WORKMAN. Born 10 June 1909, at Chingford, Essex. S. of William Arthur Workman, Holmhurst, Loughton, Essex. Educ. at Rugby School; and privately, with Rev. F. de W. Lushington, M.A., Château d'Oex, Switzerland.

Rec. by W. W. Vaughan, M.A., Head Master, Rugby School; and B. L. Hallward, M.A., Fellow of Peterhouse. Adm. 11 July 1927: began res. 5 Oct. 1927. Matric. 1 Nov. 1927.

B.A. (3rd Cl. Law Tri. Pt I, 1929; allowed Ord. degree, Pt II, 1930) 1930.

Articled Clerk to Lawrence, Graham & Co. (Solicitors), 6 New Square, Lincoln's Inn, W.C. 2, 1930–3. Joined Sanders, Phillips & Co. (printers, etc.), Chryssell Road, London, S.W. 9, in 1934. Died 23 May 1937 after a long illness.

RUDOLF MORITZ ERNEST PICK. Born 24 March 1902, at Magdeburg. S. of Emil Emanuel Pick, 14 The Chase, Clapham Common, S.W. 4. Educ. at King Edward's School, Birmingham; and St David's College, Lampeter (B.A. degree). Rec. by Rev. Canon M. Jones, D.D., Principal, and D. Dawson, M.Litt. (Peterhouse), Lecturer, of St David's College, Lampeter. Adm. 13 July 1927: began res. 5 Oct. 1927. Matric. 1 Nov. 1927. Aff. Stud.

B.A. (2nd Cl., 1st Div., Hist. Tri. Pt II, 1929) 1929. M.A. 1935.

Asst Master, Schule Schloss Salem, Baden, 1929–32. Travelling in Asia, America and elsewhere, followed by study at Berlin Univ., 1932–4. Asst Master, Central Secondary School, Birmingham, 1934–.

He matric. as Rudolf Morris Ernest PICK.

KRISHNA RAO NARAYANA RAO NAGARKATTI. Born 5 March 1905, at Haveri, Bombay Presidency. S. of Narayana Rao Venkatesh Nagarkatti (decd). Educ. at London Mission High School, Bangalore; and Central College (Mysore Univ.), Bangalore (B.Sc. degree, Mysore Univ.). Rec. by India Office. Adm. 20 Sept. 1927: began res. 5 Oct. 1927. Matric. 1 Nov. 1927. Probationer, I.C.S.

Resided till end of E. 1929.

I.C.S., with appt. as Asst Commissioner, Central Provinces, 1929–.

He matric. as Krishna Narayan NAGARKATTI.

JOHN BUNTING TOINTON. Born 14 April 1908, at Grantham. S. of Herbert Charles Tointon, West Cottage, Bourne, Lincs. Educ. at Uppingham School; and privately, with J. B. H. Beards, 17 Oak's Crescent, Wolverhampton. Adm. 5 Oct. 1927: began res. 14 Oct. 1927. Matric. 1 Nov. 1927.

Resided till M. 1930 inclusive. M.B., B.Chir. 1938.

M.R.C.S., L.R.C.P. 1937. Entered the R.A.M.C.: Lieut., 1937; Capt., 1938.

He changed his names to John Bunting BUNTING by deed poll dated 28 Feb. 1934 (*London Gazette*, 13 March 1934).

BRIAN EMILE WOOD. Born 28 Nov. 1907, at Islington. S. of Arthur Herbert Wood, Ardath, Hastings Road, Bexhill-on-Sea. Educ. privately. Rec. by D. W. Wheeler, M.A., Berrow, Carew Road, Eastbourne; and E. C. Francis, M.A., Fellow of Peterhouse. Adm. 5 Oct. 1927: began res. 13 Oct. 1927. Matric. 1 Nov. 1927.

B.A. (Ord. degree) 1930. M.A. 1934.

Architect. A.A. Dipl. 1937. A.R.I.B.A. 1937.

JOHN ARTHUR COOK. Born 11 July 1908, at Simla, India. S. of John Polson Cook, Punjab Irrigation, Public Works Dept, India. Educ. at Westminster School. Adm. 5 Oct. 1927: began res. 11 Oct. 1927. Matric. 1 Nov. 1927.

Went down after E. 1930.

Blue: Assoc. Football, 1927, 1928, 1929, 1930.

With the Anglo-American Oil Co., Ltd, 1931. Asst Master at St Cross, Walton-on-the-Hill, Tadworth, Surrey, 1931–2. With *The Daily Express*, 1932–.

Bro. of D. Cook (p. 149).

ERNEST BARKER. Adm. **Fellow**, 4 Dec. 1927. Professorial Fellow, 1927–39. Matric. and incorp. Litt.D. (from New College, Oxford), 20 Jan. 1928. Professor of Political Science, 1927–39.

Born 23 Sept. 1874, at Woodley, Cheshire. S. of George Barker (dec^d), of Woodley. Educ. at Manchester Grammar School, and Balliol College, Oxford (Class. Schol.; B.A. 1897; M.A., from Merton College, 1900; D.Litt., from New College, 1922). *Craven Schol.*, 1895.

Served during 1915–18 as Pte in Oxford Volunteer Regt, and in Ministry of Information; and during 1917–18 successively in Ministry of Munitions and Ministry of Labour.

At Oxford was Fellow (Classics) of Merton College, 1898–1905; Junior Proctor, 1908–9; Fellow and Lecturer (History) of St John's College, 1909–13; Fellow and Tutor (History) of New College, 1913–20. Principal of King's College, London, 1920–7.

Member of Consultative Committee of Board of Education, 1920–8. President, Section L, British Assoc., 1924. Stevenson Lecturer on Citizenship, Glasgow Univ., 1925–6. Lowell Lecturer, Boston, Mass., 1929. Chairman, Community Centres and Associations Committee of the National Council of Social Service, 1931–. Chairman, British Co-operating Committee of International Student Service, 1931–. President, Institute of Sociology, 1935–8.

Hon. LL.D., Edinburgh, 1921; Harvard, 1929; Calcutta, 1938; and Dalhousie, Nova Scotia, 1938. Fellow (and afterwards Life Governor), King's College, London, 1921–. Order of the White Lion, Czechoslovakia, 1927. Hon. Fellow, Merton College, Oxford, 1931–.

Author:

> *The Political thought of Plato and Aristotle.* London (1906). Revised ed., entitled '*Greek political theory: Plato and his predecessors*'. Ib. (1918).
> *The Dominican Order and Convocation: a study of the growth of representation in the Church during the thirteenth century.* Oxford, 1913.
> *Political thought in England from Herbert Spencer to the present day.* (*Home Univ. Library*, 104.) London (1915). 2nd ed., entitled '*Political thought in England, 1848 to 1914*'. (*Home Univ. Library*, 104.) Ib. (1928).
> *The Crusades.* (*World's Manuals.*) London, 1923.
> *National character and the factors in its formation.* London (1927).
> *Church, State and study; essays.* London (1930).
> *Burke and Bristol: a study of the relations between Burke and his constituency during the years 1774–80.* (*Lewis Fry Memorial Lecture*, 1930.) Bristol [1931].
> *Universities in Great Britain, their position and their problems.* London (1931).
> O. von Gierke's *Natural law and the theory of society, 1500 to 1800.* (*Five subsections from* '*Das deutsche Genossenschaftsrecht*', vol. 4.) *With a lecture on The ideas of natural law and humanity, by E. Troeltsch. Translated with an introduction by E. Barker.* 2 vols. Cambridge, 1934.
> *The citizen's choice.* Cambridge, 1937.
> *Oliver Cromwell and the English people.* (*Cambridge Miscellany*, 18.) Cambridge, 1937.
> *And other works.*

Also contributor to:

> *The Encyclopaedia Britannica.* 11th ed. Cambridge, 1910–11. And 14th ed. London, 1929.
> *The Cambridge Medieval History*, vol. 1. Cambridge, 1911.
> *The Cambridge Ancient History*, vol. 6. Cambridge, 1927.
> *European civilization, its origin and development, by various contributors; under the direction of E. Eyre.* Vol. 5. Oxford, 1937.
> *Church and community.* (*Church, Community and State*, 5.) London (1938).
> *And other works.*

Editor:

> J. M. Dent & Sons' *The Library of Greek thought.* Vol. 1–. London, 1923–.

BRUCE ODERY BOARDMAN. Born 31 Dec. 1908, at Woodford Green, Essex. S. of John Alexander Boardman, Hadley, Mornington Road, Woodford Green. Educ. at Mill Hill School. Adm. 11 July 1927: began res. 8 Oct. 1928. Matric. 1 Nov. 1928.

Went down during E. 1931.

Chief Accountant to Greenly's Ltd (advertising agents) and Crichton Studios Ltd (commercial artists, etc.), both of 5 Chancery Lane, London, W.C. 2; and Sec. and Accountant to Westminster Laboratories Ltd (pharmaceutical products), 4–12 Palmer Street, Westminster, S.W. 1.

JOHN HENRY VAUGHAN VAUGHAN, 2nd Lieut., R.E. Born 6 Jan. 1908, at Wimbledon. S. of Colonel Henry Bathurst Vaughan, I.A. (ret.), Fontcouvert,

Queen's Road, Guernsey, C.I. Educ. at University College School; Elizabeth College, Guernsey; and R.M.A., Woolwich. Rec. by War Office. Adm. 30 Nov. 1927: began res. 1 Oct. 1928. Matric. 1 Nov. 1928.

B.A. (3rd Cl. Mech. Sci. Tri., 1930; all. 3 terms as Commiss. Off.) 1930
Lieut. (1931–), R.E.

NORMAN CECIL SAINSBURY. Born 14 July 1910, at Portsmouth. S. of Philip Henry Sainsbury (decd) and Mrs Sainsbury, 17 Lyndhurst Road, North End, Portsmouth. Educ. at Portsmouth Grammar School. Adm. 16 Dec. 1927: began res. 8 Oct. 1928. Matric. 1 Nov. 1928. Entrance Major Schol., Classics.

B.A. (1st Cl. Class. Tri. Pt I (l, g), 1930; 1st Cl. Oriental Lang. Tri. Pt I (c), 1931) 1931. 1st Cl. Oriental Lang. Tri. Pt II (b), 1932. M.A. 1935. Kitchener Schol., 1929 (held for 4 years). Robert Slade Schol., 1930; re-elected, 1931. E. G. Browne Schol., Pembroke College, 1932.
Asst Under-Librarian, University Library, Cambridge, 1933–5. Asst Keeper (2nd Class), Dept of Oriental Printed Books and Manuscripts, British Museum, 1935–.

KINGSLEY MORTON RAW. Born 12 Oct. 1908, at Spratton, Northants. S. of Rev. George Raw, Spratton Vicarage, Northampton. Educ. at Northampton Town and County School. Adm. 16 Dec. 1927: began res. 8 Oct. 1928. Matric. 1 Nov. 1928. Entrance Major Schol., Nat. Sciences.

B.A. (2nd Cl. Nat. Sci. Tri. Pt I, 1930; 2nd Cl. Pt II (Physics), 1931) 1931. M.A. 1937. *Bell Exhib.*, 1928. Schol.†, 1930.
Asst Master, Bury Grammar School, 1932–5; and at Edinburgh Institution (subsequently called Melville College), 1935–.

REUBEN COHEN. Born 4 Sept. 1910, in London. S. of Nathan Cohen, 3 Convent Gardens, N. Kensington, W. 11. Educ. at Polytechnic School, Regent Street, W. 1. Adm. 16 Dec. 1927: began res. 8 Oct. 1928. Matric. 1 Nov. 1928. Entrance Major Schol., History.

B.A. (1st Cl., 2nd Div., Hist. Tri. Pt I, 1930; 1st Cl., 2nd Div., Pt II, 1931) 1931. M.A. 1935. Lady Ward Schol., 1930.
With Marks & Spencer, Ltd (chain store), 1931–; being now (1936) manager of a London branch.

HUBERT HAROLD TRANTER. Born 30 March 1909, at Wolverhampton. S. of Harry Harold Tranter, 78 Clark Road, Wolverhampton. Educ. at Wolverhampton Grammar School. Adm. 16 Dec. 1927: began res. 8 Oct. 1928. Matric. 1 Nov. 1928. Entrance Minor Schol., Maths.

B.A. (1st Cl. Math. Tri. Pt I, 1929; Jun. Opt. Pt II, 1931) 1931. M.A. 1935. Kitchener Schol., 1928 (held for 3 years). Schol.†, 1930.
Actuarial Asst in London Office of the Sun Life Assurance Co. of Canada, 1932–.

ERIC JOHNSON. Born 23 Sept. 1910, at Brierley Hill, Staffs. S. of Alec Johnson, 98 John Street, Brierley Hill. Educ. at King Edward's School, Stourbridge. Adm. 16 Dec. 1927: began res. 8 Oct. 1928. Matric. 1 Nov. 1928. Entrance Minor Schol., Maths.

B.A. (1st Cl. Math. Tri. Pt I, 1929; Wrang. Pt II (b*), 1931) 1931. M.A. 1935. Francis Gisborne Schol., 1930.
Asst Master, King Edward's School, Stourbridge, 1931–4; and (as Senior Math. Master) at Emanuel School, Wandsworth Common, 1934–.

KENNETH RAPHAEL HENRY FOLLAND. Born 10 Oct. 1909, at Birmingham. S. of Heywood Michael Henry Folland, 21a Cambridge Road, King's Heath,

Birmingham. Educ. at King Edward's School, Birmingham. Adm. 16 Dec. 1927: began res. 8 Oct. 1928. Matric. 1 Nov. 1928. Entrance Minor Schol., Classics.

B.A. (1st Cl. Class. Tri. Pt I (*l*, *g*), 1930; 2nd Cl. Pt II, 1932) 1932. M.A. 1936. Thomas Parke Schol., 1930; re-elected, 1931.
Senior Classical Master, Cowbridge Grammar School, Glam, 1932–5; and at Bridgend County School, Glam, 1935–.

FRANK WILLIAM WALBANK. Born 10 Dec. 1909, at Bingley, Yorks. S. of Albert Joseph David Walbank, 7 Bromley Road, Bingley. Educ. at Bradford Grammar School. Adm. 16 Dec. 1927: began res. 8 Oct. 1928. Matric. 1 Nov. 1928. Entrance Minor Schol., Classics.

B.A. (1st Cl. Class. Tri. Pt I (*L*, *G*), 1930; 1st Cl. Pt II, *f* (*c*), 1931) 1931. M.A. 1935. Edward Lord North Schol., 1930. Hugo de Balsham Stud. (for research in Classics), £80, 1931. *Grant of £100 from George Charles Winter Warr Fund*, 1931. Leaf Stud., £50, 1932. *Thirlwall Prize*, 1933. *Hare Prize*, 1939.
Asst Master, North Manchester Municipal High School, 1932–3. Asst Lecturer in Latin, Liverpool Univ., 1934–6; and Lecturer, 1936–.
Second cousin of F. A. Walbank (p. 150).
Author:
  Aratos of Sicyon. (*Thirlwall Prize*, 1933.) Cambridge, 1933.

LESLIE MEECH. Born 11 Oct. 1909, in London. S. of Alfred Edward Meech, 283 Tooley Street, Horsleydown, S.E. 1. Educ. at St Olave's and St Saviour's Grammar School, Bermondsey. Adm. 16 Dec. 1927: began res. 8 Oct. 1928. Matric. 1 Nov. 1928. Entrance Minor Schol., History.

Went down during E. 1929.

RALPH DULINSKY. Born 13 Dec. 1908, in London. S. of Joel Dulinsky, 8 Bernard House, Shepherd Street, E. 1. Educ. at Owen's School, Islington. Adm. 16 Dec. 1927: began res. 8 Oct. 1928. Matric. 1 Nov. 1928. Entrance Exhib., History.

B.A. (1st Cl., 2nd Div., Hist. Tri. Pt I, 1930; 2nd Cl., 1st Div., Pt II, 1931) 1931. Henry Wilshawe Schol., 1929; re-elected, 1930.
Engaged in business, 1931–3. Journalist, with Odhams Press Ltd, 1933–.
He changed his names to Ralph DULIN by deed poll dated 13 Oct. 1930 (*London Gazette*, 21 Oct. 1930).

EDWARD JOHN EVANS. Born 11 June 1909, at Torquay. S. of Major Charles Edward Evans (decᵈ) and Mrs Evans, Elm Court, Babbacombe, S. Devon. Educ. at Wellington College. Adm. 17 Dec. 1927: began res. 8 Oct. 1928. Matric. 1 Nov. 1928.

B.A. (2nd Cl., 1st Div., Mod. & Med. Lang. Tri. Pt I, French & German, 1929; 2nd Cl., 2nd Div., Econ. Tri. Pt II (O.R.), 1931) 1931. Kitchener Schol., 1928 (held for 3 years).
Went to Vladivostok, U.S.S.R., in 1932.

HUGH JAMES TRAVERS. Born 2 Nov. 1909, at Halifax. S. of Major Hugh Price Travers (decᵈ) and Mrs Travers, The Little Dene, Triangle, Yorks. Educ. at Wellington College. Adm. 17 Dec. 1927: began res. 8 Oct. 1928. Matric. 1 Nov. 1928.

B.A. (2nd Cl., 2nd Div., Hist. Tri. Pt I, 1930; 2nd Cl., 1st Div., Pt II, 1931) 1931. Kitchener Schol., 1928 (held for 3 years).
Was with T. & A. Constable, Univ. Press, Edinburgh, in 1932.

JOHN POWNALL REEVES. Born 7 April 1909, at Blackheath, London. S. of Herbert James Reeves, Danesford, Hordle, Lymington, Hants. Educ. at Haileybury College. Adm. 20 Dec. 1927: began res. 8 Oct. 1928. Matric. 1 Nov. 1928.

B.A. (2nd Cl., 2nd Div., Mod. & Med. Lang. Tri. Pt I, French, 1929; 2nd Cl., 2nd Div., Pt I, Spanish, 1930; 3rd Cl. Pt II, 1931) 1931.
China Consular Service, 1932–; with appt. as Vice-Consul, Hankow, 1935–.

WILLIAM FRANK PROUDFOOT. Born 27 Nov. 1909, at Sidcup, Kent. S. of William Donald Proudfoot, St Fillans, Sandhurst Road, Sidcup. Educ. at Leys School. Adm. 31 Dec. 1927: began res. 8 Oct. 1928. Matric. 1 Nov. 1928.

B.A. (2nd Cl., 1st Div., Hist. Tri. Pt I, 1930; 1st Cl., 2nd Div., Law Tri. Pt II, 1931) 1931. M.A. 1935. Exhib. for History, 1929; re-elected, 1930.
Solicitor (adm. Oct. 1934); practising at 3 Gray's Inn Place, W.C. 1.

BASIL LINGARD DEED. Born 15 Jan. 1909, at Cirencester. S. of Sydney George Deed, Cromwell Lodge, Maldon, Essex. Educ. at Haileybury College. Adm. 2 Jan. 1928: began res. 6 Oct. 1928. Matric. 1 Nov. 1928.

B.A. (2nd Cl. Class. Tri. Pt I (l, g), 1930; 1st Cl. Pt II, 1931) 1931. M.A. 1935. Exhib. for Classics, 1929; re-elected, 1930.
Asst Master, Berkhamsted School, 1931–.

WILLIAM ALLAN EDWARDS. Born 5 Sept. 1909, at Bolton, Lancs. S. of William James Edwards, 32 Alexander Road, Tonge Park, Bolton. Educ. at Bolton Municipal Secondary School. Adm. 2 Jan. 1928: began res. 30 Oct. 1928. Matric. 1 Nov. 1928.

B.A. (1st Cl. Engl. Tri. Pt I, 1930; 1st Cl. Pt II, 1931) 1931. Exhib. for English, 1929. John Blyth Schol., 1930. Hugo de Balsham Stud. (for research in English), £60, 1931. Adm. Research Stud. as from Oct. 1931. Le Bas Prize, 1932. Jebb Stud., 1932.
Senior Lecturer in English, Cape Town Univ., 1934–.
Author:
    Plagiarism: an essay on good and bad borrowing. (Le Bas Prize, 1932.) Cambridge, 1933.

JAMES NEVILLE MASON. Born 15 May 1909, at Huddersfield. S. of John Mason, Croft House, Marsh, Huddersfield. Educ. at Marlborough College. Adm. 2 Jan. 1928: began res. 8 Oct. 1928. Matric. 1 Nov. 1928.

B.A. (Ord. degree) 1931. Leaf Grant, 1930.

GEOFFREY RICHARD FRANCIS SCOTSON. Born 23 Nov. 1908, at Dhulia, Bombay Presidency. S. of John Thomas Scotson (Peterhouse, B.A. 1900), I.C.S., 60 Cooden Drive, Bexhill-on-Sea. Educ. at Eastbourne College. Adm. 2 Jan. 1928: began res. 8 Oct. 1928. Matric. 1 Nov. 1928.

B.A. (2nd Cl. Math. Tri. Pt I, 1929; 1st Cl. Mech. Sci. Tri., 1931) 1931. M.A. 1935. George Carter Schol. (for Mech. Sciences), 1930.
Research Engineer, with the General Electric Co., Ltd, Wembley, Middlesex, 1933–. A.M.I.E.E. 1936.

PATRICK TAIT. Born 13 April 1909, at Bangalore, India. S. of Prof. John Guthrie Tait (Peterhouse, M.A. 1890), 38 George Square, Edinburgh. Educ. at Edinburgh Academy. Adm. 2 Jan. 1928: began res. 2 Oct. 1928. Matric. 1 Nov. 1928.

Resided M. 1928 to L. 1931 and E. 1933. B.A. (3rd Cl. Class. Tri. Pt I, 1930; adm. to degree without further exam.) 1933.
Died 5 Dec. 1935 at Edinburgh.
For his father and grandfather (P. G. Tait, successively Fellow and Hon. Fellow), see Walker.

OSWALD JAMES KEY. Born 11 Oct. 1906, in London. S. of Rev. Preb. Frederick John Key (Peterhouse, M.A. 1900), Shelton Rectory, Stoke-on-Trent. Educ. at Rossall School. Adm. 18 Jan. 1928: began res. 8 Oct. 1928. Matric. 1 Nov. 1928.

B.A. (Ord. degree) 1931. M.A. 1935.
Asst Master, Campbell College, Belfast, 1931–4; and at Harrow School, 1935–.

STANLEY ROBERT McPHEE. Born 27 Jan. 1909, at Belfast, Transvaal. S. of H. H. (Fairburn-) McPhee, Mombasa, Kenya. Educ. at Milton School, Bulawayo, Rhodesia. Rec. by P. T. Robinson, M.A. (Peterhouse), Asst Master. Adm. 28 Jan. 1928: began res. 8 Oct. 1928. Matric. 1 Nov. 1928.

Went down after M. 1929.
Half-Blue: Athletics (Pole Vault), 1929.
Reported living independently at Venice.

WILLIAM LAWRENCE VERNON CALDWELL. Born 24 Oct. 1909, at Sligo, Ireland. S. of Lieut.-Col. Alick Francis Somerville Caldwell, Wayfarers, Shrublands Road, Berkhamsted, Herts. Educ. at Berkhamsted School. Adm. 13 Feb. 1928: began res. 8 Oct. 1928. Matric. 1 Nov. 1928.

B.A. (3rd Cl. Class. Tri. Pt I, 1930; 3rd Cl. Engl. Tri. Pt I, 1931) 1931. M.A. 1935.
Asst Master, Seacroft School (preparatory), Skegness, Lincs, 1931–3. Private tutor, 1933–4. Senior Master, Belhaven Hill (also a preparatory school), Dunbar, East Lothian, 1934–.

GYRTH JAMES GORDON PITT. Born 29 Aug. 1909, at Streatham, London. S. of Walter James Pitt, Harman's Corner, Borden, by Sittingbourne, Kent. Educ. at King's School, Canterbury. Adm. 24 Feb. 1928: began res. 8 Oct. 1928. Matric. 1 Nov. 1928.

B.A. (2nd Cl. Class. Tri. Pt I, 1930; 1st Cl. Pt II, 1931) 1931. Lady Mary Ramsey Schol. (Honorary) for 1931–2; but did not reside.
Asst Superintendent, Dept of Excise, Straits Settlements, 1931–.

EDWARD READING ILOTT. Born 26 June 1908, at Portsmouth. S. of Julian Mayne Ilott, Valerian, West Parade, Bexhill-on-Sea. Educ. at Tonbridge School; and privately. Adm. 25 Feb. 1928: began res. 8 Oct. 1928. Matric. 1 Nov. 1928.

Went down during L. 1932.
Asst Master, Stanmore Park (a preparatory school), Stanmore, Middlesex, 1932–3. Head Master, Beaumont House (also preparatory), Heronsgate, Herts, 1933–.

JOHN MALCOLM MUIR. Born 14 April 1909, at Putney. S. of John Muir, O.B.E., Corserine, Radlett, Herts. Educ. at St George's School, Harpenden. Adm. 19 March 1928: began res. 9 Oct. 1928. Matric. 1 Nov. 1928.

B.A. (3rd Cl. Mech. Sci. Tri., 1931) 1931. M.A. 1936.
Represented Cambridge v. Oxford in Motor Cycle Reliability Trial, 1929; and in Motor Cycle Hill Climb, 1931.
Winner of many Amateur Racing Motor Cyclist events, including Manx Grand Prix. Research Engineer, with C. A. V. Bosch Ltd, Acton, Middlesex, 1934–6. Subsequently joined an automobile firm in Cape Town. G.I.Mech.E. 1933. G.M.I.Auto.E.
Cousin of I. A. M. Muir (p. 85).

BRUCE CARTWRIGHT DE GARDANNE ALLAN. Born 11 Dec. 1910, at Mixcoae, Mexico City, Mexico. S. of Fergus Leon de Gardanne Allan (decd) and Mrs Allan, c/o The Royal Bank of Scotland, 3 Bishopsgate, London, E.C. 2.

Educ. at Wellington College. Adm. 27 March 1928: began res. 7 Oct. 1928. Matric. 1 Nov. 1928.

B.A. (3rd Cl. Nat. Sci. Tri. Pt I, 1930; 3rd Cl. Mech. Sci. Tri., 1932) 1932. M.A. 1937.
Gas Engineer, with the Compañía Mexicana de Petróleo 'El Aguila', S.A., Tampico, Mexico, 1933–.
He matric. as Bruce de Gardanne Cartwright ALLAN.

CHARLES GODFREY BELL. Born 25 Nov. 1908, at Streatham, London. S. of Rev. William Godfrey Bell (Peterhouse, M.A. 1909), 2 Clifton Hill, Brighton. Educ. at Brighton College; and privately. Adm. 27 March 1928: began res. 8 Oct. 1928. Matric. 1 Nov. 1928.

B.A. (Ord. degree) 1931. M.A. 1937.
Chichester Theol. Coll., 1932. Ordained d. 1933, p. 1935 Durham. C. of St Peter, Stockton-on-Tees, 1933–6; St Margaret, Plumstead, Dio. Southwark, 1937–.

WILFRED JOHN BEVISS. Born 31 Oct. 1908, at Axminster, Devon. S. of William Beviss, The Berea, Wambrook, Chard, Somerset. Educ. at Allhallows School, Honiton. Adm. 27 March 1928: began res. 8 Oct. 1928. Matric. 1 Nov. 1928.

B.A. (3rd Cl. Law Tri. Pt I, 1930; 3rd Cl. Pt II, 1931) 1931.
He matric. as Wilfrid John BEVISS.

HERBERT FREDERICK BRUDENELL FOSTER. Born 8 May 1908, at Queensbury, Yorks. S. of Colonel Herbert Anderton Foster, Faskally, Pitlochry, Perthshire. Educ. at Radley College. Adm. 27 March 1928: began res. 8 Oct. 1928. Matric. 1 Nov. 1928.

Went down after E. 1931.
Represented Cambridge v. Oxford at Rugby Fives, 1930, 1931. (Captain, 1931.)
Manages the family estate of Faskally. Lieut. (1932–), Scottish Horse (T.A.).

EDWARD HOOTON. Born 13 March 1910, at Lincoln. S. of Charles William Hooton, Kirthorne, Queensway, Lincoln. Educ. at Lincoln School. Adm. 27 March 1928: began res. 8 Oct. 1928. Matric. 1 Nov. 1928.

B.A. (3rd Cl. Math. Tri. Pt I, 1929; 3rd Cl. Law Tri. Pt II, 1931) 1931. LL.B. 1932. M.A. 1935.
Kitchener Schol., 1929 (held for 2 years). Squire Schol., 1929.
Solicitor (adm. Aug. 1934); practising at Birmingham.

PETER KINNERSLY. Born 16 June 1910, at Calais, St Martin's, Guernsey, C.I. S. of George Edward Kinnersly (decd) and Mrs Kinnersly, Calais, St Martin's, Guernsey. Educ. at Sherborne School. Adm. 27 March 1928: began res. 8 Oct. 1928. Matric. 1 Nov. 1928.

Went down after M. 1930.
2nd Lieut., R. Tank Corps (Supplementary Reserve), 1931; Lieut., 1934; resigned, 1934. In business at St Sampson's, Guernsey, 1936–.

ARTHUR HUBERT STANLEY MEGAW. Born 14 July 1910, at Dublin. S. of Arthur Stanley Megaw, Arden, Fortwilliam Drive, Belfast. Educ. at Campbell College, Belfast. Adm. 27 March 1928: began res. 7 Oct. 1928. Matric. 1 Nov. 1928.

B.A. (Ord. degree) 1931. M.A. 1935. Leaf Grant, 1931. Walston Stud., 1931. Grant of £100 from Craven Fund, 1932. Macmillan Studentship of British School at Athens (for research in Hellenic Studies), 1933.
Asst Director of, and Architect to, the British School at Athens, 1935–6. Director of Antiquities, Cyprus, 1936–.

BASIL HENRY PAGE. Born 7 Jan. 1910, at Ilkley, Yorks. S. of Frederick James Page, The Grange, Wodehouse Road, Bombay. Educ. at Canford School. Adm. 27 March 1928: began res. 8 Oct. 1928. Matric. 1 Nov. 1928.

B.A. (2ⁿᵈ Cl. Nat. Sci. Tri. Pt I, 1930; Cert. of Dilig. Study, 1931) 1931. M.A., M.B., B.Chir. 1936.
Half-Blue: Cross Country, 1930, and Athletics (One mile), 1931. Represented Cambridge *v.* Oxford in Relay Races (Four miles), 1928, 1930.
M.R.C.S., L.R.C.P. 1934. F.R.C.S. 1935.

CHARLES SHIPPAM. Born 13 April 1909, at Chichester. S. of Frank Shippam, Potwell House, Walberton, Arundel, Sussex. Educ. at Malvern College. Rec. by F. S. Preston, M.A., Head Master, and Rev. W. O. Cosgrove, M.A. (Peterhouse), Chaplain and Asst Master; and others. Adm. 27 March 1928: began res. 8 Oct. 1928. Matric. 1 Nov. 1928.

Went down after E. 1931.
Managing Director of C. Shippam, Ltd (provision merchants), Chichester.

NORMAN ELLIS WILKINSON. Born 22 Nov. 1910, at Harrogate. S. of George Wilkinson, Beech Mount, 23 Otley Road, Harrogate. Educ. at Oundle School. Adm. 27 March 1928: began res. 8 Oct. 1928. Matric. 1 Nov. 1928.

B.A. (2ⁿᵈ Cl. Nat. Sci. Tri. Pt I, 1931) 1931. M.A. 1935.
Studied at Jena Univ., 1931–2. Salisbury Theol. Coll., 1932. Ordained d. 1933, p. 1934 Oxford. C. of Banbury, Dio. Oxford, 1933–.

WILLIAM ROBERT BUCHANAN LEE. Born 25 June 1906, at Cape Town. S. of Vincent Buchanan Lee, Knowsley, Kloof Road, Sea Point, Cape Town. Educ. at Diocesan College, Rondebosch, Cape Town. Adm. 28 March 1928: began res. 9 Oct. 1928. Matric. 1 Nov. 1928.

B.A. (3ʳᵈ Cl. Law Tri. Pt I, 1930; 3ʳᵈ Cl. Pt II, 1931) 1931.
Called to the Bar, Inner Temple, 17 Nov. 1932.

RICHARD CHARLES OLDFIELD. Born 26 Sept. 1909, in London. S. of Prof. Sir Francis Du Pré Oldfield, 53 Palace Court, Bayswater, W. 2. Educ. at Marlborough College. Adm. 28 March 1928: began res. 8 Oct. 1928. Matric. 1 Nov. 1928.

B.A. (2ⁿᵈ Cl. Nat. Sci. Tri. Pt I, 1930; Cert. of Dilig. Study, 1931) 1931. M.A. 1935. Exhib. (Honorary) for Moral Sciences, 1931. Adm. Research Stud. as from Oct. 1933. *Arnold Gerstenberg Stud.*, 1934.
Leverhulme Research Stud. of National Institute of Industrial Psychology, 1937. Member of British Psychological Society.

NAIMPALLI SHIVA RAO. Born 31 May 1906, at Mangalore, Madras. S. of Subba Rao, Mercara Hill, Mangalore. Educ. privately. Adm. 28 March 1928: began res. 9 Oct. 1928. Matric. 1 Nov. 1928.

B.A. (Ord. degree) 1931.
Asst, Imperial Tobacco Co. of India, Ltd, Madras, 1935–.

DAVID ERSKINE COX. Born 2 Feb. 1910, at Ross, Herefordshire. S. of Major William Stanley Ramsay Cox, Ashe Leigh, Ross. Educ. at Wellington College. Adm. 4 April 1928: began res. 8 Oct. 1928. Matric. 1 Nov. 1928.

Resided M. 1928 to L. 1931 and E. 1933. B.A. (3ʳᵈ Cl. Math. Tri. Pt I, 1930; P.S. Exam. French, 1933) 1933.
Asst Master, St Edmund's School (preparatory), Hindhead ,Surrey, 1933–.

Humphrey Robert Arthur HIGGENS. Born 26 Jan. 1908, at Much Hadham, Herts. S. of Claude Robert Higgens, New Hall, Standon, Herts. Educ. at Eton College. Adm. 27 April 1928: began res. 8 Oct. 1928. Matric. 1 Nov. 1928.

B.A. (2nd Cl. Class. Tri. Pt I (*l*, *G*), 1930; 2nd Cl., 1st Div., Engl. Tri. Pt I, 1931) 1931. M.A. 1935. Half-Blue: Fencing (Sabre), 1931.
Asst Master, St Paul's School, 1935–.

John Ernest ALLEN. Adm. to incorporate,—'Order Book', 21 May 1928. Matric. and incorp. M.A. (from Wadham College, Oxford), 12 Oct. 1928.

Born 23 July 1872, at Highfield, Shepton Mallet, Somerset. S. of John Allen (dec^d), of Shepton Mallet. Educ. at Clifton College, and Wadham College, Oxford (B.A. 1899; M.A. 1924).
Called to the Bar, Inner Temple, 19 Nov. 1900. Contested S.W. Sussex Division in Liberal interest, 1905 and 1906. Member of Balkan Committee since 1905. Hon. Sec., British Association's Committee on the Effects of the War on Credit, Currency and Finance, 1915–22.
  Author:
    (With F. W. Hirst) *Legal and practical guide to county elections.* London, 1906.
    The War debt and how to meet it; with an examination of the proposed 'capital levy'. London (1919).
    (With F. W. Hirst) *British War budgets. (Economic and Social History of the World War: British Series.)* London, 1926.

Arthur Reginald JONES, Flt Lieut., R.A.F. Born 13 April 1899, at Stickford, Lincs. S. of Rev. Orton Arundel Jones, Longstone, Hope Cove, nr Kingsbridge, S. Devon. Rec. by Air Ministry. Adm. 3 July 1928: began res. 1 Oct. 1928. Matric. 1 Nov. 1928.

Resided M. 1928.
Killed 5 Aug. 1931 in an aeroplane accident at Heliopolis, Egypt; being then still Flt Lieut., R.A.F.

Cedric Horace ADAMS. Born 20 March 1910, at Southsea. S. of Alfred James Adams, Edenhurst, Timperley, Cheshire. Educ. at Clifton College. Adm. 9 July 1928: began res. 7 Oct. 1928. Matric. 1 Nov. 1928.

B.A. (Ord. degree) 1931.
Chartered Accountant.

Christopher Sydney COCKERELL. Born 4 June 1910, at Cambridge. S. of (*later* Sir) Sydney Carlyle Cockerell (Director of Fitzwilliam Museum), 3 Shaftesbury Road, Cambridge. Educ. at Gresham's School, Holt. Adm. 9 July 1928: began res. 8 Oct. 1928. Matric. 1 Nov. 1928.

B.A. (3rd Cl. Intercoll. Exam. in Mech. Sci., 1930; standard of Ord. degree, Mech. Sci. Tri., 1931) 1931. M.A. 1935. Adm. Research Stud. as from Jan. 1934.
Represented Cambridge *v.* Oxford in Motor Cycle Hill Climb, 1931; and at Shooting (Miniature Rifle), 1931.

John Stephen JAMES. Born 26 Dec. 1909, at Broxbourne, Herts. S. of John Egbert James, The Beacon, St John's, Woking. Educ. at Marlborough College. Adm. 9 July 1928: began res. 8 Oct. 1928. Matric. 1 Nov. 1928.

B.A. (3rd Cl. Law Tri. Pt I, 1930; standard of Ord. degree, Pt II, 1931) 1931.
Called to the Bar, Lincoln's Inn, 17 Nov. 1932. With Sweet & Maxwell, Ltd (law booksellers), 2 & 3 Chancery Lane, London, W.C. 2, 1934–.

John Francis Howard REES-JONES. Born 17 Nov. 1909, at Redruth, Cornwall. S. of Rev. John Rees-Jones, Newlyn Vicarage, Penzance. Educ. at Truro Cathedral School. Adm. 9 July 1928: began res. 8 Oct. 1928. Matric. 1 Nov. 1928.

B.A. (2nd Cl., 1st Div., Hist. Tri. Pt I, 1930; 2nd Cl., 2nd Div., Engl. Tri. Pt I, 1931) 1931. M.A. 1937.
St Stephen's House, Oxford, 1931. Ordained d. 1933, p. 1934 Exeter. C. of St Peter, Plymouth, 1933–6; All Saints, Tooting, Dio. Southwark, 1936–.

GRAHAM ROGERS SANSBURY. Born 4 Aug. 1909, at Streatham, London. S. of Cyril Jackson Sansbury, 69 Mount Nod Road, Streatham, S.W. 16. Educ. at Dulwich College. Adm. 9 July 1928: began res. 8 Oct. 1928. Matric. 1 Nov. 1928.

B.A. (3ʳᵈ Cl. Engl. Tri. Pt I, 1930; 2ⁿᵈ Cl. Theol. Tri. Pt I, Sec. A, 1932) 1932. M.A. 1938.
Westcott House, Cambridge, 1931. Ordained d. 1932, p. 1933 Southwark. C. of St Peter, St Helier, 1932–5; Malden, 1935–8; Chaplain, Kolar Gold Field, Mysore, Dio. Madras, 1938–.
Bro. of C. K. Sansbury (p. 92).

STEPHEN THOMAS COLVIN TURNER. Born 25 April 1910, at Nicosia, Cyprus. S. of Henry Attree Turner, Amman, via Palestine. Educ. at Marlborough College. Adm. 9 July 1928: began res. 8 Oct. 1928. Matric. 1 Nov. 1928.

B.A. (Ord. degree) 1931.
With Macgregor & Co., Ltd (timber exporters), Rangoon, 1931–2. Asst C.O., Desert Patrol, Arab Legion, Amman, Transjordan, 1933–.

WILLIAM HENRY THOMSON ANDREWS. Born 13 Oct. 1909, at Helensburgh, Dumbartonshire. S. of George Johnston Andrews, Riverstone, Helensburgh. Educ. at Trinity College, Glenalmond. Adm. 10 July 1928: began res. 13 Oct. 1928. Matric. 1 Nov. 1928.

B.A. (Ord. degree) 1932.
Director of the Enfield Rolling Mills Ltd, Brimsdown, Middlesex.

RICHARD LESLIE HARRIS LLOYD. Born 17 March 1909, in London. S. of Rev. Richard Harris Lloyd, The Vicarage, North Ferriby, Yorks. Educ. at Worksop College, and St Augustine's College, Canterbury. Adm. 10 July 1928: began res. 8 Oct. 1928. Matric. 1 Nov. 1928.

B.A. (2ⁿᵈ Cl., 2ⁿᵈ Div., Hist. Tri. Pt I, 1930; 2ⁿᵈ Cl., 1ˢᵗ Div., Pt II, 1931) 1931. M.A. 1935.
Matric. from Merton College, Oxford, 12 Oct. 1932; incorp. B.A., 19 Nov. 1932; M.A., B.Litt. 1936. St Stephen's House, Oxford, 1932. Ordained d. 1936, p. 1937 York. C. of Middlesbrough, 1936–8; Northallerton, Dio. York, 1938–.

FRANK HAWLEY. Born 31 March 1906, at Stockton-on-Tees. S. of Albert Hawley, 56 Stanley Street, Norton-on-Tees. Educ. at Stockton Secondary School and Liverpool Univ. (B.A. degree). Adm. 13 July 1928: began res. 11 Oct. 1928. Matric. 1 Nov. 1928. Research Stud.

Messrs J. S. Fry & Sons' Stud. (for research in Linguistic Studies), 1928. Went down after E. 1929. Went to Japan.

LEWIS BLIZARD HOPE-REFORD. Born 5 March 1910, at Ballinderry, Co. Antrim. S. of Dr John Hope Reford, C.M.G., Director of Medical and Sanitary Services, Uganda Protectorate. Educ. at Haileybury College. Adm. 16 July 1928: began res. 8 Oct. 1928. Matric. 1 Nov. 1928.

B.A. (Ord. degree) 1931.
Winner, with T. G. Askwith (p. 141), of the Lowe Double Sculls, 1931.
Entered the Indian Army: 2nd Lieut., 1932 (with seniority of 1930); Lieut., 1933 (with seniority of 1932).

JOSEPH DANIEL UNWIN, **Fellow Commoner**. Born 6 Dec. 1895, at Haverhill, Suffolk. S. of Frederic Daniel Unwin, The Grange, Withersfield,

Suffolk. Educ. at Shrewsbury School. Adm. 7 Aug. 1928: began res. 1 Oct. 1928. Matric. 1 Nov. 1928. Research Stud.

Ph.D. 1931.
✕ 1914–19. Capt., Northamptonshire Regt.; Capt., Tank Corps. (W 3.) *M.C. M.*

Honorary Class. Exhib., Oriel College, Oxford, 1914; but did not matric. Foreign Managing Director, British Syndicate, operating in Abyssinia, Somaliland, etc., 1919–22. Then engaged in private business; and also studying in Oxford, 1924–8. F.R.A.I. 1928.

Head of Cambridge House University Settlement, Camberwell, London, S.E. 5, 1931–6. Died 18 June 1936 at Ealing, after an operation for appendicitis.

Author:

Sexual regulations and human behaviour. London, 1933.
Notes on the Unwin family. London (1934).
Sex and culture. London, 1934.
The scandal of imprisonment for debt. London, 1935.
Sexual regulations and cultural behaviour; an address delivered before the Medical Section of the British Psychological Society, 27 March 1935. London, 1935.

Sir THOMAS ANTON BERTRAM, *Kt.* Adm. **Fellow**, 4 Oct. 1928. Internal Fellow, 1928–9. Senior Bursar, 1928–9.

Born 8 Feb. 1869, at Barnstaple, Devon. S. of Rev. Robert Aitken Bertram (dec^d). Educ. at City of London School, and Gonville and Caius College (Class. Schol.; B.A. 1890; M.A. 1894; Fellow, 1891–7). *Powis Medal*, 1890. *Chancellor's Classical Medal*, 1891. President of Union Soc., E. 1892.

Called to the Bar, Lincoln's Inn, 26 Apr. 1893. Attorney-General of the Bahamas, 1902–7. Puisne Judge, Cyprus, 1907–11. Attorney-General of Ceylon, 1911–18. K.C. (Ceylon), 1913. Cr. Kt, 1916. Chief Justice of Ceylon, 1918–25. President, Special Commissions on the Affairs of the Orthodox Patriarchate of Jerusalem, 1921 and 1925.

Died 16 Sept. 1937 at Canterbury.

Author:

(With A. Parsons) *The Workmen's Compensation Acts, 1897 and 1900.* London, 1900. 2nd ed. Ib., 1902.
(With H. C. Luke) *Report of the Commission appointed by the Government of Palestine to inquire into the affairs of the Orthodox Patriarchate of Jerusalem.* London, 1921.
(With J. W. A. Young) *The Orthodox Patriarchate of Jerusalem: report of the Commission appointed by the Government of Palestine...* London, 1926.
The Colonial Service. Cambridge, 1930.

KENNETH EDGAR BOND. Born 24 Oct. 1908, at Edwinstowe, Notts. S. of Rev. Edward Vines Bond, Beddington Rectory, Croydon, Surrey. Educ. at Haileybury College. Adm. 31 Dec. 1927: began res. 7 Oct. 1929. Matric. 1 Nov. 1929.

B.A. (Ord. degree) 1932. M.A., M.B., B.Chir. 1938
M.R.C.S., L.R.C.P. 1936.

KENNETH DOUGLAS WHITE. Born 22 Nov. 1908, at Liverpool. S. of James Harrison White, 49 Arundel Avenue, Sefton Park, Liverpool. Educ. at Liverpool Institute High School and Liverpool Univ. (B.A. degree). Adm. 18 Dec. 1928: began res. 8 Oct. 1929. Matric. 1 Nov. 1929. Entrance Major Schol., Classics. Aff. Stud.

B.A. (1st Cl. Class. Tri. Pt I, 1930; 1st Cl. Pt II, 1931) 1931. M.A. 1938. Edmund Woodward Schol., 1930. Leaf Grant, 1931.
Asst in Greek, Edinburgh Univ., 1931–3. Asst Lecturer in Greek, Leeds Univ., 1933–.

GUY OLIVER MILLER NEATBY. Born 3 June 1910, at Leytonstone, Essex. S. of Dr Thomas Miller Neatby, 102 Riggindale Road, Streatham, S.W. 16. Educ. at City of London School. Adm. 18 Dec. 1928: began res. 7 Oct. 1929. Matric. 1 Nov. 1929. Entrance Major Schol., Classics.

B.A. (1st Cl. Class. Tri. Pt I (g), 1930; 2nd Cl. Pt II, 1932), 1932. M.A. 1936. Edward Lord North Schol., 1931.
M.R.C.S., L.R.C.P. 1938.

KENNETH MITCHELL. Born 12 April 1911, at Monkseaton, Northumberland. S. of James Wilson Mitchell, Garleigh, 40 St George's Crescent, Monkseaton. Educ. at Tynemouth School, and Armstrong College, Newcastle-on-Tyne. Adm. 18 Dec. 1928: began res. 7 Oct. 1929. Matric. 1 Nov. 1929. Entrance Minor Schol., Maths.

B.A. (1st Cl. Math. Tri. Pt I, 1930; Wrang. Pt II (b), 1932) 1932. Ph.D. 1935. Francis Gisborne Schol., 1931. J. M. Dodds Stud. (for research in Mathematical Physics), £50, 1932; re-elected, £60, 1933. Adm. Research Stud. as from Oct. 1932. Leaf Grant, 1933. Goldsmiths' Co.'s Senior Stud., 1933. *Smith's Prize*, 1934.
Asst Lecturer in Applied Mathematics, Leeds Univ., 1934–8; and Lecturer, 1938–.

HEDLEY WILSON JOHNSON. Born 8 Oct. 1910, at Winchmore Hill, Middlesex. S. of Harry Cecil Johnson, Eversley, Uphill Road, Mill Hill, N.W. 7. Educ. at Mill Hill School. Adm. 18 Dec. 1928: began res. 7 Oct. 1929. Matric. 1 Nov. 1929. Entrance Minor Schol., Classics.

B.A. (2nd Cl. Class. Tri. Pt I, 1931; 3rd Cl. Pt II, 1932) 1932. M.A. 1936. Schol.†, 1931.
Asst Master, Monkton Combe School, 1933–.

HUGH BROWN. Born 22 Feb. 1910, at Shotts, Lanarkshire. S. of John Brown, School House, Clarkston, Airdrie, Lanarkshire. Educ. at Fettes College. Adm. 18 Dec. 1928: began res. 11 Oct. 1929. Matric. 1 Nov. 1929. Entrance Minor Schol., Classics.

B.A. (1st Cl. Class. Tri. Pt I (g, l), 1931; 2nd Cl., 1st Div., Engl. Tri. Pt I, 1933) 1933. Kitchener Schol., 1929 (held for 4 years). Edmund Woodward Schol., 1931. Schol.† for English, 1932.
Half-Blue: Cross Country, 1932, 1933.
Asst Master, Methodist College, Belfast, 1933–.

JAMES SIMPSON. Born 18 May 1910, at Liverpool. S. of James Simpson, 124 Adelaide Road, Liverpool. Educ. at St Francis Xavier's College, Liverpool. Adm. 18 Dec. 1928: began res. 7 Oct. 1929. Matric. 1 Nov. 1929. Entrance Minor Schol., History.

B.A. (2nd Cl., 1st Div., Hist. Tri. Pt I, 1931; 2nd Cl., 1st Div., Pt II, 1932) 1932. M.A. 1936. Schol.†, 1931.
Schoolmaster.

ARTHUR TIBBEY GERARD. Born 2 Sept. 1910, in London. S. of Thomas George Tibbey, 16 Tyson Road, Forest Hill, S.E. 23. Educ. at Dulwich College. Adm. 18 Dec. 1928: began res. 7 Oct. 1929. Matric. 1 Nov. 1929. Entrance Minor Schol., History.

B.A. (1st Cl., 1st Div., Hist. Tri. Pt I, 1931; 1st Cl. Pt II, 1932) 1932. Leaf Stud., £50, 1931. Lady Ward Schol., 1931. Given title of Scholar for 1932–3. *Members' Prize (English Essay)*, 1932.
Asst Principal, Ministry of Health, 1933–.
He changed his names from Arthur Gerard TIBBEY to Arthur Tibbey GERARD by deed poll dated 1 Aug. 1929 (*London Gazette*, 9 Aug. 1929).

ANTHONY IRVING PHELPS. Born 4 Jan. 1911, at Scorton, Yorks. S. of John Henry Dixon Phelps, St Clare, Malvern. Educ. at Felsted School. Adm. 18 Dec. 1928: began res. 7 Oct. 1929. Matric. 1 Nov. 1929. Entrance Exhib., Classics.

B.A. (2nd Cl. Class. Tri. Pt I, 1931; 3rd Cl. Hist. Tri. Pt II, 1932) 1932. M.A. 1937. Exhib., 1931.
Asst Master, Ottershaw College, Chertsey, Surrey, 1932–.

JOHN FARLEY SPRY. Born 11 March 1910, at Cambridge. S. of John Farley Spry (dec^d). Guardian: Charles Percy Walby, 161 Rue Lamorinière, Antwerp. Educ. at Perse School, Cambridge. Adm. 18 Dec. 1928: began res. 7 Oct. 1929. Matric. 1 Nov. 1929. Entrance Exhib., History.

> B.A. (2nd Cl., 1st Div., Hist. Tri. Pt I, 1931; 2nd Cl., 2nd Div., Pt II, 1932) 1932. M.A. 1936. Exhib., 1931.
> Solicitor (adm. Nov. 1935). Colonial Service, with appt. as Asst Registrar of Titles, Uganda, 1936–.

CUTHBERT HOWARD DAWKINS. Born 25 Nov. 1910, at Axminster, Devon. S. of Edwin Howard Dawkins (dec^d). Guardian: Joshua Spencer Brown, Rosemount, Musbury Road, Axminster. Educ. at Rugby School. Adm. 23 Dec. 1928: began res. 7 Oct. 1929. Matric. 1 Nov. 1929.

> B.A. (Ord. degree) 1932.
> Lay Missionary (Bible Churchmen's Missionary Soc.), Abyssinia, 1934–.

MAURICE MILSOM CHAPMAN. Born 5 Aug. 1910, at Taunton. S. of Milsom Robert Chapman, Westmead, Wellington Road, Taunton. Educ. at Clifton College. Adm. 23 Dec. 1928: began res. 7 Oct. 1929. Matric. 1 Nov. 1929.

> B.A. (2nd Cl., 1st Div., Mod. & Med. Lang. Tri. Pt I, French & German, 1930; 3rd Cl. Pt II, 1932) 1932. M.A. 1937. Leaf Grant, 1931.
> Asst Master, Ottershaw College, Chertsey, Surrey, 1934–.

GEORGE NOEL HINTON. Born 11 Dec. 1910, at Bulford, Wilts. S. of Lieut.-Col. Godfrey Bingham Hinton, C.M.G. (dec^d), and Mrs Hinton, Shepton Beauchamp, Seavington, Somerset. Educ. at Wellington College. Adm. 23 Dec. 1928: began res. 7 Oct. 1929. Matric. 1 Nov. 1929.

> B.A. (2nd Cl., 2nd Div., Engl. Tri. Pt I, 1931; 3rd Cl. Pt II, 1932) 1932. Kitchener Schol., 1929 (held for 3 years).

THOMAS WATKIN GERRARD COLLINS. Born 28 Sept. 1910, at Johannesburg, Transvaal. S. of Capt. Joseph Clarke Collins, The Residency, Middleburg, Transvaal. Educ. at Eastbourne College. Adm. 23 Dec. 1928: began res. 7 Oct. 1929. Matric. 1 Nov. 1929.

> B.A. (Ord. degree) 1932.
> Lay Missionary (Africa Inland Mission), Kenya Colony, 1934–.

WILFRID MEYNELL WOODHOUSE. Born 30 Sept. 1911, in London. S. of George Woodhouse, 19 Wigmore Street, W. 1. Educ. at St Edward's School, Oxford. Adm. 23 Dec. 1928: began res. 7 Oct. 1929. Matric. 1 Nov. 1929.

> B.A. (Ord. degree) 1932. M.A. 1936.
> Architect. A.R.I.B.A. 1935.

GEOFFREY HEYGATE LOWICK. Born 21 March 1911, at Northampton. S. of William Cory Lowick, The Avenue, Spinney Hill, Northampton. Educ. at Eastbourne College. Adm. 23 Dec. 1928: began res. 7 Oct. 1929. Matric. 1 Nov. 1929.

> B.A. (2nd Cl., 2nd Div., Law Tri. Pt I, 1931; 2nd Cl., 2nd Div., Pt II, 1932) 1932. M.A. 1938.
> Solicitor (adm. Nov. 1935); practising at Northampton.

GIJSBERT DIEDERIK ADVOCAAT. Born 25 Sept. 1910, at Petropolis, Brazil. S. of Gijsbert Diederik Advocaat, 39 Boulevard Carabacel, Nice. Educ.

at Trinity College, Glenalmond. Adm. 23 Dec. 1928: began res. 7 Oct. 1929.
Matric. 1 Nov. 1929.

> Resided till E. 1932 inclusive. B.A. (Ord. degree) 1934.
> Architect; practising at Oslo, Norway. A.A. Dipl.

GEORGE FREDERICK BLUMER. Born 22 Feb. 1911, at Stafford. S. of
Frederick Milnes Blumer, The Mount, Stafford. Educ. at King's School, Canterbury. Adm. 5 Jan. 1929: began res. 7 Oct. 1929. Matric. 1 Nov. 1929.

> B.A. (2nd Cl., 2nd Div., Law Tri. Pt I, 1931; 2nd Cl., 2nd Div., Econ. Tri. Pt II (N.R.), 1932) 1932.
> Third Class Officer, Ministry of Labour, 1932–8; and Asst Principal, 1938–. F.R.Econ.S. 1934.
> 2nd Lieut. (1937–), R. Northumberland Fus. (T.A.).
> Bro. of J. A. C. Blumer (p. 103).

JOHN SHEARME CURTIS. Born 15 May 1910, at Blackheath, London.
S. of Colonel Ivor Curtis (Peterhouse, M.A. 1900, decd) and Mrs Curtis, 66 Downs
Road, Coulsdon, Surrey. Educ. at Cheltenham College. Adm. 5 Jan. 1929: began
res. 7 Oct. 1929. Matric. 1 Nov. 1929.

> B.A. (3rd Cl. Math. Tri. Pt I, 1930; 3rd Cl. Econ. Tri. Pt II (O.R.), 1932) 1932. Ironmongers'
> Co.'s Exhib., 1929 (held for 3 years). Kitchener Schol., 1929 (held for 3 years).
> With Warner, Barnes & Co., Ltd (importers, exporters, shipping and insurance agents), Manila,
> Philippine Islands, 1932–.

DOUGLAS BARRÉ FORBES. Born 12 Oct. 1910, at Clevedon, Somerset.
S. of Barré Robert Machray Forbes, 9 Beaufort Road, Clifton. Educ. at Clifton
College. Adm. 5 Jan. 1929: began res. 7 Oct. 1929. Matric. 1 Nov. 1929.

> B.A. (2nd Cl. Class. Tri. Pt I, 1930; 2nd Cl., 2nd Div., Law Tri. Pt II, 1932) 1932. LL.B. 1934.
> Solicitor (adm. Dec. 1935); being partner in O'Donoghue & Forbes, 16 Orchard Street, Bristol.
> Bro. of W. A. Forbes (p. 91) and cousin of J. C. Gurney (p. 8).

ROBERT SHERBOTOFF GEOGHEGAN. Born 31 Dec. 1909, at Norwich.
S. of George Frederick Geoghegan, Claughton, Prideaux Road, Eastbourne. Educ.
at Eastbourne College. Adm. 5 Jan. 1929: began res. 7 Oct. 1929. Matric. 1 Nov.
1929.

> B.A. (3rd Cl. Math. Tri. Pt I, 1930; 3rd Cl. Mech. Sci. Tri., 1932) 1932.
> Engineer. G.I.Mech.E. 1934. Lieut. (1937–), R.E. (T.A.).

GEORGE EDWARD PHILIP WOOD. Born 11 April 1910, at Hibaldstow,
Lincs. S. of Rev. Edward Francis Wood, St Swithin's Vicarage, Lincoln. Educ.
at St Edward's School, Oxford. Adm. 5 Jan. 1929: began res. 7 Oct. 1929. Matric.
1 Nov. 1929.

> B.A. (Ord. degree) 1932. M.A. 1936.
> Classical Master, Merton Court (a preparatory school), Foots Cray, Kent, 1932–6; and at Oatlands
> (also preparatory), Harrogate, 1936–.

MITSUNAO HIROSE. Born 11 March 1905, at Kobe, Japan. S. of Chiaki
Hirose, 12 Sumaura-dori, 3 chome, Suma-ku, Kobe. Guardian: T. Imai, Sumitomo
Bank, 67 Bishopsgate, London, E.C. 2. Educ. at Kwansei Gakuin College of
Commerce, Kobe. Adm. 2 Feb. 1929: began res. 7 Oct. 1929. Matric. 1 Nov. 1929.

> B.A. (Ord. degree) 1932.
> With the Sumitomo Goshi-Kaisha, Osaka, Japan, 1933–.

ARCHER JOHN PORTER MARTIN. Born 1 March 1910, in London. S. of Dr William Archer Porter Martin, 27 Rothsay Road, Bedford. Educ. at Bedford School. Adm. 2 Feb. 1929: began res. 7 Oct. 1929. Matric. 1 Nov. 1929.

B.A. (2nd Cl. Nat. Sci. Tri. Pt I, 1931; 2nd Cl., 2nd Div., Pt II (Biochemistry), 1932) 1932. M.A. 1936. Ph.D. 1937. Exhib. for Nat. Sciences, 1930; re-elected, 1931. Adm. Research Stud. as from Oct. 1932.

Biophysicist, Wool Industries Research Assoc., Torridon, Headingley, Leeds, 1938–.

JOHN RUSSELL HALL. Born 8 May 1910, at Newcastle-on-Tyne. S. of Christopher Gerald Hall, 49 Cartington Terrace, Heaton, Newcastle-on-Tyne. Educ. at Royal Grammar School, Newcastle. Adm. 6 Feb. 1929: began res. 7 Oct. 1929. Matric. 1 Nov. 1929. Entrance Exhib., History.

B.A. (2nd Cl., 1st Div., Hist. Tri. Pt I, 1931; 2nd Cl., 2nd Div., Pt II, 1932) 1932. M.A. 1936. Exhib., 1931.

Senior History Master, Foyle College, Londonderry, 1933–6; and at Skinners' School, Tunbridge Wells, 1936–.

ARTHUR GORDON POYNTER LEAHY, 2nd Lieut., R.E. Born 19 Dec. 1908, at Charlton, Kent. S. of Lieut.-Col. Henry Gordon Leahy, O.B.E., Army and Navy Club, Pall Mall, S.W. 1. Educ. at Cheltenham College, and R.M.A., Woolwich. Rec. by War Office. Adm. 26 Feb. 1929: began res. 8 Oct. 1929. Matric. 1 Nov. 1929.

B.A. (2nd Cl. Mech. Sci. Tri., 1931; all 3 terms as Commiss. Off.) 1931.

Capt. (1938–), R.E.

JOHN FREDERICK ASHFORD VELLACOTT. Born 1 Dec. 1910, at Barnstaple, Devon. S. of John Lewes Hole Vellacott, Trafalgar Lawn, Barnstaple. Educ. at Bromsgrove School. Adm. 13 March 1929: began res. 7 Oct. 1929. Matric. 1 Nov. 1929.

B.A. (2nd Cl. Mech. Sci. Tri., 1932) 1932.

Was apprenticed to C. A. Parsons & Co., Ltd (engineers), Newcastle-on-Tyne. Died 29 Dec. 1933 at Barnstaple, of pneumonia.

Third cousin of P. C. Vellacott, Fellow and Tutor (p. 2; and *Walker*, p. 675).

JOHN WEBBER WALTON. Born 13 Sept. 1911, at Middleton, Lancs. S. of Frederick John Walton, Paulerspury, Towcester, Northants. Educ. at Bedford School. Adm. 13 March 1929: began res. 7 Oct. 1929. Matric. 1 Nov. 1929.

B.A. (2nd Cl. Mech. Sci. Tri., 1932) 1932. M.A. 1936.

Mechanical Engineer, with Mather & Platt, Ltd, Newton Heath, Manchester.

WILLIAM CHALMERS BURNS. Born 1 Feb. 1906, in London. S. of Robert James Burns, 45 Norland Square, Holland Park, W. 11. Educ. at Perse School, Cambridge; and Royal Academy of Music, London. Adm. 14 March 1929: began res. 7 Oct. 1929. Matric. 1 Nov. 1929. Bernard Hale Organ Scholar.

B.A. (Ord. degree) 1932. M.A., Mus.B. 1936. Leaf Grant, 1931. Re-elected Bernard Hale Organ Scholar, 1931.

L.R.A.M. 1928.

PATRICK STANLEY SAVILL. Born 17 March 1909, at Southend-on-Sea. S. of Spencer Edward Savill (dec^d) and Mrs Savill, 8 Marchwood Crescent, Ealing, W. 5. Educ. at Stowe School; and privately. Adm. 14 March 1929: began res. 7 Oct. 1929. Matric. 1 Nov. 1929.

B.A. (Ord. degree) 1932. Mus.B. 1932. M.A. 1936.

Precentor, Farnborough School, Hants, 1933–5. Musical Director of '1066 and all that' (book by R. Arkell, music by A. Reynolds), 1936–. L.R.A.M. 1933. A.R.C.O. 1934.

PHILIP FRANCIS MALIM. Born 26 June 1910, at Sedbergh, Yorks. S. of Frederic Blagden Malim, Master of Wellington College, Berks. Educ. at Wellington College. Adm. 27 March 1929: began res. 7 Oct. 1929. Matric. 1 Nov. 1929.

B.A. (Ord. degree) 1932.
M.R.C.S., L.R.C.P. 1938.

JULES MARIE HENRI DEFOER. Born 12 Sept. 1904, at Soerabaya, Java. S. of Henri Bernard Defoer, Stadhouderskade 126, Amsterdam. Educ. at Jesuit College, Amsterdam; St Willibrord's College, Katwijk a/d Rijn; and Downside Abbey, nr Bath. Adm. 27 March 1929: began res. 7 Oct. 1929. Matric. 1 Nov. 1929.

Went down after M. 1929.
Now (1936) Dom Leo Defoer, O.S.B., of Downside Abbey.

ALEXANDER FULTON STRUTHERS. Born 8 May 1911, at Elisavetpol, Caucasus. S. of Thomas Struthers, 97 Bromham Road, Bedford. Educ. at Bedford School. Adm. 27 March 1929: began res. 7 Oct. 1929. Matric. 1 Nov. 1929.

B.A. (3rd Cl. Econ. Tri. Pt I (O.R.), 1931; 3rd Cl. Pt II (O.R.), 1932) 1932.
He matric. and graduated as Alastair Fulton STRUTHERS.

JOHN ERROLL MACSWINEY. Born 7 Oct. 1911, at Boyle, Co. Roscommon. S. of Major John Charles MacSwiney, O.B.E., 45d Westbourne Terrace, London, W. 2. Educ. at Wellington College. Adm. 27 March 1929: began res. 7 Oct. 1929. Matric. 1 Nov. 1929.

B.A. (Ord. degree) 1932. M.A. 1937.
Chartered Accountant; being with Buckley, Hall, Devin & Co., 82 King William Street, London, E.C. 4. A.C.A. 1937.

LIONEL HENRY RICHARDS. Born 6 Nov. 1910, in London. S. of His Honour Judge Whitmore Lionel Richards, Woodfield, Hoole, Chester. Educ. at Wellington College. Adm. 27 March 1929: began res. 7 Oct. 1929. Matric. 1 Nov. 1929.

B.A. (Ord. degree) 1932.
Called to the Bar, Lincoln's Inn, 27 Jan. 1936. On Northern circuit.

WILLIAM HERBERT BARNETT. Born 30 Nov. 1910, at Belfast. S. of Robert Barnett, Northleigh, Fortwilliam Park, Belfast. Educ. at Campbell College, Belfast. Adm. 27 March 1929: began res. 7 Oct. 1929. Matric. 1 Nov. 1929.

B.A. (3rd Cl. Econ. Tri. Pt I (O.R.), 1931; 3rd Cl. Pt II (O.R.), 1932) 1932. M.A. 1937.
Director of W. & R. Barnett, Ltd (grain importers), Belfast.

ERIC GEORGE WILLIAMSON. Born 31 July 1910, at Much Wenlock, Salop. S. of George Richard Williamson, Wenlock, St Paul's Road, Coventry. Educ. at Bloxham School, Banbury. Adm. 27 March 1929: began res. 2 Oct. 1929. Matric. 1 Nov. 1929.

B.A. (Ord. degree) 1932. M.A. 1937.
M.R.C.S., L.R.C.P. 1936.

JOHN MALCOLM HAMMOND. Born 6 March 1910, at Plumtree, S. Rhodesia. S. of Robert Woodward Hammond (Peterhouse, M.A. 1911), Head Master of Plumtree School, S. Rhodesia. Educ. at Plumtree School, S. Rhodesia. Adm. 3 April 1929: began res. 7 Oct. 1929. Matric. 1 Nov. 1929.

B.A. (Ord. degree) 1932.
S. Rhodesia Civil Service, 1935–; being Asst Master successively at Plumtree School, Cochran School, Dombashawa School and (1937–) Tjoltjo School.
Bro. of I. S. Hammond (p. 90).

WILLIAM DOUGLAS O'HANLON. Born 6 May 1911, at Bromley, Kent. S. of Alfred O'Hanlon, Limpsfield Court, Limpsfield, Surrey. Educ. at Rugby School. Adm. 24 April 1929: began res. 7 Oct. 1929. Matric. 1 Nov. 1929.

B.A. (3rd Cl. Econ. Tri. Pt I (O.R.), 1931; 3rd Cl. Pt II (O.R.), 1932) 1932. M.A. 1937. Lay Missionary (Bible Churchmen's Missionary Soc.), Abyssinia, 1934–.

WILLIAM MAX RAFFE. Born 18 Oct. 1910, at Ipswich. S. of William Joshua Raffe, 63 Henley Road, Ipswich. Educ. at Leys School. Adm. 17 May 1929: began res. 7 Oct. 1929. Matric. 1 Nov. 1929.

B.A. (Ord. degree) 1932. Asst Master, Shrewsbury House (a preparatory school), Ditton Hill, Surbiton, Surrey, 1933–.

ERIC BOLTON. Born 21 Nov. 1909, at Lincoln. S. of Albert Ernest Bolton, Mount View, Carline Road, Lincoln. Educ. at Lincoln School. Adm. 17 June 1929: began res. 8 Oct. 1929. Matric. 1 Nov. 1929.

B.A. (Ord. degree) 1932. M.R.C.S., L.R.C.P. 1937.

JOHN MESSURIER COHU, Flg. Off., R.A.F. Born 29 April 1904, in Guernsey, C.I. S. of John Messurier Cohu. Educ. at Elizabeth College, Guernsey. Rec. by Air Ministry. Adm. 17 June 1929: began res. 1 Oct. 1929. Matric. 1 Nov. 1929.

Resided till end of E. 1930. Sqdn Ldr (1937–), R.A.F.

ARTHUR WILLIAM BAYNES McDONALD, Flg. Off., R.A.F. Born 14 June 1903, at Klerksdorp, Transvaal. S. of Dr William Maclaughlan McDonald, St John's, Antigua, B.W.I. Educ. at Epsom College. Rec. by Air Ministry. Adm. 17 June 1929: began res. 1 Oct. 1929. Matric. 1 Nov. 1929.

B.A. (3rd Cl. Mech. Sci. Tri., 1931; all. 3 terms as Commiss. Off.) 1931. Sqdn Ldr (1936–), R.A.F. A.F.C. 1938.

CHARLES BLAISE LA COSTE. Born 26 Oct. 1910, at Richmond, Surrey. S. of Capt. Charles John Constable La Coste, M.C. (decd), and Mrs La Coste, Curtis Farm, Headley, Bordon, Hants. Educ. at Wellington College. Adm. 26 June 1929: began res. 1 Oct. 1929. Matric. 1 Nov. 1929.

B.A. (Ord. degree) 1932. With the Norton Grinding Wheel Co., Ltd, Welwyn Garden City, Herts, 1932–.

PATRICK NEVE OTTAWAY. Born 12 March 1911, at St Albans. S. of Thomas Ottaway, 19 Avenue Road, St Albans. Educ. at Aldenham School. Adm. 27 June 1929: began res. 7 Oct. 1929. Matric. 1 Nov. 1929.

Killed 10 Dec. 1929 in a motor-cycle accident at Welwyn, Herts, after residing one term.

MUHAMMAD HAMID ALI. Born 4 Sept. 1906, at Lucknow. S. of Muhammad Hashmat Ali, Hazratganj, Lucknow. Educ. at Church Mission Birkett High School, Lucknow; Government Jubilee Intermediate College, Lucknow; and Canning College, Lucknow Univ. (B.A. degree). Adm. 29 July 1929: began res. 7 Oct. 1929. Matric. 1 Nov. 1929. Probationer, I.C.S.

Resided till end of E. 1931. I.C.S., 1931–; with appt. as Joint Magistrate and Deputy Collector, Bengal, 1934–.

PHILLIPS PATRICK GREY. Born 1 July 1903, at Matlock, Derbyshire. S. of Thomas Patrick Grey, 105 Herrick Road, Loughborough. Educ. at Aldenham School and Loughborough College. Adm. 18 Sept. 1929: began res. 7 Oct. 1929. Matric. 1 Nov. 1929. Probationer, Colonial Service.

Resided till E. 1930.
Held short service commission in the R.A.F., 1924–9, with final rank of Flg. Off. Colonial Service, Nigeria, 1930–; now (1936) with appt. as Asst District Officer.
He matric. as Phillip Patrick GREY.

JOHN CHARLES BURKILL. Adm. **Fellow**, 1 Oct. 1929. Internal Fellow, 1929; re-elected Internal Fellow, 1934. Sc.D. 1939. Lecturer in Mathematics, 1929–. Director of Studies in Mathematics, 1929–31. Asst Tutor, 1929–30. Tutor, 1930– (being Senior Tutor, 1934–). Tutorial Bursar, 1930–2.

University Lecturer in Mathematics, 1929–.

Born 1 Feb. 1900, at Holt, Norfolk. S. of Hugh Roberson Burkill, Winteringham, Lincs. Educ. at St Paul's School, and Trinity College (Math. Schol.; B.A. 1921; M.A. 1925; Fellow, 1922–8). *Abbott Schol.*, 1919. *Allen Schol.*, 1922. *Smith's Prize*, 1923.
✕ 1918–19. 2nd Lieut., R.E.
Professor of Pure Mathematics, Liverpool Univ., 1924–9.

RICHARD ERSKINE BONHAM-CARTER. Born 27 Aug. 1910, at Poltalloch, Kilmartin, Argyll. S. of Capt. Alfred Erskine Bonham-Carter (dec^d) and Mrs Bonham-Carter, Castle Sweyne Cottage, Achnamara, Argyll. Educ. at Clifton College. Adm. 4 Oct. 1929: began res. 7 Oct. 1929. Matric. 1 Nov. 1929.

B.A. (Ord. degree) 1932.
M.R.C.S., L.R.C.P. 1936.

ALAN EDWARD COHEN. Born 22 Oct. 1910, at Manchester. S. of Max Edward Cohen, Shawbrook, Levenshulme, Manchester. Educ. at Rugby School. Adm. 4 Oct. 1929: began res. 1 Oct. 1929. Matric. 1 Nov. 1929.

B.A. (1st Cl. Nat. Sci. Tri. Pt I, 1932) 1932. In E. 1932 given title of Scholar for 1931–2.
M.R.C.S., L.R.C.P. 1935. Died 4 May 1936 at the London Hospital.

WILLIAM GARDNER HUTTON. Born 15 Feb. 1910, at Leeds. S. of James William Hutton, 293 Burley Road, Leeds. Educ. at St Peter's School, York. Adm. 4 Oct. 1929: began res. 1 Oct. 1929. Matric. 1 Nov. 1929.

B.A. (Ord. degree) 1932. M.A. 1938.
M.R.C.S., L.R.C.P. 1936.

REGINALD JOSEPH TWORT. Born 21 March 1911, at Bagshot, Surrey. S. of Reginald Frank Twort, 1 Albyn Place, Aberdeen. Educ. at Fettes College. Adm. 4 Oct. 1929: began res. 1 Oct. 1929. Matric. 1 Nov. 1929.

B.A. (1st Cl. Nat. Sci. Tri. Pt I, 1932) 1932. M.A. 1938. Exhib. for Nat. Sciences and Medicine, 1931. Leaf Grant, 1932. Given title of Scholar for 1932–3.
M.B., Ch.B., Aberdeen, 1936. Resident Medical Officer, Royal Infirmary, Aberdeen, 1936–.

CHARLES EVELYN WATSON. Born 12 Feb. 1911, at Simla, India. S. of Lieut.-Col. Charles Scott-Moncrieff Chalmers Watson, 33 Mayo Gardens, Lahore. Educ. at Cheltenham College. Adm. 4 Oct. 1929: began res. 1 Oct. 1929. Matric. 1 Nov. 1929.

B.A. (Ord. degree) 1932.
M.R.C.S., L.R.C.P. 1935. Entered the R.A.M.C.: Lieut., 1936 (with seniority of 1935); Capt., 1937 (with seniority of 1936).

THOMAS GARRETT ASKWITH. Born 24 May 1911, at Cheam, Surrey. S. of Thomas Nowell Askwith (dec^d) and Mrs Askwith, Oakmead, Burley, Ringwood, Hants. Educ. at Haileybury College. Adm. 5 Oct. 1929: began res. 7 Oct. 1929. Matric. 1 Nov. 1929.

B.A. (Ord. degree) 1932. M.A. 1936. Probationer, Colonial Service, M. 1935 to E. 1936.
Winner of Fairbairn Sculls, 1931. Winner, with L. B. Hope-Reford (p. 132), of the Lowe Double Sculls, 1931. Winner of Colquhoun Sculls, 1931. Blue: Rowing, 1932, 1933. (Hon. Sec., C.U.B.C., 1932–3.)
Rowed in the Leander (=Cambridge) crew which won the Grand Challenge Cup at Henley, 1932; and in same crew, representing Great Britain, in the Olympic Games at Los Angeles, 1932. Winner of Diamond Sculls at Henley, 1933. Rowed in the Leander crew, representing Great Britain, in the Olympic Games at Berlin, 1936.
Colonial Service, with appt. as Asst District Commissioner, Kenya Colony, 1936–.

REUBEN O'NEILL PEARSON. Born 22 Feb. 1910, at Tanley, Cartmel, Lancs. S. of Reuben O'Neill Pearson (dec^d) and Mrs Pearson, Tanley, Cartmel. Educ. at Shrewsbury School. Adm. 5 Oct. 1929: began res. 8 Oct. 1929. Matric. 29 Nov. 1929.

B.A. (Ord. degree) 1932.
Entered the Regular Army,—R.A.S.C. 2nd Lieut., 1933 (with seniority of 1931); Lieut., 1934.

CHARLES EDMUND CARRINGTON. Adm. to incorporate,—'Order Book', 28 Oct. 1929. Matric. and incorp. M.A. (from Christ Church, Oxford), 19 Dec. 1929.

Born 21 Apr. 1897, at West Bromwich, Staffs. S. of Very Rev. Charles Walter Carrington. Educ. at Christ's College, Christchurch, New Zealand; and Christ Church, Oxford (B.A. 1921; M.A. 1929). ✗ 1914–19. Capt., R. Warwickshire Regt. *M.C.*
Asst Master, Haileybury College, 1921–4 and 1926–9. Lecturer in History, Pembroke College, Oxford, 1924–5. Educational Sec., University Press, Cambridge, 1929–36; and Educational Manager of its London Publishing House, 1936–. Major, T.A. Res. of Officers.
Author:
  The War record of the 1/5th Battalion, The Royal Warwickshire Regiment. Birmingham, 1922.
  A subaltern's War; being a memoir of the Great War... [*Publ. under the pseudonym 'Charles Edmonds'.*] London, 1929.
  (With J. H. Jackson) *A history of England.* Cambridge, 1932. (2nd ed.) Ib., 1934. (3rd ed.) Ib., 1936. [Parts also publ. separately.]
  (With S. C. Roberts) *The Cambridge book of the Silver Jubilee of King George V*, 1910–35. Cambridge, 1935.
  T. E. Lawrence. [*Publ. under the pseudonym 'Charles Edmonds'.*] [London] 1935.
  The life and reign of King George V; a book for boys and girls. Cambridge, 1936.
  (With M. Carrington) *A pageant of kings and queens.* Cambridge, 1937.

ROGER MACHELL COX. Born 13 June 1911, at Plymouth. S. of Arthur Henry Machell Cox, Knightstone, Yelverton, S. Devon. Educ. at Clifton College. Adm. 31 Dec. 1928: began res. 4 Oct. 1930. Matric. 3 Nov. 1930.

B.A. (2nd Cl., 1st Div., Hist. Tri. Pt I, 1932; 2nd Cl., 1st Div., Pt II, 1933) 1933.

HOWARD BENJAMIN MORRIS. Born 16 Nov. 1911, at Trelleck, Monmouth-shire. S. of Benjamin Morris, Cottage Farm, Itton, nr Chepstow, Mon. Educ. at Monmouth Grammar School. Adm. 19 Dec. 1929: began res. 6 Oct. 1930. Matric. 3 Nov. 1930. Entrance Major Schol., Maths.

B.A. (1st Cl. Math. Tri. Pt I, 1931; Wrang. Pt II, 1933) 1933. Francis Gisborne Schol., 1932.
Asst Master, Bryanston School, 1933–5. Killed 14 Feb. 1937 fighting for the Government forces in the Spanish Civil War.

KENNETH WELLESLEY. Born 15 June 1911, at Weston-super-Mare. S. of Alfred Arthur Wellesley, 182 Gammon's Lane, Watford, Herts. Educ. at Watford Grammar School. Adm. 19 Dec. 1929: began res. 6 Oct. 1930. Matric. 3 Nov. 1930. Entrance Major Schol., Classics.

> B.A. (1ˢᵗ Cl. Class. Tri. Pt I (G, L), 1932; 1ˢᵗ Cl. Pt II (c), 1934) 1934. M.A. 1937. Leaf Grant, 1932. *Montagu Butler Prize*, 1932. *John Stewart of Rannoch Schol. in Greek and Latin*, 1932. Lady Mary Ramsey Schol., 1932; re-elected, 1933. *Prox. acc. for Porson Schol.*, 1933.
> Asst Master, Bede Collegiate School, Sunderland, 1934–6; and at Cambridge and County High School, 1936–.

DAVID ROSENTHAL. Born 31 March 1911, at Manchester. S. of Morris Rosenthal, 203 Broughton Lane, nr Broughton, Salford, Lancs. Educ. at Manchester Grammar School. Adm. 19 Dec. 1929: began res. 6 Oct. 1930. Matric. 3 Nov. 1930. Entrance Major Schol., Classics.

> Resided till E. 1933 inclusive. B.A. (1ˢᵗ Cl. Class. Tri. Pt I (g, l), 1932; 1ˢᵗ Cl. Hist. Tri. Pt II, 1935) 1935. Thomas Parke Schol., 1932.
> Known as David ROLAND, 1936–.

ERNEST WILLIAM TODD. Born 9 April 1912, at Peckham, London. S. of Charles Amos Todd, Springvale, 10 Pickwick Road, Dulwich Village, S.E. 21. Educ. at Wilson's Grammar School, Camberwell, S.E. 5. Adm. 19 Dec. 1929: began res. 6 Oct. 1930. Matric. 3 Nov. 1930. Entrance Minor Schol., Maths.

> B.A. (2ⁿᵈ Cl. Math. Tri. Pt I, 1931; Sen. Opt. Pt II, 1933) 1933. M.A. 1937. Schol.†, 1932.
> Studied at the London School of Economics, 1933–4. Actuarial Asst in London Office of the Scottish Amicable Life Assurance Soc., 1935–.

DUDLEY ERIC RICHARDS. Born 12 July 1911, at Wavertree, Liverpool. S. of David Evan Richards, 83 Brookdale Road, Sefton Park, Liverpool. Educ. at Liverpool Collegiate School. Adm. 19 Dec. 1929: began res. 6 Oct. 1930. Matric. 3 Nov. 1930. Entrance Minor Schol., Classics.

> B.A. (1ˢᵗ Cl. Class. Tri. Pt I (G), 1932; 1ˢᵗ Cl. Oriental Lang. Tri. Pt I (b), and 2ⁿᵈ Cl. Pt II (c), 1934) 1934. Edmund Woodward Schol., 1932; re-elected (for Oriental Languages), 1933. Kennett Schol., Queens' College, 1934; but relinquished this for E. G. Browne Schol., Pembroke College, 1934.
> Research Schol., Manchester College, Oxford, 1935–6. Asst Tutor with Messrs Thurbon and Jones-Williams, Ledbury, Herefordshire, 1937–.

ARTHUR PROPPER. Born 3 Aug. 1910, at Islington. S. of Isidore Propper, 4ᵃ Lewis Buildings, Liverpool Road, Islington, N. 1. Educ. at Owen's School, Islington. Adm. 19 Dec. 1929: began res. 6 Oct. 1930. Matric. 3 Nov. 1930. Entrance Minor Schol., History.

> B.A. (3ʳᵈ Cl. Hist. Tri. Pt I, 1932; 1ˢᵗ Cl. Pt II, 1933) 1933. Leaf Grant, 1932. Exhib., subsequently Schol.†, 1932.
> With W. S. Crawford Ltd (advertising agents), 233 High Holborn, London, W.C. 1, 1933–.

ERIC WILLIAM HENRY BRIAULT. Born 24 Dec. 1911, at Acton, Middlesex. S. of Henry George Briault, 60 Queen's Park Road, Brighton. Educ. at Brighton, Hove and Sussex Grammar School. Adm. 19 Dec. 1929: began res. 6 Oct. 1930. Matric. 3 Nov. 1930. Entrance Minor Schol., History.

> B.A. (2ⁿᵈ Cl., 1ˢᵗ Div., Hist. Tri. Pt I, 1932; 1ˢᵗ Cl. Geog. Tri. Pt I, 1933) 1933. M.A. 1937. Leaf Grant, 1932. Robert Slade Schol., 1932.
> Half-Blue: Cross Country, 1931, 1932. Blue: Athletics (Three miles), 1933.
> Asst Master, Queen Elizabeth's Grammar School, Barnet, 1933–.

CHARLES HENRY CHAPMAN. Born 6 March 1911, at Sydenham, London. S. of John Chapman, 35 Lawrie Park Road, Sydenham, S.E. 26. Educ. at Christ's Hospital. Adm. 19 Dec. 1929: began res. 6 Oct. 1930. Matric. 3 Nov. 1930. Entrance Exhib., Classics.

B.A. (2nd Cl. Class. Tri. Pt I (g), 1932; 3rd Cl. Pt II, 1933) 1933. Exhib., 1932.
Asst Master, Coatham School, Redcar, 1933–.

CHRISTOPHER DERING COLCHESTER. Born 24 Feb. 1912, at Croydon, Surrey. S. of Maurice Herbert Colchester, Selborne Cottage, 10 West Hill, Sanderstead, Surrey. Educ. at Rugby School. Adm. 19 Dec. 1929: began res. 6 Oct. 1930. Matric. 3 Nov. 1930. Entrance Exhib., Nat. Sciences.

B.A. (3rd Cl. Math. Tri. Pt I, 1931; 1st Cl. Mech. Sci. Tri., 1933) 1933. Exhib. for Mech. Sciences, 1932.
Engineer in Telephone Section, Research and Development Dept, Marconi's Wireless Telegraph Co., Ltd, Chelmsford, Essex, 1933–.

PATRICK MURDOCH JOHNSTON. Born 5 Oct. 1911, at Murree, Punjab, India. S. of Major Claude Errington Longden Johnston (decd) and Mrs Johnston, Timothy's Tithe, Bramber Road, Seaford, Sussex. Educ. at Wellington College. Adm. 19 Dec. 1929: began res. 6 Oct. 1930. Matric. 3 Nov. 1930. Entrance Exhib., History.

B.A. (2nd Cl., 1st Div., Hist. Tri. Pt I, 1932; 2nd Cl., 1st Div., Pt II, 1933) 1933. Kitchener Schol., 1930 (held for 3 years). Exhib., 1932.
H.M. Consular Service: apptd Probationer Vice-Consul, 1934; and has served successively in Paris, Hamburg and (1936–) Valparaiso.

PHILIP PERCIVAL BROWN. Born 9 Nov. 1911, at Charlesworth, Derbyshire. S. of Percy Bayley Brown, 59 Alexandra Road, Southport. Educ. at Rossall School. Adm. 21 Dec. 1929: began res. 6 Oct. 1930. Matric. 3 Nov. 1930.

B.A. (2nd Cl., 2nd Div., Hist. Tri. Pt I, 1932; 2nd Cl., 2nd Div., Law Tri. Pt II, 1933) 1933. LL.B. 1935. M.A. 1937.
Solicitor (adm. Nov. 1936); practising at Southport.
He changed his names to Philip Percival BAYLEY-BROWN by deed poll dated 12 April 1933 (London Gazette, 21 April 1933).

ALEXANDER CRAWFORD WELLESLEY WALTON. Born 3 Jan. 1912, at Bexhill-on-Sea. S. of Brig.-Gen. William Crawford Walton, C.B., C.M.G., I.A. (ret.), Bardowie, Queen's Road, Weybridge, Surrey. Educ. at Wellington College. Adm. 21 Dec. 1929: began res. 6 Oct. 1930. Matric. 3 Nov. 1930.

B.A. (Ord. degree) 1933. M.A. 1937.
Engaged in architectural research in Greece, etc.
Author:
    Architecture and music; a study in reciprocal values. Cambridge, 1934.

ALEXANDER FORBES. Born 4 Dec. 1911, at Aberdeen. S. of Alexander Forbes, 17 Queen's Road, Aberdeen. Educ. at Trinity College, Glenalmond. Adm. 21 Dec. 1929: began res. 6 Oct. 1930. Matric. 3 Nov. 1930.

Went down during E. 1931.
Was a Bombardier, R.A., in 1934.

JAMES SINCLAIR ROBERTSON. Born 16 Sept. 1911, at Bowdon, Cheshire. S. of Alan Douglas Robertson, Woodville, Altrincham, Cheshire. Educ. at Rugby School. Adm. 21 Dec. 1929: began res. 6 Oct. 1930. Matric. 3 Nov. 1930.

B.A. (3rd Cl. Econ. Tri. Pt I (N.R.), 1931; 3rd Cl. Pt II, 1933) 1933. M.A. 1937.
On the Manchester Stock Exchange, 1935–; being partner in Marsden, Close-Brooks & Robertson, 26 Pall Mall, Manchester.

ARTHUR JOHN MINCHIN. Born 21 March 1912, at Cloughjordan, Co. Tipperary. S. of John Edward Minchin, Thornvale, Cloughjordan. Educ. at Wellington College. Adm. 21 Dec. 1929: began res. 6 Oct. 1930. Matric. 3 Nov. 1930.

> B.A. (3ʳᵈ Cl. Nat. Sci. Tri. Pt I, 1933) 1933.
> Farming at Kitale, Kenya Colony.

WALTER NORMAN WISE. Born 14 March 1912, at Johannesburg, Transvaal. S. of Walter John Wise, Ardeen, 79 Woodcote Road, Wallington, Surrey. Educ. at Mill Hill School. Adm. 21 Dec. 1929: began res. 3 Oct. 1930. Matric. 3 Nov. 1930.

> B.A. (3ʳᵈ Cl. Econ. Tri. Pt I (N.R.), 1931; 3ʳᵈ Cl. Pt II, 1933) 1933.
> With Walter Wise & Co. (S. African merchants), Johannesburg, 1934–.

HENRY JOHN BRANDRETH GREEVES. Born 2 May 1911, at Farndale, Yorks. S. of Rev. Henry Brandreth Greeves (Peterhouse, M.A. 1921), Walkington Rectory, Beverley, E. Yorks. Educ. at St Peter's School, York. Adm. 21 Dec. 1929: began res. 6 Oct. 1930. Matric. 3 Nov. 1930.

> Resided till E. 1933 inclusive. B.A. (Ord. degree) 1936.

JACQUES ROBERT CHRISTIAN HOBOKEN. Born 10 April 1911, at Cannes, France. S. of Jacques Hoboken, Springhill, Winkfield, Berks. Educ. at Aston Clinton Park, Bucks. Adm. 21 Dec. 1929: began res. 6 Oct. 1930. Matric. 3 Nov. 1930.

> B.A. (Ord. degree) 1933.

HILARY NOBLE BALL. Born 15 May 1912, at Brasted, Kent. S. of Arnold Harding Ball (decᵈ). Stepfather: Arthur William Roe, Lambsland, Rolvenden, Kent. Educ. at Charterhouse. Adm. 21 Dec. 1929: began res. 6 Oct. 1930. Matric. 3 Nov. 1930.

> B.A. (Aegr. Nat. Sci. Tri. Pt I, 1933) 1933. M.A. 1937.
> Mushroom farming in Kent, 1935–.

THOMAS EDWIN WILEY DURRANS. Born 24 May 1911, in London. S. of Dr Thomas Harold Durrans, 73 Chandos Avenue, Oakleigh Park, N. 20. Educ. at Malvern College and Lausanne Univ. Adm. 21 Dec. 1929: began res. 6 Oct. 1930. Matric. 3 Nov. 1930.

> B.A. (3ʳᵈ Cl. Mod. & Med. Lang. Tri. Pt I, French, 1931; 3ʳᵈ Cl. Pt I, Spanish, 1932; 3ʳᵈ Cl. Pt II, 1933) 1933. M.A. 1938.
> Asst Master, Collington Rise School (preparatory), Bexhill-on-Sea, 1933–4; at Gadebridge Park School (also preparatory), Hemel Hempstead, Herts, 1934–5; and (as Senior Spanish Master) at Merchiston Castle School, Edinburgh, 1935–.

CHARLES WILLIAM STEWART HARTLEY. Born 5 Oct. 1911, at Bedford. S. of Dr Arthur Conning Hartley (decᵈ) and Mrs Hartley, 56 De Parys Avenue, Bedford. Educ. at Wellington College. Adm. 21 Dec. 1929: began res. 6 Oct. 1930. Matric. 3 Nov. 1930.

> B.A. (3ʳᵈ Cl. Nat. Sci. Tri. Pt I, 1933) 1933. Dipl. in Agric. Sci. 1934.
> Colonial Agricultural Schol., 1933–5; held successively at School of Agriculture, Cambridge (1933–4), and at Imperial College of Tropical Agriculture, Trinidad (1934–5). Colonial Service, with appt. as Agricultural Officer, Malayan Agricultural Service, 1935–.

ALEXIS MICHAEL DENHOLM. Born 3 April 1912, at Bo'ness, Linlithgow-shire. S. of William Andrew Denholm (dec^d) and Mrs Denholm, Tidings Hill, Bo'ness. Educ. at Fettes College. Adm. 11 Feb. 1930: began res. 6 Oct. 1930. Matric. 3 Nov. 1930.

> B.A. (Ord. degree) 1933.
> Represented Cambridge v. Oxford at Shooting (Rapid and Snap), 1931.
> With Scantlebury & Hemingway, Ltd (timber brokers), London, 1934–5; being their representative in Finland, 1935. Stockbrokers' Clerk, with Stevenson & Barrs, Derby, 1935–.

HUBERT MALCOLM CAMERON SMITH, 2nd Lieut., R.E. Born 10 Oct. 1909, at Mount Abu, Rajputana, India. S. of John Hubert Smith, Bhuj, Kutch, India. Educ. at King's School, Canterbury; and R.M.A., Woolwich. Rec. by War Office. Adm 21 Feb. 1930: began res. 7 Oct. 1930. Matric. 3 Nov. 1930.

> B.A. (3rd Cl. Mech. Sci. Tri., 1932; all. 3 terms as Commiss. Off.) 1932.
> Lieut. (1932–), R.E.

WILLSON WHITING. Born 16 April 1909, at Devon, Pennsylvania. S. of Allen Edward Whiting, Devon, Pa. Educ. at St Paul's School, Concord, New Hampshire; and Yale Univ. (Yale College, B.A. degree). Adm. 14 March 1930: began res. 3 Oct. 1930. Matric. 3 Nov. 1930. Aff. Stud.

> Went down after E. 1931.
> Bro. of A. E. Whiting (p. 112).

ALAN WILLIAM BAKER. Born 6 April 1911, at Nelson, New Zealand. S. of William George Baker, Eastern Extension Telegraph Co., Electra House, Moorgate, E.C. 2. Educ. at Eastbourne College. Adm. 21 March 1930: began res. 6 Oct. 1930. Matric. 3 Nov. 1930.

> B.A. (3rd Cl. Mech. Sci. Tri., 1933) 1933.
> Asst Electrical Engineer to Manchester Corporation Transport Dept, 1936–. G.I.E.E. 1934.

ROBERT PAUL CAMPBELL. Born 28 April 1912, at Glasnevin, Dublin. S. of John Ritch Campbell, Cuilin, Bray, Co. Wicklow. Educ. at Haileybury College and Lausanne Univ. Rec. by Rev. W. R. Lloyd, M.A. (Peterhouse), Asst Master and Chaplain, Haileybury College; and others. Adm. 28 March 1930: began res. 6 Oct. 1930. Matric. 3 Nov. 1930.

> B.A. (2nd Cl., 1st Div., Mod. & Med. Lang. Tri. Pt I, French, 1931; 2nd Cl., 1st Div., Pt I, German, 1932; 2nd Cl., 2nd Div., Pt II, 1933) 1933.
> With Paul & Vincent, Ltd (manufacturers of artificial manures, etc.), Dublin.

NICHOLAS ASTELL KAYE. Born 11 Aug. 1912, at Strathpeffer, Scotland. S. of Henry Wynyard Kaye (dec^d) and Mrs Kaye, Lark Hill, Abingdon, Berks. Educ. at Bradfield College. Adm. 28 March 1930: began res. 6 Oct. 1930. Matric. 3 Nov. 1930.

> B.A. (3rd Cl. Econ. Tri. Pt I (N.R.), 1931; standard of Ord. degree, Pt II, 1933) 1933. Kitchener Schol., 1931 (held for 2 years).
> With the Brazilian Warrant Agency and Finance Co., Ltd, 1933–.

THOMAS PAULETT PARTINGTON. Born 4 Jan. 1912, at St John's Wood, London. S. of Thomas Edward Partington, 62 Cottenham Park Road, Wimbledon, S.W. 20. Educ. at Haileybury College. Rec. by Rev. W. R. Lloyd, M.A. (Peterhouse),

Asst Master and Chaplain; and others. Adm. 28 March 1930: began res. 6 Oct. 1930. Matric. 3 Nov. 1930.

B.A. (Ord. degree) 1933. M.A. 1937.
Asst Master, Wood Norton School (preparatory), nr Evesham, Worcs, 1933-6; and at Doon House (also preparatory), Westgate-on-Sea, Kent, 1936–.

GEORGE EGBERT SINCLAIR STEVENSON. Born 25 Dec. 1911, at Lakewood, New Jersey. S. of Major George Edmond Sinclair Stevenson, Royal West Kent Regt, Bangalore, India. Educ. at Cheltenham College. Rec. by J. C. Gurney, O.B.E., M.A. (Peterhouse), House Master; and others. Adm. 28 March 1930: began res. 6 Oct. 1930. Matric. 3 Nov. 1930.

B.A. (2nd Cl., 1st Div., Mod. & Med. Lang. Tri. Pt I, French & German, 1931; 3rd Cl. Law Tri. Pt I, 1932; 3rd Cl. Pt II, 1933) 1933. M.A. 1937.
Solicitor (adm. Dec. 1936); practising with Slaughter & May, 18 Austin Friars, London, E.C. 2.
He matric. as George Egbert Sinclair STEVENSON.

PHILIP WHITTALL KEUN. Born 20 July 1911, at Smyrna. S. of Frederick George Keun, 11 Avenue de la République, Tunis. Educ. at Clifton College. Adm. 28 March 1930: began res. 6 Oct. 1930. Matric. 3 Nov. 1930.

B.A. (2nd Cl., 2nd Div., Mod. & Med. Lang. Tri. Pt I, French, 1931; 2nd Cl., 1st Div., Pt I, Spanish, 1932; 2nd Cl., 2nd Div., Pt II, 1933) 1933.
Tea Planter, Diyagama East Estate, Agrapatana, Ceylon (Boustead Bros Agency), 1935–.

IVAN STEVAN IVANOVIĆ. Born 9 June 1913, at Osijek, Yugoslavia. S. of Dr Ivan Rikard Ivanović. Stepfather: B. N. Banaz, 26 Albert Court, London, S.W. 7. Educ. at Westminster School. Adm. 28 March 1930: began res. 6 Oct. 1930. Matric. 3 Nov. 1930.

B.A. (3rd Cl. Econ. Tri. Pt I (N.R.), 1931; standard of Ord. degree, Pt II, 1933) 1933. M.A. 1937.
Represented Cambridge v. Oxford in Relay Races (Hurdles), 1931, 1932. Half-Blue: Athletics (120 yards Hurdles), 1932, 1933. Blue: Athletics (220 yards Hurdles), 1933. Half-Blue: Water Polo, 1933. Represented Cambridge v. Oxford at Swimming (Breast Stroke), 1933. Represented Oxford and Cambridge v. Harvard and Yale, and also v. Princeton and Cornell, at Putting the Shot, 1933.
Represented Yugoslavia at Hurdles, 1933, 1934, 1935, 1936; and in the Olympic Games at Berlin, 1936.
With Jugoslav Lloyd Ltd (shipping), 1934–; being now (1936) stationed at Buenos Aires.

ALEXANDER FRANCIS RAWDON SMITH. Born 26 March 1912, at Rhyl, N. Wales. S. of Dr George Francis Rawdon Smith, 17 Greenbank Drive, Liverpool. Educ. at Rugby School. Adm. 28 March 1930: began res. 6 Oct. 1930. Matric. 3 Nov. 1930.

B.A. (Ord. degree) 1933. Ph.D. 1936. M.A. 1937. Adm. Research Stud. as from Oct. 1933. *Senior Studentship of Royal Commissioners for the Exhibition of 1851*, 1936.
Research Stud., Medical Research Council, 1934–6. Rockefeller Foundation Fellowship (in Physiology), 1937. Member of Physiological Society, 1937.
Author:
    Theories of sensation. (Cambridge Biological Studies.) Cambridge, 1938.

RALPH STUART ARUNDELL DONNITHORNE. Born 2 Aug. 1912, in London. S. of Clarence Edward Stuart Comyn Donnithorne (Peterhouse, B.A. 1903), Grove House, Redgrave, Diss, Suffolk. Educ. at Lancing College. Adm. 28 March 1930: began res. 6 Oct. 1930. Matric. 3 Nov. 1930.

B.A. (2nd Cl., 2nd Div., Mod. & Med. Lang. Tri. Pt I, French, 1931; exempted through illness from Pt I, Spanish, 1932; 3rd Cl. Econ. Tri. Pt II, 1934) 1934.
Articled to Charles Eves, Lord & Co. (Chartered Accountants), Capel House, 62 New Broad Street, London, E.C. 2, 1934–.
Cousin of G. V. A. Seccombe-Hett (p. 121).

JOHN EDWARD LASCELLES. Born 9 June 1911, at Thelveton, Norfolk. S. of the Hon. William Horace Lascelles, Swanton House, Swanton Novers, Melton Constable, Norfolk. Educ. at Gresham's School, Holt; and privately, with Rev. R. Hurd, M.A. (Peterhouse), Vicar of St Thomas, Heigham, Norwich. Adm. 29 March 1930: began res. 6 Oct. 1930. Matric. 3 Nov. 1930.

B.A. (3rd Cl. Hist. Tri. Pt I, 1932; 3rd Cl. Pt II, 1933) 1933.
Schoolmaster; with appt. as Asst Master, Etonhurst Preparatory School, Weston-super-Mare, 1936–.

LESLIE EDWARD MITCHELL CLAXTON. Born 26 Dec. 1910, at Ludhiana, Punjab, India. S. of Philip Claxton, Indus Canals, Dera Ghazi Khan, Punjab. Educ. at St Paul's School. Adm. 29 March 1930: began res. 6 Oct. 1930. Matric. 3 Nov. 1930.

B.A. (3rd Cl. Math. Tri. Pt I, 1931; 3rd Cl. Theol. Tri. Pt II (e), 1933) 1933.
Cuddesdon Theol. Coll., 1934. Ordained d. 1935, p. 1936 London. C. of Holy Trinity, Hounslow, Dio. London, 1935–.

JOHN STILL BENNETT. Born 22 March 1911, at St Albans. S. of Sir Charles Alan Bennett, K.C. (Judge of Chancery Division High Court of Justice), Middle Meadow, Beaconsfield, Bucks. Educ. at Clifton College. Adm. 8 April 1930: began res. 6 Oct. 1930. Matric. 3 Nov. 1930.

B.A. (3rd Cl. Law Tri. Pt I, 1932; 3rd Cl. Pt II, 1933) 1933.
Called to the Bar, Lincoln's Inn, 28 Jan. 1935. On Western circuit. Practising at Chancery Bar.

HIYANE EKSATSIRA BERNADO DE MEL. Born 3 Dec. 1912, at Colombo, Ceylon. S. of (later Sir) Henry Lawson De Mel, C.B.E., J.P., Elsmere, Horton Place, Colombo. Educ. at Royal College, Colombo. Adm. 28 April 1930: began res. 6 Oct. 1930. Matric. 3 Nov. 1930.

Went down after E. 1933.
With H. L. De Mel & Co. (general importers and exporters, and steamship, estate and insurance agents), Colombo, 1934–.

BORIS PEĆAREVIĆ. Born 12 Aug. 1910, at Volosca, now Italy. S. of Dr Juraj Pećarević, Žerjavićeva ul.18, Zagreb, Yugoslavia. Educ. at Gymnasium, Zagreb; and Vienna Univ. Adm. 27 May 1930: began res. 6 Oct. 1930. Matric. 3 Nov. 1930.

Went down after E. 1931.

THOMAS GRAVES CLARKE. Born 19 Aug. 1911, at Liverpool. S. of Capt. George Alfred Erskine Clarke, Vicar's Hill, Boldre, Lymington, Hants. Educ. at Cheltenham College. Rec. by J. C. Gurney, O.B.E., M.A. (Peterhouse), House Master; and others. Adm. 5 July 1930: began res. 6 Oct. 1930. Matric. 3 Nov. 1930.

Went down after E. 1931.
On the London Stock Exchange. In 1937 was adopted as prospective National Conservative candidate for the Parliamentary constituency of North Camberwell.

RICHARD MINOR. Born 23 Oct. 1911, at Darlington. S. of Philip Minor (dec^d) and Mrs Minor, 47 Fife Road, Darlington. Educ. at Haileybury College. Adm. 5 July 1930: began res. 6 Oct. 1930. Matric. 3 Nov. 1930.

B.A. (2nd Cl. Nat. Sci. Tri. Pt I, 1932; 3rd Cl. Pt II (Botany), 1933) 1933. M.A. 1938. Kitchener Schol., 1930 (held for 3 years).
Asst Master, St George's College, Quilmes, F.C.S., Argentine Republic, 1935–.

KHWAJA ABDUR RAHIM. Born 14 Sept. 1908, at Amritsar, Punjab, India. S. of Khwaja Ghulam Mohammad, Sub-Judge, Daska, District Sialkote, Punjab. Educ. at Government College, Lahore (B.A. degree, Punjab Univ.). Adm. 26 July 1930: began res. 6 Oct. 1930. Matric. 29 Nov. 1930. Aff. Stud. Probationer, I.C.S.

B.A. (1st Cl. Oriental Lang. Tri. Pt II (*b*), 1932) 1932. In E. 1932 given title of Scholar for 1931–2. I.C.S., with appt. as Asst Commissioner, Punjab, 1932–. He changed his names to ABDUR RAHIM in Sept. 1935.

JOHN RICHARD POPE. Born 22 May 1911, at Shadwell, Leeds. S. of Richard Hudson Pope, 16 St Winifred's Road, Harrogate. Educ. at St Peter's School, York. Adm. 8 Aug. 1930: began res. 6 Oct. 1930. Matric. 3 Nov. 1930.

B.A. (Exempted through illness from Class. Tri. Pt I, 1932; 2nd Cl., 2nd Div., Engl. Tri. Pt I, 1933) 1933. M.A. 1937. Asst Master, Junior King's School, Canterbury (Milner Court, Sturry), 1933–4; at Oatlands (also a preparatory school), Harrogate, 1935–6; and at Ovingdean Hall (also preparatory), Brighton, 1936–. A.M.R.S.T. 1934. F.R.G.S. 1934.

FRED ASHTON. Born 25 April 1908 at Glossop, Derbyshire. S. of Robert Ashton, Fir Lea, Sheffield Road, Glossop. Educ. at Glossop Grammar School and Liverpool Univ. (B.Sc. degree). Adm. 15 Aug. 1930: began res. 6 Oct. 1930. Matric. 3 Nov. 1930. Aff. Stud.

B.A. (Sen. Opt. Math. Tri. Pt II, 1932) 1932. M.A. 1937. Medical Student and Tutor in Mathematics in 1936.

WILLIAM KEITH CHAMBERS GUTHRIE. Adm. **Bye-Fellow**, 2 Oct. 1930. **Fellow** (Research), 1932; elected Internal Fellow, 1935. M.A. 1932. Director of Studies in Classics, 1930–5. Lecturer in Classics, 1935–.

University Lecturer in Classics, 1935–. Pro-Proctor, 1935–6. Junior Proctor, 1936–7. Additional Pro-Proctor, 1937–8. Orator, 1939–.

Born 1 Aug. 1906, at Clapham, London. S. of Charles Jameson Guthrie, 22 Franconia Road, Clapham, S.W. 4. Educ. at Dulwich College, and Trinity College (Class. Schol. and Eric Evan Spicer Schol.; B.A. 1928). *Browne Schol.*, 1927. *Craven Stud.*, 1928. 1st *Chancellor's Classical Medal*, 1929. *Amy Mary Preston Read Schol.*, 1930.
Author:
    Orpheus and Greek religion: a study of the Orphic movement. (*Methuen's Handbooks of Archaeology.*) London (1935).

REGINALD THOMAS MAY. Born 26 April 1911, at Acton, Middlesex. S. of Claude William May, 6 Messaline Avenue, Acton, W. 3. Educ. at Aldenham School. Adm. 3 Oct. 1930: began res. 7 Oct. 1930. Matric. 3 Nov. 1930.

Resided till E. 1933 inclusive. B.A. (Ord. degree) 1935. M.R.C.S., L.R.C.P. 1936. Surgeon Lieut., R.N., 1937–.

JAMES FRANCIS BURFORD. Born 1 Oct. 1911, at Brooklyn, N.Y. S. of J. Wilfred Burford, Compañía Petrolera Lobitos, Lobitos, via Talara, Peru. Educ. at Eastbourne College. Adm. 7 Oct. 1930: began res. 6 Oct. 1930. Matric. 3 Nov. 1930.

B.A. (Ord. degree) 1933. In the Public Works Dept, Hong Kong. Assoc.M.Inst.C.E. 1938.

DOUGLAS ANDREW CAINE. Born 20 Nov. 1911, at Alderley Edge, Cheshire. S. of Douglas Caine, Copley, Bertram Drive, Hoylake, Cheshire. Educ. at St Edward's School, Oxford. Adm. 7 Oct. 1930: began res. 9 Oct. 1930. Matric. 29 Nov. 1930.

Went down after M. 1931. Farming at Summercourt, Cornwall.

WALTER MICHAEL DOUGLAS CAREY. Born 11 Sept. 1911, at Liverpool.
S. of Walter Carey, 36 Downs Park West, Bristol. Educ. at Clifton College. Adm.
7 Oct. 1930: began res. 1 Oct. 1930. Matric. 3 Nov. 1930.

B.A. (2ⁿᵈ Cl. Mech. Sci. Tri., 1933) 1933. M.A. 1937.

DAVID COOK. Born 31 March 1911, at Littlehampton, Sussex. S. of John
Polson Cook, Punjab Irrigation, Public Works Dept, India. Educ. at Malvern
College. Adm. 7 Oct. 1930: began res. 6 Oct. 1930. Matric. 3 Nov. 1930.

Went down after E. 1932.
Bro. of J. A. Cook (p. 123).

IAN TEMPERLEY STAMP. Born 13 May 1911, at Hampstead. S. of Francis
Underwood Stamp (decᵈ) and Mrs Stamp, Hillside Cottage, Berkhamsted, Herts.
Educ. at Haileybury College and Grenoble Univ. Adm. 7 Oct. 1930: began res.
2 Oct. 1930. Matric. 3 Nov. 1930.

B.A. (3ʳᵈ Cl. Class. Tri. Pt I, 1931; 2ⁿᵈ Cl., 2ⁿᵈ Div., Mod. & Med. Lang. Tri. Pt I, French, 1932;
2ⁿᵈ Cl., 2ⁿᵈ Div., Pt I, Spanish, 1933) 1933. Leaf Grant, 1933.
After going down studied at the Konsularakademie, Vienna. On staff of the London Chamber of
Commerce, 1935–6. Sub-editor, Empire News Dept, B.B.C., 1936–.

EDWARD MASSY WESTMORLAND WOOD. Born 30 July 1912, at Kashmir,
India. S. of Cdr Arthur Westmorland Wood, R.N. (ret.), Jodhpur, Rajputana,
India. Educ. at Haileybury College. Adm. 10 Oct. 1930: began res. 6 Oct. 1931.
Matric. 2 Nov. 1931.

B.A. (3ʳᵈ Cl. Law Tri. Pt I, 1933; 3ʳᵈ Cl. Pt II, 1934) 1934.
Customs and Excise, Federated Malay States and Straits Settlements, 1934–7. Sudan Civil Service,
Customs Dept, 1937–.
Nephew of T. P. Wood and H. G. W. Wood (*Walker*, pp. 649 and 674).

DENYS CHRISTOPHER TAYLER. Born 12 July 1912, at Bradford-on-Avon.
S. of Henry Christopher Tayler, The Abbey House, Bradford-on-Avon. Educ.
at Marlborough College. Adm. 19 Dec. 1930: began res. 6 Oct. 1931. Matric.
2 Nov. 1931. Entrance Minor Schol., Maths.

B.A. (1ˢᵗ Cl. Math. Tri. Pt I, 1932; Sen. Opt. Pt II, 1934) 1934. Exhib., 1933.
Was Asst Master, Trent College, 1934–5. Died 26 Sept. 1935 at Bradford-on-Avon, from blood
poisoning.

ERIC THOMSON GOODWIN. Born 30 July 1913, at Wolverhampton. S. of
John Edward Goodwin, Thirlmere, 1 Blenheim Road, North Harrow, Middlesex.
Educ. at King Edward VI. Grammar School, Stafford; and Harrow County School.
Adm. 19 Dec. 1930: began res. 6 Oct. 1931. Matric. 2 Nov. 1931. Entrance Minor
Schol., Maths.

B.A. (1ˢᵗ Cl. Math. Tri. Pt I, 1932; Wrang. Pt II (*b**), 1934) 1934. M.A., Ph.D. 1938. Francis
Gisborne Schol., 1933. Adm. Research Stud. as from Oct. 1934. J. M. Dodds Stud. (for research
in Maths), £50, 1934; re-elected, £60, 1935; and again, £100, 1936. *Rayleigh Prize*, 1936.
Asst Lecturer in Mathematics, Sheffield Univ., 1937–.

JAMES TAYLOR SINCLAIR. Born 4 Feb. 1912, at Fulham. S. of James
Taylor Sinclair, 78 Barons Court Road, W. 14. Educ. at St Paul's School. Adm.
19 Dec. 1930: began res. 5 Oct. 1931. Matric. 2 Nov. 1931. Entrance Minor
Schol., Classics.

B.A. (2ⁿᵈ Cl. Class. Tri. Pt I (*l, g*), 1933; 2ⁿᵈ Cl. Theol. Tri. Pt I, Sec. A, 1934) 1934. M.A. 1938.
Exhib., 1933. *George Williams Prize*, 1936.
Winner of Fairbairn Sculls, 1934.
Senior Classical Master, Orleton (a preparatory school), Scarborough, 1936–.

REGINALD THEODORE JOURDAIN. Born 5 June 1912, at Silchar, Assam, India. S. of Rev. Reginald Towle Jourdain, Woodham Vicarage, Woking. Educ. at St Edward's School, Oxford. Adm. 19 Dec. 1930: began res. 6 Oct. 1931. Matric. 2 Nov. 1931. Entrance Minor Schol., Classics.

B.A. (2nd Cl. Class. Tri. Pt I (*l, g*), 1933; 2nd Cl. Theol. Tri. Pt I, Sec. A, 1934) 1934. M.A. 1938. Exhib., 1933.
On staff of St Michael's College (Native Teachers' Training College under Universities Mission to Central Africa), Likoma Island, Nyasaland, 1935-6. Chichester Theol. Coll., 1937.
Bro. of E. D. T. Jourdain (p. 120).

BRIAN HARVEY GOODWIN WORMALD, subsequently **Fellow**. Born 24 July 1912, at Sutton Coldfield, Warwickshire. S. of Rev. Charles Octavius Richard Wormald, The Rectory, Solihull, Warwickshire. Educ. at Harrow School. Adm. 19 Dec. 1930: began res. 6 Oct. 1931. Matric. 2 Nov. 1931. Entrance Minor Schol., History.

B.A. (1st Cl. Hist. Tri. Pt I, 1933; 1st Cl. Pt II, 1934) 1934. M.A. 1938. Leaf Stud., £15, 1933. Lady Ward Schol., 1933. Adm. Research Stud. as from Oct. 1934. Hugo de Balsham Stud. (for research in History), £100, 1934; re-elected, 1935. *Members' Prize (English Essay)*, 1935. Strathcona Stud., St John's College, 1936. *Prince Consort Prize*, 1938.
Fellow (Research), 1938–.

ALFRED LOCKWOOD GADD. Born 10 July 1912, at Martin Mill, nr Dover. S. of Charles Alfred Gadd, 18 Hill Road, Folkestone. Educ. at Harvey Grammar School, Folkestone. Adm. 19 Dec. 1930: began res. 6 Oct. 1931. Matric. 2 Nov. 1931. Entrance Minor Schol., Mod. Languages.

B.A. (1st Cl. Mod. & Med. Lang. Tri. Pt I, French, 1932; 2nd Cl., 1st Div., Pt I, German, 1933; 1st Cl. Pt II, 1934) 1934. Leaf Grant, 1933. Schol.†, 1933.
Asst Master, Bedford School, 1934-5; and at King's School, Rochester, 1935-.

FELIX ALAN WALBANK. Born 9 Feb. 1913, at Eldwick, Bingley, Yorks. S. of Felix Joseph Walbank (dec^d) and Mrs Walbank, 71 Park Road, Bingley. Educ. at Bradford Grammar School. Adm. 19 Dec. 1930: began res. 6 Oct. 1931. Matric. 2 Nov. 1931. Entrance Exhib., Classics.

B.A. (1st Cl. Class. Tri. Pt I (*l, g*), 1933; 2nd Cl., 1st Div., Engl. Tri. Pt II, 1934) 1934. M.A. 1938. John Blyth Schol., 1933. Leaf Grant, 1934.
Senior English Master, Carre's Grammar School, Sleaford, Lincs, 1934-.
Second cousin of F. W. Walbank (p. 126).

ARTHUR HUGH SAVILE REID. Born 13 Sept. 1912, at Shrewsbury. S. of Lieut.-Col. Charles Savile Reid, D.S.O., Chernocke House, Fleet, Hants. Educ. at Wellington College. Adm. 19 Dec. 1930: began res. 6 Oct. 1931. Matric. 2 Nov. 1931. Entrance Exhib., Classics.

B.A. (1st Cl. Class. Tri. Pt I (*l, g*), 1933; 2nd Cl., 2nd Div., Geog. Tri. Pt I, 1934) 1934. M.A. 1938. Kitchener Schol., 1931 (held for 3 years). John Cosin Schol., 1933.
Half-Blue: Squash Rackets, 1932, 1933. Half-Blue: Rackets, 1933, 1934.
Traffic Apprentice, London and North Eastern Railway Co., Darlington, 1934-5. Asst District Traffic Manager, Sudan Railways, Wad Medani, Sudan, 1935-.

GEORGE JAMES BOYDEN. Born 4 Feb. 1913, at Peckham, London. S. of Henry George Boyden, 402 Baring Road, Grove Park, Lee, S.E. 12. Educ. at Dulwich College. Adm. 19 Dec. 1930: began res. 6 Oct. 1931. Matric. 2 Nov. 1931. Entrance Exhib., Classics.

B.A. (2nd Cl. Class. Tri. Pt I (*l, g*), 1933; 1st Cl. Pt II, 1934) 1934. Leaf Grant, 1933. Exhib., 1933. In E. 1934 given title of Scholar for 1933-4.
Asst Master, Colfe's Grammar School, Lewisham, 1936-.

WOODWARD EDWIN PAYNE. Born 2 June 1913, at Forest Gate, Essex. S. of George Payne, 286 Green Street, Forest Gate, E. 7. Educ. West Ham Municipal Secondary School. Adm. 19 Dec. 1930: began res. 6 Oct. 1931. Matric. 2 Nov. 1931. Entrance Exhib., History.

B.A. (1st Cl. Hist. Tri. Pt I, 1933; 1st Cl. Pt II, 1934) 1934. Alistair Bevington Schol., 1933. Leaf Grant, 1934.
Asst Master, Grange High School for Boys, Bradford, Yorks, 1935. Asst Principal, Air Ministry, 1936–.

IAN ROY. Born 2 Aug. 1912, at Manchester. S. of John Roy (decd) and Mrs Roy, 42 Richmond Avenue, Sedgley Park, Prestwich, Manchester. Educ. at Manchester Grammar School. Adm. 19 Dec. 1930: began res. 6 Oct. 1931. Matric. 2 Nov. 1931. Entrance Exhib., History.

B.A. (2nd Cl., 1st Div., Hist. Tri. Pt I, 1933; 2nd Cl., 2nd Div., Pt II, 1934) 1934. Leaf Grant, 1933. Exhib., 1933.
Asst Inspector of Taxes, Inland Revenue Dept, 1935–6. Asst Principal, Home Office, 1936–.

FELIX THEODORE FRIES. Born 9 Jan. 1913, in London. S. of Felix Fries, 91 Prebend Gardens, Stamford Brook, W. 6. Educ. at Latymer Upper School, Hammersmith. Adm. 19 Dec. 1930: began res. 8 Oct. 1931. Matric. 2 Nov. 1931. Entrance Exhib., History.

B.A. (2nd Cl., 1st Div., Hist. Tri. Pt I, 1933; 1st Cl. Pt II, 1934) 1934. Leaf Grant, 1933. Exhib., 1933. Adm. Research Stud. as from Oct. 1934. Hugo de Balsham Grant (for research in History), £100, 1934; and again, 1935.
Engaged on historical research for *The Times*, 1937.

RONALD FRANCIS BOYD CAMPBELL. Born 28 Aug. 1912, at Exmouth, Devon. S. of Major Roy Neil Boyd Campbell, D.S.O., O.B.E., I.A. (ret.), Mount House, Hartley, Plymouth. Educ. at Berkhamsted School. Adm. 19 Dec. 1930: began res. 6 Oct. 1931. Matric. 2 Nov. 1931.

B.A. (2nd Cl., 2nd Div., Hist. Tri. Pt I, 1933; 3rd Cl. Geog. Tri. Pt I, 1934) 1934. M.A. 1938.
Asst Master, Berkhamsted School, 1934–. F.R.G.S. 1934. Lieut. (1937–), Berkhamsted School O.T.C. (T.A.).

FRANK MARTIN CATTELL. Born 7 Sept. 1912, at Wallington, Surrey. S. of Frank Alfred Cattell, Sherwood, 3 Carew Road, Wallington. Educ. at Malvern College. Adm. 19 Dec. 1930: began res. 6 Oct. 1931. Matric. 2 Nov. 1931.

B.A. (2nd Cl. Class. Tri. Pt I (l), 1933; 2nd Cl. Pt II, 1934) 1934.
With Barclays Bank Ltd.

ROBERT ANTHONY CLINTON-THOMAS. Born 5 April 1913, at Dehra Dun, United Provinces, India. S. of Brigadier Robert Henry Thomas, D.S.O. Stepfather: Colonel Harold John Couchman, D.S.O., M.C., c/o Lloyds Bank, 6 Pall Mall, S.W. 1. Educ. at Haileybury College. Adm. 19 Dec. 1930: began res. 6 Oct. 1931. Matric. 2 Nov. 1931.

B.A. (2nd Cl., 2nd Div., Hist. Tri. Pt I, 1933; 2nd Cl., 1st Div., Pt II, 1934) 1934.
I.C.S., with appt. as Asst Commissioner, Punjab, 1937–.

TERENCE WILMOT HUTCHISON. Born 13 Aug. 1912, at Bournemouth. S. of Paul Robert Hutchison (decd) and Mrs Hutchison, 18 The Ridgeway, Golders Green, N.W. 11. Educ. at Tonbridge School. Adm. 19 Dec. 1930: began res. 6 Oct. 1931. Matric. 2 Nov. 1931.

B.A. (3rd Cl. Class. Tri. Pt I, 1932; 1st Cl., 2nd Div., Econ. Tri. Pt II, 1934) 1934. M.A. 1938.
In M. 1934 given title of Scholar for 1933–4.

GEOFFREY ALLEN ROWTON. Born 21 Jan. 1913, at Cleveleys, Thornton, Lancs. S. of Harold Stanley Rowton, 7 Devanha Gardens, Aberdeen. Educ. at Aberdeen Grammar School. Adm. 19 Dec. 1930: began res. 4 Oct. 1931. Matric. 2 Nov. 1931.

B.A. (3rd Cl. Hist. Tri. Pt I, 1933; 3rd Cl. Law Tri. Pt II, 1934) 1934.
Undergraduate, Aberdeen Univ., 1934–; and Law-Apprentice with Henry J. Gray & Connochie, Advocates, Aberdeen, also 1934–.

CHRISTOPHER LLOYD ROYSTON STEADMAN. Born 22 Nov. 1912, at Bracebridge, Lincoln. S. of Capt. William Milton Steadman (dec^d) and Mrs Steadman, 1 Camden Crescent, Dover. Educ. at Haileybury College. Adm. 19 Dec. 1930: began res. 6 Oct. 1931. Matric. 2 Nov. 1931.

B.A. (2nd Cl., 2nd Div., Hist. Tri. Pt I, 1933; 2nd Cl., 2nd Div., Geog. Tri. Pt I, 1934) 1934. Kitchener Schol., 1931 (held for 3 years).
Entered the Regular Army,—R.A.S.C. 2nd Lieut., 1935 (with seniority of 1933); Lieut., 1936.

GUY WILLIAM WILLIS STEVENS. Born 11 July 1912, in London. S. of Alfred William Stevens, 15 St John's Wood Court, N.W. 8. Educ. at Canford School. Adm. 19 Dec. 1930: began res. 15 Oct. 1931. Matric. 2 Nov. 1931.

B.A. (2nd Cl. Nat. Sci. Tri. Pt I, 1933; Cert. of Dilig. Study, 1934) 1934. 3rd Cl. Nat. Sci. Tri. Pt II, 1935. M.A., Ph.D. 1938. Adm. Research Stud. as from Oct. 1935.

TREDWAY SEYMOUR SYDENHAM SYDENHAM-CLARKE. Born 19 Jan. 1913, at Kotagiri, Nilgiri Hills, S. India. S. of Ernest Alfred Sydenham-Clarke, Langton Priory, Guildford, Surrey. Educ. at Charterhouse. Adm. 19 Dec. 1930: began res. 6 Oct. 1931. Matric. 2 Nov. 1931.

B.A. (2nd Cl., 1st Div., Mod. & Med. Lang. Tri. Pt I, German, 1932; 2nd Cl., 2nd Div., Pt I, Spanish, 1933; 2nd Cl., 2nd Div., Pt II, 1934) 1934.
Represented Cambridge v. Oxford at Winter Sports (Ski-ing), 1933.
Ceylon Civil Service, 1936–.

JOHN ARNOLD HARROP WOLFF. Born 14 July 1912, at Hale, Cheshire. S. of Arnold Harrop Wolff, Ross Mill Farm, Hale Barns, Cheshire. Educ. at Haileybury College. Adm. 20 Dec. 1930: began res. 6 Oct. 1931. Matric. 2 Nov. 1931.

B.A. (2nd Cl., 2nd Div., Law Tri. Pt I, 1933; 2nd Cl., 1st Div., Pt II, 1934) 1934. Ironmongers' Co.'s Exhib., 1932 (held for 2 years). Probationer, Colonial Service, M. 1934 to E. 1935.
Blue: Hockey, 1935.
Colonial Service, with appt. as District Officer, Kenya Colony, 1936–.

ANTONY DOUGHTY BROWNE. Born 21 Nov. 1912, in London. S. of Montague Doughty Browne, The Wood House, Branksome Avenue, Bournemouth. Educ. at Wellington College. Adm. 20 Dec. 1930: began res. 6 Oct. 1931. Matric. 2 Nov. 1931.

B.A. (Ord. degree) 1934.
Architect.

KENNETH SERGEANT HELLRICH. Born 24 March 1912, at Ealing, Middlesex. S. of Victor Ernest Charles Hellrich, Kingswood Cottage, Bellfield Avenue, Harrow Weald. Educ. at Berkhamsted School. Adm. 20 Dec. 1930: began res. 6 Oct. 1931. Matric. 2 Nov. 1931.

B.A. (2nd Cl., 2nd Div., Hist. Tri. Pt I, 1933; 2nd Cl., 1st Div., Archaeol. & Anthropol. Tri., Sec. A, 1934) 1934.
Customs and Excise, Federated Malay States and Straits Settlements, 1934–.

JOHN RUSSELL FAWCUS. Born 27 May 1911, at Ewell, Epsom. S. of Russell Evans Fawcus, Tumber House, Headley, nr Epsom. Educ. at Cheltenham College; and privately. Rec. by J. C. Gurney, O.B.E., M.A. (Peterhouse), House Master, Cheltenham College; and others. Adm. 20 Dec. 1930: began res. 6 Oct. 1931. Matric. 2 Nov. 1931.

B.A. (Ord. degree) 1934.
Half-Blue: Lawn Tennis, 1934.

PAUL TEMPLE COTTON. Born 7 May 1912, at Runcorn, Chester. S. of Lieut.-Col. Harold Temple Cotton, D.S.O. (dec^d), and Mrs Temple Cotton, Hill Arrish, Branscombe, Devon. Educ. at Wellington College. Adm. 20 Dec. 1930: began res. 6 Oct. 1931. Matric. 2 Nov. 1931.

B.A. (2nd Cl. Nat. Sci. Tri. Pt I, 1934) 1934. Kitchener Schol., 1931 (held for 3 years). *Grant of £40 from Worts Fund*, 1935. Probationer, Colonial Service, M. 1935 to E. 1936.
Represented Cambridge v. Oxford at Jiu-Jitsu, 1932, 1933, 1934. (Captain for the year 1933-4.)
Colonial Service, with appt. as Cadet, District Staff, Nyasaland Protectorate, 1936-.

RICHARD STANDISH ELPHINSTONE HINDE. Born 28 April 1912, at Dublin. S. of Richard Hinde, 10 Laurel Road, Wimbledon, S.W. 20. Educ. at Monkton Combe School. Adm. 20 Dec. 1930: began res. 6 Oct. 1931. Matric. 2 Nov. 1931.

B.A. (Ord. degree) 1934. M.A. 1938.
Wycliffe Hall, Oxford, 1934. Ordained d. 1935, p. 1936 Leicester. C. of Holy Trinity, City and Dio. Leicester, 1935-; and Deputy Chaplain, H.M. Prison, Leicester, also 1935-.

CHARLES EDWARD NEILD WYATT. Born 5 March 1913, at Alexandria, Egypt. S. of Stanley Charles Wyatt, 134 Avenue du Maréchal Foch, St Germain-en-Laye, Seine et Oise, France. Educ. at Felsted School. Adm. 20 Dec. 1930: began res. 6 Oct. 1931. Matric. 2 Nov. 1931.

B.A. (3rd Cl. Econ. Tri. Pt I, 1932; 3rd Cl. Law Tri. Pt II, 1934) 1934.
Blue: Hockey, 1934.
Articled to J. H. Champness, Corderoy & Co. (Chartered Accountants), 10 St Swithin's Lane, London, E.C. 4, 1934-.

HAROLD KENNEDY MACDONALD. Born 24 Feb. 1912, at Edinburgh. S. of James Harold Macdonald, Goodtrees, Murrayfield, Edinburgh. Educ. at Loretto School. Adm. 20 Dec. 1930: began res. 6 Oct. 1931. Matric. 2 Nov. 1931.

B.A. (Ord. degree) 1934.
Law-Apprentice with Dundas & Wilson, Clerks to the Signet, Edinburgh, 1934-.

KENNETH PHILIP MARSHALL. Born 2 Sept. 1912, at Langford, nr Bristol. S. of Philip Twells Marshall (Peterhouse, M.A. 1905), Langford Place, Langford. Educ. at Charterhouse. Adm. 20 Dec. 1930: began res. 6 Oct. 1931. Matric. 2 Nov. 1931.

B.A. (Ord. degree) 1934. M.A. 1938.
Asst Master, St Anselm's (a preparatory school), Croydon, Surrey, 1936-.
For his father, grandfather (G. W. Marshall) and three uncles (G. Marshall, I. Marshall and W. Marshall), see *Walker*.

LESLIE HALYBURTON TAGGART. Born 3 April 1913, at Manila, Philippine Islands. S. of William Philip Goodlet Taggart, c/o Chartered Bank of India, Australia & China, 38 Bishopsgate, London, E.C. 2. Educ. at Sedbergh School. Adm. 20 Dec. 1930: began res. 6 Oct. 1931. Matric. 2 Nov. 1931.

3rd Cl. Econ. Tri. Pt I, 1932. Went down after E. 1933.
With the Chartered Bank of India, Australia & China, 1933-.

INDEX

Names are indexed under the forms which applied at the date of admission, cross-references being given from certain variant forms. Titles of office (e.g. Capt., Rev.) are omitted. Those who are or have been Master, Fellow, Emeritus Fellow, Bye-Fellow or Fellow Commoner of the College have been so denoted. Names of parents, persons recommending men to the College, etc., are not indexed.

For EU product safety concerns, contact us at Calle de José Abascal, 56–1°,
28003 Madrid, Spain or eugpsr@cambridge.org.